Nineteenth-Century Russian Literature

NINETEENTH-CENTURY RUSSIAN LITERATURE

Studies of Ten Russian Writers

Edited by
JOHN FENNELL

UNIVERSITY OF CALIFORNIA PRESS

Berkeley and Los Angeles 1973

University of California Press
Berkeley and Los Angeles

All rights reserved
© *1973 by Faber and Faber Ltd*

Library of Congress Catalog Card Number: 72-89800
ISBN: 0-520-02350-1

Printed in Great Britain by
William Clowes and Sons Ltd, London, Colchester and Beccles

Contents

Introduction

THE purpose of this collection of essays is not to provide the reader with anything like a history of Russian literature in the nineteenth century, but to investigate certain aspects of certain writers, which, it is hoped, will prove useful to anyone who is studying, or who is interested in, Russian literature. The choice of authors is restricted by space; so too is the choice of aspects which are examined in depth. In some cases contributors have had to limit their field of investigation both to certain works and to particular facets of those works. Pushkin's prose, for example, his lyrical poetry, his *skazki*, his so-called 'miniature dramas', have all been sacrificed for a study of *Evgeny Onegin, Boris Godunov* and the narrative poems—and primarily for a study of the purely formal aspects of these works; while certain features of Lermontov's poetry are examined in detail, there is no discussion of his novel *A Hero of Our Time* or of his dramas; and the architectonics of the novels of Tolstoy and Dostoevsky are not given more than a cursory mention.

Not all the contributors have approached their subjects in the same manner or spirit, and the reader may well be disconcerted by the apparent lack of uniformity in treatment. No two persons can approach literature in quite the same way, and different literary subjects obviously require different critical treatments. The chapter on Gogol', for example, is largely an exploration of the tension between the normal and the paranormal, between reality and nightmare, between essence and appearance in Gogol''s work; it is an attempt to guide the reader through the frightening and exciting world of Gogol''s creation past the booby traps so delicately placed in his path; the novels of Turgenev, on the other hand, are analysed largely from the point of view of their structure and their socio-political themes. The section on Pushkin in the main investigates the devices used by Pushkin to achieve particular effects, while the chapter on Chekhov

9

tends to deal more with the central themes of Chekhov's writings: the problem of realism, the study of man's consciousness, the shift of meaning from the surface of the text to the sub-text, and the concentration on the internal rather than the external development of action in both his plays and his stories. Each contributor has approached his own subject in the manner which he considers to be the most important and valuable and which he also happens to find most interesting and satisfying to himself. In other words, each has concentrated on what appears to him to be the 'essential' in an author, with reference to those works which he thinks are fundamental or particularly important for understanding him as a creative writer and as a person. The aim has been not so much to place writers in the perspective of their literary background, as to interpret each author's central preoccupation and themes and to examine what seems to be the most important feature of his creative work.

In general, readily accessible biographical details have been omitted on the assumption that the reader can find out for himself the necessary facts from easily obtainable 'Lives'. There are no potted biographies. Only in so far as biographical information is helpful for a proper understanding of some aspect or other of the author's work are details of his life, his character, his political and literary propensities or his habits given. Dostoevsky's attitude to society, for example, or to revolution or to religion, his oscillations between belief and disbelief, his obsession with 'facts' and fiction are examined in some detail precisely because Dostoevsky is pre-eminently a biographical writer. At the same time mere 'telling the story' has been avoided in most cases; it has been assumed that the reader will have little difficulty in acquainting himself with the plot of a novel or the subject-matter of a play. In other words it has been taken for granted that most readers will approach this book after having already acquired at least the basic knowledge about the authors' lives and the contents of their main works.

Finally a word on the question of language. As many readers may have little or no knowledge of Russian, quotations in Russian have been kept to a minimum. Where, however, it is essential to quote in the original—for example where the study of a particular author or text calls for more detailed stylistic analysis (such as the examination of Fet's imagery or Pushkin's polyphony)—then the closest possible, though not necessarily the most elegant, rendering into English is given next to the Russian. At the end of each chapter is a select bibliography of works cited in the footnotes and works recommended for further reading.

In transliterating Russian words the 'British' system of latinization advocated in the *Slavonic and East European Review* (*see* W. K. Matthews, 'The Latinisation of Cyrillic Characters', vol. 30, 1952, No. 75, pp. 531–49) has been used. One or two minor exceptions, however, have been made to this system: (i) *e* and *ë* are always transliterated *e* (thus *Evgeny*, and not *Yevgeny*); (ii) the endings-ий and -ый are always rendered by -*y* in proper names (*Dostoevsky*); (iii) the 'soft sign', the letter ь, is rendered by an apostrophe (*Gor'ky, Gogol'*); (iv) in the spelling of feminine names ending in -*iya*, the spelling -*ia* has been used throughout (*Maria, Sofia*).

J. FENNELL

PUSHKIN

J. FENNELL

CRITICS NEVER SEEM TO TIRE OF POINTING OUT THAT PUSHKIN was the most universal of all Russian writers, universal in the sense that he tried his hand at virtually every form of literature known to the Russians at the beginning of the nineteenth century and experimented with new modes, new subject-matter. He tackled *all* the genres, from the short story to the drama, from the pastiche to the novel in verse, from the critical essay to the epic poem. Obviously to deal satisfactorily with this vast range in so small a space is impossible. The best one could hope for would be a few clichés on certain aspects of all Pushkin's genres, and the only instructive conclusion one could reach would be that Pushkin's scope was indeed huge, all-embracing, as if one didn't know that already.

For the purpose of this essay, therefore, it has been decided to skirt large areas of Pushkin's creative territory and settle upon three fields only: his *poemy* or long narrative poems, his novel in verse *Evgeny Onegin*, and his drama *Boris Godunov*. Narrow and disappointing as this field will no doubt appear to many readers, it must be still further narrowed, for it would be impossible to investigate *all* aspects of either the *poemy*, or *Evgeny Onegin*, or *Boris Godunov*, let alone all three. We must therefore restrict ourselves once again. It is not proposed to approach these works extrinsically, in other words to consider them as evidence of Pushkin's attitude towards his social environment or as a reflexion of history, of society, of social developments; it is not intended to discuss the influence of Pushkin's writing on contemporary society, the mutual relationship between his literature

13

and current ideas; it is not even planned to investigate how the known facts of Pushkin's life, habits and propensities influenced his creative work, or to hazard his 'intentions' in writing this or that piece, or to enquire how his poetry can be said to 'illustrate' his own life and experience. Instead it is proposed to study them intrinsically and to concentrate on an analysis and evaluation of the works themselves.[1]

The *poema*, or narrative poem, was the verse genre most widely practised by Pushkin. It enjoyed—especially the heroic-epic version of it—enormous popularity and prestige in eighteenth-century Russia. At the beginning of the nineteenth century, however, tastes changed. The neo-classical epic, as well as other sub-genres of the *poema*, ceased to thrill the reading public or to attract the professional poets. Instead the lyrical Romantic *poema* captivated imaginations. Byron's *Childe Harold* and the 'Eastern Poems' swept Russia as they had swept Western Europe before. The heroic epic, with its lofty subjects and matching stilted style, its conventional idealized heroes with whom the impersonal author has no emotional contact, its slow-moving episodic narrative which throws no light on the faceless characters but merely serves to illustrate the unreal, almost mediaeval, struggle between good and evil, between black and white—all this was replaced by a *poema* with a new content, a new, subjective attitude to life, a new interest in man's inner conflicts and emotions.

The lyrical Byronic epic attracted Pushkin's attention at an early stage in his career. Apart from one youthful attempt at the heroic-comic, *Ruslan and Lyudmila* (1817–20),[2] and the witty, erotic, blasphemous parody, *Gavriliada* (1821), all Pushkin's first essays in the genre were based on the Byronic pattern. His so-called 'Southern Poems'—*The Prisoner of the Caucasus* (*Kavkazskiy plennik*) (1820–1), *The Robber-Brothers* (*Brat'ya-razboyniki*) (1821–2) and *The Fountain*

---

[1] For general studies of Pushkin the following are especially recommended: Bayley, *Pushkin;* Tomashevsky, *Pushkin. Kniga pervaya* and *Pushkin. Kniga vtoraya;* Gukovsky, *Pushkin i problemy; Pushkin i russkie romantiki;* Slonimsky, *Masterstvo;* Blagoy, *Masterstvo* and *Tvorcheskiy put'.* On Pushkin's language the following are recommended: Vinogradov, *Yazyk Pushkina* and *Stil' Pushkina;* Grigor'eva and Ivanova, *Poeticheskaya frazeologiya.* One of the most useful books of reference and bibliography is *Pushkin. Itogi i problemy.*

[2] On the question of the genre of *Ruslan and Lyudmila* as well as the influence of Ariosto and Voltaire, see Slonimsky, 'Pervaya poema', pp. 187–94, 199–201. One of the best studies of the poem is Slonimsky, *Masterstvo*, pp. 187–216.

of Bakhchisaray (Bakhchisarayskiy fontan) (1821–3)—are impregnated with the spirit and technique of the 'Eastern Poems'. The influence of Byron can be seen in the plot, the structure, the subjective treatment of the characters, the narrative method and other features as well.[1] This pervasive influence was both obstructive and unproductive. It held Pushkin back, binding him to many of the cliché-ridden effusions of his schoolboy poetry and forcing him to perpetuate the tiresome habit of conveying other people's emotions by means of other people's stale commonplaces. Of course, there are flashes of realistic description and unmistakably Pushkinian phraseology, and there is plenty of mellifluous diction. For all the second-hand nature of much of the writing we cannot forget that this is after all Pushkin—bad Pushkin, perhaps, and some of it poetry which Pushkin himself later regretted having written,[2] but still with glimpses of the mature poet.[3] It was only in *The Gipsies (Tsygany)* (1824) that Pushkin abandoned his Byronic manner and for the first time in a sustained piece of writing showed the direction much of his mature work was to take.

When considering the subject-matter of many of Pushkin's major writings one is struck by the fact that certain intellectual demands are being made on the reader and that the reader is forced willy-nilly to become involved in some problem or other inherent in the narrative.

---

[1] For a detailed analysis of the Byronic elements in Pushkin's 'Southern Poems', see Zhirmunsky, *Bayron i Pushkin.*

[2] On 14th October 1823, he wrote to Vyazemsky '*Bakhchisarayskiy fontan,* between ourselves, is trash' (for Pushkin's letters, see *SS*, vols. 8, 9; in English: Shaw, 'Letters').

[3] See for example the tendency to string together concrete objects in his descriptions of the Circassians and their way of life in *The Prisoner of the Caucasus*:

> На нем броня, пищаль, колчан,
> Кубанский лук, кинжал, аркан
> И шашка...

He had about him armour, a gun, a quiver, | A bow from the Kuban', a dagger, a lasso | And a sabre ...

or

> Все путь ему: болото, бор,
> Кусты, утесы и овраги...

He traversed all: bog, forest, | Shrubs, cliffs, ravines ...

(Note that all quotations are taken from the Soviet ten-volume edition of Pushkin (*SS*), 1959–62.)

Now this does not occur to any noticeable degree in the epic *poemy* of the eighteenth century. In them one is given an ideal picture, a struggle, say, between good and evil, the outcome of which is obvious from the start. In the Byronic poem the reader merely observes and shares the hero's emotions and spiritual conflicts. We are simply invited to witness the record of anguish, ecstasy, passion, or whatever it may be, but seldom asked to pass judgement or to query motives. This is all done for us by the author who obligingly, if irritatingly, forestalls our own response by letting us share in *his* emotional approach to the situation. In Pushkin's early 'Southern Poems' no intellectual demands are made. There are no problems to solve. *The Prisoner of the Caucasus* is little more than an illustration of the traditional Romantic juxtaposition of civilization and primitive society: we witness the captive's misery, boredom, disillusionment; we note the contrast with the naive native girl; we observe his callous behaviour and enjoy the lush descriptions of nature. But that is all. There is no question of passing moral judgements, condemning, approving, deciding who is right and who is wrong. Much the same applies to *The Fountain of Bakhchisaray*. We are given a glamorous picture of the harem with a psychological study of envy and jealousy thrown in. But we are not called upon to judge the posturing hero or indeed to ask ourselves any significant questions about the story.

The Gipsies, however, is a 'problem piece', the first in Russian literature, and if we are to obtain satisfaction from it we must firstly decipher the problems and then find a solution to them. Pushkin does not commit himself explicitly; he remains aloof. But nevertheless he scatters clues and we find ourselves asking such questions as What is Freedom? What is the power of Fate? Is only the slave of passions defenceless against Destiny? Or are all men subject to 'blind cunning Fate'?

It is precisely this implicit posing of questions and this demand made on the reader to involve himself which make *The Gipsies* so unlike any of Pushkin's previous *poemy*. But a still greater breach with the 'Romantic-Byronic' past is marked by the formal elements of *The Gipsies*—the structure, the narrative technique and the style.

A distinguishing feature of the earlier *poemy* is their structural weakness. They lack symmetry and proportion. One can scarcely talk of the 'structure' of *Ruslan and Lyudmila*, for example—it is little more than a collection of anecdotes loosely strung together. *The Prisoner of the Caucasus* is remarkable structurally only for its imbalance. Pushkin seems to have little control over his material: in Part II the Captive takes fifty-eight lines to pour out his heart to the Circassian girl, while nearly 200 of the 371 lines of Part I are used for grandiose nature descriptions or sketches of the customs of the natives. Still more uncontrolled is the structure of *The Fountain of Bakhchisaray*, a jumble of exotically garish scenes barely connected with each other and seemingly thrown together in an attempt to dazzle and to break free from the laws of classical architectonics. But in *The Gipsies* there is a considerable tightening up, an economy and compactness, a structural balance between various parts of the work: words echo words; situations mirror each other with what Blagoy calls 'mathematical consistency'.[1] At times the compactness shatters any illusion of reality there may have been: at the very beginning of the action, for example, Zemfira manages to pack into eight lines (43–50)[2] an astonishing amount of information about Aleko, excellent stuff for the swift advancement of the plot, but quite out of keeping with her highly strung, passionate nature.[3] One must not of course imagine that in *The Gipsies* Pushkin jettisons all the structural devices of the Romantic *poema*; as Zhirmunsky has shown in his *Bayron i Pushkin*, many of the Byronic techniques—the scene-setting overture, the abrupt entry *in medias res*, the omniscient author's reminiscence which serves as the hero's 'pre-history', the dramatic scenes, to quote a few—are retained by Pushkin. But the overall impression is one of restraint, balance and clarity.

The narrative technique of Byron's 'Eastern Poems' is largely conditioned by the centripetal nature of the subject-matter. Concentration on the psyche of the hero demands an omnipresent and omniscient author, commenting, interrupting, questioning, exclaiming, digressing, conditioning and, above all, assimilating with the central character. Now it is true that in Pushkin's early 'Southern Poems' there is a modicum of aloofness foreign to the 'Eastern Poems'.

---

[1] For a good analysis of the structure of *The Gipsies*, see Blagoy, *Tvorcheskiy put'*, Chap. 7, Sec. 3.
[2] Note that numbers here and elsewhere refer to line numbers within the text.
[3] Cf. the Old Man's equally improbable telescopic speech of welcome (51–62).

But neither *The Prisoner* nor *The Fountain* can be described as in any sense objective pieces of narrative.

In *The Gipsies*, on the other hand, Pushkin seems to be trying to get as far away as possible from the subjective narrative technique of his early works and to distance himself from characters, story and reader, to make himself remote and unidentifiable. By far the largest part of the poem consists of purely objective narrative—either scenery or action painting (the gipsies' camp, for example (1–30, 73–89) or the description of their way of life (225–54))—or of dramatic dialogue with stage directions. There is no involvement, no intimacy. Only the setting is given, and the words and actions of the dramatis personae have to carry the argument. However, some form of psychological explanation is essential. The author has to emerge occasionally and to inform us of certain things—of Aleko's background and pre-history (120–39), for example. But this is kept to a minimum, and a great deal of psychological motivation and interpretation is given us in what might be described as disguised narrated speech, in which the third person singular is used in place of the first person, thus making an interior monologue part and parcel of the author's uninterrupted flow of narrative. For example, in the first passage describing Aleko after he has joined the gipsies we read: 'Gloomily the young man gazed at the now-empty plain, and he did not dare to explain to himself the secret cause of his sorrow. Black-eyed Zemfira is with him; now he is a free dweller of the world.' (94–9) After the physical description of Aleko gazing at the plain ('gloomily' describes his features, his stance; not necessarily his emotions), the words 'and he pondered:' could be supplied and the remainder of the passage could be read as direct speech (i.e. in the *first* person singular)— 'I dare not explain . . . Zemfira is with me . . .' etc. This method of disguising soliloquy as part of the narrative not only enables the author to keep up his flow without breaking off for a fragment of direct statement and thus to economize and avoid 'Romantic spread', but also creates a certain degree of authorial detachment.[1] Indeed, almost the only passage in *The Gipsies* in which Pushkin intrudes on the narrative in order *personally* to portray the innermost thoughts of a character is when he describes Aleko's sleep and awakening just before the murder (440 sq.). Here he both informs us of Aleko's mental condition ('fear seizes

[1] For Pushkin's use of this technique elsewhere, see Vickery, 'Three Examples'.

18

him'; he is 'oppressed by foreboding') and even gives us an inkling of what his dream was like ('in his mind a vague vision plays'), all things which of course an extrinsic recorder of speech and action could not be expected to know or relate.

Although Pushkin in *The Gipsies* cuts his role as omniscient revealer of other people's thoughts and emotions right back, he is still unable to rid himself of the equally, if not more, obtrusive role of poet-commentator. But again, these intrusions are far less numerous than in earlier works. Only on one occasion[1] does he allow himself the luxury of an unmotivated lyrical irruption into the fairly calm narrative stream: at the end of the vivid picture of the raising of the gipsy camp in the morning after Aleko's arrival, Pushkin, as if unable to leave good alone, comments on the scene: '. . . It is all so brisk and restless, *so foreign to our dead pleasures, so foreign to this empty life, which is as monotonous as the song of slaves.*'[2] (90–3) This personal comment, this angry, isolated relation of the poem to the poet's world, strikes a jarring note. An entirely new dimension is gratuitously added, gratuitously because Pushkin is going to make the same point anyhow in the various speeches of Aleko and the Old Man, and make it *indirectly* and all the more effectively.

Apart from this isolated personal comment there are of course other authorial interruptions. But their aim is quite different. It is not to comment on life, to reveal the *true* author behind the story (which is certainly the aim of Pushkin's remarks on 'our dead pleasures'), or to make the reader compare conditions of fiction and life. The aim is functional. They serve to shift the scenery, to move from one phase to another, or to stress one particular theme. For example, the allegorical 'God's little bird' song (104–19) which introduces Aleko's pre-history is preceded by two rhetorical questions: 'But why does the young man's heart quake? By what care is he oppressed?' (102–3) These immediately call up the communicative author, not to give his views as was the case ten lines earlier, but to serve as a plot-pusher, a bridge between Aleko's vain ruminations on the causes of his 'secret misery' and the omniscient author's description of his background. It is

---

[1] Apart from the Epilogue, that is. Pushkin reserves the Epilogue in all three 'Southern Poems' for lyrical comments. Note that in *The Fountain* the Epilogue begins without a heading at line 505, *Pokinuv sever nakonets* . . . [Having abandoned the north at last . . .]

[2] My italics (J.F.).

just as artificial a device as the *Ptichka bozhiya* allegory. The same sort of thing occurs at the end of Aleko's pre-history when Pushkin again intrudes ('But, God, how passions played with his docile soul! . . .' etc. 140–5). This time the purpose is perhaps slightly more personal and revelatory of the author's thoughts, or rather his designs on the reader, in that it serves to weight the Fate theme. But it is still basically a *structural* device in so far as it helps to warn the reader of the conclusion to expect. In other words, when Pushkin emerges in person in *The Gipsies* and declares his presence openly by addressing the reader or exclaiming to the world in general, he is on all occasions, with the one exception mentioned above, merely employing a variant of an artifice beloved of the eighteenth-century fiction-writer. True it is slightly less crude than the question and answer technique, such as we find in say *The Corsair*:

> *Who o'er his placid slumber bends?*
> *His foes are gone, and here he hath no friends;*
> *Is it some seraph sent to grant him grace?*
> *No, 'tis an earthly form with heavenly face!*

and certainly rarer and more discreet than the rhetoric which be-spatters *The Prisoner* and *The Fountain* or the euphuistic '*druz'ya moi*'s and '*chitatel''*s of *Ruslan and Lyudmila*, but it serves the same function.

The reason for Pushkin's striving for this type of objectivity in *The Gipsies* is to be found in the poem's purpose. The more demands a work makes on the reader, the more the author is obliged to avoid, hide or disguise any partiality he may feel. He must not give the game away. The very fact that Pushkin is here attempting a problem piece and forcing participation on his readers compels him to distance himself from his subject, his characters and, ultimately, his readers.

Now it is often true to say that the further back an author places himself the more freely he can manipulate different 'voices' within his work. The Romantic writer who is always ready in the wings, stepping forward to interfere with the narrative, tends to restrict all his explanations and comments to one voice—his own, or that of his implied author (which of course may differ from his own). And Pushkin in his early works makes all other voices sound like his own authorial voice. The light bantering tone of *Ruslan and Lyudmila* hardly alters throughout, in spite of the deliberate mixture of genres.

20

The earlier 'Southern Poems' are equally monophonic, although in *The Prisoner* there are already glimpses of a descriptive style which stands in sharp contrast to, say, the hero's effusions or the banal utterances of the heroine. *The Gipsies,* on the other hand, is Pushkin's first major work in which he consistently, and successfully, attempts to differentiate between stylistic layers and to use different voices for different purposes. It is not only his most 'objective' work to date; it is his first truly polyphonic work.

Four basic 'voices' can be distinguished: those of the 'objective narrator', the Old Man, Aleko and Zemfira. Of course these are not exclusive. Other minor stylistic currents are also discernible: the folkloric, for example (see the two songs) and the diverse tones of the authorial intruder, which vary according to the topic or character under scrutiny.

The 'objective Narrator's voice'—the voice with which Pushkin describes background and actions—is austere and laconic. The vocabulary is unemotional and undecorative. The aim is to present a picture which describes with precision what is visible and audible; consequently the descriptive elements—the adverbs and adjectives— are monosemantic; they have no overtones: 'cold' means low in temperature and not 'unemotional', 'frigid' or 'gloomy'. All words convey exact, precise information; they give no impression of emotions felt by the author. Occasionally a picture is given greater expressiveness by the use of a 'subjective' or 'intellectual' adjective added to a concrete noun. The tame bear is described (245) as gnawing its 'frustrating' or 'irksome' (*dokuchnuyu*) chain, not its 'thick', 'iron' or 'heavy' chain; this immediately evokes the angle of the bear's head or the glint in its eye. The descriptive elements used in the burial scene (493–7)—*robko* [shyly], *vstrevozhennoy* [alarmed], *skorbnoy* [mournful]—fulfil the same function and allow the reader's imagination more scope than the unvarnished depiction of most scenes. The syntax matches the vocabulary in austerity and simplicity. The sentence structure is startlingly bare and artless. Take for example the six lines describing the gipsy encampment (7–12):

> Между колесами телег,
> Полузавешанных коврами,
> Горит огонь; семья кругом

21

Готовит ужин; в чистом поле
Пасутся кони; за шатром
Ручной медведь лежит на воле.

Between the wheels of the waggons, | Half covered-over with rugs, | A fire burns; around it a family | Cooks its supper; in the open steppe | The horses graze; behind the tent | A tame bear lies in freedom.

Here, apart from the swift-flowing participial clause in the second line, the syntax is reduced to the subject + predicate combination (*sem'ya gotovit uzhin*: a family cooks its supper). The remarkably prosaic nature of the descriptive passages is increased by enjambement (note how the last four lines of the above quotation all flow into each other) and by the typically Pushkinian tendency to catalogue (see especially 14–17; 80 sq.). But what stamps such passages most as prosaic is the almost total absence of metaphor. In the first thirty lines of the poem and in the description of the striking of the camp (73–89), for example, only two moribund metaphors can be found— *niskhodit sonnoe molchanie* [sleepy silence descends]; *volynki govor* [the sound, lit. 'talk', of pipes]—and they are virtually dead.[1]

The Old Man's 'voice' is close to that of the author-narrator. This is hardly surprising, for he is the one character whose views Pushkin patently shares; he can indeed be called his mouthpiece. The lexis is similar to the narrator's. Even when dealing with such abstract concepts as pride, freedom or will in his final speech to Aleko (510–20), he manages to lend his words a concrete flavour. Instead of vague adjectives ('we are lawless, unvindictive, unemotional' etc.) he uses nouns and verbs: 'We have no *laws*; we do not *torture*, we do not *put men to death*; we have no need of *blood* or *groans*.' The syntax of most of his speeches is again remarkable for its simplicity. The tale of Mariula (370–409), for example, which begins with a naive little jingle

Послушай: расскажу тебе
Я повесть о самом себе,

Listen: I will tell you | A tale about myself.

---

[1] This is not to say there is *no* imagery in any of the descriptive passages. Indeed there are some very hackneyed metaphors and periphrases reminiscent of Pushkin's schoolboy works. See 487, 502–3, 533 (a relic from *The Prisoner* 252), 239–40, 250. There are no bold or original metaphors.

contains in all its forty lines only one subordinate clause (372–3).
The three lines describing his awakening on the morning after
Mariula's departure (400–2)

> Я мирно спал; заря блеснула;
> Проснулся я, подруги нет!
> Ищу, зову — пропал и след

*I was sleeping peacefully; dawn flashed; | I woke up; my beloved
was not there! | I look for her, call her—all trace has vanished.*

consists of seven abrupt syntactical units in twice as many words.
At times the syntax becomes unnaturally compressed, as for example
in his first speech (51–62) when in a series of machine-gun like utterances he outlines a programme of Aleko's activities, or when he drops
his pearls of aphoristic folksy wisdom before Aleko (414–7).[1] Metaphors are rare in his speech, but he has a propensity for nature similes
—for instance he uses an extended comparison with the moon while
explaining the nature of woman to Aleko; and in the best mediaeval
folkloric tradition the moon is anthropomorphized (343–58).

Only once does Pushkin slacken his grip on the Old Man—when he
has him rouse the lovers with the cliché 'abandon your couch of bliss'
(72). Otherwise the portrait is carefully sustained. True he makes
him round off the story of Ovid with three lines of almost impenetrable syntactic opaqueness (214–6) and has him use coy periphrasis
and hackneyed metaphors to describe his own youth (379–80; 381–2;
389–90): but the complexities of the first are an imitation of Ovid's
style, while the artificialities of the second represent an attempt to
stress the romantic nature of youth and to contrast it with the plain
realism of maturity. We are left with the picture of simplicity, natural
wisdom, proximity to nature and absence of false emotionalism.

The voice of Aleko—i.e. his own speech and the words used by the
narrator to describe him—is sharply contrasted with that of the
objective narrator and the Old Man. As the representative of false,
artificial civilization, of 'stuffy towns' (*dushnye goroda*), he uses, and
is described in, an artificial, borrowed language. His vocabulary is

---

[1] Note that the Old Man sometimes uses short attributive adjectives in keeping
with the folkloric tradition: *gor'ki slezy* [bitter tears] 210; *v zimnyu noch'* [on a
winter's night] 292; *minuvshi leta* [in past years] 295. Cf. the use of short adjectives
in the folksy *Ptichka bozhiya* poem.

abstract, imprecise and emotional. He hardly opens his mouth without uttering such words as *volnenie* [excitement], *bezumnyy* [mad], *nezhnyy* [tender], *unynie* [gloom], *pustinnyy* [deserted], *utomitel'nyy* [exhausting], *milyy* [dear]—words which reflect the condition of his soul, its emptiness perhaps. When he wakes up on the night of the murder (443 sq.) he stretches out his hand *jealously*, but his *timid* hand seizes the *cold* sheets. Pushkin goes on to describe his emotions in a series of conventional melodramatic clichés: he gets up *with trepidation*; fear *seizes him*; *hot and cold* run through his body; he is *fearful* to look at, etc., etc., and we are reminded of the astonishing brevity with which the parallel awakening of the Old Man is described.[1] As one would expect, the syntax is far more complex than that of the objective narrator or the Old Man. Aleko's heated outburst in answer to the Old Man's string of calm simple aphorisms (414–17) is masterly in its confusion and intricacy. But the main distinguishing feature of Aleko's 'voice' is his use of rhetorical devices. He talks in bursts of exclamations, parallelisms, oxymorons, repetitions; indeed at times his language is so artificial and abstruse that one wonders what a simple girl like Zemfira could have made of it (see particularly 168–76; 217–24). Metaphors abound, although most of them are well-worn clichés and merely stress the artificiality of his speech.

There is little to say about the language of Zemfira. It occupies only about a tenth of the poem, and Pushkin seems to have given it as little thought as he gave the delineation of her physical appearance or character. It is as simple as he can make it. The short sharp prosaic bursts of speech (e.g. the night scene, 305 sq.), the uncomplicated sentence structure, the plain 'concrete' vocabulary (see especially her touchingly naive description of what *she* thinks life in the cities must be like, 164–7) and the almost total absence of imagery tell us all that we need to know about this primitive, instinctive child of nature.

If so much space has been devoted to *The Gipsies* it is not so much because of its intrinsic merits as because of its importance in the history of Pushkin's development as a writer. It marks the half-way stage— the breach with the 'Romantic-Byronic' past and the beginning of new literary interests, a preoccupation with new stylistic techniques. As a largely experimental work it has its faults—strident melodrama,

---

[1] Note too the deliberate contrast of *calm* nature—*Spokoyno vse* ... [all is peaceful . . .] 452–3—in which four sentences are crowded into two lines.

a woodenness of character-portrayal, here and there inconsistencies of style—but these do not detract from the reader's aesthetic appreciation, as does the overall impression of coldness: the more Pushkin aspires towards objectivity in his sloughing off of Byronism the remoter the work becomes from the author and the less it tells us about him. In the succeeding *poemy*—and indeed in much of his mature work— Pushkin abandons this unnatural Olympian pose; he draws close and reveals himself, or rather varying aspects of himself, to his readers. It is as though he began to realize that this self-inflicted isolation was foreign to his generous nature: he must show his thoughts, not disguise them by means of artificial distancing devices. He must give the reader a picture of himself and make him aware of his presence, whether as wit, philosopher, historian, patriot or poet.

At first glance *Count Nulin* (*Graf Nulin*) (1825) appears to be as objective a work as any. Authorial intrusion seems minimal. It looks like nothing but an exercise in the 'low style', full of 'prosaic ravings', 'contemptible prose' and the 'variegated rubbish of the Flemish School';[1] an attempt merely to paint the squalor and boredom of provincial life and to strip it of romantic glamour. But *Count Nulin* does not consist solely of prosaic descriptions of the farmyard; it has a plot centred on a faintly erotic anecdote, and fluttering behind it all is the frivolous, light-hearted, witty and highly-skilled narrator, holding back information where necessary, nudging us, winking, hinting. He intrudes again and again, either to guide us through the narrative, to push on the plot, to follow the Count around and explain his motives,[2] or to comment with sophistication and mock sententiousness and to draw his readers into the fun. The frothy, unserious, at times conventional (*druz'ya moi!* [my friends!]) authorial remarks reveal precisely that gay image of himself which Pushkin wanted his readers to receive.

For all Pushkin's joyous self-revelation in *Count Nulin*, we can hardly call him *engagé*: there is really nothing beyond say the pleasures of hunting—revealed in a few lines—to be involved in; and he is still too much the professional story-teller to drop all pretence and reveal

---

[1] Expressions used by Pushkin to describe certain elements of his style in *Evgeny Onegin*.
[2] Note that he tells us very little of what goes on in Natal'ya's mind. To comment on *her* emotions would give the game away.

himself as the *artist* revelling in the creative joys of painting a totally unsentimental picture of nature (the grey drab colours of the farmyard, the noises, the smells almost) or of evoking *physically* an emotional crisis (the angry frightened heroine's reaction to Nulin's sexual assault:

> Она Тарквинию с размаха
> Дает — пощечину, да, да!
> Пощечину, да ведь какую!

With all her might she gives Tarquin | A box on the ear, yes, yes! | A box on the ear and what a one!)

In *Poltava* (1828), however, Pushkin involves himself up to the hilt, this time as the passionate patriot-historian.

Just as in *Count Nulin* no demands were made on the readers— we were merely *entertained* by a witty raconteur—so here we are not asked to pose or answer any questions, to judge the behaviour of Maria or Mazepa. We are simply guided through the narrative by the omnipresent Pushkin, given his appreciation or criticism, and even supplied with his explicit interpretation in an epilogue (in the passage of time the Mazepas of this world are forgotten, the Peters survive). As we inferred from *The Gipsies* that the more demanding a work, the remoter the author tends to make himself, so here we can observe the converse: the less the reader is expected to work, the more the author-narrator is likely to intrude.

And intrude he does. True, it is an impersonal intrusion; there are no 'I's, 'my's or 'our's. But we have every other form of irruption into the text. His hand is felt at every turn. He sees, knows and describes everything. He shifts from scene to scene, from character to character. He interprets his puppets' thoughts, explains their motives and reactions. As plot-manipulator he emerges with the by now familiar rhetorical questions ('But where is the Hetman! . .' After the battle in Part III he asks seven rhetorical questions and then proceeds to answer them); he even comments on the dramatic irony of Maria's ignorance at the end of Part I ('O, if only she knew! . . But the murderous secret is still hidden from her'). But it is as biased historical commentator that Pushkin makes his presence most felt. From the very first we are told what to think about Mazepa. There is nothing ambiguous about him. It is not just oblique criticism put into the thoughts and words of Kochubey (though there is plenty of this); Pushkin tells us what a villain he is, subjectively sprinkling him with such epithets as 'cunning', 'evil', 'blood-thirsty', 'criminal', etc. He even addresses him personally ('O destroyer of holy innocence!...' Part III). And at the same time he tries to make us feel pity for the noble Kochubey and admiration for the glorious Peter. Nothing is left for us to do but enjoy the soft evocations of nature (*Tikha Ukrainskaya noch'* [Calm is the Ukrainian night] etc.), and admire the solemn majesty of the ode-like rhetoric, to follow the love story around which the work is centred, and to be caught up with poor Maria in her awful predicament.[1] Pushkin the hero-worshipper, the patriot, by making his presence felt continuously, has freed us of any effort. We do not even have to question his sincerity or reliability as narrator.[2]

Although Pushkin's last *poema*, *The Bronze Horseman*, poses problems as vital and engaging as any in *The Gipsies*, although it seemingly gives no explicit answers but leaves a series of question marks, and although it compels the reader to collaborate if he is to receive full satisfaction, nevertheless it is impregnated with Pushkin's presence. Pushkin emerges as the *personal* author, not just the omniscient narrator dipping into the minds of his characters ('A restless care disturbs [the Count]') or the commentator putting his views across in the third person ('Mazepa is evil, treacherous, cunning, etc.'). Thus paradoxically *The Bronze Horseman* is at the same time the most and the least revealing of all his *poemy*: the more we read it the more we know about Pushkin and yet the more we become confused about its ultimate meaning.

How should we interpret this simple-looking little *povest'*? What do the statue, the elements, the 'hero' symbolize? From Belinsky to the present day hardly a critic has refrained from giving his own interpretation, or from confirming or rejecting his predecessors' views. There have been political, socio-political, religious, metaphysical, literary, historical exegeses. Ingenious 'signals' have been picked up and codes deciphered. *The Bronze Horseman* has been used

[1] Note that the narrator withholds from us the vital information concerning her reaction to her mother's revelations. She faints melodramatically in Part II and we do not see her again until after the battle when she is mad.

[2] On *Poltava*, see Slonimsky, *Masterstvo*, pp. 273–93 (good general appreciation); Blagoy, *Masterstvo*, pp. 199–203 (good on structure). On style, see Vickery, 'Three Examples'; Sokolov, '*Poltava*'. Cf. Tynyanov, *Arkhaisty*, pp. 271–2.

to demonstrate most theories concerning Pushkin's life and thought. Pushkin, it would seem, can be made to emerge from the work in any guise that suits the literary historian.

There is no purpose to be gained here by speculating on the meaning of the poem or on Pushkin's purpose in writing it. We can only address the reader to some of the voluminous literature on the subject,[1] suggest that he follow the complex history of its genesis and its connection with other works (*Ezersky | My Hero's Genealogy—Rodoslovnaya moego geroya—*and *My Genealogy—Moya rodoslovnaya*) traced by the Soviet scholar O. S. Solov'eva,[2] and limit ourselves once again to a discussion of some of the work's formal aspects in the hope that such an investigation may help the reader to find his own 'solution' to *The Bronze Horseman*.

The Bronze Horseman is a *povest'*, a short story in verse told by an omnipresent and omniscient narrator. This is made quite explicit in the succinct 'frame' passage at the end of the Introduction:

> Была ужасная пора,
> Об ней свежо воспоминанье...
> Об ней, друзья мои, для вас
> Начну свое повествованье.
> Печален будет мой рассказ.[3]

There was a dread time, | The memory of it is still fresh . . . | About it, my friends, for you | I will begin my narrative. | My tale will be sad.

---

[1] For a useful summary in English of various interpretations, see Lednicki, *Pushkin's Bronze Horseman*, pp. 1–6. See also Bryusov, *Moy Pushkin*, pp. 63 sq.; Slonimsky, *Masterstvo*, pp. 300–7; Blagoy, *Masterstvo*, 203–22; Kharlap, 'O Mednom vsadnike'; Gerbstman, 'O syuzhete'.

[2] Solov'eva, '*Ezerskiy i Mednyy vsadnik*'.

[3] The original draft version of this passage contained a description of Pushkin's own emotional condition

> Смутясь, я сердцем приуныл
> И на минуту позабыл
> Свое сердечное страданье,

In confusion I became despondent in my heart | And for a minute I forgot | The suffering of my heart,

reminiscent of his original draft introduction to *The Fountain of Bakhchisaray*. This was rejected no doubt as totally out of keeping with the image of the poet built up in the Introduction. The draft passage from *The Fountain*, thinks Slonimsky, was rejected as clashing with the 'lyrical tone' of the work. See Slonimsky, *Masterstvo*, pp. 294–5; cf. Timofeev, '*Mednyy vsadnik*', p. 225.

The author has of course already established his presence. Having started the *poema* disguised as a courtly ode-writer, aloof, but none the less communicating Peter's thoughts and omnisciently sweeping over the traditional 'hundred years' (*Proshlo sto let*)[1] between the foundation of the city and the present day, he emerges at last as the undisguised authorial 'I'. From the start of the great lyrical confession of love for the city (*Lyublyu tebya, Petra tvoren'e* . . . [I love you, city of Peter's creation . . .] 43) to the sombre beginning of the narrative proper in Part I, Pushkin thrusts himself upon our imagination. The evocations of the city are shown through his eyes and his eyes alone. After seven lines crammed with rich musical (see below pp. 35–6) and rhetorical devices (chiasma, repetition, hypallage, oxymoron) Pushkin lowers the tone to the utmost simplicity of prosaic utterance— almost to understatement—to portray himself as the focal point of the whole poem, reading, writing, lampless in his room:

> Когда я в комнате моей
> Пишу, читаю без лампады...

When in my room | I write or read without a lamp . . .

Vision follows vision, each enriching not only our image of the city but also our knowledge of the poet: with every line the picture of Pushkin grows vivider in our eyes, until by the end of the last majestic outburst—the final passionate apostrophe to Petropolis—we have experienced the whole gamut of his poetic emotions. He has established himself in our minds as the poet capable of experiencing delight at the humble pleasures of the city (*beg sanok* . . . [the sledges coursing . . .] 61; *devich'i litsa* . . . [the faces of girls . . .] 62, etc.) and rapture at its majestic aspects (67–83). From now on we know that the 'I', whether stated or implied, is Pushkin.

For the rest of the poem Pushkin, whether interpreting the agony of the populace (*Osada! pristup!* . . . [Siege! Assault! . . .] 190 sq.), allowing Evgeny's feelings to pour out in interior monologue or narrated speech, or even explaining the anthropomorphized Neva's motives (*I sporit' stalo ey nevmoch'* [She could no longer endure the struggle] 170), has immediate access to and contact with his reader.

---

[1] For the possible origins and reminiscences of this set formula, see Pumpyansky, '*Mednyy vsadnik*', pp. 97–8; cf. Lednicki, *Pushkin's Bronze Horseman*, pp. 18–19.

Only on one occasion are we given momentarily to mistrust him, when he indulges in faint irony at the expense of the hack Khvostov (344–6).[1] Otherwise we know where we are. There is no ambiguity. *Bednyy, bednyy moy Evgeniy* [My poor, poor Evgeny!] is not just a cliché. It means what it says: Evgeny is the object of Pushkin's profound compassion. And of course when it comes to the grand authorial comments there is no mistaking Pushkin's voice. He no longer needs to comment with the authority of his own voice. Instead he smoothly glides from the thoughts of his hero into his own. At the end of Part I, for example, he rounds off Evgeny's despairing monologue, dramatically rendered in narrated speech (*Bozhe, Bozhe! tam—Uvy!* ... [O God, O God! There, alas! ...] 241–8), with a rhetorical question asked by Evgeny (*Ili vo sne | On eto vidit?* [Or is he dreaming this?]—i.e. *Ili vo sne ya eto vizhu?* [Or am I dreaming this?]) and follows it with the great despairing question, uttered in true Pushkinian tones:

> ...иль вся наша
> И жизнь ничто, как сон пустой,
> Насмешка неба над землей?

Or is all our | Life nothing but an empty dream, | Heaven's mockery at earth?

The same thing occurs in Part II when mad Evgeny approaches the statue (404–23): the author shows us his thoughts—Evgeny recognizes the scene of the tragedy 'and the [marble] lions and the square ...' (409)—and then launches into a rhetorical monologue which in its sheer majesty of expression is clearly Pushkin's own (*i togo, | Kto* ... [and him who ...] 409–10) down to ... *podnyal na dyby* [... reared up] 423). Again, there is no 'I'; indeed Pushkin, by mentioning Evgeny's sudden lucidity (*Proyasnilis' | V nem strashno mysli* [His thoughts became terribly clear] 404–5), almost deludes us into believing that these are the madman's thoughts.

---

[1] The episode in which Alexander I appears on the balcony and sends his generals to save the drowning people may also be ironical. A. Gerbstman considers that the passage is in direct contrast with the 'Petrine' episodes and that the basic theme of the whole work is the juxtaposition of Peter and Alexander. See Gerbstman, 'O syuzhete'.

But only for a moment. There can be no mistaking the lofty intonations. Only Pushkin could exclaim

О мощный властелин судьбы!

O mighty master of Fate!

If the masterly narrative skill with which Pushkin establishes his own impression and image on the work distinguishes *The Bronze Horseman* from the other *poemy*, so too does the interweaving of stylistic patterns. We have remarked above that in *The Gipsies* Pushkin's chilly remoteness helped him to manipulate several voices; such polyphony and contrapuntal style is far less noticeable in all succeeding *poemy* except *The Bronze Horseman. Count Nulin* and *The Little House in Kolomna (Domik v Kolomne)* (1830) are both basically monophonic works, not only because the subject dealt with in both is restricted to a particular milieu which it scarcely leaves; but also because a particular, somewhat narrow, 'Pushkin' is always making himself felt. Even in *Poltava*, which embraces a variety of scenes, milieus and social strata, and where, it is true, one can pick out two or three separate linguistic strains,[1] there is still no striking stylistic differentiation between the various themes; there are no characteristic 'voices'.[2]

In *The Bronze Horseman*, however, Pushkin for the first time achieves what might be called a synthesis of authorial intimacy and stylistic polyphony. Now much has been written about the contrasting and blending of stylistic patterns in *The Bronze Horseman*. In particular Pushkin's sharply contrasting treatment of what are called the 'Petrine style' and the 'Evgeny style' has been dealt with in detail: the lofty descriptions of Peter and his bronze image, with their archaisms, rhetoric and alliteration reminiscent of the courtly odes

---

[1] Slonimsky, for instance, distinguishes between what he calls the 'popular song', the 'Ukrainian-political' and the 'odic' streams. *Masterstvo*, pp. 276–9.

[2] The unfinished *Tazit* (1829–30), the second 'Caucasian' *poema* and stylistically the closest of Pushkin's mature works to the early 'Southern Poems', is written almost entirely in one key; *Andzhelo* (1833), a very free adaptation of 'Measure for Measure', is little more than a stylized representation of an Italian renaissance *novella* and consequently, like most Pushkinian stylizations, is strictly monophonic.

31

of the eighteenth century[1] and the naked prosaic descriptions of Evgeny and his thoughts and actions have been more than once studied by the Pushkin specialists[2] and need no further comment here. But what might be called the 'third manner'—the style used to describe the elements and certain aspects of St. Petersburg—has received considerably less attention from the critics. It is of course not always easy to say where the boundary between this and the other two styles runs. At times this 'third manner' looks like a fusion of the 'Petrine style' and the 'Evgeny style': the second half of the Introduction (43 sq.), for example, modulates from the jingle of

Когда я в комнате моей
Пишу, читаю без лампады (50-1)

When in my room | I write or read without a lamp

to the majestic alliterative rumble of

Твоей твердыни дым и гром (76),

The smoke and thunder of your fortress,

at the same time containing lines reminiscent of the cosy townscapes of *Evgeny Onegin* (see especially 63–6).[3] Those passages, however, which have as their central 'character' the river, the rain, the wind or even the time of year are on the whole distinguishable from the rest of the poem.

It has often been remarked that *The Bronze Horseman* is the most 'atmospheric' of Pushkin's works, and there can be little doubt that this is largely due to the intensity of these 'elemental' passages. How is the effect achieved? The vocabulary is modern—archaisms such as *khladom* [cold] (98), *bregami* [banks] (171) or *peni* [foam] (382)

---

[1] See Pumpyansky, '*Mednyy vsadnik*'; Aronson, 'K istorii'; Bryusov, *Moy Pushkin*, pp. 85 sq. For some interesting remarks on the syntactic similarity of the 'Petrine' *abba* quatrains in *The Bronze Horseman* and the concluding quatrains of the odes of Lomonosov see Vickery, '*Mednyj vsadnik*'.

[2] E.g. Blagoy, *Masterstvo*, pp. 206 sq.; Slonimsky, *Masterstvo*, pp. 297 sq.; Timofeev, '*Mednyy vsadnik*', pp. 225 sq.; Pumpyansky, '*Mednyy vsadnik*', p. 93.

[3] Vickery ('*Mednyj vsadnik*', p. 140) considers that lines 67–91 are 'Petrine'. N. S. Pospelov, however, considers the whole of the third paragraph of the Introduction (43–83) syntactically homogeneous. See Pospelov, *Sintaksicheskiy stroy*, pp. 171–248.

are exceptional; it is simple—so simple that at times one can catch the intonations of popular speech (*duri* [madness], *nevmoch'* [unable], *poutru* [in the morning] 169–71); it is unemotional and concrete; and it is precise—words tend to be semantically unambiguous. Even if a polysemantic word appears at first reading ambiguous because of its position in the sentence, the ambiguity is soon dissolved by the context. An attribute such as *mrachnyy* when qualifying *val* (wave) at the beginning of a sentence could have several connotations apart from its purely denotary sense of 'dark': 'fearful', 'gloomy' or 'sullen', for instance; and in

Мрачный вал
Плескал на пристань (381-2)

The sullen wave | Splashed against the embankment

it could mean any of these, until the wave is metaphorically personified by *ropshcha peni* [reproachfully grumbling] and by the graphic simile of the unsuccessful petitioner, and 'sullen' becomes the appropriate epithet.[1] The syntax matches the vocabulary in simplicity (e.g. *Uzh bylo posdno i temno* [Already it was late and dark] 103), almost the only form of subordination being gerundial clauses (*pechal'no voya* [sadly howling]). It is the richness of the imagery combined with the subtlety of the 'orchestration' that gives the work its evocative atmospheric power.

The imagery is remarkably bold and often startlingly original. It is based exclusively on the pathetic fallacy. Nature is personified throughout either by metaphors or by similes. In the nine lines at the beginning of Part I, for example, the inanimate is animated in a series of vivid images: November breathes; the Neva tosses like a sick man in his restless[2] bed; the rain beats angrily; the wind howls gloomily. In the first five lines of the introduction to Part II the Neva is personified by metaphor, this time as an evil-doer returning from some cataclysmic act of destruction (earlier, in the description of the flood, the waves 'climb into windows like thieves' 191, cf. 341): the animation is intensified by an extended simile (265–73) in which a

---

[1] Note that in the next line *Mrachno bylo* could mean either 'it was dark' or 'it was gloomy', although the primary sense of 'dark' seems more likely in view of *vo t'me nochnoy* [in the darkness of the night] in 388.

[2] Note how the unexpected hypallage increases the effectiveness of the simile.

band of marauders are pictured bursting into a village and returning home laden with loot, each of the four lines describing their retreat syntactically and lexically balancing the Neva's metaphorical withdrawal. A few lines further on the scene of the crime is converted to a battlefield: the waves are now 'full of the triumph of victory' (279) and the Neva now 'breathes heavily' (echoing the breathing of November in line 98) 'like a horse galloping home from battle' (forestalling the image of the battlefield to come in line 305). We are never allowed to forget that Nature is as alive and active as Evgeny. Verbs, adjectives and adverbs continually bring the elements to life or keep them alive, the effectiveness of the metamorphosis being frequently heightened by the addition of a subjective-emotional epithet—to say that the wind howled *gloomily* or *sadly* implies an *additional* element of personification: the wind is not just a person howling, but a gloomy or a sad one; or again, the 'violence' by which the Neva is exhausted (261) is described as 'insolent' (*naglym*), an adjective which properly qualifies a human being—an imaginary bandit—and brings 'violence' to life.

Again and again the effectiveness of the imagery and the intensity of the mood are heightened by the virtuosity of the 'sound-painting'— the astonishing arrangement of syllables, vowels and consonants to convey various effects. In no *poema*, indeed in no long work of Pushkin was such ambitious 'orchestration' attempted as in *The Bronze Horseman*. It is not just a question of simple *sound-imitation* by means of onomatopaeic effects (*Shipen'e penistykh bokalov* [The hiss of foaming goblets], for example) or words devoid of onomatopoeic effects—e.g. *Serdito bilsya dozhd' v okno* [Angrily the rain beat against the window]—where the words taken separately have no peculiarly sonorous qualities but when taken together produce the desired acoustic effect by virtue of the peculiar combination of consonants and vowels. This technique is indeed frequently used to illustrate the sounds conveyed by the words: the boom of the cannons (*Tvoey tverdyni dym i grom* [The smoke and thunder of your fortress]—*dyn, dym, grom*), the howling of the wind (*vyl . . . unylo* 161), the gurgling of the water (*Kotlom klokocha i klubyas'* [Bubbling like a cauldron and swirling] 181). But Pushkin also manipulates his sounds simply in order to achieve certain sound-patterns and thus to heighten the effect of a line or a passage. At times he does this in order to imprint

34

a phrase upon the reader's mind, in the same way as he uses variation of metre to lend lustre or weight to a line of particular significance. We have only to compare

Насмешка неба над землей (250)

Heaven's mockery at earth

with the variant forced upon Pushkin by the censor

Насмешка рока над землей

Fate's mockery at earth

to see how effective and memorable the original alliteration is. But mostly it is applied to whole passages, as for example the second half of the description of the flood (*Pogoda pushche svirepela . . .* [The weather raged more fiercely . . .] 179 sq.).

The pattern is often extraordinarily complex, and it is not proposed to examine the technique or to attempt to improve on Bryusov's analysis.[1] Suffice it to stress that the more one examines the text of *The Bronze Horseman*, the more intricate the pattern appears. At a first reading of the 'hymn' to St. Petersburg, for example,

Люблю тебя, Петра творенье,
Люблю твой строгий, стройный вид,
Невы державное теченье,
Береговой ее гранит,
Твоих оград узор чугунный,
Твоих задумчивых ночей
Прозрачный сумрак, блеск безлунный . . .

I love you, [city of] Peter's creation, | I love your stern, harmonious aspect, | The majestic flow of the Neva, | Her granite banks, | The iron tracery of your railings, | Your pensive nights' | Transparent twilight and moonless gleam . . .

one might notice the alliteration of *strogiy | stroynyy*, or the combination of liquid consonants in p*r* oz*r*achnyy sum*r*ak, b*l*esk bez*l*unnyy. But a deeper study would reveal such effects as the insistent play on *t* (*t–tr–tvr*) in *Lyublyu tebya Petra tvoren'e*, the parallel alternations of the dentals and their palatalized consonants (*d→zh: t→ch*) in

[1] Bryusov, *Moy Pushkin*, pp. 63–94, 229–63.

derzhavnoe techen'e, and the interplay of *r* and *g* in b*e*r*e*govoy–granit–ograd–uzo*r* chugunnyy.

It is of course virtually impossible to say what makes Pushkin's 'sound-painting' devices so aesthetically effective and distinguishes them from the distressing vulgarity of say Bal'mont[1] or mere cleverness. But undoubtedly a large part of their effectiveness is due to this 'hidden' quality, to the unobtrusive tact with which Pushkin exploits them and to the subtle interplay of meaning and sound.

Perhaps a further study of these formal aspects of *The Bronze Horseman* will help the reader to understand why its impact on generations of critics has been so powerful and why it is so often called the 'greatest' of all his works. To summarize, we can provide a few superlatives of our own which may prove more helpful than 'greatest'. Of all Pushkin's *poemy, The Bronze Horseman* is the most intimate and personal. It is the most successful experiment with contrasting, blending and interplay of stylistic layers. It contains the most developed and the most evocative imagery; and its texture is enlivened by the richest 'orchestration' and sound-painting. Of course many more superlatives could be added to the list and the second term of comparison of many of them could be extended. 'Of all Pushkin's *poemy*' could read 'of all Pushkin's works'.

EVGENY ONEGIN

The immensely complex work that is *Evgeny Onegin* has engendered a bewildering variety of critical interpretations. It has been called 'an encyclopaedia of Russian life' (Belinsky), 'first of all and above all a phenomenon of style . . . not "a picture of Russian life"' (Nabokov), 'the first Russian realistic novel' (Gor'ky) and even 'the first truly great realistic creation of all world literature in the

---

[1] Cf. the lines quoted in Unbegaun, *Russian Versification*, p. 119:

> Вечер. Взморье. Вздохи ветра.
> Величавый возглас волн.
> Буря близко. В берег бьется
> Чуждый чарам черный челн.

Evening. Sea-shore. Sighs of the wind. | The majestic cry of the waves. | A storm is near. The shore is buffeted | by the black bark which knows no charms.

nineteenth century' (Blagoy), 'a broad and just portrayal of the world of lies, hypocrisy and emptiness' (Meylakh), 'the most intimate of all Pushkin's works' (Blagoy again), 'a novel of parody and a parody of the novel' (Shklovsky). The problem of interpretation is not simplified, as it rarely is, by Pushkin's various extraneous utterances. In a letter of 4th November, 1823 written just after the completion of Chapter I, for instance, he describes his work as 'not a novel but a novel in verse—the devil of a difference! Like *Don Juan*', while eighteen months later he writes: 'you compare the first chapter of my novel with *Don Juan*. No one respects *Don Juan* more than I do . . . but it has nothing in common with *Onegin*.'[1] In his 'Preface' to *Evgeny Onegin*, added to the work in 1827, he talks, with enraging vagueness, of 'multicoloured chapters, half funny, half sad, of the common people (*prostonarodnykh*), ideal, the carefree fruit of my enjoyments'.

We may be able to get a clearer idea about the nature of *Evgeny Onegin*, if we consider Pushkin's attitude, as expressed *within* the work, to the narrator, to his characters, to the events described, to the reader, and above all to the novel, if not to poetry itself. This relationship is remarkably intricate and, it would appear at first sight, contradictory: the distance between the narrator and the object of his narrative seems now vast, now tiny; the identification of Pushkin with the narrator—now credible, now suspect; the narrator himself—now ironic and detached, now passionate and involved.

Evgeny Onegin is the most 'intrusive' of all Pushkin's works: the narrator continually thrusts himself to the fore. From time to time he may retreat into the wings in order to describe an action or let his characters speak for themselves. But never for long. Back he comes, often with what looks like unquenchable garrulity, to chat, to comment, to explain, to reminisce, and to treat his readers to huge asides.

Now had Pushkin confined his narrative method to objective, impersonal 'showing' (e.g. 'It is now dark: [Evgeny] gets into a sleigh. "Look out, look out!", the shout rings out' etc., etc., 1/16), to omniscient 'telling' or interpretation (e.g. 'The Russian *khandra* [spleen, ennui] overcame him little by little', 1/38) and to an intimate author-reader relationship used for commenting or for shifting the story

---

[1] Letter of 24th March, 1825, to A. Bestuzhev. All Pushkin's remarks on *Evgeny Onegin* are printed in Brodsky, *Evgeniy Onegin*, pp. 17–29.

37

forward ('But what of my Onegin?', 1/35), then we might have been able readily to suspend our disbelief and to accept the illusion of the story's reality and the credibility of the author. But Pushkin complicates matters. Towards the end of Chapter I he introduces himself as a *character* in the story.

Up to this point Pushkin has already laid the foundation for the character of Evgeny by closely observing his behaviour and the workings of his mind. At the same time he has given us a great deal of information about himself—about his spleen, boredom, indifference, about his love of pleasure and his rakish life, about his infinite regret for the past and his 'romantic' amours, about his habits, his likes and dislikes, and so on. Then, in Stanza 45, he informs us: 'I made friends with him at that time' (i.e. during Evgeny's period of boredom with life in St. Petersburg—*before* the action of the story begins), and proceeds to compare his own character with Evgeny's, to reminisce on their meetings together and finally, in Stanza 51, to part from him ('But we were separated by fate for a long time'). Except in the 'Fragments from Evgeny's Journey' (see below, p. 39), 'Pushkin', the character in the story, never emerges again.

From the narrative point of view this unmotivated parting of 'Pushkin' and Onegin is essential, and we are obliged to forget 'Pushkin': the subsequent story could not have been told by an 'I' who personally knew one of the characters, unless all pretence of omniscience were dropped. 'Pushkin', the friend of Evgeny, could not have done what only Pushkin the author could do—namely pry into his characters' minds, record their thoughts in monologues and observe their behaviour when out of Evgeny's presence. Why then does Pushkin introduce this perplexing ghost?

Of course it might be explained by 'carelessness' (cf. 'the carefree fruit of my enjoyments' of the 'Preface') or speed of writing, an unwillingness at this early stage of the novel to think ahead to future technical complications; or it might even be attributed to a slapdash, devil-may-care touch of Byronism.[1] But although such carelessness could easily have been removed, Pushkin made no attempt to eliminate

---

[1] There is a similarly disquieting intrusion in Canto I of *Don Juan* where Byron assures his readers not only that his story is true but that he actually '*Saw* Juan's last elopement with the devil' (1/203). This, however, can be attributed to 'playfulness' on Byron's part, or an inability to resist rhyming 'devil' with 'Seville'.

Evgeny's awkward friend from the story at a later date; indeed he included in his original eighth chapter (replaced by the present Chapter 8 and printed separately as 'Fragments from Onegin's Journey') the so-called 'Odessa stanzas' in which Pushkin again appears briefly as a character in his own right: 'I lived at that time in dusty Odessa . . .'[1] Perhaps the real reason for the inclusion, or at any rate the ultimate retention, of this additional 'character' was in fact to blur or destroy the illusion of reality? A consideration of Pushkin's authorial intrusions in the novel as a whole may help us further in this direction.

Why does Pushkin intrude at such length and with such frequency throughout the work? Two obvious answers present themselves. First of all, a 'novel in verse' or a 'free novel', as Pushkin called it (8/50)—that is, a novel bound by no limits, no rules of genre, a novel 'like *Don Juan*' in fact—was the ideal vehicle for personal commentary. There were no tiresome conventions to hem the author in. Here was an opportunity to discourse on subjects which intrigued, worried, fascinated or puzzled him, to go off on seemingly arbitrary and capricious tangents in any direction, to expatiate on love, literature, art, society, fate, women, friendship and so on.

Of course such garrulity is deceptive. However capricious Pushkin's disquisitions appear at first glance, they are in fact carefully woven into the fabric of the novel. What looks like a loose clutter of structural units separated by rambling digressions turns out, on closer scrutiny, to be a work of classical tautness and proportions.[2] Time and again the narrator intrudes not just to indulge in compulsive ad-libbing, but to move the narrative, to change the subject and the mood, to increase or decrease the tempo, even to explain away narrative difficulties. One example will suffice. In Chapter 4 a series of seemingly irrepressible discourses on random topics turns out to be a skilfully controlled bridge-passage between one theme and another. After

---

[1] This line is followed by ten stanzas describing life in Odessa as Pushkin remembered it from his stay there in 1823–4. The last line of the 'Fragments' runs 'And so I lived at that time in Odessa . . .', which is the first line of a series of stanzas which survived only in MS form. In these Pushkin states that he had 'forgotten about the gloomy rake, the hero of my tale', who never corresponded with him. He then briefly describes his meeting with Evgeny, and, a few lines further on, has them part once more.

[2] On the 'mathematically exact compositional structure' of *Evgeny Onegin*, see Blagoy, *Masterstvo*, pp. 178–98; Lotman, 'Khudozhestvennaya struktura'.

describing with sentimental clichés and devastating irony (4/25, 26) how Lensky and Ol′ga pass their time together, Pushkin slips into a light, bantering digression on albums (4/27–30)—still in the same 'stylistic key' as the Lensky-Ol′ga theme, though with slightly more sophistication and wit. Gradually the subject changes and with it the tone: from albums to madrigals, from madrigals to elegies, from elegies to odes; and by Stanza 32 we are involved in an esoteric literary debate (32, 33). In the following stanza (34), subtly linked with its predecessor by two splendidly conventional lines aping the periphrastic formulae of the eighteenth-century ode

> Поклонник славы и свободы,
> В волненьи бурных дум своих,

An admirer of fame and freedom, | In the excitement of his stormy thoughts.

Pushkin returns to Lensky, but only to deflate him in the next two lines:

> Владимир и писал бы оды,
> Да Ольга не читала их.

Vladimir might have written odes, | But Ol′ga would not have read them.

The mock-serious digression which follows, with its four lines of conventional poetic jargon:

> И впрям, блажен любовник скромный,
> Читающий мечты свои
> Предмету песен и любви,
> Красавице приятно-томной!

And indeed blessed is the modest lover | Who reads his daydreams | To the object of his songs and love, | A pleasantly-languorous beauty!

capped by two of down-to-earth deflation:

> Блажен.. хоть, может быть, она
> Совсем иным развлечена.

Blessed . . . though perhaps she | Is diverted by something quite different.

remind us that we are once more back in Pushkin's own intimate world. This is confirmed by Stanza 35, which is full of homely simplicity (*staroy nyane*[1] [old nanny]; *skuchnogo obeda* [boring dinner]; *zabredshego soseda* [a neighbour who has dropped in]; *pugayu stado dikikh utok* [I scare a flock of wild ducks]) mixed with irony and wit: again the mock serious 'poetic' is punctured by the simplicity of the 'prose'. The periphrastic:

> Но я плоды моих мечтаний
> И гармонических затей

But I [read] *the fruits of my fantasies | And of my harmonious devices*

is followed by

> Читаю только старой няне

Only to my old nanny

and nine more equally unaffected 'prosaic' lines, while the concluding couplet consists of the lofty, archaic, Derzhavin-like:

> Вняв пенью сладкозвучных строф

Hearkening to the chant of sweet-sounding strophes

followed by the artless:

> Они слетают с берегов.

They fly away from the banks.

This combination of cosiness and irony, simplicity and bathos, attunes us for the Onegin theme which follows immediately (Onegin in the country, leading a life similar to Pushkin's at Mikhaylovskoe[2]). The transition is complete. The digressions have guided us from one major theme to another.

---

[1] Note how the phraseology (*Podrugi yunosti moey* [Companion of my youth]) repeats that of *Zimniy vecher* [Winter Evening] written at the same time in Mikhaylovskoe (*dobraya podruzhka | Bednoy yunosti moey* [Dear Companion | Of my poor youth]). Cf. *Nyane* [To my Nanny] (1826): *Podruga dney moikh surovykh* [Companion of my bleak days].

[2] In 1826 (27th May) Pushkin wrote to Vyazemsky: 'In Canto 4 of *Onegin* I depicted my own life'.

We have seen that authorial intrusions in *Evgeny Onegin* are used both as an outlet for Pushkin's views on a variety of topics and as a structural device. But a third use can also be discerned: the 'lyrical author' is displayed, it seems, in order to create a sense of what one critic[1] has called the 'second reality', or the reality of the creative process. Now *Evgeny Onegin* is a highly 'literary' work. It is full of allusions to authors, books, styles, genres, literary conflicts; it contains parodies, imitations, quotations; there are obscure esoteric references to literary circles. It is a work which needs a commentary to enable the reader to unravel the more obstruse allusions. As such it might be considered an imitation of *Don Juan*, and indeed the literariness of *Don Juan* no doubt attracted and influenced Pushkin. But Pushkin takes his 'literariness' a stage further. He makes the reader constantly aware of the poet in the background, manipulating, creating, comparing, and thus points up the conventional nature of the 'first reality' of the work, the reality of the plot, the love story, the setting; he undermines reality, as it were. A landscape, for example, is not necessarily painted to provide a backcloth against which the *personae* are going to perform. It is painted rather as a model of the artist's style and technique. Take for example the beginning of Chapter 5. Tat'yana wakes up in Stanza 1 to see a wintry landscape from her window. We *believe* in the scene as she is made to witness it: in other words, the illusion is created because we see it through her eyes. But with the first word of the second stanza this is no longer the case. The exclamatory *Zima!* [Winter!] makes us immediately aware that it is now Pushkin the artist intruding with a *generalized* picture of winter, just as 'concrete' and 'realistic' as the catalogue of objects viewed by Tat'yana in Stanza 1, but no longer forming a realistic setting for the characters or the action of the story. As if to drive this point home, Pushkin starts Stanza 3 with a comment on his painting ('But perhaps pictures of this kind will not attract you: all this [you will say] is lowly nature; there is not much that is elegant here'), and even goes on to compare his technique with that of this contemporaries Vyazemsky and Baratynsky. In other words we are made to feel that the nature picture of Stanza 2, for all its 'realism', is not part of the décor at all, but an example of Pushkin's art. Pushkin is showing us what he can do. Our attention is distracted entirely from Tat'yana, who has to be

[1] Stilman, 'Problemy'.

artificially re-introduced in Stanza 4 ('Tat'yana . . . loved the Russian winter') before we can be lulled back into the illusion of the Tat'yana setting.

The same sort of thing occurs in Chapter 4. Having described Onegin's country life and habits with intimate and convincing detail (4/37, 39), Pushkin moves over to the changing seasons and in Stanza 41 produces another 'model', another realistic and 'concrete' picture, this time of autumn. And again we realize that this is not a setting for Evgeny at all, but a set-piece as it were. The point is emphasized by Pushkin in the following stanza where he interrupts his highly realistic description to make a jocular comment in parenthesis:

> И вот уже трещат морозы
> И серебрятся средь полей...
> (Читатель ждет уж рифмы *розы*;
> На, вот возьми ее скорей!)

And now the brittle-hard frosts have set in, | Shining silver amidst the fields . . . | (The reader is already expecting the rhyme 'roses'; | Here you are then, take it quickly!) (In Russian 'roses' rhymes with 'frosts'.)

Of course this is not to say that we are never aware of the setting or that the characters always perform against an artificial background. Again and again we are made to feel the atmosphere, the physical presence of the characters against a material setting. But we are never allowed to enjoy the illusion for long, for the illusion is always being undermined by the stylistic devices of the author, just as it was undermined by the early introduction of 'Pushkin' the friend of Evgeny. One may be carried away by the tense atmosphere of the duel—by the cold technical brilliance of the pistol-loading scene (6/29), by the doom-laden movements of the contestants moving heavily towards each other (*Pokhodkoy tverdoy, tikho, rovno* . . . [With firm gait, calmy, evenly . . .] 30), the awful finality of dead Lensky's immobility and the blood 'steaming' from his wound (32); but the final feeling one carries away from the scene is one not of pity, anguish, horror, but of amazement at Pushkin's poetic versatility. In what should be one of the most solemn moments of the whole poem, Pushkin pours forth a 'torrent of unrelated images'[1] and second-hand clichés to describe poor dead Lensky in his own style:

> Младой певец
> Нашел безвременный конец.
> Дохнула буря, цвет прекрасный
> Увял на утренней заре,
> Потух огонь на алтаре!..

The young singer | Has found an untimely end. | The storm wind blew, the fair blossom | Faded at the dawn of day, | The flame on the altar went out! . . .

and then follows it up with the great extended image of the empty house—quiet, utterly simple, majestic and haunting:

> Теперь, как в доме опустелом,
> Всё в нем и тихо и темно;
> Замолкло навсегда оно.
> Закрыты ставни, окны мелом
> Забелены. Хозяйки нет.
> А где, Бог весть. Пропал и след.

Now, as in a deserted house, | All within is both quiet and dark; | It has become silent for ever. | The shutters are closed. With chalk the windows | Are whitened. The owner is not there. | But where she is God knows. All trace is lost.

'Pushkin's own contribution, a sample as it were of what *he* can do', as one critic has remarked.[2] We have been involved not so much in the events as in the manner of their telling. We have been made conscious—and this time without any intrusive hint from the author—of Pushkin's manipulation of style and poetic technique.

If we compare the methods of *Evgeny Onegin* with those of *Count Nulin*, the point will be made clearer. For all the witty, sophisticated intrusions, *Count Nulin* is a highly *realistic* work: there are no contrasts in style, no comments on the verse, language or manner, no literary allusions. The result is a vivid impression of the squalor, boredom, dirt and artificiality of the deglamorized life of the country

---

[1] Nabokov, *Eugene Onegin*, vol. 3, pp. 52–3.
[2] Ibid.

landowner and his wife. The background is painted to create an illusion of reality, and Pushkin takes good care not to shatter it. When Natal'ya Pavlovna looks out of *her* window, we know that the farmyard is what *she* sees. We know that the impression made on us is the same as that made on her. The scene may have been conceived by Pushkin as just another essay in the 'Flemish' style, but he never lets us into the secret. There is no parading of talent. We are not made aware of his presence as the artist in the background. The same applies even to *The Bronze Horseman*. In spite of Pushkin's contrasting and blending of stylistic elements we are never allowed to glimpse the poet at work. We are made to believe in the atmosphere of 'autumnal chill' and to accept it as the background for Evgeny's wandering. We are never aware of Pushkin 'making it strange'.[1]

Pushkin's stressing of the written, literary nature of *Evgeny Onegin*, his making the reader conscious of his presence as the creative artist in the background, does not diminish the importance or even the sincerity of the views he expresses—on society, love, friendship or fate, for example; it does not lessen the social or the historical significance of the work. For many readers it may make no difference to their immediate perception of the novel proper—i.e. the interaction of the characters against their given background; indeed it should be possible to read *Evgeny Onegin*—and no doubt many do—ignoring the destructive elements and 'weeping' with 'Pushkin' for Tat'yana.[2]

---

[1] The only verse work of Pushkin's comparable to *Evgeny Onegin* in this respect is *The Little House in Kolomna* (*Domik v Kolomne*) (1830). Not only does it begin with eight stanzas in which technical problems of versification are discussed, but the narrative is interrupted by such comments as:

> Бледная Диана
> Глядела долго девушке в окно [another girl at the window!]
> (Без этого ни одного романа
> Не обойдется; так заведено!)

Pale Diana | Gazed long at the girl in the window | (Without this not one novel | Can manage; thus it is decreed!)

[2] R. Matlaw in his perceptive article on Tat'yana's dream describes Pushkin's 'crie de coeur' in 3/15

> Татьяна, милая Татьяна!
> С тобой теперь я слезы лью ..

Tat'yana, dear Tat'yana! | With you I now shed tears.

as 'a parody of author involvement in sentimental fiction'. Matlaw, 'The Dream', p. 493.

45

In no other work does Pushkin allow his consciousness of *style* to be felt so acutely by the reader as in *Evgeny Onegin*. Our attention is constantly being drawn to the technique of description, to the manipulation of phraseology, to the choice of colours for townscapes and landscapes, to the choice of syntax for action, movement, conversation, to the choice of clichés for objects of parody and ironic treatment. Yet it is difficult to label the various styles, to talk of the 'Romantic', or the 'mock-classical', or the 'realistic', because these terms are often imprecise, and one particular 'style' may consist of a deliberate mixture of diverse elements. It would perhaps simplify the problem if we were to consider two main 'manners' of writing which seem to run through *Evgeny Onegin*, sometimes exclusive of each other, sometimes temporarily coalescing, but for the most part in strict juxtaposition, if not actual conflict. The problem is to supply them with a name: one might be called loosely the 'poetic' manner, the manner typical of Pushkin's own early effusions, of Zhukovsky and the Russian 'pre-Romantics'—the stringing together of periphrases, some from the pseudo-classical treasury of Russian eighteenth-century poetry, some from the Karamzinist school of the beginning of the nineteenth century—of tired stereotypes evocative of sentiment and emotions, of vague polysemantic metaphors depicting the 'inexpressible disturbance of the soul'.[1] The other might be called the 'prosaic' manner—realistic, objective, unemotional, undecorative, concrete, concise, to use a few of the epithets which can be applied to it—the manner with which Pushkin began to experiment in *The Gipsies* for what we called the 'objective narrator's voice' and which is so much in evidence in *Count Nulin*, *The Little House in Kolomna* and the 'Evgeny passages' of *The Bronze Horseman*.

The most striking element of the 'poetic' manner is the use of clichés formed by joining together mutually evocative adjectives, nouns, verbs and adverbs. The clusters thus formed (particularly if one or all of the elements are 'abstract' or 'subjective') do little or nothing to increase our knowledge of the original concept. Thus, in the field of emotions—the most fertile for such conventional growths—*grust'* [grief] is barely enriched by trite epithets like *nezhnaya* [tender], *beznadezhnaya* [hopeless] or *taynaya* [secret], and we know little more about the nature of a person's love when the verb *'lyubit''* [to love], say,

[1] Gukovsky, *Pushkin i russkie romantiki*, p. 47.

46

is qualified by *tomno* [languorously], *strastno* [passionately] or *plamenno* [ardently]. It is as though the poet has at his fingertips a number of words to express emotions from despair to bliss to which he can add vague, imprecise qualifiers at will. The results are often as meaningless and uninformative as the combination of traditional set themes used by the mediaeval writer to describe a saint's childhood or a battle.

Even more widespread are the conventional periphrases which decorate the 'poetic' style of *Evgeny Onegin*. These range from the heavy classical conceits (*Nemolchnyy shopot Nereidy* [Nereid's unceasing whisper] 8/4; or *Priyut zadumchivykh Driad* [The shelter of pensive dryads] 2/1) to such complex and often subtle combinations as:

> Лесов таинственная сень
> С печальным шумом обнажалась (4/40)

The mysterious shade of the forests | Was baring itself with mournful sound.

in which the adjectives (particularly *pechal'nym* [mournful]) refer rather to the effect produced on the onlooker than to the nouns they qualify; and they include innumerable circumlocutions to describe natural phenomena such as 'the wondrous choir of heavenly luminaries' (5/9) or the bee which 'flies from its waxen cell to fetch the tribute of the fields' (7/1), as well as the ubiquitous images of heat, fire, storm and waves to denote passion.

Pushkin's views on such stylistic artificialities, as far as prose is concerned at any rate, were unequivocal. In an unfinished article written before *Evgeny Onegin* (in 1822) he attacked those Russian writers who, 'considering it base to explain the most ordinary things simply, think to enliven childish prose with additions and flaccid metaphors. They never say "friendship" without adding "this sacred feeling, the noble flame of which etc.". Instead of "early in the morning" they write "barely had the first rays of the rising sun illumined the eastern edges of the azure heaven" . . . I read in a review of some theatre-lover: "this young nursling of Thalia and Melpomene, generously endowed by Apollo"—My God—put "this good young actress".'[1] How can we then explain the profusion of clichés, 'flaccid

---

[1] *SS*, vol. 6, pp. 255–6.

metaphors' and periphrases which we find in *Evgeny Onegin*? Why is there such an abundance of 'languorous glances', 'tormented hearts' and 'seething passions'? Why 'Diana's face' (1/47) and not the moon? Why the loans from Parny, Millevoye, Zhukovsky, Milonov, Kyukhel'beker and countless other second-rate early Romantics? The answer is to be found in the use which Pushkin makes of his 'poetic' style.

Primarily it is used for parody. In his description of Lensky and Ol'ga, Pushkin mercilessly ridicules them as if to highlight their artificiality, their tawdriness and their insincerity. Lensky pours out his thoughts before the duel in a string of grandiloquent hackneyed metaphors:

> Не потерплю, чтоб развратитель
> Огнем и вздохов и похвал
> Младое сердце искушал,
> Чтоб червь презренный, ядовитый
> Точил лилеи стебелек,
> Чтобы двухутренний цветок
> Увял еще полураскрытый... (6/17)

I shall not permit the libertine | With the fire of sighs and flattery | To tempt her young heart, | Nor the despicable poisonous worm | To nibble at the lily's tender stalk, | Nor the flower on its second morn | To fade away still half-unfolded . . .

Even more preposterous are his verses (6/21–2) which read like a travesty of Pushkin's own efforts to dazzle his school-friends. Ol'ga, on whose eventual dismissal from the story Pushkin wastes not more than thirteen lines (7/10), fares no better: in the three stanzas which introduce her (2/21–3) we are treated to a veritable orgy of gallic stereotyped expressions. To warn his readers that such effusions are not to be taken seriously (as if authorial comment were necessary!) Pushkin inserts his own wry deflationary remraks. Lensky's pre-duel interior monologue is capped with:

> Все это значило, друзья:
> С приятелем стреляюсь я (6/17)

All this meant, my friends, | 'I am going to fight a duel with my friend'.

His verses are described as 'dim and limp', while Ol′ga's description is rounded off with

> Все в Ольге...но любой роман
> Возьмите и найдете верно
> Ее портрет... (2/23)

All this is in Ol′ga . . . But take any novel | And for sure you will find | Her portrait . . .

Only the 'torrent of unrelated images' which describe Lensky's death receives no comment: the contrast of the majestic 'empty house' is sufficient.

The 'poetic' manner, however, is by no means confined to pure parody; we find it used, for example, in passages where no mimicry or outright mockery are intended, but where one may still suspect an ironic attitude of the author to his subject. When Tat′yana's emotions, aroused by her imagination or by her reading of sentimental novels, are uncontrolled, they are given the full 'poetic' treatment. At her namesday party she is so overcome with emotion that she nearly swoons (5/30). Pushkin describes her with two nature similes ('paler than the morning moon, timider than the hunted deer'), talks vaguely of her 'darkling' (*temneyushchikh*) eyes, and finally tosses together the images of fire and tempest to convey her agitation ('passionate heat blazes stormily within her')[1]. Still more banal are the images used to describe her disturbed condition after the rendezvous with Evgeny in the garden (4/23). The 'mad sufferings of love' 'agitate the young soul thirsting for sadness'; Tat′yana 'burns with inconsolable passion'; 'sleep shuns her bed' and her youth 'grows dim'. We have only to compare this stream of romantic exuberance with the phraseology used to depict the Tat′yana of Chapter 8 to realize how effective this 'poetic' style can be for creating an image of immaturity and uncontrolled (and often derivative) emotionalism. When Tat′yana is

---

[1] Note that when, at the end of the stanza, her 'will and the power of reason' prevail, she is described in quite different language:

> Она два слова
> Сквозь зубы молвила тишком
> И усидела за столом.

Two words | She uttered quietly through her teeth | And remained seated at the table.

portrayed as above pettiness, contemptuous of the artificialities of society, mistress of her feelings, *mature*—then the language becomes concrete, prosaic, majestically solemn and icily simple. In Stanza 14 a string of negatives (*ne . . . ne . . . ne . . ., bez . . . bez . . . bez . . . bez . . .*) showing what qualities were absent in her make-up is capped with

Все тихо, просто было в ней —

Everything about her was quiet, simple

words which not only describe the mature Tat'yana but also the language itself. When Tat'yana meets Evgeny again in Stanza 18, her self-control is brought to light by the absolute calm and simplicity of the vocabulary and syntax:

Но ей ничто не изменило:
В ней сохранился тот же тон,
Был так же тих ее поклон.

Ей-ей! не то, чтоб содрогнулась,
Иль стала вдруг бледна, красна...
У ней и бровь не шевельнулась;
Не сжала даже губ она (8/18-19).

But nothing betrayed her: | She preserved exactly the same tone, | Her bow was just as serene.
In very truth, far from shuddering | Or becoming suddenly pale or crimson, | She did not even move an eyebrow, | Nor did she even compress her lips.

The 'prosaic' style needs no detailed description here: the basic elements have already been examined above in the discussion of the 'objective narrator's voice' in *The Gipsies*. The principles are much the same: elimination of unnecessary epithets; absence of 'abstract' and vague parts of speech, of periphrases, clichés and hyperbole, etc.; economy of words; simplified syntax with a minimum of subordination; frequent enjambement between lines and quatrains;[1] a tendency to catalogue, particularly concrete objects (see especially 7/31, 38).

---

[1] For the question of the syntactical disruption of the normal division of the *Onegin* stanza into four quatrains and a couplet, see Lotman, 'Khudozhestvennaya struktura'; Vinokur, 'Slovo i stikh'; Pospelov, *Sintaksicheskiy stroy*.

To these can be added a considerable lowering of the tone and the introduction of purely conversational elements—both lexical (vulgarisms) and syntactical (ellipsis, infinitives expressing inceptive past tense, interjections in place of main verbs, frequentative use of perfective verbs, etc.).

The 'prosaic' style is most frequently used for description of action. Interest or excitement is kept at a high pitch by some or all of the devices mentioned above. The classic example is Tat'yana's headlong rush through the garden to meet Evgeny in Chapter 3:

> Вдруг топот!...кровь ее застыла.
> Вот ближе! скачут...и на двор
> Евгений! "Ах!" — и легче тени
> Татьяна прыг в другие сени,
> С крыльца на двор, и прямо в сад,
> Летит, летит; взглянуть назад
> Не смеет; мигом обежала
> Куртины, мостики, лужок,
> Аллею к озеру, лесок,
> Кусты сирен переломала,
> По цветникам летя к ручью.
> И, задыхаясь, на скамью
>
> Упала... (38-9)

Suddenly the clatter of horses' hoofs!...Her blood froze. | Nearer and nearer! The horses are galloping...And into the courtyard | [Drives] Evgeny! 'Ah!' [she cries], and lighter than a shadow | Tat'yana jumps into the other entrance hall, | From the porch into the courtyard, and straight into the garden | She flies, she flies; to look back | She does not dare; in an instant she ran through | Borders, [across] small bridges, a little field, | Down the avenue leading to the lake, through a copse, | Breaking down lilac shrubs, | Flying over flower-beds towards the brook. | And gasping for breath, upon the bench ...|
She fell ...

Apart from the stereotyped *krov' ee zastyla* [her blood froze], which is still attached by rhyme to the ultra-romantic first two lines of the stanza, the language is very close to common speech. The vocabulary is plain and 'concrete'; the syntax is simplicity itself—verbs are omitted (*i na dvor | Evgeniy!* [into the courtyard—Evgeny]) or replaced by interjections (*"Akh!"*; *Tat'yana pryg* [Tat'yana jumps]); there is no subordination unless we count the gerunds *letya* [flying] and *zadykhayas'* [gasping for breath]; 'concrete' nouns are piled up (*kurtiny, mostiki, luzhok* ... [borders, small bridges, a little field] etc.); enjambements—interlinear, interquatrain and even interstanza—completely disrupt the pattern of ordered poetry and break the hypnotic rhythm of the stanza. Similar passages describing action are not hard to find—Tat'yana's dream (see especially 5/14, which begins with three verbless sentences followed by four clauses in which the graphic perfectives, *zatsepit* [catches], *vyrvet* [tears], *uvyaznet* [gets stuck], *vyronit* [drops], heighten the feeling of suspense and frustration);[1] the staccato end to 5/45 where Lensky in a fury decides to fight Evgeny; the astonishingly down-to-earth pistol-loading scene (6/29).

'Action' passages are of course not the only vehicles for the 'prosaic' style. Frequently land- and townscapes receive the same treatment—perhaps with less ellipsis, but with an equal simplicity of vocabulary and syntax, a tendency to enjambement and 'cataloguing' and an avoidance of abstract, emotional phraseology—see for example the brittle vivid picture of winter in 5/2, or the 'Flemish' 'farmyard' description (*Lyublyu peschanyy kosogor* [I love a sandy hill-side]) in *Fragments from Evgeny's Journey*, or again the description of winter in 4/42.[2]

But for the most remarkable examples of simplicity and naturalness of language we must turn to the conversations, particularly to the words of Tat'yana's *nyanya* (3/17–20, 33–5) and Evgeny's housekeeper (7/17–18). Both Filippovna's and Anis'ya's utterances are as far removed from conventional 'poetic' or bookish jargon and as close to popular speech as Pushkin could get without sinking into tedious naturalistic imitation. With customary tact Pushkin avoids pure reproduction of peasant speech. There is no phonetic mimicry, for

---

[1] For the duplication of themes and expressions in Tat'yana's flight through the garden and her dream, see Matlaw, 'The Dream', pp. 495–6.

[2] See also 1/35 and 7/38 for townscapes. Note that descriptions of spring tend to be clothed in conventional romantic phraseology, eg. 7/1.

example. His effects are achieved with the aid of a few 'signal'[1] words (*zashiblo* [I've lost my memory], *byley* [true tales], *nebylits* [fables], *chereda* [sorry pass], *moy svet* [my sweet]—3/17–18; *sizhival* [used to sit], *obedyval* [used to dine], *zhival* [lived], *kostoch-kam* [dear bones]—7/17–18). Of course it's not just a question of stripping their speech of ornamentation and simplifying the syntax: it is the *rightness*, the *exactness* of so many of the expressions and gestures which in a few words make Filippovna and Anis'ya as memorable as any peasant type painstakingly built up by Nekrasov in hundreds of lines. When for example Tat'yana explains dramatically but imprecisely that she is 'sick at heart':

> 'Ах, няня, няня, я тоскую,
> Мне тошно, милая моя:
> Я плакать, я рыдать готова!..' (3/19)

'O nanny, nanny, I feel miserable, | I feel sick at heart, my dear; | I'm about to cry, to sob! . . .

Filippovna's reaction:

> — Дитя мое, ты нездорова;
> Господь помилуй и спаси!

'My child, you are unwell; | The Lord have mercy and save us!'

is exactly right. Romantic yearnings are quite beyond her ken: 'sickness of heart', a fevered look and tearfulness are in Filippovna's mind a symptom of physical illness. And when the stuttering confession comes out:

> '...Я... знаешь, няня... влюблена'

'I . . . you know, nanny . . . I'm in love'

the bewildered *nyanya* can only resort to a trembling sign of the cross and a prayer:

> — Дитя мое, Господь с тобой! —
> И няня девушку с мольбой
> Крестила дряхлою рукой.

'My child, the Lord be with you!' | And the nurse with a prayer | Made the sign of the cross over the girl with her frail hand.

---

[1] The expression is Tomashevsky's. See 'Voprosy', Sec. 6.

The 'prosaic' manner is rarely allowed to stand in isolation for long. Time and again it is placed by Pushkin in direct contrast, even in conflict, with the 'poetic'. Tat'yana's flight through the garden (3/38) is sandwiched between lines of striking banality ('her soul ached and her languorous gaze was full of tears'—'her heart, full of torments, keeps a dark dream of hope'); the haunting, liquid, moon-washed picture of Tat'yana and her *nyanya* (3/20) which concludes their first conversation is a strange mixture of well-defined 'Flemish' strokes:

> ...и на скамейке...
> С платком на голове седой
> Старушку в длинной телогрейке —

... and on the bench ... | With a kerchief on her grey head | The old woman in her long jacket ...

and vague blurred pastel shades:

> ...луна сияла
> И темным светом озаряла
> Татьяны бледные красы,
> И распущенные власы,
> И капли слез...

... the moon shone, | And with dark light illumined | the pale charms of Tat'yana | And her loosened hair | And drops of tears ...

The 'romantic' concluding couplet:

> И все дремало в тишине
> При вдохновительной луне

And everything slumbered in quiet | In the light of the inspirative moon —

which sets the seal to the predominantly 'poetic' scene consisted in the original draft of a soft 'moon' line:

> И все молчало при луне —

And everything was silent in the moonlight

followed by the stark:

Лишь кот мяукал на окне.

Only a cat miaowed at the window.

Perhaps Pushkin felt the contrast here to be too strong; at least the revised version left the reader in a certain amount of ambiguity as to the author's attitude to the picture. Unromantic miaowing was too obvious a pointer to authorial irony.

Why this perpetual juxtaposing of stylistically different elements, this conflict between 'poetry' and 'prose'? Is it just to shatter the illusion of reality, to stop the reader from taking this or that character or passage too seriously? Is it to enforce awareness of the artificiality of the 'romantic' or the solemn by placing them cheek by jowl with the 'realistic' or the vulgar? Or is it primarily the result of an overwhelming desire to demonstrate poetic skills, to exhibit art, to revel in words and to show how language, verse, metre and rhyme can be manipulated and moulded to produce certain effects?

We might go one step further and ask: Is not the fundamental theme of *Evgeny Onegin* Pushkin himself? Not necessarily a Pushkin lamenting the irretrievable passing of time and weeping for wasted youth or inability to find a meaning in life,[1] but a Pushkin observing and recording the process of his maturation as a poet and rejoicing in the ripeness of his 'prose' rather than lamenting the greenness of his 'poetry'? The clues are there. The identification of his muse with his heroine in the beginning of Chapter 8 and his comparison in *Evgeny's Journey* of the exuberance of his 'Crimean period' ('At that time I thought I needed wildernesses, the pearly crests of waves, and the sound of the sea, and rocks piled high, and the "ideal" of a proud maiden, and nameless sufferings'—all the baggage of the Romantic poet) with the sobriety of his mature style ('I have poured much water into my poetic goblet') point unmistakably to his absorption with the question of his development as a poet. Perhaps after all Pushkin meant us to take this 'complex symphony of stylistic layers'[2] first and foremost as a monument of—and to—poetic craftsmanship.

[1] Such are the general conclusions of Vickery ('Byron's *Don Juan*') and Gustafson ('Metaphor') on the fundamental meaning of *Evgeny Onegin*.
[2] Gukovsky, *Pushkin i problemy*, p. 176.

BORIS GODUNOV[1]

Belinsky called *Boris Godunov* Pushkin's Waterloo, 'in which he deployed his genius to its full breadth and depth and yet suffered a decisive defeat',[2] We may disagree with Belinsky's attribution of defeat to Pushkin's slavish imitation of Karamzin and the 'absence of a true live poetic idea which would give wholeness and fulness to the tragedy',[3] but we must admit that the play *was* a defeat, in that it did not achieve what Pushkin hoped it would achieve ('The success or failure of my tragedy will influence the reform of our dramatic system', he wrote[4]). Yet at the same time it was a victory on a number of fronts.

Before we can define the nature of the victory or assess the importance of the defeat, we must consider briefly what Pushkin's views on the drama were, what he demanded from the dramatist and what he was attempting to do in *Boris Godunov*.[5] Firstly, Pushkin rebelled against the tyranny of 'rules' in drama. The dramatist, in his opinion, should not be bound by the three classical unities, rigid observation of which could only result in improbabilities and absurdities. 'I have sacrificed two classical unities [i.e. of place and time]', he wrote, 'and barely kept the last [of action]'.[6] Secondly, the dramatist, realizing that full verisimilitude is unattainable on the stage ('where can you find verisimilitude in a building divided into two parts . . . one of

---

[1] *Boris Godunov*, planned as the first part of a trilogy on the Time of Troubles and written between December 1824 and November 1825, was received unfavourably by Nicholas I and only printed in 1831. It was first staged in 1870.

The most useful works on *Boris Godunov* are Gukovsky, *Pushkin i problemy*, Chap. 1; articles by Gorodetsky, Slonimsky and Vinokur in '*Boris Godunov*' (ed. Derzhavin); Gorodetsky, *Dramaturgiya*. For Pushkin's other attempt at tragedy, *Vadim*, of which only 22 lines were written, see Gorodetsky, *Dramaturgiya*, pp. 74–85.

[2] Belinsky, *Polnoe sobranie sochineniy* (1935–59), vol. 7, p. 505. Later in the same article Belinsky defines the positive aspects of *Boris Godunov*, but restricts his observations to such vague terms as 'excellent form', 'artistic style', 'noble classical simplicity', 'inimitable pictures of Russian life' (ibid, pp. 526–30).

[3] Ibid., p. 526.

[4] *SS*, vol. 6, p. 431.

[5] Pushkin's views are expressed mainly in his 'draft of an Introduction to *Boris Godunov*', consisting of various early letters and drafts (*SS*, vol. 6, pp. 299–302), and in his articles on Pogodin's *Marfa Posadnitsa* (ibid., pp. 359–67).

[6] Ibid., p. 281.

which is occupied by 2,000 people who by convention are not seen by those on the stage?'),[1] must strive at least for *psychological* realism: 'Truth of passions, verisimilitude of feelings in given circumstances— this is what our mind demands from the dramatic writer':[2] in other words he must aim at realistic depiction of character, which, in Pushkin's eyes, can only be achieved by avoiding monotony and addiction to type. Shakespeare is the pattern: 'The people created by Shakespeare are not, as is the case with Molière, representatives of some passion or other, of some vice—but live beings, filled with many passions, many vices. Circumstances develop before the audience their variety and their many-sided characters. With Molière the miser is miserly and that's that. With Shakespeare Shylock is miserly, shrewd, vengeful, child-loving, witty . . .'[3] Thirdly, the dramatist must free himself from the 'unity of style', 'this fourth indispensable unity of the French tragedy'.[4] A uniform—and usually stilted— language in the mouths of monarchs, messengers and children alike is the hall-mark of the artificial courtly French drama. The 'truly popular' tragedy—i.e. the Shakespearian, on the other hand, is distinguished by its linguistic variety: 'With Racine Nero does not simply say: "Je serai caché dans ce cabinet" but: "caché près de ces lieux je vous verrai, Madame". Agammemnon wakes his confidant and says to him pompously:

> *Oui, c'est Agammemnon, c'est ton roi qui t'éveille.*
> *Viens, reconnais la voix qui frappe ton oreille.*

We are used to this; we think that this is how it should be. But it must be admitted that if Shakespeare's heroes explain themselves like grooms it does not strike us as strange, for we feel that even great people ought to express simple ideas like simple people.'[5] Not only must the language be varied, but the dialogue must be made more natural; the classical one-line exchanges must be replaced by 'truth of conversation' (*istina razgovorov*). Lastly, if the drama is historical— and Pushkin envisaged no other type of drama—then historical realism must be preserved. The author must not impose his own views, must not comment or indulge in 'allusions'. His picture must

---

[1] Ibid., p. 360. [2] Ibid., p. 361.
[3] *SS*, vol. 7, p. 210. [4] *SS*, vol. 6, p. 281.
[5] Ibid., p. 362.

be entirely objective: 'Not [the dramatist], not his political opinions, not his secret or open prejudices—none of these should speak in tragedy: but people of bygone days, their minds, their prejudices. It is not his business to justify or condemn, to prompt the heroes' speeches. His duty is to resurrect the past age in all its truth'.[1]

Many critics dismiss *Boris Godunov* as structurally weak if not chaotic, and, quoting Pushkin's dictum ('I have arranged my tragedy according to the system of our father Shakespeare'),[2] attribute this weakness to the influence of Shakespeare. Unity of time and place are not observed—the action covers seven and a half years (February 1598 to June 1605); scene-locations include Moscow, the Lithuanian frontier, Poland and the Ukraine. At first glance it would appear that the unity of action has been adandoned. There seems to be no symmetry of plot; no exposition, no development, no climax, no dénouement; not one emotion is displayed but several, and Boris is by no means the sole centre of interest. Indeed, his death, far from being the climax of the play, has nothing whatever to do with the dynamics of the plot. Yet for all the apparent 'aimlessness' of structure there *is* a unity within the play, a 'unity of interest', one might call it. If Boris's struggle with his conscience is considered to be the fulcrum of the action and his death the climax, then the whole play appears episodic: Boris, after all, only appears in six of the twenty-three scenes, and many of the episodes have nothing to do with the torments of a guilt-ridden ruler or with the question of who killed the infant Dmitry. But if, in spite of the title of the play, we consider Boris's private tragedy to be a secondary theme, and if we take the change of dynasty—the collapse of the old order, the end of the first phase in the history of Muscovy, the dramatic confrontation of East and West —as the *basic* theme of the drama, then what appears at first glance to be little more than a random collection of colourful scenes takes shape as a play. We can observe exposition (the accession scenes, the early Otrep'ev/Pretender scenes), growth (the Polish scenes, 11, 12, 13; the beginning and end of the Tsar's Council, 15; the battle scenes, especially 19; and the beginning of the death scene, 20), climax (Basmanov's defection, 21) and dénouement (the 'revolution' of the mob, 22, and the death of Boris's son Fedor, 23). At the same time the subsidiary theme—Boris's struggle with his tormented conscience—

[1] *SS*, vol. 6, p. 365.   [2] Ibid., p. 281.

runs parallel to, but seldom interferes with, the main action and is developed as a secondary tragedy of its own.

As for the question of psychological realism, we must recall Pushkin's insistence on the need to destroy monotony of character and addiction to type. Although none of the characters in *Boris Godunov* can be considered as 'types', few are sufficiently developed or given enough scope to show their 'many-sidedness'. We do not know enough about them; indeed, we scarcely have time to observe more than one facet: Marina's overwhelming ambition, Basmanov's intelligence, Shuysky's slyness or Patriarch Iov's stupidity, for instance.

With Boris, however, Pushkin is true to his principles. We may criticize Pushkin for depicting him statically—there is no noticeable development in him or his outlook over the seven years of the play's action—or for showing him predominantly in one and the same mood throughout, or for giving us too little insight into his reaction to other people's words—most of his utterances are monologues. But there can be no doubt about the multiformity of his character. We are shown Boris the tsar with his lofty concept of the autocrat's role and his genuine desire to rule well and justly; we are shown a Boris devoted to his children, deeply religious yet superstitious, humane and endearing; and we are shown Boris the murderer, whose appalling guilty conscience and fear of a vengeful God[1] give him no rest. Whether Pushkin has produced a convincing figure or a puppet is for each individual reader to decide. But side by side with any eponymous historical hero of eighteenth-century and early nineteenth-century tragedy—a Mikhail of Chernigov, a Dmitry Donskoy, an Ivan III or a false Dmitry—Pushkin's Boris stands out as a revolutionary figure, the first flesh-and-blood character in Russian tragedy.

With the portrait of the Pretender the principle of 'many-sidedness' is pushed to extremes. 'Grigory Otrep′ev', 'Dmitry', 'False-Dmitry', 'Pretender'—such are the names given him at various stages of the play—is the most elusive and chameleon-like character in *Boris*

---

[1] Even when comforting Ksenia (10) he is haunted by his sense of guilt:

> Я, может быть, прогневал небеса,
> Я счастие твое не мог устроить.

I, perhaps, have angered the heavens, | I could not bring about your happiness.

Godunov. Rejecting Karamzin's one-sided image of him ('cunning deceiver', 'villain', 'contemptible tramp', 'abhorrent sensualist' etc.), Pushkin portrays him as a 'poor monk' and an inspired leader of men, a poetry-loving aesthete and a tough general, a chivalrous knight and a proud Russian. From scene to scene he shifts and changes; even in the course of a single speech he is capable of betraying a double personality: in Scene 11, for example, he talks with what Pushkin would have us believe to be the mincing elegance of a Pole

> ...твой гостеприимный замок
> И пышностью блистает благородной
> И славится хозяйкой молодой. —
> Прелестную Марину я надеюсь
> Увидеть там.

... your hospitable castle | Is resplendent with noble magnificence | And is famed for its young chatelaine. | The charming Marina I hope | To see there.

and with the grandeur of a Muscovite

> ...А вы, мои друзья,
> Литва и Русь, вы, братские знамена
> Поднявшие на общего врага,
> На моего коварного элодея
> Сыны славян, я скоро поведу
> В желанный бой дружины ваши грозны.

... But you, my friends, | Lithuanians, Russians, you who have raised the brotherly banners | Against our common foe, | Against my cunning evil-doer, | O sons of the Slavs, soon will I lead | Your awesome bands into the long-desired battle.

Are we meant to believe in the reality of his kaleidoscopic character? Is verisimilitude the prime factor in his depiction? The answer may be that the illusion of reality is being deliberately sacrificed to serve a different purpose: to illustrate Pushkin's attitude to the role of personality in history; rather than a psychologically convincing character-study perhaps we should see in him the symbol of a 'non-leader' capable of heading a vast popular movement, *not* because he has the requisite qualities of a ruler or because he is shrewd, experienced and wise like the ineffectual Boris, but because he can adapt himself to circumstances and because he recognizes that he is nothing more than 'the pretext for conflicts and war' (13), the adaptable agent of historical inevitability.

The problem of psychological realism is closely connected with that of style. How to achieve 'verisimilitude of language', how to break down the 'unity of style', how to differentiate between characters by means of their individual manner of speaking, how to overcome, or make the public aware of, the linguistic absurdities imposed on the historical dramatist by the conventions of the theatre—these were the tasks which faced Pushkin for the first time in his literary career.

'Truth of conversation' (*istina razgovorov*) which Pushkin deman- ded from the dramatist, presented few complications: the incongruous string of one- or two-line declamatory monologues which passed for dialogue in the tragedies of a Sumarokov, a Katenin or an Ozerov merely had to be replaced by a flowing exchange of thought: questions which are answered, exclamations which evoke responses in the interlocutor, repetitions of words which pick up the thread of preceding remarks, and so forth.[1] The real difficulty which faced Pushkin lay in the choice of an overall language for the play. Should he use the literary or the spoken language of his own age? And if the latter, should it be the language of the salon or the peasants? Should he adopt the declamatory lofty style of Russian tragedy? Or should he attempt a reproduction of the language of the late sixteenth and early seventeenth centuries, alternating between the vernacular—'Old Russian', and the 'chancellery language' (*prikaznyy yazyk*)—and Old Church Slavonic? The answer, of course, had to be a compromise, a synthesis, with Pushkin's own poetical language at the base.

Now clearly some characters are allocated a larger proportion of this or that linguistic element.[2] Pimen's language, for instance, has a greater density of archaic and Old Church Slavonic elements than that of any other character; the funny monks, Varlaam and Misail, are allowed to speak in a language full of vulgarisms and rhyming popular

[1] See for example the conversation between Vorotynsky and Shuysky in Scene 1 or the prose dialogue in Scene 8. For an examination of Pushkin's technique, see Vinokur, 'Yazyk *Borisa Godunova*', Part 1, in '*Boris Godunov*' (ed. Derzhavin).

[2] For a definition and analysis of the various linguistic strata in *Boris Godunov*, see Vinokur, op. cit.; cf. Grinkova, 'O yazyke tragedii A. S. Pushkina *Boris Godunov*', in *Izuchenie yazyka*, pp. 72–104.

saws; while the *d'yak* Shchelkalov's speech in Scene 2 is, suitably enough, predominantly Old Russian in its syntax and lexis. But such lexical 'pointers' to class, origin or occupation as archaisms, modernisms, vulgarisms etc. are not necessarily confined to those characters who might be expected to benefit the most from them or be differentiated by them. The Patriarch's speech (especially in Scene 6) is far from being predominantly Old Church Slavonic in flavour; Marina Mnishek, for all her 'Western' nature ('elle est horriblement Polonaise', wrote Pushkin),[1] is just as prone to archaisms as are, say, Shuysky or Vorotynsky; while Boris, even in his most majestic moods, may use modernisms or even vulgarisms. Differentiation of character, in other words, is not necessarily achieved by a greater or lesser apportionment of this or that linguistic element. Each character has his or her 'voice', but each voice is capable of a considerable range of variation. A particular emotional stimulus may call for a word, a phrase or an image outside, and quite out of keeping with, the basically 'ecclesiastical', 'majestic', 'Muscovite' or 'Polish' nature of the particular character's speech-habit. In this way the characters acquire a larger degree of flexibility, are able to express a greater variety of psychological nuances. One has only to compare the monochrome tones of Aleko, who may be linguistically differentiated from the other characters in *The Gipsies* but whose utterances are totally predictable, with the expressive range of Boris, the Pretender or Marina to see how the latter are psychologically enriched and brought to life by this linguistic flexibility.

Of course Pushkin could be accused of destroying historical verisimilitude by permitting such seemingly indiscriminate apportionment of varying stylistic elements. Boris, it might be claimed, should use only the lofty tones of a Muscovite autocrat. Indeed, the contemporary critic Bulgarin, always ready to pounce, poured scorn on the rhetorical outburst at the beginning of Boris's monologue in Scene 7:

> Не так ли
> Мы смолоду влюбляемся и алчем
> Утех любви, но только утолим
> Сердечный глад мгновенным обладаньем,
> Уж, охладев, скучаем и томимся?..

[1] *SS*, vol. 6, p. 293.

*Is it not thus | That from early youth we fall in love and hunger
for | The joys of love, but only quench | The hunger of our hearts
with momentary possession, | And, growing cold, already become
bored and languish? . . .*

Such words, he claimed, made sense in 'the mouth of a Knight
Togenburg',[1] but 'in the mouth of a Russian tsar this is an anachronism! In the seventeenth century, after the rule of the pious Feodor
Ioannovich, in a society from which the female sex was excluded,
no one knew or even so much thought about "momentary possession"!' This is true; and in a sense Pushkin *is* destroying an element of
realism. But then full dramatic verisimilitude, as Pushkin realized,
is in any case an impossibility: realism of one sort must be sacrificed
for realism of another. Compromise is inevitable, and variation of
stylistic elements in the speech of individual characters constitutes
a compromise.

Although Pushkin may be compromising here and elsewhere,
it is the type of compromise he can afford to make, for the stylistic
variations, apart from increasing psychological realism, serve other
purposes as well. The introduction of the above-quoted passage,
containing such expressions as *vlyublyaemsya* [we fall in love],
alchem utekh lyubvi [we hunger for the joys of love], *utolim* [we quench],
and *serdechnyy glad* [the hunger of our hearts], into Boris's great
solemn monologue can, for example, be considered as an illustration
of the recurrent Pushkinian theme of maturation: just as the process of
Tat'yana's ripening is paralleled with that of Pushkin's Muse in the
beginning of Chapter VIII of *Evgeny Onegin* and just as in *The Gipsies*
Pushkin sprinkles the Old Man's speech with periphrastic clichés to
illustrate his *romantic* youth (see above, p. 23),[2] so here the juxtaposition of *alchem utekh lyubvi* with the rest of the monologue may
be interpreted as symbolic of the development of the poet.[3]

Furthermore, paradoxical though it may seem, variegation of
style, while undermining one aspect of historical realism, at the same

[1] A reference to Zhukovsky's sentimental ballad *Rytsar' Togenburg* (1818),
an imitation of Schiller's *Ritter Toggenburg*.
[2] Other examples of this can also be found elsewhere in Pushkin's poetry. See,
for example, Stepanov's appreciation of the poem *Ya pomnyu chudnoe mgnoven'e*
[I remember a wondrous moment] (Stepanov, *Lirika*, pp. 327–46).
[3] Note that in the same speech Boris touches on another highly personal
Pushkinian theme, the relationship between ruler/poet and the people.

time increases other aspects of it. What looks like an anachronism may be helping to build up the overall picture of historical reality and indeed to 'resurrect the past age in all its truth'.

In his *Pushkin i problemy realisticheskogo stilya* Gukovsky submits that Pushkin achieves historicity in *Boris Godunov* by using differing stylistic strata to illustrate the contrast of civilizations. Muscovy is juxtaposed with the West in a series of pictures: Ksenia's lament for her betrothed in Scene 10 is contrasted with the love scene between the Pretender and Marina (13); Pimen, the Russian chronicler (5), with the Polish poet in Kraków (11); the feast in Shuysky's house (9) with the dance in Mnishek's castle (12), etc.[1] An examination of the style of each of these contrasting pictures will show just how sharply defined are the cultural differences. In Shuysky's feast, for example, Pushkin does not merely recapture the ceremonial of a Muscovite boyar's household with the almost liturgical movement of the actors—Shuysky stands up; all stand up; a prayer is read; a toast is drunk; the host accompanies the departing guests to the door—but he also manages to convey the solemn atmosphere by the language: the boy's prayer with its judicious admixture of lexical and syntactical archaisms and the two short speeches of Shuysky—plain, direct, unemotional—are completely in keeping with the spirit of the age. There are no jarring anachronisms. Even though a prayer would not have sounded quite like this and a boyar in the sixteenth or seventeenth century would not have used quite the same vocabulary and grammar, the scene is entirely convincing as a period piece. No illusions are broken; no suspension of disbelief is called for. The ball scene in Mnishek's castle, on the other hand, presents a striking contrast. To the strains of a Polonaise the couples dance by on the stage; a 'cavalier' converses with his 'lady' and compares Marina Mnishek to a 'marble nymph'; he talks of her 'holding us in captivity', to which his 'lady' replies 'a pleasurable captivity' (*priyatnyy plen*); Mnishek ruminates on the old days and holds forth on 'charming hands', 'cheerful beauty', 'bold youth', 'the thunder of music', etc. The whole scene reeks of artificiality. By means of such euphuisms as *Prelestnykh ruk ne zhmem i ne tseluem* [Charming hands we no longer press or kiss] or pedantic affectations like *panna Mnishek zaderzhit nas v plenu ... Priyatnyy plen* [Panna Mnishek will hold us in captivity. ... A pleasant captivity], Pushkin

[1] For other contrasting scenes, see Gukovsky, *Pushkin i problemy*, pp. 43 sq.

takes us out of the solid, grave world of conservative Muscovy and plunges us into the frivolous artificiality of early seventeenth-century Polish life. Of course the compromise is far greater here. Pushkin can hardly expect us to accept this picture of 'the West' as entirely credible. But nevertheless it serves its function—of providing a contrast between civilizations and of highlighting the austerity and solemnity of a Muscovy which Pushkin had studied and which he knew intimately.

The contrast of East and West is brought out still further in Pushkin's presentation of the Pretender. As we have seen above, he is capable of talking like a Westerner and like a Muscovite in one and the same speech: the artificiality of his words addressed to Mnishek (*Tvoy gostepriimnyy zamok* ... [Your hospitable castle ...]) is similar to the romantic diction of the Ball scene, while the remainder of the speech, addressed to '*Litva i Rus''* [Lithuanians and Russians], is reminiscent of Boris's most solemn utterances. In the same scene (11) he converses in the loftiest of tones with Kurbsky's son, whereas his words to the poet betray the intonations of a renaissance prince (*parnasskie tsvety* ... [the flowers of Parnassus ...] *ne votshche v ikh plamennoy grudi / Kipit vostorg* [not for nothing in their ardent breasts / Rapture seethes], etc.). In the garden scene (13) his language modulates from the extreme romanticism of his first monologue to the fiery pride of his two final speeches addressed to Marina. In an atmosphere of soft breezes and 'the deceptive moon' he is capable of talking of 'unconquerable trembling', the 'quivering of tense desires', love dulling his imagination, Marina's 'sweet bewitching voice'. But when stung to fury by Marina's sneering words he not only speaks like a Muscovite tsarevich, he *becomes* Dmitry.[1] Marina's taunts:

> Клянешься ты! итак, должна я верить—

You swear! So, I must believe—

evoke the great outburst beginning

> Тень Грозного меня усыновила,
> Димитрием из гроба нарекла,
> Вокруг меня народы возмутила
> И в жертву мне Бориса обрекла —

---

[1] Only here and at the end of Scene 16 where he appears triumphant on horseback does Pushkin name the Pretender 'Dimitry'.

PUSHKIN

The shade of [Ivan] the Terrible has adopted me, | Has from the grave named me Dimitry, | Has stirred up the peoples around me | And has destined Boris to be my victim.

in which not only is the language lofty and dignified with its majestic metaphor ('The shade of [Ivan] . . . has adopted me') and solemn vocabulary (the archaic *narekla* [named] and the resounding verbs *usynovila* [adopted], *vozmutila* [stirred up], *obrekla* [destined]), but the metre is vigorous and brilliant with its regular omission of the second and fourth stresses, and the alternating rhyme stands out in the midst of a sea of blank verse.

The play is full of these striking stylistic contrasts. As 'poetry' and 'prose' clashed in *Evgeny Onegin*, so in *Boris Godunov* the main linguistic conflict is between the language of Muscovy—ranging from the solemn, lofty and archaic to the popular and even the vulgar— and the language of the 'West'—'literary', bookish, 'romantic', stereotyped and at times barely distinguishable from the poetic diction of Pushkin's youth.

In vain Pushkin hoped that the 'reform of the Russian dramatic system' would be 'influenced by the success or failure of *Boris Godunov*'. Those of his contemporaries and successors who tried their hand at historical tragedy either lacked the talent to produce anything more than pale imitations of Pushkin—often filled with tendentious allusions and invariably wanting in any historical sense or 'feel' for the period portrayed—or merely continued the unproductive traditions of the pre-Pushkinian tragedy; while gifted playwrights left historical drama strictly alone and applied their talents to other theatrical genres.

Yet for all its lack of influence on subsequent drama, *Boris Godunov* was a triumph, if only in as far as Pushkin achieved what he set out to achieve. However heavily Pushkin leaned on the work of previous dramatists and on Karamzin's History for ideas, phraseology and even themes—the result was none the less revolutionary both in the concept of drama and in the concept of historicity. Here for the first time in Russian literature was a dramatist who was able to bring tragedy to life and a historian who realized that history is not a series of occurrences motivated solely by the will or caprices of individuals, but a chain of events governed by laws whose existence he sensed but into whose nature he did not enquire.

66

PUSHKIN

On completing *Boris Godunov* Pushkin wrote to Vyazemsky (c. 7th November, 1825): 'My tragedy is finished; I reread it aloud to myself, and I clapped my hands and cried Well done, Pushkin, well done, you son of a bitch!' *(ay da Pushkin, ay da sukin syn!)*. His emotions are understandable.

SELECT BIBLIOGRAPHY

Aronson, M., 'K istorii *Mednogo vsadnika*', *Vremennik Pushkinskoy komissii*, 1, Moscow–Leningrad, 1936, pp. 221–6.

Bayley, J., *Pushkin. A Comparative Commentary*, Cambridge, 1971.

Blagoy, D., *Masterstvo Pushkina*, Moscow, 1955.

 Tvorcheskiy put' Pushkina, Moscow–Leningrad, 1950.

'*Boris Godunov*' *A. S. Pushkina*, ed. K. Derzhavin, Leningrad, 1936.

Brodsky, N., '*Evgeniy Onegin. Roman A. S. Pushkina*, 4th edn., Moscow 1957.

Bryusov, V., *Moy Pushkin*, Moscow–Leningrad, 1929.

Gerbstman, A., 'O syuzhete i obrazakh *Mednogo vsadnika*', *Russkaya literatura*, 1963, No. 4, pp. 77–88.

Gorodetsky, B., *Dramaturgiya Pushkina*, Moscow–Leningrad, 1953.

Grigor'eva, A. and Ivanova, N., *Poeticheskaya frazeologiya Pushkina*, Moscow, 1969.

Gukovsky, G., *Pushkin i problemy realisticheskogo stilya*, Moscow, 1957.

 Pushkin i russkie romantiki, Moscow, 1965.

Gustafson, R., 'The Metaphor of the Seasons in Evgenij Onegin', *Slavic and East European Journal*, Vol. 6, 1962, No. 1, pp. 6–20.

Izuchenie yazyka pisatelya, ed. N. Grinkova, Leningrad, 1957.

Kharlap, M., 'O *Mednom vsadnike* Pushkina', *Voprosy literatury*, 1961, No. 7, pp. 87–101.

Lednicki, W., *Pushkin's Bronze Horseman*, University of California Press, 1955.

Lotman, Yu., 'Khudozhestvennaya struktura *Evgeniya Onegina*', *Uchenye zapiski Tartuskogo gosudarstvennogo universiteta. Trudy po russkoy i slavyanskoy filologii, IX, literaturovedenie*, Tartu, 1966, pp. 5–32.

Matlaw, R., 'The Dream in *Yevgenij Onegin*, with a note on *Gore ot uma*', *Slavonic and East European Review*, Vol. 37, 1959, No. 89, pp. 487–503.

Nabokov, V., *Eugene Onegin. A Novel in Verse by Aleksandr Pushkin. Translated from the Russian, with a Commentary by Vladimir Nabokov*, 4 vols., London, 1964.

Pospelov, N., *Sintaksicheskiy stroy stikhotvornykh proizvedeniy Pushkina*, Moscow, 1960.

Pumpyansky, L., '*Mednyy vsadnik* i poeticheskaya traditsiya XVIII veka', *Vremennik Pushkinskoy komissii*, 4–5, Moscow–Leningrad, 1939, pp. 91–124.

PUSHKIN

Pushkin, A. S., *Sobranie sochineniy v desyati tomakh* (*SS*), Moscow, 1959–1962.

Pushkin. Itogi i problemy izucheniya, eds. B. Gorodetsky, N. Izmaylov, V. Meylakh, Moscow–Leningrad, 1966.

Shaw, J., *The Letters of Alexander Pushkin*, 3 vols., Bloomington and Philadelphia. 1963.

Slonimsky, A., *Masterstvo Pushkina*, Moscow, 1959.

'Pervaya poema Pushkina', *Vremennik Pushkinskoy komissii*, 3, Moscow–Leningrad, 1937, pp. 183–202.

Sokolov, A., *'Poltava* Pushkina i *Petriady'*, *Vremennik Pushkinskoy komissii*, 4–5, Moscow–Leningrad, 1939, pp. 57–90.

Solov'eva, O., *'Ezerskiy* i *Mednyy vsadnik*. Istoriya teksta', *Pushkin. Issledovaniya i materialy*, 3, Moscow–Leningrad, 1960, pp. 268–344.

SS, see Pushkin, *Sobranie sochineniy*.

Stepanov, N., *Lirika Pushkina*, Moscow, 1959.

Stilman, L., 'Problemy literaturnykh zhanrov i traditsiy v *Evgenii Onegine:* k voprosu perekhoda ot romantizma k realizmu', *American Contributions to the Fourth International Congress of Slavicists*, The Hague, 1958, pp. 321–67.

Timofeev, L., *'Mednyy vsadnik* (iz nablyudeniy nad stikhami poemy)', *Pushkin. Sbornik statey*, ed. A. Egolin, Moscow, 1941, pp. 214–59.

Tomashevsky, B.,*Pushkin. Kniga pervaya* (*1813–1824*), Moscow–Leningrad, 1956.

Pushkin. Kniga vtoraya. Materialy k monografii 1824–1837, Moscow–Leningrad, 1961.

'Voprosy yazyka v tvorchestve Pushkina', *Pushkin. Issledovaniya i materialy*, I, Moscow–Leningrad, 1956, pp. 126–84.

Tynyanov, Yu., *Arkhaisty i novatory*, Leningrad, 1929 (reprint Slavische Propyläen, Vol. 31, 1967).

Unbegaun, B., *Russian Versification*, Oxford, 1956.

Vickery, W., 'Byron's *Don Juan* and Pushkin's *Evgenij Onegin:* The Question of Parallelism', *Indiana Slavic Studies*, Vol. 4, The Hague, 1967, pp. 181–91.

'Mednyj vsadnik and the Eighteenth-century Heroic Ode', *Indiana Slavic Studies*, Vol. 3, The Hague, 1963, pp. 140–62.

'Three Examples of Narrated Speech in Pushkin's *Poltava'*, *Slavic and East European Journal*, Vol. 8, 1964, No. 3, pp. 273–83.

Vinogradov, V., *Stil' Pushkina*, Moscow, 1941.

Yazyk Pushkina. Pushkin i istoriya russkogo literaturnogo yazyka. Moscow–Leningrad, 1935.

Vinokur, G., 'Slovo i stikh v *Evgenii Onegine'*, *Pushkin. Sbornik statey*, ed. A. Egolin, Moscow, 1941, pp. 155–213.

Zhirmunsky, V., *Bayron i Pushkin. Iz istorii romanticheskoy poemy*, Leningrad, 1924.

GOGOL'

A. DE JONGE

APPARENTLY THE ONLY POINT OF AGREEMENT SHARED BY ALL
interpreters of Gogol' is the recognition that no two interpretations
of his work are alike. This is not to say that it has the range and richness
that makes it all things to all men, in the sense that this may be true
of, say, Shakespeare. It is possible to run different interpretations of
Shakespeare in parallel, whereas the various views of Gogol' seem to
cancel each other out. Thus he has been seen as the father of social
realism, above all interested in giving an accurate portrayal of contemporary Russia. He has also been seen as a profound religious
thinker whose interest in the contemporary was perhaps comparable
to Dante's interest in Florence, but whose chief concern it was to
reveal the presence in this world of Antichrist, and to advocate the
establishment of an Orthodox theocracy; a view of Russia not un-
connected with a view of Moscow as the third Rome. Admittedly the
realist interpretation accepts that Gogol' indulged in lapses into
romantic fantasy, and the religious view concedes that he could be an
unrivalled observer of the contemporary scene. But nevertheless, the
two views stand in direct contradiction to one another and are
virtually impossible to reconcile. The realist interpretation is not
surprisingly the one that has enjoyed the greater popularity in both
pre- and post-revolutionary Russia. It was first formulated by Belinsky, who tended to find in Gogol' that which was grist to his particular
revolutionary mill: a picture of a corrupt bureaucracy, a series of
portraits of irresponsible landowners cut off from reality and living at
the expense of their serfs in a grotesque fantasy world—a picture of hell

69

which Belinsky found difficult to distinguish from a picture of the Russia of Nicholas I. The relevance of this interpretation to the history of Russian literary and political criticism is considerable, and it is on this basis that the great bulk of Soviet scholarship has been founded.

The opposing view was first expressed with any conviction by Merezhkovsky. It is not surprising that the religious interpretation should have emerged in the spiritualistic climate of the Russian intelligentsia at the turn of the century. This approach is as militant and uncompromising as was that of the realists, and in its way it offers an equally powerful and convincing reading.

In the course of the twentieth century there emerged a third approach that favoured a formalistic examination of the work as an assembly of aesthetic devices. Strangely enough this treatment was first formulated by Andrey Bely, who combined an elaboration of the Merezhkovsky line with a series of penetrating linguistic analyses based on close reading and statistics; a method subsequently taken up in the twenties by the Formalists themselves.

Thus there are, broadly speaking, three approaches to Gogol': realist, religious and aesthetic. Hardline versions of each tend to dismiss the possibility of finding anything of value in the others. The formalist treatment, which suggests that an examination of what the author intended is neither possible nor interesting, is something of an abdication; the others represent uncompromising commitments to certain aspects of the work at the expense of others, said to be of secondary importance. The relative significance of a particular aspect becomes consequent on the interpretation in question. Thus every view of Gogol' seems to have been shaped by a readiness to find what it wants to find, and only that.

The first question to be answered, therefore, is how was it possible for his work to generate so many conflicting interpretations? We must acknowledge the existence of each view, not as being the true, the correct view, but as evidence of one of the ways in which the work can be read. That it can manifestly be read in a number of mutually contradictory ways is a point of considerable importance. It may even be that to understand how such widely differing interpretations of the same corpus of writing could arise is to find the key to that writing. It is on this approach that the following critical account will be founded. It is hoped that this will succeed in explaining the existence of interpretations that differ as widely as do those of Belinsky and Merezh-kovsky. For the fact that the work can enjoy such widely differing interpretations at the hands of critics who were, admittedly, all special pleaders, points to its definitive characteristic; its essential ambiguity. An analysis of the writing in terms of its ambiguity provides the key not only to what Gogol' wrote, but to why he wrote, to the reasons that prompted him to embark on the extraordinary enterprise of 'creative writing', to devote his life to the invention of fictions: characters, situations and events whose only reality consists in their existence as linguistic signs on a sheet of paper.

Although this may be a question posed by the work of any artist, it is particularly relevant to a writer such as Gogol', not only because, with his Ukrainian background and upbringing, he was estranged, both geographically and culturally, from the main line of development of a literary tradition, but because there was, to all intents and purposes, no such tradition for him to follow. It is relatively easy to conceive of writing prose fiction in emulation of masters such as Turgenev or Dostoevsky, but Gogol''s writing can be related to no major work of Russian literature. Although scholars may suggest models on which he has drawn, the fact remains that Gogol', viewed in the historical perspective of 'great literature', may be said to have invented Russian literary prose virtually single-handed. He stands at the beginning, not in the middle of a line of development, and it is this that renders the question of why he wrote one of some importance.

Nikolay Vasil'evich Gogol'-Yanovsky was born in 1809. His parents were fairly prosperous Ukrainian landowners. His father, who dabbled in amateur dramatics, as author, director and actor, died when Gogol' was sixteen. His mother was an impractical woman with a somewhat tenuous grasp on reality. She had the typically Russian characteristic of viewing fact through a focus of emotion. Although she never understood a word of what her son wrote, she greeted his literary career with uncritical admiration, ascribing to him works he could not possibly have written, and even suggesting that he had invented the steamship. There is perhaps more than an echo here of Khlestakov's extravagant claims in *The Inspector General*. Gogol''s heredity was conducive to the confusion of dream and reality.

In 1828 he leaves the family estate to go to St Petersburg with the avowed intention of entering the civil service. In a letter to a friend he

71

had already made it clear that he was driven not by personal ambition, but by a desire to be of service. It is with that in mind that he had chosen the department of justice.[1] The letter employs the highflown language that Gogol' always adopts when discussing his idealistic aspirations, and, as always, it rings false, as if the author were unconsciously deceiving himself with his own rhetoric. Already we find one of his most puzzling and important characteristics. Time and again he will write, in conceptual terms, of his ideals of service, of his desire to be a crusader in the cause of authentic values, but whenever he slips into this lofty and abstract mode, his writing gives the impression that something is missing, that it is undermined by a strain of unconscious hypocrisy. But hypocrisy notwithstanding, it may be seen that even at this early age his professed ambitions lay in this direction. One of the most important features of his view of his role is his preoccupation with how things should be, as opposed to how they are. What will henceforward be referred to as the *normative* tendency, the need to preach as opposed to the need to describe, is a major constituent of his work.

There is a sense in which those Soviet critics who have described Gogol' as the observer of contemporary reality have failed to see that it is open to the marxist critic to find him a realist of a very different kind. Gogol''s account of the world as it is is always related to a sense of the world as it should be. His account of contemporary reality describes the latter as being devoid of authentic values; it is, in marxist terms, alien and unreal. His normative tendency may usefully be considered in this respect as the product of an 'unhappy consciousness' which seeks to restore the world to reality by creating an awareness of authentic values, effecting a revolution in the collective consciousness, such that there would no longer be any discrepancy between the world as it is and as it should be. For it is the tension between these two concepts that provides the mainspring of Gogol''s creative drive.

The complete failure to treat of the world as it is may well be one of the reasons for the total failure of his first creation, a 1,200 line verse idyll, *Gants Kyukhel'garten* (1829). As with all his one-sided treatments of the ideal it strikes a false note, and was quite rightly dismissed by contemporary critics. Gogol''s reaction was typical. Not for the last time he attempted to destroy every copy of the work, and left the

[1] *Letters*, p. 26.

72

country soon afterwards. Gogol' the realist was singularly ill-equipped to face reality.

In 1832 he published a collection of Ukrainian stories, *The Evenings in a Village near Dikan'ka* (*Vechera na khutore bliz Dikan'ki*), his first prose work. Although it does not bear qualitative comparison with the later writing, it is not unimportant. For the most part tuppence-coloured stories of local village life, apparently based on an oral tradition, they are presented through the mediation of a series of story-tellers who meet regularly at the house of one Rudy Pan'ko. The language is loaded with Ukrainian—Gogol' provides a glossary for the benefit of his Russian readers—and the writing has a largely rustic turn of phrase. There is a real attempt at speech characterization; moreover the marked differences in stylistic level from story to story presumably correspond to the styles of the various narrators. However, this realistic narrative mode is sometimes interrupted by the author who indulges in some essentially lyrical purple passages.[1] Such writing already reveals one of his principal stylistic characteristics, namely his remarkable capacity to impart sustained rhythmic tension to long loosely constructed sentences.

An important feature of these stories is their humour. It was this that impressed his contemporaries. It is alleged that even his printers were reduced to helpless laughter. Gogol''s normative ambitions never prevented him from remaining the funniest of writers. Yet the humour of *The Evenings* is not typical of the mature Gogol'. It relies largely on slapstick, with little sense of black comedy, of the absurd. Amorous Cossacks have their courtship interrupted and are obliged to hide in ludicrous situations; disapproving parents are tricked into letting their offspring marry unsuitable partners. The situations are contrived and the humour lacks the bite of the later works.

No less important than the humour is the occasional intrusion of the supernatural, in the shape of ghosts, sorcerers or the devil himself. But with one or two exceptions this has a purely aesthetic function. It is a source of entertainment, and could scarcely be said to reflect the author's own *angst*. In the introduction the narrator promises a work that will 'terrify us with its apparitions from the beyond, with the kind of marvels that were once created in our Orthodox land in the good old days'. Despite the occasional glimpses of a diabolic parallel

[1] E.g. the beginning of Chapter Two of *The May Night* (*Mayskaya noch'*).

world that may intrude on these rustic romps, the supernatural on the whole gets a more light-hearted treatment than it is to enjoy in the later work. But even so, the interplay between reality and illusion, natural and supernatural does play its part.

The stories appear to reflect a world that Gogol' knew at first hand. A set of funny stories about his homeland might well have seemed an appropriate subject to a young Ukrainian anxious to make his mark on the capital. Yet the work is something more than a mere product of circumstance. Thus it was written in St Petersburg and not in a village near Dikan'ka. Gogol''s realism is never the product of immediate experience. He seems to require geographical distance between him and his subject.[1] It is no coincidence that *Dead Souls* was written in Rome. His work is almost always based on a second-hand 'hearsay' reality. What passes for observation is often the product of invention and imagination. Thus when working on *The Evenings* he sends his mother repeated requests for detailed information about Ukrainian folkways, such information being 'very very necessary to him'.[2] This method of composition, whereby the subject is viewed from afar and based on secondhand observation, is Gogol''s characteristic way of working. As important in this respect as his absence from the Ukraine was his presence in St Petersburg. The capital, which will feature in his later writing as a diabolic and essentially unreal place, a world of madmen and zombies, is already seen in this light. He describes it as an eerily quiet town, quite lacking in identity, a town in which foreigners feel at home and Russians feel like foreigners.[3]

It is this awareness of the unreal city that turns him to the description of authentic values in the shape of *kazachestvo* [the Cossack community, the Cossack ethos]. This remains for him an image of the freedom of the spirit. His Cossacks drink, dance and play on an epic scale and represent a world in which happiness and fulfilment are possible, a world standing in direct opposition to the petrified capital. This creation of a largely imaginary picture points to another important aspect of his writing: his use of art as therapy. He cannot find what

---

[1] 'Contained in my very nature is the ability to imagine a world graphically only when I have moved far away from it.' *Letters*, p. 111.
[2] Ibid., p. 30.
[3] Ibid., p. 29.

he wants in the workaday reality of St Petersburg, so he invents it instead; creates life as it should be in his writing. It is significant in this respect that many of these stories end in happy marriages. Whereas the dominant note of the later work is one of disintegration as the world breaks up into meaningless fragments, these stories treat principally of harmony and integration. The real world they describe is a meaningful organic whole, whereas the occasional intrusions of a hostile supernatural often take the form of the disruption of the laws of space and time, undermining apparently stable reality and suggesting that the ordered world is, suddenly, quite literally falling apart.

The stories' humour may also be related to their therapeutic function. Gogol' often describes laughter as a defence against the triviality and emptiness of the world. There is a very real sense in which he may be thought of as creating these fictions against his own sadness. Once again realism may be seen to constitute a flight from reality.

The stories also anticipate the later work in respect of their lack of stylistic consistency. Gogol''s narrative has great tonal range. He can move freely from passages written in the highest of styles, bravura pieces with all the stops pulled out, as in the opening passages of Chapters One and Two of *The Fair at Sorochintsy* (*Sorochinskaya yarmarka*), to another stylistic level that contrasts sharply—the vivid, idiomatic language of the protagonists: a way of writing that relies either on direct speech or on narrative so heavily loaded with idiom that the stylistic result is the same. The effect of this contrast in levels is partly comical, and, since the main purpose of the story is to amuse, this is as it should be. But it has another no less important role. By switching stylistic levels he varies the pace of the story. The sensuous passages read slowly, and this creates a kind of stylistic backdrop that sets off the rapidly moving slapstick comedy. Now one could hardly maintain that an approach to narrative based on this sense of formal balancing contains any kind of confessional element representing the unmediated voice of the author himself. Choice of style is largely determined by formal considerations such as the balance between description and action. These will play a more important role than the author's personal view of his subject. Gogol' is thus unlikely to make a clean breast of his feelings in his writing; if he is reflected in these works, it is at one remove.

That choice of style is largely determined by subject-matter is illustrated in the most ambitious of these stories *The Terrible Vengeance* (*Strashnaya mest'*). Gogol' aims here at creating an atmosphere of legend and folk epic. The piece illustrates his treatment of the clash between *kazachestvo* and the supernatural—a theme that is to find its definitive treatment in *Viy*. In *The Terrible Vengeance* his language creates a specific atmosphere, drawing on stylistic devices associated with an oral and epic tradition; enumeration, repetition, rhetorical question, inversion of subject and verb. Techniques of imagery and narrative have the same stylistic flavour: battles are described in traditional epic terms as feasts, Katerina mourns her dead husband in the code of the *plach* or lament, another rhetorical set-piece, whereas the highflown nature of the style is admirably illustrated by the famous opening to Chapter Ten, describing the Dnepr. One of the great purple passages of Russian prose, it has a declamatory tone supported by a remarkable command over sentence rhythms. Indeed, throughout the story Gogol' goes to great lengths to vary his rhythms, most obviously by the alternation of long and short sentences. As a result the prose is never monotonous, the reader is held by the rhythm of his reading as much as by what he reads.[1]

But for all his skill Gogol' cannot quite avoid giving an impression of Ossianesque *ersatz*. The language never truly comes to life, moreover the narrative seems clumsy and contrived. That Gogol' finds it difficult to handle complex narrative forms is subsequently confirmed by *The Portrait* (*Portret*). Both pieces require two narrative levels, one relating a series of mysteriously linked events, which it is the task of the second level to reveal. In *The Terrible Vengeance* the protagonists of the main action play no part in its elucidation, and the latter appears to be a kind of afterthought.

But for all that the story does convey a remarkable sense of blackness and desolation, and consistently maintains a doom-laden atmosphere which makes it clear from the start that positive values, embodied in the spirited Cossack, Burul'bash, will never triumph over the forces of evil. Gogol' creates a distinctly tragic feeling and tone. Indeed the theme has tragic connotations, dealing as it does with the visitation upon our own heads of our fathers' sins. Joined with this

[1] For an extensive treatment of this aspect of Gogol''s style, see Bely, *Masterstvo Gogolya*, pp. 71–6.

in the final exposition is the terrifying image of the original sinner being judged by his male ancestors as Minos is to judge Phaedra after her death. Petro is placed in elemental contact with the earth, out of which he vainly tries to draw himself as his ancestors gnaw his bones. Gogol''s treatment of the ancestor theme takes one down to an archetypal bedrock of the imagination, as he seems to deal with the themes of transgression and retribution in their most elemental form. Thus it is not for nothing that the sorcerer, referred to incidentally as Antichrist, is guilty not only of treason and apostasy, but also of incestuous lust, the most fundamental transgression of all. It is because the story confronts us with such archetypal themes and images that, despite its technical shortcomings, it conveys a sense of imaginative authenticity that renders it something much more powerful than a mere rhetorical and aesthetic exercise in *Gothick* horror.

It is with the story of *Ivan Fedorovich Shpon'ka and his Aunt* (*Ivan Fedorovich Shpon'ka i ego tetushka*) that we first hear the voice of the mature Gogol'. The piece is in some ways comparable to the finest episodes of *Dead Souls*, for Gogol' here finds what is to become his definitive idiom. Much can be learnt from an examination of its language and compositional technique. Its principal stylistic feature is a long, loose, rambling sentence packed with detailed information largely irrelevant to the story line. Gogol' creates an atmosphere of inconsequence and non-event by means of a certain narrative soft-focus. He will lend considerable prominence to an element by describing it at length—a familiar pointing-up device. It would be a legitimate assumption on the part of a reader familiar with conventional narrative codes that such prominence is a sign that the element in question will play a part in the story's subsequent development. But this is not so. Gogol' creates a contrast between the rhetorical prominence created by a certain stylistic treatment and the sheer lack of significance of the passage so treated. It is largely on this formal contrast that the story is based. Gogol' has inverted Chekhov's recipe for narrative, whereby if an author begins his piece by describing a gun hanging on a wall, then sooner or later that gun must go off.[1] In Gogol''s world the gun never does. His descriptions have a negative relevance; they belong to the story because they do not relate to it. Thus in the letter his aunt writes to Shpon'ka more stylistic promi-

[1] Quoted by Shklovsky, *O teorii prozy*, p. 105.

nence is given to the fact that an unusually large turnip has grown in the garden than to her suggestion that it is time her nephew ran his estate himself. The effect of this perspective is to suggest that apparent triviality and irrelevance are in some way central to the story, as indeed they are, since the story is precisely *about* insignificance and triviality.

A stylistic treatment that makes an empty joke of non-event and non-existence has far-reaching ramifications. It is no coincidence that other aspects of the mature writing emerge at the same time, since they are presumably generated by the same imaginative pre-occupations. Thus together with the rhetoric of inconsequence we find great importance attached to food and physical comfort. When Shpon'ka dines with Storchenko much prominence is given to a description of the menu. Storchenko's conversation subordinates the spirit to the stomach. It consists almost entirely of how to grow food, and he talks in one breath of sowing potatoes and of what clever people there used to be.[1] The aunt places people in the same sub-ordinate relationship to food, asking Shpon'ka what he ate before asking him whom he met. The story emphasizes gluttony and physical comfort—a world of soft feather-beds (Storchenko's lips are described as pillows)—not far removed from the world of Oblomov's dream. However much such a world might appeal to Gogol', it tends to stifle spiritual energy and thus runs counter to his normative ambitions. Because this way of life does not support positive values it is described in terms of irrelevant detail, and takes on the force of a shaggy dog story of genius. Gogol''s rhetoric of insignificance has a thematic motivation: he employs negative humour when describing negative values. Thus he sometimes introduces slightly unnerving details into his descriptions, witness the pig, usually for Gogol' a messenger of chaos, who greets Shpon'ka's homecoming by grunting 'louder than usual'. A similar effect is achieved by the account of Shpon'ka's courtship. Rather than kneel before his lady and confess to an inextinguishable flame of passion, he remarks that there are a great many flies in summer. This, the summit of a rhetoric of inconsequence, is also a typical example of the general collapse into timidity and

---

[1] This rhetoric of 'gastronomic parataxis' whereby obsession with food is so all-embracing that it destroys any sense of perspective, placing the spiritual and the material on the same level, plays a most important part in the rhetoric of *Dead Souls*, notably in the episode describing Petr Petrovich Petukh in Part Two.

insignificance that Gogol' considers, in the final analysis, to be the outcome of a lack of psychic energy.

Shpon'ka's dream takes us into the nightmare world that, for Gogol', underlies reality. Although the world of night retains the status of a dream in this piece, and only obtrudes directly into reality in later works, its structural role is identical. Just as *The Overcoat* (*Shinel'*) will move from the real to the surreal with its sharply contrasting conclusion, so this work follows the same pattern. The bald matter-of-fact tone of the bulk of the story, its flat treatment of character and action, stands in direct opposition to its panic-stricken conclusion. It is based on the juxtaposition of violently contrasting elements; we move from day to night, from reality to nightmare before we know where we are. Gogol' achieves the effect of a progression, as he draws us ever further into the world of the absurd; a movement from reality to something else that is to play a vital role in the later work. The movement is here achieved by means of the ever-increasing degree of linguistic anomaly with which the word 'wife' is used; its referents become more and more bizarre until it is finally made to refer to a piece of cloth. There is a gradual descent into a world of non-significance, in which meaning has been lost. As is so often the case in Gogol', chaos is rendered through the collapse of language.

The story sustains this sense of chaos to the end, for its ending is a non-ending. The unfulfilled promise of a sequel fits with the feeling tone of the writing. It creates a sense of disintegration and frustration in the reader who feels 'This can't be all, there must be more to it', only to discover his mistake, for Gogol' is describing a world in which that *is* all there is.

Shpon'ka introduces the theme of the transition from a normal to a paranormal world. In all the stories that treat directly of the supernatural we find this slide into a world in which the laws of space, time and causality no longer apply. When, in *St John's Eve* (*Vecher nakanune Ivana Kupala*), Petro enters the sorcerer's magic world, the enchanted flower he drops floats through the air, the treasure he digs for sinks deeper into the earth. The laws of this diabolic world are by definition the opposite of the laws governing our world. However, while still under the enchantment he commits a real murder with real consequences for his future.

That the diabolical world is the opposite of ours, standing in a

79

negative relation to it, is borne out by the conclusion of *The Enchanted Place* (*Zakoldovannoe mesto*). Nothing grows there as it should, melons are not melons, cucumbers not cucumbers; they are *the devil knows what*. This introduces the important theme of *ne to* [not what you suppose, not what you might think], the concept of negation that transforms seemingly stable reality into the something else that the devil alone knows. Gogol' never writes the word devil lightly, for it is he who is ultimately responsible for the undermining and disruption of reality.

However the interplay between the two worlds still enjoys a fairly lighthearted treatment in these tales. For the reality he describes, country life in the Ukraine, is viewed as an authentic reality that opposes the nightmare world we may sometimes glimpse. On the whole the melons of Dikan'ka really are melons; it is only when they grow in enchanted places that they may turn into something else. But in the later works there are no sets of positive values to withstand the nightmare. The capital is itself one gigantic enchanted place, whose reality, in the normative sense, has been completely eroded; there is no longer any distinction to be made between reality and nightmare, they have become one and the same.

Gogol''s next collection of stories, *Mirgorod*, was composed between the years 1832–4, although the longest piece, *Taras Bul'ba*, only found its present form in 1842. The story represents an attempt at creating a powerful picture of life as it should be. The only practical outcome of Gogol''s plan to write a history of the Ukraine, it develops a view of heroic *kazachestvo* already implied by *The Evenings*. Gogol' situates his account in a historical perspective, but does not respect historical verisimilitude, freely mingling the events of the fifteenth, sixteenth and seventeenth centuries.[1] He is describing an essentially ideal world as opposed to a historical reality, hence his imaginative treatment with its use of heroic exaggeration. This attempt at the epic is more successful than was *The Terrible Vengeance*, for the language is on the whole less contrived and pitched at a lower level, and there is a greater sense of epic scale. His hero is *kazachestvo*, and to render its quality, its unbounded energy, its love of battle and bottle, its scorn for non-

[1] For the chronology of *Taras* see Gukovsky, *Realizm*, pp. 164–5.

essentials such as over-ornate weapons, its fervent and uncompromising Orthodoxy, Gogol' uses direct speech characterization and vivid description of the way of life of the Cossack community. This is perhaps the one occasion on which his unqualified account of positive values gains any animation. Whether he describes Bul'ba and his sons riding across a sea of grass, or life in the camp itself, he succeeds in conveying a sense of vitality, striking a note of collective purpose in an integrated community that stands in contrast to the portraits of moral sloth and degradation which generally characterize his work.

He deliberately seeks an epic frame within which to set his account of things as they should be. His characters all have a strong moral sense, taking the form of a sense of difference between 'us' and 'them', Orthodox and heathen; an opposition which brooks no compromise, for to compromise is to surrender. Gogol''s language, particularly when he moves into high style, is a strange blend of folk idiom and a Homeric narrative mode; notably in his account of the siege of Dubno with its set pieces—the taunting before battle, battle itself as a series of single combats, and so on.

But even here positive values do not go unchallenged. Characteristically, Bul'ba's world is set in the past, and we gain a sense of its passing. By the end *kazachestvo* is a shadow of its true self; the *sech'* has been broken up, many Cossacks have sworn allegiance to Polish infidels, and Taras, the last champion of the old order, has become an outlaw. When he is finally hunted down his world dies with him. Equally his own life is coloured with personal disappointment. One son, Andriy, forsakes the uncompromisingly masculine Cossack way of life, wherein woman's only role is that of grieving mother. He yields to sexual temptation and is punished by his father's hand—an echo of the avenging ancestor of *The Terrible Vengeance*. The other son, Ostap, is executed in a foreign city, with his father an impotent onlooker. Thus negative values triumph on every level. Bul'ba pursues a downward path till he has outlived his sons and practically outlived *kazachestvo*. One feels that with the end of the book one witnesses the end of the Cossacks' golden age.

The most interesting treatment of negative values comes with the account of Andriy's betrayal. Sex, as usual in Gogol', is a destructive force. It deprives Andriy of his *kazachestvo*, turns him into an infidel knight, over-dressed in plumes and armour, and makes him pay the penalty for his apostasy. The account of how he finds his way, through a tunnel, from the Cossack camp into the besieged city, is perhaps one of the most interesting of all Gogol''s descriptions of transition from one world to another. Although ostensibly a realistic piece, much importance is attached to conveying a sense of the imaginative texture of the hero's subterranean journey; he passes into a world of darkness only to emerge in a Catholic, and hence pagan, church. Andriy journeys into an underworld of *ne to*; the other world of the plague-stricken, starving city, a terrifying, petrified place in which richly clad corpses litter the streets, and which Gogol' describes as a kind of hallucination, the city appearing in a stark unreal light that recalls the haunted vision of Edgar Allan Poe.

The author again achieves a maximum of imaginative fascination with yet another description of a city, Warsaw, the scene of Ostap's execution. Thus its ghetto is described in grotesque but extraordinarily vivid language. His speech characterization imparts to the Jews a striking combination of guile and obsequiousness. The description of the execution itself is remarkably animated, paradoxically more effective than any other passage in the story. This introduces a phenomenon of crucial importance to our understanding of Gogol'. His aesthetic talents are at a maximum when he writes about negative values, whereas the more he seeks to describe their positive counterparts, the more lifeless his prose becomes. He here renders the essentially dead world of the feelingless spectators with their dehumanized reactions; a butcher looking on with expert eyes, a young nobleman explaining to his lady in feelingless detail precisely what will be done to the Cossacks. In fact we are pausing for a moment in the world of dead souls, and the writing gains in strength accordingly.

If *Taras Bul'ba* is the account or the Cossack ideal, then the story of *The Two Ivans* (*Povest' o tom, kak possorilsya Ivan Ivanovich s Ivanom Nikiforovichem*) stands in direct opposition to it, describing the Cossacks as they are now.[1] This study of human pettiness only takes on its full force in relation to a vision of the ideal. From the warlike energetic brotherhood of the past we move to the recumbent life of the present. The two Ivans' long-standing friendship is founded not on any positive bond, but on habit and propinquity, and it is broken

[1] A point made by Gukovsky, *Realizm*, pp. 219 sq.

not by apostasy, but by a word. The story is a study in degeneration and disintegration within a community—an essentially sleepy world of slothful indolence. Thus the pacific nature of its citizens is brought out by the fact that neither Ivan has any use for the weapons Ivan Ivanovich so covets, and by the fact that the only soldiers in the piece are old soldiers.

In this story we see Gogol''s narrative technique at its strongest. It has the simplest of backbones. Two friends have a quarrel which reaches the point of no return when one of them utters a definitive insult. War is declared; after a series of hostile acts the two ex-friends resort to litigation, which fails to yield immediate satisfaction. A final attempt at reconciliation fails and they grow old in a greying world, in perpetual expectation that some court or other is about to find in their respective favours. Gogol' uses the plot line as a pretext for some evocative descriptive writing. We find vivid pictures of the two Ivans, including characterization of their speech and personalities, and are shown the world in which they live in some detail. The author is very conscious of the visual dimension, describing one scene as being worthy of an artist's brush. Indeed there is a real sense in which he is painting word-pictures for us. He creates a powerful impression of the sleepy Ukrainian town and its inhabitants, displaying a keen eye for often loaded detail. In the middle of a neutral description of the square in front of the courthouse he points out that it is always full of hens pecking away at grains of corn inadvertently dropped by prospective plaintiffs. He also creates vivid sketches of secondary characters, such as the mayor who is lovingly described at the beginning of Chapter Five, complete to the missing button on his uniform, the circumstances in which he lost it, and the measures he took to recover it. The passage is a remarkable blend of observation and comic invention. Gogol' holds his readers by the sheer wealth of details which have a whimsical relevance to the overall picture. Rather than paint in broad strokes, he creates a mosaic of finely observed elements. His descriptions tend to be in close-up. This imparts to his writing a vivid animation that is further increased by his extraordinary ear for the rhythms of direct speech. He displays great feeling for dialogue, notably in the exchanges between the two Ivans, and in the courthouse scene. He manages to capture the specificity of spoken Russian, bringing out its range of partial synonyms, its richness of idiom, its essentially concrete feel, that elusive quality which, for lack of a better word, might be termed its linguistic *fatness*.

Thus Gogol' the observer has an important part to play in the piece, but the story also constitutes a critique of observed reality. The two Ivans quarrel about a warlike object that has no place in their world. The nature of the object emphasizes that the quarrel turns on the encounter between covetousness and a dog in the manger; moreover, through its lack of relevance, the gun acts as a criticism of a society which has lost all sense of *kazachestvo*, and only retains a sense of idle acquisitiveness and an instant readiness to take umbrage. Their moral sloth is such that the Ivans even abandon direct action; they both delegate their pursuit of vengeance to the courts, thus introducing us to the world of petty officialdom. Gogol', whose normative instincts had at one time turned his thoughts towards a career in the department of justice, sees the actual world of the civil service as the most frightening example of life as it is; a world from which all sense of human values has been banished, leaving nothing behind but an arid structure of hierarchy and formalized procedure which invites comparison with the world of Kafka. It is into this world that the two Ivans are driven by their all-consuming sense of spite, and from the moment they set foot in it they are lost. Not only does litigation make them express themselves in the absurd rhetoric of legalistic jargon, thereby destroying their language, perhaps their only vital quality, it deprives them of their very humanity. When they last appear they have lost virtually every element of their initial characterization; two old men may be alive, but the two Ivans are no more. Indeed the town itself has changed. Gogol' no longer tells us how marvellous it is, he brings out melancholy connotations, describing the grey, rainy place it has become, and ending his story on a note of unbearable sadness.

Were this to be a complete account of the piece it might justifiably be viewed as a forerunner of the Chekhovian short story. The technique of relating a trivial incident in the everyday life of a small town in such a way that despite its bald realism it becomes a cipher for some usually depressing aspect of the human condition is a familiar one. Those critics who find Gogol' a realist in this special sense are quick to draw attention to this story, but as always they are obliged to do him some violence in order to fit him to their particular Procrustean bed. Realistic observation has an undeniable role to play, but as always this strain of writing is undermined by occasional touches that remind us that, for Gogol', realism is a means and never an end in itself. The world of Mirgorod is as much a product of the imagination as the world of Taras Bul'ba. Thus the painstaking comparison of the two Ivans that opens the story slips into absurdity when Gogol' refutes the rumour that Ivan Nikiforovich was born with a tail. Moreover certain aspects of Gogol's' rhetoric make us question the basis of his observations. Thus he creates a pattern of comparison whereby Ivan Ivanovich was tall and thin, Ivan Nikiforovich short and fat, and so on. But then he introduces two items that have no basis for comparison whatsoever: Ivan Ivanovich gets angry when a fly lands in his soup, whereas Ivan Nikiforovich likes to take tea in the bath. Although this note is never sustained, Gogol' will introduce it occasionally—when he tells us that one Anton Prokof'evich inadvertently wore a certain pair of trousers that constituted an irresistible invitation to the dogs of Mirgorod to bite him in the leg. But perhaps the most sinister disruption of normality takes the shape of Ivan Ivanovich's pig which, suddenly galloping into the courthouse, seizes and makes off with Ivan Nikiforovich's petition. In Gogol''s world pigs work hand in glove with the devil—it was in the guise of a pig that he was rumoured to have appeared in *The Fair at Sorochintsy*. Gogol' has grown more sophisticated; simile has become metaphor and the pig stands alone. But the fact that his satanic connotations are left understood should deceive no one. The pig plays a diabolical role, for his onslaught brings chaos in its wake, exasperates the tension, helping to set in motion the series of legal complications that lead to the eventual undoing of the two Ivans.

Neither in reality nor in the world of realistic short stories do pigs eat legal documents. That they do so in Mirgorod illustrates the gulf that divides Gogol' from later generations. His realism is an essential feature of his fictional world, but it is only one feature among others. He clearly derives great pleasure from his word-pictures, but however much he may love such pictures for their own sake, he requires his art to be something more than an immediate record of perceived reality. Although a story such as this makes no direct moral judgement, the fact remains that everything that Gogol' writes after *The Evenings* stands with reference to an awareness of moral issues; it is in the final analysis Gogol''s moral sense that is the essential motivation of his aesthetic activity.

Viy is a more sophisticated treatment of one of the important themes of *The Evenings*; the interplay between the natural and the supernatural. It is a study in contrasts, an exercise in the creation of comparative atmospheres that reveals Gogol''s obsession with the relationship between the two worlds and with the nature of their threshold. He strikes a remarkable balance between the 'diurnal' and 'nocturnal' elements, switching us from one to the other with the greatest ease. Whichever world we may be in, its presence seems so all-embracing that we are temporarily unable to admit the existence of its counterpart. Throughout the story he maintains two discrete but complementary narrative spheres, and it is in this that his technical achievement lies.

The opening section with its vivid account of life in a Kiev seminary resembles the description of the education of Bul'ba's sons. Although not directly relevant to the adventures of Khoma Brut, this section has a number of functions. It reveals Gogol', the Scott-like historical novelist, using his imagination to reconstruct a world from which his readers are divorced by space and time. Hence the loving care he brings to the detailed description of the seminarists' way of life. Secondly, the account of the milieu suffices to characterize the hero, telling us the sort of person he is, boisterous, happy-go-lucky and brave. The stronger his personality the more telling will be his reactions. Finally, Gogol' needs this very vivid account of the diurnal world, in order to set the description of the nocturnal world against it, thereby making the switch into terror the more frightening. The story, incidentally, takes us back into the world of *kazachestvo* and masculine values, which are once again destroyed by the feminine and unequivocally sexual onslaught of the forces of night.

Gogol' here presents his hero in a manner characteristic of his work in general. It might best be thought of in cinematic terms. The account of seminary life constitutes a long shot, lending no prominence to any one character. We move into medium shot with the picture of the three seminarists travelling together. Once again no prominence is lent to Brut. It is not until they are in the witch's house that the camera moves into close-up, isolating the hero. The process of moving in the camera is furthered by a subsequent change of viewpoint, as the

86

following episode, the encounter with the witch, is seen through Brut's own eyes. Gogol' retains a certain freedom of movement, sometimes showing us reality from the standpoint of the neutral observer, sometimes, at moments of particular tension, making us live it with and through the hero. He can thereby vary narrative texture and achieve climactic effects by increasing involvement at the appropriate moment. Moreover he is able to treat the worlds of night and day in different ways. Day on the whole calls for the objective language of the observer, night for the subjective language of the participant.

The first transition from day to night is accompanied by strong erotic overtones. Indeed the 'Shpon'ka trauma' of acute sexual anxiety is a vital element of the piece. It brings about the gradual change from normality to nightmare in one of the most accomplished passages that Gogol' ever wrote. First Brut loses physical control over himself, his perceptions are then gradually modified till, slipping into another world, he is ridden by the witch not over grass, but over water, and a strange sun takes the place of the moon. This is accompanied by a 'devilish sweet feeling', a scarcely veiled suggestion of sexual pleasure. The passage makes enormous use not only of imagination but of sentence rhythms. It consists of a series of sentences beginning 'He felt', 'He saw', of increasing length. As they grow longer their pattern creates an impression of distortion, finally conveying the sense of the smoothest of transitions into another world.

With the return of day, Brut is left with the crucial question: 'Was it a dream?' The story poses a series of basic unresolved questions about the relationship between waking and dreaming. We cannot say whether he 'really' saw Viy or not. He may have dreamt it, but dream or not it killed him. The rest of the story, from the first to the last encounter with the witch, continues this study of the interplay between the two worlds. This reaches a climax in the contrasting events of day and night in the Cossack village. The daytime is devoted to drinking, eating and playing, and contrasts sharply with the events of night. Thus the Cossacks tell stories of the supernatural as opposed to experiencing it, they play games in which the winner rides the loser, in playful contrast to Brut's sinister night-ride. As soon as darkness falls the mood shifts; it is as if day had never existed, and what began, towards dusk, as a sense of vague unease, builds to panic as Brut leaves the friendly kitchen and approaches the church. As he does so for the last time Gogol' crowns his description with a familiar loaded expression: 'It was a hellish night.' As usual he means what he says.

The events in the church are somewhat puzzling. Gogol''s treatment of his hero's destruction poses certain problems. Why do his prayers not prevail against the forces of evil? Why should he be destroyed? Who or what is Viy? Why does Brut look at it despite the warning voice? Any answer must needs be speculative. Gogol' seems to have been less interested in resolving questions of guilt and responsibility as such, than he was in exploring a world in which they were posed automatically. Thus the answer to Brut's fate would seem to lie in sexual transgression. This fits with Gogol''s other treatments of the theme. It is here suggested that it is so powerful a force that not even faith can withstand it. Brut's instinct to look, despite the advice of the still small voice, might represent instinct flying in the face of reason. Tough seminarist though he may be, Brut is powerless to help himself in the nocturnal world. The significance of Viy is harder to determine. With its heavy lidded eyes, iron face and earthen body it has elemental connotations reminiscent of the evil ancestor-figure of *The Terrible Vengeance*. No longer rooted in the earth, it has acquired some power of movement. It is a kind of evil, clairvoyant judge, but one who requires its victim's complicity, a look must be exchanged, if it is to find him out. Viy is the opposite of the good and the beautiful, an earthbound ancestral bogeyman, the embodiment of our passions and desires, that will, given half a chance, come to find us.

The Old-fashioned Landowners (*Starosvetskie pomeshchiki*) is the most delicate of these stories. Yet this apparently bland account of a rustic idyll and its termination is one of the most unnerving pieces Gogol' ever wrote, so gently does he sketch in the *ne to*, the hostile elements undermining the garden of Eden. That these are not given the flamboyant treatment they enjoy in *Viy* makes the picture the more alarming; in Gogol''s world it is a case of better the devil you see than the one you sense behind you.

It is doubtless this story's resemblance to the mature writing that has given cause to its widely differing interpretations. The point at issue is the character of the landowners. For the neo-Belinsky line they are emblems of moral sloth; alienated exploiters living in a fantasy world, unable to cope with reality, they have become human vegetables. That they live in such a world is undeniable. They never leave their estate and completely lack the *razmakh*, the exuberance of Bul'ba's world. So rooted are they in their here and now, that the prospect of any radical change in their life is viewed, notably by Afanasy Ivanovich, as inconceivable and hence comic. The realist interpretation is confirmed by Gogol''s emphasis on the vital role played in their lives by habit and comfort. On her deathbed Pul'kheria Ivanovna lacks the spiritual equipment to think of her immortal soul: she can only think in terms of what she knows, and of what will become of her husband. He only feels a true sense of loss on his return to an empty house, and in future years is most strongly reminded of her when he thinks of what she used to cook for him. Because he lives through habit he is dehumanized when that habit is interrupted; absence, not death, is the source of his grief. Yet a totally negative view does not account fully for the impression Gogol''s picture leaves on us. Although, sociologically speaking, the couple may be landowners, they do not exactly grind the faces of the poor. They live in the midst of such plenty that, far from extracting surplus value from their employees, it is they who provide the surplus. They are robbed without mercy, but there is always enough to go round. In their world it is a case of each according to his appetite. Moreover, they are virtually the only couple that Gogol' describes as displaying a genuine feeling for one another. The comradeship of *Taras Bul'ba* seems superficial in comparison. They are kind and hospitable, Philemon and Baucis living a materialistic idyll in a small garden of Eden; an existence whose keynotes are harmony and integration, they have a home, a centre.[1]

The essential ambiguity of Gogol''s treatment is most apparent in his description of the role of comfort and food. We are back in Oblomov land—a warm nursery atmosphere described with loving care, it has all the characteristics and limitations of an idyllic Russian childhood. Its attraction for Gogol' must have been immense. Food always played a major role in his writing and in his life. But his attitude to food and his treatment of his characters' way of life is ambiguous, as is confirmed by the sinister fact that Gogol', the mighty eater, died to all intents and purposes of excessive fasting. Perhaps this gives us

---

[1] For an analysis of the role of idyllic connotations see: Poggioli, 'Gogol''s *Old-fashioned Landowners*'.

the clue to his treatment of this life. It appears ambiguous because he found it so. However warm, gentle and comfortable it might have been, it was also pathetically vulnerable. Philemon and Baucis were living on the brink of disaster, their way of life all too easy to undermine.

But this is not to say that Gogol' condemns them out of hand. That he treats them indulgently is shown by the style. It lacks the absurd, slightly savage surrealism, the irony masquerading as humour, with which he describes the two Ivans. The principal characteristic of this story is its gentleness. He employs long sensuous sentences whose peaceful rhythms admittedly border on sloth. Yet the keynote, emphasized by the frequent use of diminutives, is one of warmth, *uyutnost'*. This is born out in the imagery by the motif of musicality, always associated for Gogol' with lyricism and happiness. Their world sings for them; not only are there the famous singing doors which the narrator recalls with such affection, there is also the music that accompanies them whenever they set out in their carriage.

But although the music of happiness provides a dominant note, this happiness is set in the past. The narrator, whose voice is heard throughout, emphasizes from the start that the way of life he describes is no more. The retrospective account of happiness is undermined by time and Gogol''s nostalgic sadness. Moreover the description of their home conveys the slightest sense of unease, achieved by delicate use of the device of the 'non-shooting gun'. The author enters into a degree of detailed description that borders on irrelevance, and this disturbs and disorients the reader. The world looks stable enough, and yet the descriptions are unfocused enough to be unsettling. Unsure of their function we tend to question them. The guns seem unloaded, but what if one goes off?

It does. A gun in the shape of a cat, described by Pul'kheria Ivanovna as 'a gentle creature that would harm no one', goes off with a vengeance. For Eden is not what it seems. When introducing us to it Gogol' suggests that their way of life was so peaceful that one might conclude that passions and evil forces are a figment of our imagination. In fact they reach even into this charmed circle, just as they broke into the circle Khoma Brut drew around him. The cat is an interesting medium for their manifestation. On its return from the woods it has become the embodiment of a savagery and energy quite foreign to the old couple's world; no longer a gentle creature but a predator, it constitutes a threat by virtue of its very difference. It may well be an embodiment of 'passions and desires' with latent sexual connotations, for there is a Russian saying *Bludliv kak kot, pugliv kak zayats* [lascivious as a cat, timid as a hare], and it is perhaps through such a focus that Gogol' sees the cat. It contrasts with their world in every way. There no one is ever hungry, the cat is starving; no one ever eats meat—it is only after his wife's death that we see Afanasy Ivanovich sawing at a chicken—the cat is a predator. Thus it represents a contrast on the gastronomic plane, perhaps the most important feature of their way of life.

The clue to Gogol''s conception of the undermined world is provided by the sinister phrase with which he introduces the theme, when he suggests that small causes may often produce great effects. Gogol''s world is ruled by a secret causal system which can take over conventional reality at a moment's notice. Appearances are infinitely deceptive; in this world, as in Kafka's, one should not wait to be chased before starting to run.

Thus it is on the contrast between apparent peace and actual precariousness that the rhetoric of this fiction is founded. We again find the tension between essence and appearance that, in one form or another, supports all his writing. This emerges most strongly in his treatment of the supernatural; the narrator intervenes to recall his experience of hearing a disembodied voice call to him in broad daylight; an experience more terrifying than any encounter on a dark and stormy night. *The Old-fashioned Landowners* represents the orchestration of this brand of horror. Where *Viy* dealt with the contrast between night and day, we now find the erosion of day itself, and it is this that makes the piece so disturbing. Brut was at least safe in the daylight, but here there is no refuge. The story is built on the contrast between the seemingly realistic account of a life of non-event and the suggestion of an infernal parallel world which may occasionally intrude in the shape of a cat or a still small voice. The treatment of Afanasy Ivanovich's reaction to his wife's death shows a similar contrast on a purely psychological level. The man who lived like a vegetable experiences a degree of grief that time cannot efface. Passionless habit is paradoxically stronger than passion. A flat sense of everyday reality contrasts with violent passion, normality with the extraordinary. The balance of opposites plays a structural role on two levels: the psychology of Afanasy and the relationship between the natural and the supernatural. Just as passion lacks the intensity of grief created by interrupted habit, so the wild night is less frightening than broad daylight. Things are never what we expect.

In one sense the story follows the pattern of *The Two Ivans*, in that both conclude with a narrator's return and his account of a slow but deadly degeneration. Afanasy Ivanovich's life has fallen apart, the estate lapses into ruin, while the effect of his grief is, paradoxically, to destroy his humanity. For there is something inhuman about his sense of loss. He lapses into a state that anticipates the total wreck of Plyushkin. In this story, as in *The Two Ivans*, we move from an account of a more or less integrated community, represented by a relationship founded on habit, to the gradual dehumanization of a central character in a world that is falling apart. In each case the concluding note is one of grief. Happiness only exists in the past, but the forces of evil always triumph to leave us in a decaying present.

One of the reasons for the strength of this story is Gogol''s less obvious treatment of the supernatural. He finds in *Mirgorod* a flat realism which, although admitting considerable linguistic extravagance, reduces the overt role of the supernatural as such. But its apparent disappearance is only a surface phenomenon. For paradoxically, and this is perhaps the most important of all manifestations of Gogol''s use of contrast as an aesthetic device, the less he writes about the infernal dimension in so many words, the more stifling its presence becomes.

It was between 1833 and 1836 that Gogol' published the so called 'Petersburg Stories': *The Nose (Nos)*, *The Overcoat (Shinel')*, *Nevskiy Prospekt*, *The Portrait (Portret)*, *The Diary of a Madman (Zapiski sumasshedshego)*. The latter three pieces first appeared together with a series of essays in a collection entitled *Arabesques (Arabeski)*. The Petersburg stories represent the summit of his achievement in the genre, and it is no coincidence that they deal with the diabolic world of the unreal city. Gogol' no longer has any sense of home or centre to withstand his nightmare. His stories are a series of case histories describing misfortunes that befall individuals isolated in a world founded on illusion, non-reality, which, in social terms, takes the form of the sacrifice of humanity to money, status and that *reductio ad absurdum* of all aspiration, the civil service hierarchy. Their theme is the collapse of the received view of an ordered world about the ears of some luckless individual who obtains a terrible glimpse of chaos and disorder.

Thus *Nevskiy Prospekt* is founded on the interplay of dream and reality. But where Gogol' has hitherto described the intrusion of a world of nightmare into the reality of the waking world, he here employs a different technique. He describes the confusion of real and ideal, followed by an attempt to find in the artificial paradise of dreaming a surrogate ideal which the reality of waking cannot provide. Although this is the standard romantic strategy of escapism, Gogol' turns romanticism on its head. He does not opt for the world of dream, find in it some transcendental value; instead the fact that his hero is obliged by circumstances to dream rather than to live constitutes a critique of a world in which, in Baudelaire's terms, 'Action is not sister to the dream.'

The essential characteristic of the hero Piskarev is his inability to understand the world as it is. He has a minimal grasp on reality and is utterly deceived by the glitter of the essentially unreal Nevskiy Prospekt. On discovering that the madonna he has followed seems to welcome his pursuit, he asks the crucial question is he dreaming? In this case, alas, he is not. In the past Gogol' has frequently translated us from reality into a dream world. Here the reverse occurs. The careful description of the brothel-parlour through Piskarev's eyes effects a gradual transition from idealistic dream to nightmare reality; a transition subsequently balanced by a corresponding movement away from reality in the account of Piskarev's second meeting with the woman at a ball. There she appears the incarnation of all he wishes her to be, but this is only a dream. Significantly Gogol' employs the same realistic style to describe both episodes. It is only at their conclusion that we discover the true status of the experience. The writing places us in the same situation as Piskarev, who is no longer able to distinguish between real and imaginary experience. For in this world there are no land-marks to help us maintain our mental stability and distinguish reality from illusion.

It is presumably to avoid ending on a note of romantic pathos that

Gogol' concludes the piece with a low-life coda also based on sexual disappointment. We move from Piskarev, whose adventures had been related in a high flown idealistic style, to the exploits of Lieutenant Pirogov, whose very name spells bathos.[1] Gogol' here uses a vivid popular style, ending on a trivial note designed to point up the true nature of the Nevskiy Prospekt. For it is St Petersburg's smartest street that is the true central character. The first time he describes it Gogol' employs a more or less realistic method. Realism is only undermined in one respect, namely by his account of the passers-by who are described entirely in terms of attributes such as whiskers or moustaches. The lapse into linguistic fantasy is emphasized by the suggestion that only employees of the Foreign Ministry may wear black whiskers, other civil servants being obliged to sport red ones. But more important than this obvious comic touch is the fact that people are no longer described as people; they have become disembodied fragments, moustaches, hats, sleeves. The world literally disintegrates before our eyes. From a seemingly harmonious whole it flies apart into a series of fragments or metonymies. For the rhetorical motif *par excellence* that renders negative value, brings out the world's absurd surreal senselessness, is the metonymy, the part that has become divorced from its whole and is therefore void of meaning.

The second description of the street is in contrast with the first. Despite the tendency to collapse into metonymy, the first passage did tell us what the street looked like. The second does the opposite. Gogol' suggests that whatever we think we see, we are wrong. Nothing is what it appears, and the greatest source of illusion is woman. The Nevskiy Prospekt 'breathes deception', above all at night, when the devil lights the lamps to show us 'everything as it is not'. The Nevskiy Prospekt is a place where seeing is not believing.

The Nose is also founded on contrast, the contrast between the extraordinary nature of the events described and the matter-or-fact tone of their relation. Thus the story opens by establishing the date of the event, setting the mood of deadpan narration which renders this story of a wandering nose so unnerving. As usual, comedy and the

---

[1] It is interesting that Gogol' originally called the principal character Palitrin (*palitra* meaning an artist's palette). The change to Piskarev suggests that he wished to stress weakness and inadequacy, in that *pisk* describes the sound made by a frightened mouse.

absurd have negative connotations, not the least of these taking the shape of the story's eponymous hero. If *Nevskiy Prospekt* touched on metonymy, *The Nose* is the story of a metonymy come to life. The nose is the supreme symbol of disintegration and collapse into chaos, which not even the human form can withstand. Man may be made in God's image, but whose image is a nose made in?[1] It is significant that at the outset the barber describes the metonymy as *ne to. Khleb delo pechenoe, a nos sovsem ne to* [Bread's a baker's business. A nose is not].

The disembodied nose has produced various interpretations. There is an alleged connection with sexual anxiety.[2] There is also the fact that Gogol' was nose obsessed. He has confessed to a 'fierce desire to turn into nothing but a nose';[3] although the context suggests that this is in order to be able the better to smell the fragrance of spring, it may well be that he too wanted to become a metonymy—a dreamlike fragment of himself. At one stage he had planned to call this piece *The Dream*. It is unlikely to be a coincidence that the Russian for dream, *son* is *nos* spelt backwards.[4] Perhaps this is the story of a dream in reverse.

At all events, Gogol' describes a world so absurd, so lacking in authenticity that, quite literally, anything can happen. It lacks all causality as we know it, events bear no relation to one another. We never learn what, if any, connection there is between the barber's discovery of Kovalev's nose in a loaf of bread, and Kovalev's discovery of his loss. This lack of meaning is emphasized at the end of Chapter One, when Gogol' obscures the narrative in a sudden fog. The nose is found, as it was lost, inexplicably, and inexplicably it returns to its place.

That absurdity is the keynote is confirmed by the way in which Kovalev reacts to his loss. It is a source of social embarrassment, inconvenience, never of existential terror. His only fear is lest his nose leave town. In such a world there is nothing absurd in his attribution of his loss to an outraged mother whose daughter he had jilted. He

---

[1] For an examination of the nose's diabolical connotations see: Ul'yanov, 'Arabesk ili apokalipsis'.

[2] See Friedman, 'The Nose', and Spycher, 'N. V. Gogol''s *The Nose*'.

[3] *Letters*, p. 74.

[4] Ul'yanov, op. cit. pp. 219–20; also Bowman, 'The Nose'. For a comprehensive structuralist exegesis of the entire works of Gogol' in terms of his obsession with with noses see Weber, *Thématiques*.

happened to have been mistaken, but it was a perfectly illogical and hence reasonable assumption to have made.

Lack of meaning is rendered by the familiar stylistic device of irrelevance. Gogol' frequently isolates totally irrelevant details—the barber's shop sign, Kovalev's personal appearance and habits (all we know of him is that he used to have a pimple on his nose when he had a nose), the shaggy coat of the horse drawing Kovalev's cab, the way in which his doctor used to clean his teeth. Gogol' uses this technique to criticize a senseless hostile world in which the chief of police is corrupt and spectators idly throng the streets in the hope of glimpsing Kovalev's nose, which is merely the curiosity of the month. It is above all a world obsessed with the dignity of rank. Kovalev can take personal insults, but will not tolerate reflections on his position in the hierarchy. When introducing him Gogol' mentions his rank sixteen times in one page. Kovalev is particularly disturbed to meet his nose on the Nevsky Prospekt since its uniform outranks him. It is through the rhetoric of rank that he addresses it, telling it that it should 'know its place'. His reaction is that it is unseemly for him, Kovalev, to be noseless, in view of his rank and his wide range of feminine acquaintance. He maintains a macabre stiff-necked righteousness, reacting to his loss with a sense of outrage, for outrage and complacency are the sum total of his emotional range, and with the return of the nose the first immediately yields to the second.

The tone of the story suggests that this episode is but a mild amplification of workaday absurdity; the nose is a metonymy that represents the whole absurd world of the capital. But it is a metonymy that has come to life and acquired identity. Hence its reply to Kovalev's charge that it is his nose. It answers that it is *sam po sebe*, no longer a fragment but a 'thing in itself'. This apogee of absurdity is emphasized by the most sinister collapse of all; the collapse of language. At the centre of the author's manipulation of the absurd lies his use of linguistic anomaly. *Nos* occurs in contexts that destroy the word's power to refer to nonlinguistic reality; the sign ceases to signify, instead it acts as an image of the ultimate threat, the dissolution and destruction of language itself. The nose is described frowning at Kovalev. Either it is a nose and cannot frown, or it can frown and is not a nose. Kovalev refers to it as a *chelovek*; a contradiction in terms that questions the meaning of *nos*, and also perhaps the meaning of *chelovek*. It is a perpetual source of misunderstanding: the clerk in the newspaper office first assumes that Kovalev is talking about a Mr Nosov. Podkolesina, in reply to Kovalev's charge of stealing his nose, also misunderstands him. Whenever the question of the nose is raised the result is non-communication and linguistic collapse. The policeman who returned the nose saw it boarding the Riga coach. Its papers being in order, he first took it for a gentleman, but on closer inspection identified it as a nose. The nose is then removed from his pocket. This, a crucial passage, cuts at the very fibres of reality. If such confusion is possible, anything is possible, and there can be no stable meaning in the world. We are not even allowed to dismiss the story as a fantasy. The narrator admits that it is improbable, but assures us that such things happen, seldom, but they happen.

But the nose is only an instrument, not an agent. As usual it is the devil who is responsible for the confusion. Thus virtually every time the barber or Kovalev seek an explanation for these events they conclude that 'the devil knows'. We are in familiar territory: Kovalev's face is yet another enchanted place, the *ne to* where there is no reality, not even the reality of language, where a nose is not a nose, any more than a melon was a melon, the devil alone knows what it is.

The Diary of a Madman is the account of a collapse into madness. The move from the diurnal to the nocturnal world is described largely in the rhetoric of an inner event. The diary records the process of disintegration with Gogol''s usual combination of detailed observation and speech characterization. Poprishchin's turn of phrase in the early pages is often reminiscent of the idiomatic expressions of the civil servants of *The Inspector General* and *Dead Souls*. But in due course the facts of observed reality are so reassembled that an asylum becomes the court of Spain, the fact that one cannot see the nose on one's face is proof that our noses have left for the moon. But these wild ramblings are set not only against a background of vivid realistic description—of His Excellency's office, of the chief clerk's hair style—they are also carefully motivated. Although the account of the collapse has its own fascination as the dates move from 'October the third' to 'I don't recall the date, and there was no month, it was the devil knows what', it is the motivation of the madness that gives the story its particular quality. As is so often the case in Gogol', the character's name betrays his nature. In Poprishchin there is *poprishche* [career]. We have the spectacle of someone who loses his sanity by living through his position in the civil service. Like Kovalev he is a victim of his snobbery and bureaucratic ambitions which combine to destroy his mind. Gogol' goes to some lengths to establish his character's dignity and sense of rank. His principal professional interest is the state of His Excellency's pens, and the act of writing has particular significance for him. He is surprised that dogs can write, since only gentlemen write properly; merchants, serfs even, may be semi-literate, but their writing is 'mechanical' and lacks punctuation. Poprishchin's snobbery emerges in his disgust at the disrespect of servants, his reaction to the vulgar smell of cooking cabbage, and above all in his sexual response to his chief's daughter, which is rendered through a rhetoric of rank. When he retrieves her handkerchief it is 'fragrant with the rank of general', moreover he refers to her as Her Excellency. To the demoralizing influence of the civil service are added the diabolic connotations of sexual desire. These emerge when, in one of his madder moments, he has a flash of terrible revelation, discovering that woman is in love with the devil, and the devil alone.

The lapse into madness differs from Gogol''s habitual treatment of transition. In the first place it takes longer. Moreover, until the conclusion Poprishchin displays no sense of anxiety or alarm. Much of the comic effect results from the matter-of-fact way in which he records his experiences. On first hearing the dogs converse he is admittedly surprised, but instead of asking himself if he was dreaming, he wonders whether he was drunk. Having established that he was sober he accepts subsequent events without question, up to the point when a Spanish grandee administers an accolade in the shape of a severe beating. The treatment of a man's unhesitating acceptance of a world of illusion suggests a terrifying parody of *Don Quixote* in which Dulcinea has become a civil servant's daughter, the knight a doleful ageing clerk. In the course of his descent Poprishchin loses all grasp on time and place, and finally all ability to articulate reality by means of language. He suggests that the human brain is not in one's head but is born on a wind from the Caspian sea—a view of anatomy that is frightening rather than comic in view of Gogol''s own quite serious assertion that the cause of his physical ailments was that his stomach was upside down.

Much of the story's comic effect derives from the exploitation of the 'Don Quixote' device. Poprishchin cannot distinguish between his reality and that of other people. His frustrated sexual and professional ambitions convince him that he is the king of Spain—the asylum his court. He is amused that a servant be stupid enough to think him mad because he wishes to have a word with her mistress's dog. But in the midst of this madness Gogol' employs a subtle technique of reversal. It is when his condition is greatly advanced that Poprishchin comes, in a moment of insane clarity, to question his position in the world not through the rhetoric of rank, but as a human being. On learning that Sophie is about to marry a chamberlain he actually questions the value of rank as such. Paradoxically he gains a glimpse of normative reality, distinguishes between form and substance, precisely at the moment when his collapse into insanity becomes total.

Gogol' obtains some interesting effects from the dogs' correspondence. Not the least of these is its mixture of styles. The letters move, in mid-sentence, from affected sentimentality to the joys of eating marrow-bone jelly. But Gogol' does not use the letters for comic effect alone. In one dog's observation of its master, strangely overjoyed to receive a piece of odourless ribbon which tastes a little salty, or of Sophie's appearance after a ball—pale and tired, she doubtless got nothing to eat—Gogol' is using the device of revealing the absurdity of conventional behaviour by showing it through the eyes of an animal.[1] But the letters play a third role. They provide a relief from Poprishchin's ramblings and apparently constitute another point of view. They reveal him for the unattractive and ridiculous little man he is, show us Sophie laughing at him. This is the familiar technique which furnishes two views of a character, his own and someone else's; but who, in this case, is the someone else? Not only is the viewpoint of the letters quite different from that of the hero, they provide information to which he could not have had access; they cannot be the product of his fantasy, he is no more likely to have written them than the dogs themselves. Gogol' has undermined the whole fabric of his story with one stroke. The piece purports to be the account of Poprishchin's fantasies, yet dream has encroached on reality to an unsuspected degree. If the letters were real, then the dogs must have talked and

[1] For further analysis of this technique with reference to Tolstoy's animal stories, see Shklovsky, *O teorii prozy*, pp. 13. sq.

perhaps Poprishchin really was the king of Spain. The fact that Gogol' has imparted a measure of objective reality to the letters once again questions the nature of the reality that we take for granted. We can no longer ask what the letters 'really' were, for Gogol' describes a world in which the word 'really' has lost its meaning.

The conclusion is famous for its sudden move into high pathos as the madman appears to return to sanity and grasp the full horror of his situation. In a passage strikingly close to the lyric conclusion of Part One of *Dead Souls*, Poprishchin calls for a carriage to carry him at a gallop down some infinite road.[1] He then makes a desperate appeal to his mother to save her sick son—he even recognizes his insanity—only to break the mood of high seriousness as his attention is drawn to the Bey of Algiers' nose. The author is again using stylistic contrast as an aesthetic device. Poprishchin only shows a full sense of human values at the height of his madness; where before we laughed at him we now feel sympathy. But we are not allowed to sustain this emotion; after this brief glimpse of humanity we revert to total madness and irrelevance in a characteristic dying fall. It is the role not the content of this passage that is of particular importance. Its significance is manifestly a function of its relation to what has gone before. It makes us momentarily reassess our attitude to Poprishchin, playing on our humane feelings, opening up another range of reactions, only to sweep these aside at once. The passage is only significant in its context, with reference to what has preceded it and to the final sentence. It is an important element in the story, but an element only; to take it out of context and suggest that it represents what Gogol' 'really' felt about Poprishchin would be indefensible. Yet it is precisely such an attitude that numerous critics have adopted to a longer but otherwise comparable 'humane passage' in *The Overcoat*.

Dostoevsky's 'We have all come out of Gogol''s *Overcoat*' is one of the most famous apocryphal sayings in Russian literature.[2] It may have been the manner of Dostoevsky's emerging, with his pathetic analyses of little people overwhelmed by poverty in the big city, that has lead to the propagation of the *Overcoat* myth, whereby this, Gogol''s first 'realist' work, portrays the first 'small man' of Russian

---

[1] An attitude to travel which was Gogol''s own. He writes of 'The road my sole medicine' and longs to be a courier on a Russian post-chaise. *Letters*, p. 97.
[2] See below, p. 237.

literature, crushed by a hostile world. Gogol' seeks to enlist our sympathy, stimulate our social conscience and *do nothing else*. Unfortunately this interpretation fails to account for the conclusion. Its supporters are obliged to dismiss this as a weakness, an unfortunate relapse into Gogol''s early manner. But if we step outside this somewhat restricted view of Gogol' the realist, it becomes clear that the piece is in no sense radically different from the earlier work, but is rather an intensification of some of its aspects. It may be more realistic than any other in the cycle, in the sense that it contains a greater proportion of descriptive detail in a low-life setting. But this realism is counterweighed by an uncompromising assertion of absurd and fantastic elements. Indeed the abrupt and superficially unmotivated transition into a fantasy world constitutes such a violent break with the preceding realism that the fantasy takes on if anything a greater prominence than it enjoyed in stories such as *The Nose* that used a surrealistic code from the outset. Structurally, with its abrupt transition from one level to another, *The Overcoat* is very similar to *The Old-fashioned Landowners*, and it will emerge that this comparison is valid in more ways than one. Thus one can no more give a satisfactory account of the piece in terms of its realistic elements alone than one could in the instance of *The Landowners*.

As always, Gogol' bases his story on the juxtaposition of a series of contrasts. He is once again concerned with transition, and it is in terms of a series of oppositions and transitions employed as structural devices that the story may most usefully be considered.

The author's use of paradoxical contrast emerges most strongly in the character of Akaky Akakievich. He appears scarcely human, is devoid of feeling, leads the most insignificant of lives, yet, paradoxically he is the subject of a genuinely moving if not tragic story. Everything about him, even his name, is apparently ridiculous.[1] He lives a non-existence, consisting entirely of copying documents. He has no interests, no desires, no awareness. His world is built of habit. But Gogol' is at pains to point out that he is content. He serves with love. Living on a pittance he is happy and secure in a closed world of his own creation. Such a view of his situation invites direct comparison with the world of the old-fashioned landowners. They too lived in

---

[1] For an analysis of latent connotations of religious martyrdom in his name, see Seemann, 'Eine Heiligenlegende als Vorbild von Gogol''s *Mantel*'.

apparent security in a closed world of their own, a world whose keynote was an unquestioning, passion-free contentment. Akaky Akakievich is as oblivious to the outside world as they were. He only resents his teasing colleagues when they interfere with his writing. They are otherwise powerless to penetrate his charmed circle. He has no other interest, not even food. Just as the landowners were so fond of food that they never opened a book, he is so absorbed by writing that he never cares what he eats. But again a life of apparent security is threatened by disaster. Passion, in the shape of an overcoat, will change his habits and destroy his stability. The instant the tailor tells him that he needs a new coat he loses his grasp on reality; everything swims before his eyes, he raises his voice for the first time in his life, and walks down the street '*as if in a dream*'. His way of life changes overnight. He even starts paying regular visits to his tailor whereas he never used to leave home. He develops a negative interest in food: what he ate used to be unimportant, but now he is absorbed by what he does not eat. His contact with the coat brings him alive. It makes him go out for his first social evening, drink champagne and even enjoy a flicker of sexuality. The loss of his coat makes him become almost violent with obstructive clerks, and it is of course the coat that is the eventual cause of his death. Gogol' has again employed a combination of contrast and transition. Akaky is at first barely human, yet has achieved a measure of security and contentment that many might envy. He acquires a coat, becomes apparently more human, more aware, yet with this new awareness comes his destruction. As usual things are not what they seem; Akaky's apparent revitalization is the instrument of his downfall.

What of the coat itself, what part does it play in the pattern? It is described as a kind of wife to him, the very thought of it is a source of companionship, providing spiritual sustenance. The sacrifices he makes to acquire it are described in almost religious terms. He fasts to earn it, and it eventually brings him a civil servant's martyrdom. In retrospect the narrator describes it as a *svetlyy gost'* [radiant guest] that momentarily illuminated his life, only to bring on disaster. For, structurally speaking, the coat plays the same role as did the cat in *The Old-fashioned Landowners*. It is another instance of the strange order of things that subtends the world of apparent normality. It may seem a source of spiritual solace, but it is really *ne to*. Its association with sexuality—another parallel with the cat motif—is important here. Not only does it arouse sexual desires in Akaky when he wears it, it is a wife, with all the connotations that that word had for Gogol'. In Shpon'ka's nightmare a wife became a piece of cloth, here a piece of cloth becomes a wife. Thus, no coincidence this, it is in connection with the tailor that our old friend the devil crops up. Petrovich will try to charge the devil knows what prices; when he refuses a second time to repair the old coat it is as if the devil drove him to it. Unclean forces make him set the price he does on the new coat. Moreover when the thought of his new coat nearly makes Akaky make a mistake in his work, his instinctive and correct reaction is to cross himself. Despite appearances the coat is a concealed source of sensuality and evil that inevitably brings about its owner's undoing.

Standing in complementary opposition to Akaky the lowly official who is paradoxically human is the Important Person, yet another example of a potentially reasonable human being reduced by his sense of rank to a *litso* [face, by extension: person, functionary], a metonymy. He is everything his counterpart is not. Where Akaky expresses himself in meaningless particles and prepositions, the Important Person's vocabulary is equally restricted, being virtually confined to imperatives. Where Akaky's position creates for him a secure and harmonious environment, that of the Important Person is a source of misery, preventing him from enjoying himself lest he betray his rank. Where Akaky has a ridiculous name his counterpart has a ridiculous absence of name. Where Akaky is humble the Important Person is a bully. However he does not simply represent authority crushing the small man, he plays a structural role in the narrative, one that is in every way equal and opposite to that played by Akaky.

It is precisely such a role that is played, on another level, by the conclusion. It is by definition the reversal of everything that has gone before. Fantastic as opposed to realistic, it portrays Akaky's ghost as having no respect for authority. as the embodiment of psychic energy. It strikes fear into all that see it, even the policemen, who contrast strongly with the policemen Akaky dealt with when alive. But the reversal of roles is carried even further. For in the conclusion the Important Person re-enacts the role originally played by Akaky, Akaky's ghost that first played by the Important Person. For in the second encounter, like Akaky, the Important Person goes to a party, drinks two glasses of champagne, decides to visit his mistress, is robbed of his overcoat and is terrified of Akaky's ghost. But where his experience frightened Akaky to death, the Important Person is re-formed by his, becomes a better man; hence is frightened into life.

Thus the construction offers a confrontation between two equal and opposite elements, realism and fantasy, that stand in a reciprocal relationship to one another. The story is another exercise in turning reality on its head. Yet there is more to it than an exercise in mere formalism. Gogol' suggests that the fantastic conclusion is a reward for his hero's wretched life. Thus the two sides of the narrative constitute yet another examination of the relationship between life as it is, and life as it should be. Gogol' uses the realistic strain to describe the appalling nature of the, normatively speaking, unreal world of St Petersburg. It is only through the focus of fantasy that he can treat of the 'real' world of positive values, in which rank does not automatically command respect, in which the ghosts of little men can have the energy of a Taras Bul'ba, and in which important people can prove capable of moral regeneration. Paradoxically what appears to be the world of fantasy is in fact the world of normative reality.

This relation between the real and the fantastic emerges early in the story in the so-called 'humane passage'. For it is in the midst of Gogol''s account of the teasing of Akaky, who has been described as a grotesque caricature of humanity, that a young official sees in his face a look that says 'I am your brother', gaining a glimpse of nor-mative reality at a moment when Akaky's situation would appear to be as divorced from that reality as possible. As with *The Diary of a Madman* it is in the most grotesque and fantastic passages that we glimpse positive values, whereas the realistic writing renders their negative counterparts. Thus the two sides have complementary roles to play; the piece is no more a realistic short story with an unfortunate fantastic coda than was *The Nose*.

The interplay of stylistic levels confirms the view that the story is built on the juxtaposition of complementary narrative strains. There are broadly speaking three levels, bound together by the voice of the narrator.[1] Gogol' employs a quasi-oral narrative mode, undelaying

[1] For a brilliant analysis of this aspect of the language, see Eykhenbaum, 'Kak sdelana *Shinel'* Gogolya'.

the piece with the rhythms of direct speech to create a narrative unity. But within this unity there are differing elements. Most important is the surrealistic irony with which the narrator deals with the grotesque world of officialdom—in the digressionary opening, or in the account of how intrepid policemen were ordered to take the ghost dead or alive. We encounter familiar devices such as contradiction in terms, irrelevance, and above all certain tricks of language such as the ironic use of the particle *dazhe* [even] to qualify the most trivial complements in order to emphasize the negative sense of values peculiar to this absurd world. He similarly uses indeterminates, *gde-to, kak-to, kogda-nibud'* [somewhere, somehow, at any time], in apparently realistic contexts such as the opening paragraph; this rhetoric imparts a sense of imprecision and irreality to his descriptions. Set against this style of writing are passages that describe elements of the action in an orthodox realistic manner. Significantly, Gogol' first uses this mode after Akaky has decided on a new coat. As he is apparently brought to life by his decision, so his speech and indeed the narrative itself strike a new and purposeful note. We now encounter closely observed and relevant detail; the writing is vivid and atmospheric, witness Akaky's walk through the streets at night, and is not allowed to lapse into irrelevance. This only recurs with the introduction of the Important Person and bureaucracy, and irrelevance of course returns with a vengeance in the final episode, which is full of digressionary elements.

The Important Person is a particular target for word play. The possibilities of his designation are fully explored by Gogol'. Thus, when discussing important people, he manages to empty the adjective of all meaning by a series of puns and pseudo-puns, until the emptiness of language becomes an image for the emptiness of rank itself.

The third stylistic element is largely found in the pages that precede Akaky's decision. He is introduced in a careful combination of the realistic and the absurd—his name, his pedigree, the punning on Bashmachkin. This blend of vivid descriptive detail with absurd digression is illustrated by Gogol''s comparison of Akaky's neck to the plaster cats women apparently mounted on their hats! He then proceeds to describe, in quite realistic language, the sorry state of his clothes. A similar blend of relevance and irrelevance is used to describe Petrovich. There is a vivid account of the approach to his room, which is followed by the absurd portrait of his wife; he is himself described with care, but the description opens with a metonymy as we focus on the nail of his big toe. This combination of the two elements which is followed first by a strain of realism and then by a fantastic conclusion, seems to constitute a stylistic preparation for the two discrete narrative modes that obtain for the rest of the story. It provides a linguistic clue to the theme, namely the interpenetration of the trivial and the tragic, an examination of the sets of negative and positive elements that go to make up the peculiar way in which Gogol''s imagination interprets the world.

The Petersburg stories provide a partial answer to a question raised at the beginning of this study—why did Gogol' write. They portray a world in which nothing can be taken for granted, a world void of sense and harmony. They suggest that our carefully constructed view of reality enjoys only a precarious stability. This world can, at a moment's notice, fly apart into a series of senseless metonymies. Confronted with the danger of a disintegrating reality Gogol' seems to have found in the act of writing a means of retaining a tenuous grasp on some kind of reality or other; the reality of language. It is the utmost importance in this respect that the harmonious world in which we first encounter Akaky is a world made of writing. This is his sole interest, it provides stability and reality, and it is through the focus of the act of writing that he sees his surroundings; *his writing creates his reality for him.*[1] In the same way Gogol' may portray a world in which there is no order, harmony or stability, yet paradoxically his description of that world has the stability and harmony of form. If he is certain of nothing else he can, taking chaos as his subject and making order from it, at least be certain of the reality of his own creation.

Although his two major farces *The Gamblers* (*Igroki*) and *Marriage* (*Zhenit'ba*) are masterpieces of their kind it is *The Inspector General* (*Revizor*) that makes Gogol' the greatest comic playwright since Molière, with whose work the piece bears comparison both in terms of its use of farce and its projection of moral values. It is with this play

---

[1] 'But if Akaky did look at anything, all he saw were his own neat evenly written lines, and it was only if a horse's head materialized out of nowhere to lean on his shoulder and blow hard through its nostrils onto his cheek that he would notice that he was in the middle of the street and not in the middle of a line.'

that Gogol', notably in later years, makes his first overt claims to a moral purpose. Although this accords with his ever-increasing tendency to preach, we should not dismiss his suggestion that the town be seen as our mental town, the characters as the passions that pillage our souls. Of course such an allegorical interpretation does not provide an entirely satisfactory reading, any more than would the suggestion that the piece was simply the indictment of contemporary bureaucratic corruption. The truth lies to one side of these interpretations and yet it includes them both. Perhaps the greatest strength of the mature Gogol' is his ability to write in a way that is both directly narrative, vivid and realistic, and at the same time general to the point of allegory. Both here and in *Dead Souls* allegory seems to lurk beneath the surface, constantly on the point of emerging without ever quite doing so. Gogol' induces a moral awareness in his readers but is too skilled an artist ever to moralize in so many words by moving onto an allegorical level as such.

It is important to establish from the outset that whatever the town may or may not be, it is not a real place in the sense that St Petersburg was real. Gogol' had little direct experience of Russian provincial life. His creation is essentially the product of his hearsay reality. All we know is that it is in the centre of Russia—one can ride for three years in any direction and not reach a frontier. There is something unreal, dreamlike, about its location. In his epilogue (*Teatral'nyy raz'ezd*) he emphasizes that it is a collective place, that his characters are universals and not specific satirical targets. One of the ways in which he hints at this allegorical level without realizing it is by means of a blend of generality of conception and specificity of detail. The town may be anywhere but its inhabitants have definite characteristics. Like the people of *Dead Souls*, they are realistic characters in a setting that has a strangely unrealistic, almost mythic, feel to it.

That Gogol' is once again offering a portrait of negative values is confirmed by a passage in the epilogue which explains that he omitted to introduce a single positive character as a source of relief, lest this destroy the realism of the negative ones. Thus he is anxious to secure our belief in his inventions as representing life as it is: a belief we would all too gladly shake off. However he admits to the presence of one positive character, namely laughter. His conception of the aesthetic role of humour has progressed from the self-directed therapy of *The Evenings* to become a moral force. He suggests in the epilogue that it is our ability to laugh that renders the triviality and emptiness of existence terrifying, and that without laughter the world would go to sleep. Thus laughter is a means of preserving our humanity and our moral consciousness. It is a form of criticism, an instrument of moral judgment, and this explains its role in both *The Inspector General* and *Dead Souls*.

Such a view accords well with the importance that the theme of judgement held for Gogol' and with its role in this piece.[1] We, as a laughing audience, stand in judgement on the characters. Moreover, the theme of injustice is an essential element of the play itself. Even as mayors go, say the merchants, this one is a monster of injustice. It is significant that the most prominent minor character is Lyapkin-Tyapkin the judge, who is more interested in dogs than in justice, and who confesses that he can never sift truth from falsehood when hearing evidence. When the mayor describes the state of the town he refers to venial sins (*greshki*). He is himself 'in many ways a sinner' and Zemlyanika he knows to be a sinner, since he's an intelligent man. But despite his awareness of corruption, the mayor's projects for reform are only concerned with appearance. He has no sense of the inner man, freely admitting in Act 1, Scene 1 that he can say nothing about the 'inner order'. This absence of any spiritual sense is one of the most important features of Gogol''s indictment. Indeed sin and judgement play a vital role in this play. Gogol' seems to echo Biblical rhetoric when the mayor says that the Inspector can 'come at any hour'. The play itself is the account of a pseudo-judgement at the hands of Khlestakov. The officials make the cardinal error of assessing him on appearance, and are finally only too pleased to be judged by him, because such judgement is easy. But the whole piece stands with reference to the awesome figure of the real Inspector who is by definition everything Khlestakov is not; the embodiment of absolute justice. He has powerful allegorical connotations—perhaps the reason why he never appears on stage—and the play concludes in a kind of temporal paradox whereby he remains for ever about to appear in the

[1] That Gogol' seems to have been obsessed with the theme of judgement is born out by a letter to his mother reminding her of the profound and terrifying impression made on him as a child by her account of the Last Judgement. *Letters*, pp. 45–6.

next second. If, as Merezhkovsky suggests, Khlestakov is Antichrist, then the Inspector is the genuine article. But rather than impose an unequivocally allegorical interpretation of his identity it would appear more likely that Gogol''s imaginative construction has been shaped by the pattern of false Messiah and Last Judgement. To say that he has used a Biblical code is not to say that he intended a Biblical message. He has written a play not a parable.

As with all his best work the play's construction is remarkably simple. It is of course based on the device of mistaken identity. But where comic playwrights tend to use such a device to create a series of complications in the plot, Gogol' is more concerned with an analysis of the mistake itself. The play proper begins with Dobchinsky and Bobchinsky announcing the arrival of a young man who must, for irrefutable reasons—he won't leave his room or pay his bill, he is young—be the Inspector General. The play ends with the mayor's asking himself how he could ever have mistaken for an Inspector General a coxcomb who was in every way his opposite. It is on this diametric opposition between 'is' and 'appears' that the drama is founded. The familiar theme of the confusion of reality and fantasy is here turned to comic effect, since it is the officials' guilty conscience that reduces their sense of reality to the point where they will accept the first stranger in town for his very opposite. Gogol''s exploration of their mistake takes the shape of a detailed examination of the phenomenon of non-communication. So panic-stricken are they that they interpret events in terms of the most extraordinary patterns of cause and effect: the thought of impending judgement has destroyed their grasp on reality. Thus both judge and postmaster see the Inspector's advent as a sign that Russia is about to declare war on Turkey. Bobchinsky and Dobchinsky deduce Khlestakov's identity from the fact that he stared at their food. The persistent misinterpretation of Khlestakov's every action is a continual source of comedy. When he offers Luka Lukich a cigar in Act 4 the gesture is so pregnant with significance that the poor man is quite unnerved by the decision should he accept it or not. The officials cannot understand Khlestakov even when he tells the truth. When he tells them that he was almost made a collegiate assessor, a rank only halfway up the ladder, they all stand to attention out of respect. They cannot understand him, only hearing what they expect to hear. Thus the mayor's first encounter with Khlestakov is a model of non-communication. They never succeed in exchanging thoughts, they can only swap noises. So obsessed with his own problems is each character that he is unable to grasp what the other is saying. For Khlestakov is as confused as anyone. It is only comically late in the play that he suspects a mistake. In earlier episodes he expresses surprise and delight at his reception, and, a typical Gogolian device, he finds the mayor's hospitality to visitors perfectly credible, only saying that he welcomed the local practice of showing travellers round; in other towns he was shown nothing.

The characters' minimal grasp on reality again emerges when, in the heat of the moment, they offer the most delightful and absurd justifications. When the mayor believes that he has been denounced by the N.C.O.'s wife whom he had had flogged, he blurts out that she had flogged herself. A similar reluctance to allow reality to obstruct the pleasure principle emerges in the mayor's wife's hesitant rejoinder to Khlestakov's avowal of instant timeless passion: 'Excuse me, but I am to some extent . . . married.' The whole pattern of non-communication and misunderstanding is ironically summed up by the mayor who unconsciously points to the cause of his misfortune when, in the last act, he says: 'Words cannot hurt'. For this is precisely what they have done throughout this play. It is words and not deeds that have brought about the officials' collective undoing.

For Khlestakov consists of nothing but words. At the beginning of the play he is an empty windbag. The officials inspire him, make him what they want him to be. They give him the breath of life, creating him in the image of their guilty conscience. Gogol' is to employ the same device in *Dead Souls* when each official in the town of N will interpret Chichikov's non-existent purchases in terms of his particular sense of guilt. In both instances the characters reveal themselves by imparting significance to a person or concept originally by definition almost without significance. This emerges in Gogol''s instructions as to how Khlestakov is to be played. He is not a stock character from knock-about farce, to be played as 'braggarts and scapegraces are played'.[1] The actor must play him with as much simplicity and sincerity as possible. He is not a confidence trickster or villain in an active sense. It is his situation that turns him into an unconscious confidence trick.

[1] *Letters*, p. 55.

He has no personality or will of his own, is quite incapable of concentrated thought. This is clear from Gogol''s description of how he speaks. 'His speech is jerky, words come out quite unexpectedly . . . He is simply stupid; he babbles only because he sees that they are disposed to listen; he lies because he has had a hearty dinner and drank a considerable quantity of wine. He is frivolous only when he approaches the ladies. The scene in which he starts lying at random should receive special attention. His every word . . . is a completely unexpected impromptu, and therefore should be expressed abruptly'.[1] He is thus largely created by circumstances. There is no consistency to him unless it be *poshlost'* [mean-spirited vulgarity, mediocrity], *khamstvo* [boorishness]. His ambitions consist entirely of false needs, they concentrate exclusively on appearance. A windbag, he is bold till faced with reality, whereupon he is instantly deflated. But you can't keep a good balloon down: he rapidly adapts to fresh circumstances and is soon inflated by the attentions of the mayor and his colleagues. In the boasting scene image succeeds image until all sense of proportion is lost. His soup arrives hot from Paris, 35,000 couriers speed to his door, and he finally achieves a sinister ubiquity, 'I am everywhere, everywhere' he cries. His keynote is bluster and one of the principal sources of the comedy is that for once he is in a situation in which bluster pays off and is taken at its face value. In his first encounter with the mayor he interprets the offer of a change of quarters as a threat of imprisonment. His first reaction is a panic-stricken blustering that puts the fear of God into the luckless mayor. Finally his complete lack of consistency, the fact that he lives solely from moment to moment, emerges in his farcical and idiosyncratic courtship of the mayor's wife and daughter.

But of course Khlestakov is not just a comic character. He has sinister not to say diabolic connotations. These are brought to a head in the last act when Zemlyanika says 'It's as if some kind of fog confused us, it was the devil's doing.' More sinister, if less obvious, is Osip's answer to Khlestakov's question, how can it be that the other guests at the inn are eating whereas he is not, as if he were not like them. Osip replies 'But of course they are not like you'. Although he goes on to point out that the other guests pay, the reply has more sinister undercurrents. Thus Gogol' once described 'our mutual

[1] Ibid., loc. cit. See also p. 165.

friend the devil' as 'a blusterer [who] consists entirely of hot air',[1] a description that fits Khlestakov well. His particular brand of devilry takes the shape of a complete lack of substance; insignificant and mediocre, he is nothing but froth and it is what others project into him that swells him to monstrous proportions. He is moreover a parody of humanity. He has the capacity to ape and hence devalue the spiritual dimension. An unconscious hypocrite, he says he hates two-faced behaviour. He alone in the play touches on the spiritual. He has a remarkable literary talent, producing instant masterpieces because his thoughts have an 'extraordinary lightness'. His soul 'thirsts for enlightenment', and finally he describes himself in his letter, in a terrible parody of Gogol''s own aspirations, as longing for spiritual sustenance, needing to take up some noble cause. That Gogol' had much in common with his hero emerges in his own correspondence. 'It is time, it is time at last to do something serious, oh, what an incomprehensibly amazing significance all the incidents and circumstances of my life have had! How salutary all the unpleasantnesses and disappointments were for me! They had something elastic in them; touching them it seemed to me, *I bounded higher*'.[2] All Khlestakov is here, even the extraordinary lightness. The same quality emerges in another letter which opens with a spiritual admonition, only to proceed to try to touch its recipient for 18,000 roubles. Indeed Gogol' recognizes this quality in himself, notably with respect to his last book *Selected Passages*, of which he writes: 'Really there is something Khlestakovian in me.'[3]

Gogol' constructs the play in a manner similar to *Dead Souls*; the arrival in town of a sinister stranger acts as a device that brings out the true nature of a whole rogue's gallery set in a world of diabolical provincial mediocrity. He shows remarkable technical skill in revealing the failings of each character. For, strictly speaking, the others are scarcely involved in the action of the play which consists of a continuing confrontation between Khlestakov and the mayor. The other officials are made to form a kind of dynamic tableau, a chorus of reactions. This emerges very clearly in Act 4, in which they each appear in turn. The structure of every scene is the same, but so skilfully does Gogol' vary the pace and speech characterization

[1] *Letters*, p. 137.   [2] Ibid., pp. 57–8. Italics mine.
[3] Ibid., p. 174.

that there is no sense whatsoever of static repetition. Instead the act moves very gently into an ever-increasing atmosphere of vague irreality culminating with the populace calling to Khlestakov through the window with their bristling forest of petitions. Indeed a great proportion of the play could be considered a kind of dynamic picture, and it is of course as a direct contrast to this, its most important compositional quality, that Gogol' ends the piece with a sustained static freeze.

The author's highly developed sense of his medium is perhaps to be explained in part by his family association with amateur dramatics, partly by his own gifts of mimicry. But be that as it may he displays here, as elsewhere indeed, a remarkable gift for stagecraft. He has a great awareness of the dramatic medium as such, with an eye not just on the actors but also on the producer. Not only does he give careful instructions as to how his characters behave, particularly as to how they should come on and go off, he has also written the parts in a way that gives the actors great scope to embroider them with gesture and expression, and to use the stage as a physical space, for example in the kind of grouping and re-grouping required by the action of Act 4, Scene 1. Moreover he makes much use of farcical stage business. It is Bobchinsky and Dobchinsky who act as the centre of the knockabout aspect of the piece, usually serving as the springs of visual action. Moreover the author supplies the kind of detail that normally has to be provided by a producer. We are told when and how Bobchinsky looks in on the mayor's first interview with Khlestakov; this piece of business is built to a climax as he falls into the room, and is later picked up when we see Bobchinsky with a plaster on his nose on his next entrance. More scope for stage business is created as the various officials take it in turns to read extracts from Khlestakov's letters, stopping as it comes to mention, and to judge, the reader in question. Like Molière he uses farcical elements to lend verve to his play, to give it the pace that will carry the audience, helping the actors to maintain a *rapport* with them, and indeed to make them laugh.

Gogol''s other great comic resource remains of course his language. He has a remarkable talent for the recreation of the rhythm and idiom of direct speech in a way that appears less a direct reproduction than its amplification. His dialogue is so true to life yet so much larger than life that it borders on the grotesque. This emerges in the speech of the mayor, which serves as a superb means of characterization. He has a wide range of tones; when talking to his colleagues his speech is composed of authoritative instruction cloaked in a form of heavy-handed and ironic politeness as he dwells on their sundry failings. Beneath this blend of authority and delicacy lies a strong undercurrent of fear which emerges in flashes of impatience. When talking to Khlestakov he uses a deferential tone which disguises an ever-increasing measure of alarm, while his asides show him seeking his opponent's measure. However, his normal tone is pithy, highly coloured and idiomatic, employing *pogovorki* [sayings] without ever lapsing into cliché. Thus after Khlestakov's boasting scene, when the mayor's wife is irritating enough to inform her husband that far from being frightened she simply felt herself to be in the presence of a gentleman, the mayor snaps back:

> Ну, уж вы — женщины! Всё кончено, одного этого слова
> достаточно!.. Вдруг брякнут ни из того ни из другого словцо.
> Вас посекут, да и только, а мужа и поминай как звали.
>
> (Act 3, Scene 9)

> *Oh you women! That's done it! That one word's all we needed!..*
> *All you've got to do is blurt something out—you'll just get*
> *flogged, but the husband—well, he's as good as dead.*

What is most striking about this style is the prominence that Gogol''s use of language imparts to verbs. Although this is a characteristic of the Russian language as such, it would be fair to say that if there is one specific feature that focuses the particular flavour of Gogol''s style, it is the verb. Time and again it is this that gives a particular phrase its richness. Gogol' has an extraordinary command over the range and nuance that formation by prefixation gives to Russian verb forms. Although, as was suggested, this is an intrinsic feature of Russian, so that one must beware of describing as peculiarly Gogolian turns of phrase that are part of a common linguistic heritage, the fact remains that Gogol''s style does give prominence to what is at least potentially one of the most important features of the language. This is perhaps one of the reasons why his style conveys the peculiar effect of having realized essential Russianness, of having created a model of the Russian language writ large. It is principally the speech of the mayor that brings out this quality to the full. Thus he has two tirades in Act 5, one cursing the merchants in Scene 2, the other cursing Khlestakov in the final scene, in which he gives full tongue. The speeches consist almost entirely of exclamations, and are so loaded with idiom that they provide what amounts to an illustration of Russian invective, and are hence, by definition, quite impossible to translate.

Khlestakov's speech stands in oppositional contrast to that of the mayor. It is at its most characteristic when he is flirting—a mixture of ill-assimilated gallicism and a parody of the rhetoric of passion. In his letter he employs a combination of racy slang, *obchistil menya krugom* [cleaned me out] and phoney French *zhuiruyu* [*je jouis*]. But on the whole his language is neutral and conventional, the product of circumstance. Where the mayor's speech is peculiar to him, one of his most striking characteristics, Khlestakov speaks in a purely conventional way, precisely because he has no character. His speech also contrasts with that of Osip, the only character in the play who understands the situation from the start. Osip, by his language, emphasizes his grasp on reality, for it is idiomatic and very much to the point. He uses ambiguity to avoid answering embarrassing questions; thus when the mayor's servant asks him whether his master is really a general he replies: 'He's a general, but not the kind you know' (*General, da tol'ko s drugoi storony*). Because Gogol' wishes to show him as being in control of the situation he never devalues his language by excessive eccentricity or rhetoric. It remains vivid and down-to-earth.

Speech characterization is also used to effect with the merchants and harridans of Act 4. He creates a view of them through their language. The presence of the merchants is justified dramatically by the way in which their language fills out the picture by creating an atmosphere of 'merchantness'. The N.C.O.'s wife similarly introduces a proletariat dimension, notably through the phonetic transcription of her speech—*necha* and *shtraft* for *nichego* [nothing] and *shtraf* [fine], and the highly-coloured language in which she expresses herself.

Gogol'"s play is ostensibly about the fate of a number of petty officials in a town in the middle of nowhere, yet it has wider implications. These emerge in certain passages that touch on the play's relation to the audience. Not the least of these is the epigraph: 'Don't

115

blame the mirror if you see an ugly mug.' Whom is the author address-ing? The characters? Hardly, since the epigraph stands outside the play. It is more likely that he is addressing his potentially critical public. The implication is that the play is a mirror in which we see ourselves. It is we who are responsible for the blackness of what we see. This creates a strange involvement whereby we actually become part of the play, an involvement that re-emerges in the last act, notably in the mayor's angry cry to the audience: 'What are you laughing at? You're laughing at yourselves!' It emerges more subtly in the pre-ceding scene. There has, as usual, been talk of pigs in this play. Zemlyanika, envying the apparent good fortune of the mayor's family, talks of happiness crawling into a pig's mouth. Another character criticizing the new-found dignity of the mayor's wife says: 'Seat her at table and she'll put her feet on it.' (A variant of the Russian saying: Seat a pig at table and it puts its feet up.) Gogol' employs a piggy rhetoric to bring out the awfulness of his characters. But, when the mayor realizes Khlestakov's identity, and stares around him in a panic-stricken fog, he says: 'I can't see a thing, just pigs' snouts instead of faces.' Whose snouts are these? It does not take much imagination, in the light of the epigraph, to visualize the mayor once again turning to the audience and seeing across the footlights, not a sea of faces, but a sea of snouts. Gogol' emphasizes our involve-ment yet a third time when, a few lines later, the mayor says that all that is now needed is for some miserable liberal scribbler to turn the whole adventure into a play. The effect of this remark is to turn the piece into a kind of perpetual motion machine; every time we reach the conclusion we learn that the action we have just witnessed will, subsequently, become the subject of a play. This is of course the play we shall see or read next time we begin at Act 1, Scene 1. An appro-priate image for this self-perpetuating cycle would be the infinity of ugly faces created by the juxtaposition of two Gogolian mirrors. But the mayor goes on to prophesy how a future audience will react; they will grin and clap, which is precisely what the audience should be doing as he makes his speech, But the mayor uses a future tense, the audience *will*, i.e. at a future date; so what are we doing, and who are we? Gogol' suggests that although the episode will eventually acquire the status of a purely aesthetic reality, a fiction performed by actors for an audience, it is for the moment something else—an implication strengthened by the fact that it is directly after this that the mayor warns us we are laughing at ourselves. Perhaps we are real protagonists in a real action, as likely in our own way as any mayor to mistake Khlestakov for the Inspector General.

With *Dead Souls* Gogol' finds a form that permits him to project his sense of anguish onto a very different scale, bringing into play a hitherto virtually untapped aspect of his imagination—his sense of the epic. Where *Taras Bul'ba*, like all Romantic attempts at historical epic, remains artificial, *Dead Souls* creates a vision of contemporary reality situated with reference to the world as it should be, that is on a truly epic scale. He has sought for this quality deliberately, describing his work not as a novel but as a *poema*. This seems to have meant for him 'a smaller kind of epos', an intermediate genre between the novel and the epic proper.[1] Moreover when, in *Selected Passages*, he expresses his admiration for the *Odyssey*, he finds in it those very qualities that make for the epic feel of his own work, namely scope, spread, value as a moral emblem, an absorbing narrative, a strong ethnic flavour; it renders all the simple truth of man's adventures (*chelovecheskogo pokhozhdeniya*).[2] It is significant in this respect that the secondary title of *Dead Souls*, under which, for reasons of censorship, it was first published, was *The Adventures of Chichikov* (*Pokhozhdeniya Chichikova*). It is useful, before plunging into this depiction of grotesque landowners and officials, to think of this world and its bland hero as a nineteenth-century *Odyssey*, a portrayal of universal values whose scope reaches well beyond provincial life in Nicholas's Russia.

In one sense the book is indeed about Gogol''s Russia; he wished to 'show, albeit from one side, the whole of Russia.'[3] Yet this is not the Russia of first hand experience; it is a Russia of the mind, the product of Gogol''s sense of 'Russianness'. That this is another imaginative work based on heresay reality emerges in his account of his reading it to Pushkin. His imagination had originally created the most terrifying collection of monsters, so that he had to moderate its extravagance in later drafts. But, more important, he was surprised and delighted at

---

[1] See Proffer, *The Simile and Gogol's 'Dead Souls'*, p. 76.
[2] See *Selected Passages*, Letter 7.
[3] *Letters*, p. 52.

117

Pushkin's reaction when he was taken in and actually assumed that the book had a realistic basis.[1] It is this successful deceit that points up the role of the great mass of realistic writing, the apparent outcome of detailed observation. It is a means to an end, a device that secures from the reader a certain kind of acceptance. Much as Gogol' the observer may value the recording of facts and details for their own sake, these observations always stand in reference to something else, act as builders of verisimilitude. For the book contains some three levels of reality. There is the seemingly neutral account of life as it appears to the uncritical observer: this might be illustrated by Chichikov as he first appears—a charming, well-mannered, middle-aged bachelor travelling for doubtless respectable reasons of his own. Then there is the level of life as it really is—the more we see of Chichikov the more sinister he becomes, his superficial charm and manners no longer appear the outward signs of inner decency, they become the packaging round a vacuum. Finally there is the third level of life as it should be, which the book in its present form only touches on in the concluding fragment, that points to a largely hypothetical regenerated Chichikov. However, we know that Gogol' had planned the second part as a purgatorial phase that preceded a total regeneration in the third part, in which Chichikov was presumably destined to reach some spiritual Ithaca. Thus we have life as it appears, as it is, and as it might be. But because fiction is Gogol''s medium, the allegorical level never obtrudes; instead it looms in the background and provides a constant source of enrichment, imparting a heightened significance to the surface-structure narrative. His characters momentarily take on gigantic proportions, affording us tantalizing glimpses of a monstrous *ne to*, only to become Nozdrev or Sobakevich again. It is because Gogol' seldom stresses their moral significance in so many words that his work remains a work of fiction and does not lapse into homily. This ability to handle allegory, maintaining both its presence and its subordination to the fiction, obliging the reader to seek it through action and character, represents the summit of Gogol''s achievement as an author.[2]

[1] See *Selected Passages*, Letter 18.
[2] A technique similar to that used by Melville in *Moby Dick*. Although ostensibly a book about whaling, it is suggested that Ahab's obsessive pursuit of the white whale is somehow pregnant with an unspecified allegorical significance. We are conscious of an allegorical dimension without ever quite knowing what it is.

Gogol''s creation stands in its own right as a complete, autonomous, 'parallel world', through which we sometimes glimpse flashes of something else. Chichikov is Chichikov, but he can also be *ne to*. A curious structural model for the interplay between the two levels is provided by Gogol' himself, when, at the beginning of Chapter 6, he describes the setting of Plyushkin's house. It has the kind of excellence that can only be achieved by a blend of art and nature 'When they combine and when nature adds a final touch to the often pointless accumulations of man's labour, relieving heavy masses, destroying the crude regularity and the poverty of conception that reveal the bare bones of the plan, imparting a marvellous warmth to what was originally created cleanly and neatly, in cold cerebration.' Gogol''s superstructure of narrative, his realistic details, his love of description for its own sake, have precisely the function he here ascribes to nature, coming between us and the allegory or naked plan, and imparting an organic warmth to what might otherwise appear an abstract cipher.

But it is typical of the author's tendency to build his fictions on juxtaposed contrasts that Chichikov, the character on whom he lavishes the greatest volume of detail, and whom he is above all concerned to render vivid, should be presented precisely as an abstract cipher. Like Khlestakov, he is not quite real; he is a parody. He looks and sounds human, but lacks the essential attributes of humanity. Whatever Gogol' may have planned for his regeneration, he is, in Part One, presented in a strongly diabolic rhetoric. But Gogol''s devilry does not smell of sulphur. Chichikov, who, if not the devil himself, is remarkably close to him, has nothing extreme about him. He is neither one thing nor the other, not too fat, not too thin; his complete lack of distinctive features render him *abnormally normal*. Thus his speech usually consists of clichés. With the single exception of an internal monologue conducted in Sobakevich's house, in which one hears the unmediated voice of Gogol' himself, Chichikov never speaks his mind. Language for him is a means of deception, never of communication or self-expression. It is because Chichikov lives in a world of externals that Gogol' describes his appearance so meticulously. He is obsessed with appearance, for appearance is what he is. Thus his blend of self-love and self-respect is rendered through his contemplation of his face, and notably of his chin, in the looking-glass.

119

Staring at his reflection is his version of introspection, because his reflection is all there is. Hence also his love of the special soap that imparts a remarkable whiteness to the skin, and hence the numerous descriptions of the famous frock-coat. His spiritual life consists in a meditation on outer cleanliness. Thus even when he was obliged to keep dirty company, he always retained a love of cleanliness in his soul. But Gogol' means outer cleanliness; Chichikov's sense of purity does not extend to the inner man. For Chichikov creates the illusion of personality out of appearance and rhetoric. He has long since lost the capacity to feel, he can only mime emotion. As an arch-hypocrite and confidence man he can turn reality on its head. Thus in a fragment of Part Two we see him telling a certain Lenitsyn that the transaction he proposes only looks crooked, but in fact is legal. Of course the reverse is true, but then Chichikov makes the incredible credible. The episode brings out another aspect of his trickery; it takes two to play. Chichikov's victims want to be victims; they all have their reasons for parting with their dead souls. There is a reciprocal action between the confidence man and his 'mark'. Neither can function without the other.

Chichikov's driving force is the quest for self-fulfilment. He is endowed with tremendous qualities: intelligence, patience, a capacity for ruthless self-denial in the interests of his ultimate goal. But these essentially moral qualities are directed towards a materialistic fulfil-ment, because, in Part One at least, Chichikov is cast in the image of the world as it is. The embodiment of the spirit of nineteenth century bourgeois capitalism, his ambition can be summed up in a word: acquisition. At the end of Chapter 7, as he registers his purchases, he gives a little speech on the virtues of acquisition, for this is the canon by which he lives. This principle, his most important attribute, is respected by a metonymy, the only metonymy of importance in the book—Chichikov's casket, his *shkatulka;* with its precise form, its careful divisions, its role as a container of strange and often useless objects, and its secret drawer for money that opens and shuts with the speed of light, this Victorian version of a brief-case is indeed a sinister image for the material substance of Chichikov himself.

Chichikov does not seek to acquire out of greed. His motives are more mysterious. He seeks through acquisition to impart a measure of authenticity to his life; it is a quest for substantiation. His concern with his heirs is of the same order. He must get rich in order to earn their approval; he must have heirs to prove that he was real, not just an ephemeral 'bubble on the water'. He is obsessed by the need to prove his existence to himself. He seeks to do so by acquisition, but it is a characteristically Gogolian paradox that he should devote his life to acquiring something that does not exist. His purchases exist on paper only, they are linguistic signs, not people. Thus it is when Chichikov meditates upon his acquisitions that Gogol' finds a strange blend of heroic and comic writing that is at one time on an epic and grotesque scale. In Chapter 7, Chichikov daydreams about them as if they were real; this is followed at the beginning of the next chapter by a passage in which the whole town discusses how Chichikov should handle his new peasants. Such passages focus the central theme of the work, Chichikov, in a superb lyric passage, almost brings them to life as he copies their names, then the town treats the names as if they were indeed alive. The real becomes unreal, the unreal takes on the appearance of reality, on a truly epic scale.

Gogol' is concerned that Chichikov and the nature of his quest remain an enigma for his readers for as long as possible. As we work our way into the book the question of his identity becomes increasingly pressing, till it is brought to a head by the desperate questions the officials ask each other, and their realization that *they do not know who Chichikov is.* Gogol' again uses the technique of contrasting levels of reality when he resolves the question of his hero's identity in two different ways. The postmaster explains that he is a one-legged bandit, Captain Kopeykin, and this, the fantastic side of the picture, is completed by the suggestion that he is Antichrist and Napoleon.[1] The realistic side is supplied by the narrator's account of Chichikov's past life. It is important to realize that both explanations enjoy equal status. To reject the first as unreasonable and to favour the second because it 'makes sense' is, in Gogol's' terms, to fail to penetrate appearances; in short, the kind of attitude that led the officials to take Chichikov at face value, when he was really, as the postmaster finally agreed, 'the devil knows what'.

[1] Chichikov is again associated with Antichrist in a fragment at the end of Part Two; a heresy springs up among some peasants which announces the birth of Antichrist 'who gives the dead no rest, and purchases dead souls'. Chichikov becomes a master of voodoo, turning his purchases into zombies, the 'undead'.

Thus Chichikov appears to be a nondescript middle-aged swindler whose good manners and sense of dignity do not prevent him from giving a little jump for joy, in private, at moments of great excitement. We have a strong sense of his visual presence joined with the suggestion of an ineffable something else—the undermining force of *ne to*. The landowners are similarly treated. They are described with a painstaking attention to the details of their appearance and circumstances. The interplay between personality and environment is impeccably done. Much use is also made of speech characterization: not only their speech but Chichikov's, since he varies his mode of address according to his company, is most revealing, notably when they reply to his strange request. Manilov employs a superb range of saccharine-coated euphemisms, Sobakevich, brutally direct, is as ready to deal in the dead as in any other staple, whereas Korobochka, with her peasant's speech, is terrified that she will sell them too cheaply. The dead souls act as a catalyst that reveals their owners' true nature.

Gogol' describes Chichikov's visits with great care, and will suddenly focus on the smallest detail: the cutlery he uses in the inn (Chapter 6), the fact that Sobakevich's wife had hands smelling of cucumber. As usual this kind of writing creates a state of false security, encouraging us to accept what we read as being in some sense more 'real' than was, say, *The Nose*. But as usual realism is undermined. Just as we come to recognize that there is something too normal about Chichikov, so the characters he meets come to acquire a grotesque quality. Despite their naturalistic surroundings, they are essentially unnatural. Manilov is too sweet, Nozdrev too unbalanced and over-resplendent with good health; Sobakevich is a crude rough copy of humanity and with Plyushkin we have reached the lowest circle of hell.[1] The key to the emblematic nature of these characters is contained in Gogol''s account of Plyushkin's degeneration. It concludes with the warning never to let one's human qualities slip, for they can never be recovered. In one way or another these characters are all studies in dehumanization, loss of reality. This emerges in Gogol''s use of language. It is the way in which he describes them that makes them border on the grotesque. Not only does he exaggerate Manilov's mincing sentimentality, amplifying it until it becomes abnormally

[1] A point emphasized by the importance of the image of the cellar in the description of Plyushkin's house. See Proffer, op. cit., p. 111.

prominent, not only does he ensure that we realize that Sobakevich is rough-hewn to the point of being inhuman, he employs his surrealistic strain to undermine the apparent reality of his descriptions. We find all the familiar booby-traps that discourage us from accepting anything at face value. Thus his use of irrelevance is brought to a climax by the regrettably brief but glorious appearance of the boot-loving lieutenant from Ryazan'. Gogol' also hints at the existence of a secondary causal system; Chichikov is first described as having a serious air and blowing his nose very loudly; Manilov's reaction to Chichikov's request is to puff out smoke in a *very* thin stream. Moreover Gogol' imparts an alarming degree of consciousness to inanimate objects; the clock in Korobochka's house 'decides it wants to strike', Sobakevich's furniture cries out its ressemblance to its master. People on the other hand are described in terms of insects or inanimate objects, the rhetoric emphasizing the allegorical theme of loss of humanity. A face may be described as a samovar, a melon or a cucumber. Another of his undermining devices emerges when the melon-like face is developed into the kind of melon from which balalaikas are made in Moldavia and which are played ... etc. Perhaps the most famous instance of such digression occurs in Chapter 1. The guests at the governor's ball are described as flies; a comparison developed to extraordinary length, it loses its status as a simile and becomes an anecdote in its own right. The digression is an aesthetic device that stresses the pointlessness of Gogol''s world, making us see it through an insect rhetoric. This idiosyncratic use of imagery lends his narrative an unnerving touch of the grotesque.

The note of allegory and universality occasionally struck in his treatment of the characters also emerges in Gogol''s sparing use of generalization. His reference to Plyushkin's loss of humanity was a case in point. Similarly he suggests that there is more to Korobochka than sheer peasantry, and that a smart St Petersburg hostess might be closer to her than we would suspect. Nozdrev is described as being ever with us, if in different clothes. Again Gogol' stresses the difference between 'is' and 'appears', adding that for many people different clothes mean a different person. Gogol' addresses us directly on other occasions. Gaiety turns to sadness if one contemplates it too long, happiness gallops through our lives leaving us gazing wistfully after it. These generalizations have a consistency of tone. Although widely dispersed they serve to impart to the often sublimely comic action a persistent note of underlying melancholy. They also serve to remind us that there is another level that subtends the narrative.

Of course the greatest source of multiple meaning and ambiguity are the dead souls themselves. These are both the deceased and those that traffic in them. Indeed the latter often appear more lifeless than the former. When Chichikov conjures up the lives of the peasants whose names he has bought, they acquire all the colour and vigour that their vendors lack in 'real' life. Chichikov raises the dead, they come mysteriously alive through language. The dead souls constitute a source of paradox for Chichikov who makes death his livelihood. On the threshold between being and not being, they are for Gogol' the epitomy of *ne to, ne se* [neither one thing nor the other]. They are 'not exactly peasants', Chichikov tells Manilov. To Sobakevich he describes them not as dead but as 'not existing'. He rightly tells Korobochka that they are 'an affair not of this world'. It is the summit of Gogol''s indictment that Chichikov is so alienated from normative reality that he treats as real something which by definition cannot exist. This emerges in the hair-raising bargaining between Chichikov and Sobakevich, for whom 'a human soul is no more than a boiled turnip'. Chichikov is obliged to go against the very bent of his imagination, constantly reminding Sobakevich that the souls don't exist, that they consist of nothing but words, that they are useless, a dream. He finds no answer to Sobakevich's rejoinder that since he is buying them they must have a use; for they are indeed real to him—even though he is later shown, when meditating on his purchases, to be somewhat disturbed by the thought that these 'were not completely real'. The question of their status is finally resumed in one of the epic highlights of Russian literature, as Korobochka rolls into the town of N at dawn, in a conveyance filled with food and feather beds, in order to ascertain the price fetched by dead souls on the open market. In short the souls are perhaps the most important image that Gogol' ever created. They act as a focus for the subtle confusion of real and unreal that occurs on every level, from the level of language—are they a metaphor?—to the level of metaphysics—what is a soul? For the book persistently questions the nature of reality, particularly the reality of language. The words 'dead souls' have been seen to raise the question of which linguistic rank they exist on. When is a metaphor not a metaphor? A similar question is posed by the digressions. There is a moment when Nozdrev, in an aggressive mood, is compared to a fool-hardy young officer leading a reckless forlorn hope against an unassailable redoubt. The description is longer and more detailed than is justified by its status as a simile for Nozdrev's behaviour. It is a fragment of digressionary reality every bit as vivid and self-support-ing as the account of the main action. How does it relate to this? The problem raises the question of whether one piece of writing can be deemed to be more or indeed less real than another, the question of what is the status of a metaphor. This in turn questions the status of fiction itself. The same question is posed by another device that recurs throughout the book: the device of using the same word in two different ways in successive sentences. Thus in the passage just alluded to Gogol' describes the redoubt as a real object in its own right, only to go on to say that this particular redoubt was by no means impregnable, that in fact the redoubt was shaking in its shoes, thereby reducing the word to a simile for Chichikov. Time and again he employs a similar technique. As with his digressions, such writing makes us question the reality of what we read, ask ourselves what is relevance, what is reality, and finally what are we reading? In this, seemingly the most realistic of Gogol''s works, there is a constant invitation to lose grip on reality altogether.

There is to be found in *Dead Souls* an attention to positive values that distinguishes the book from his earlier writing. We know that he intended to provide a positive conclusion, which, for reasons which will emerge, he found unwritable. But there is also a positive strain in Part One: the strain of Russianness. Gogol' displays throughout a love of generalization about the Russian peasant, the Russian language, and it is when he deals with the theme of his country rushing headlong into the future drawn by some mystic troika, that he achieves a measure of lyricism that is only to be equalled by the finest poetry of Aleksandr Blok. But more important than this direct intrusion of his sense of normative reality in the shape of his country's destiny is the echo of this theme in the language. He has captured as never before the specificity of the Russian language, particularly its popular idiom—for example in the section in which Dyadya Mityay and Dyadya Minyay try to move the horses (Chapter 5). If there is a positive hero in this book, then it is the Russian language as it is used in passages such as this, with its use of fat untranslatable verb forms such as *prishpandor'*. It is in this kind of writing, in Gogol''s capacity for inventing surrealistically expressive names such as Stepan Probka (Steven Cork), or in his exaltation of the 'lively Russian word' that the richness and poetry of his vision are realized. It is the kind of mood that Pushkin evokes in lines such as:

Что-то слышится родное
В скучных песнях ямщика...

Something close to the heart can be heard | In the long-drawn-out songs of the coachman . . .

Gogol' finds his love of his country through his love of the extraordinarily strong flavour of its language. When one thinks back on this aspect of the book it is perhaps above all Selifan's words to his horses that focus it (Chatper 3). Although ostensibly a realistic account of coachman's talk, the piece becomes a kind of linguistic daydream which renders once and for all its particular blend of vivid expression and absurd peasant poetry in its concluding lines, as Selifan, calling to his horses, strings adjective on adjective and seems to cover the whole expanse of the Russian language itself, until, with what is perhaps the finest of all Gogol''s surreal dying falls: 'He finally reached the point when he started to call them secretaries.'

If laughter was the positive hero of *The Inspector General*, then language as it is used here is the positive hero of *Dead Souls*. It is through language, the only thing that Gogol' felt he could be sure of, that he reached for the normative reality that he was otherwise unable to attain.

This leads us to the final episode, the culmination of Gogol''s life in spiritual bankruptcy and what amounts to suicide. It is of the greatest significance that these events are closely linked with his burning of the manuscript of the second part of *Dead Souls*: twelve years work. Although the desire to destroy his work was a recurrent obsession,[1] it comes to a head with what must have been his sense of failure at his attempt to treat directly of positive values in the second part of the intended trilogy. He had already experienced such failure

---

[1] As early as 1837 he longs for a moth that would eat up all the copies of his published works, which he describes as nonsense. *Letters*, p. 67.

126

twice before; both in literature and in life his quest for the spiritual had disappointed him. His famous or infamous last published work *Selected Passages from Correspondence with Friends* (*Izbrannye mesta iz perepiski s druz'yami*) (1847) was a direct attempt to produce a blueprint for normative reality without the mediation of fiction. Its basis is not uninteresting: it constitutes an ideological system which, like his love of language, is founded on the concept of essential Russianness. He requires his art to 'establish a spiritual harmony that realizes the heroic national qualities of his people'.[1] Yet the expression he gives to that harmony combines a terrible Khlestakovian parody of moral value, filled with extraordinary lightness, with a vision of normative reality indistinguishable from that produced some four centuries earlier by Sil'vestr in his *Domostroy*. The result is contrived and arid. When Gogol' moralizes directly he loses all sense of the comic, the lyric, the realistic and the epic—the four elements that make up the flavour of his best writing. But there is a deeper reason for his failure, one illustrated by his second disaster. In 1848 he makes a trip to the Holy Land in search of spiritual comfort. But when visiting the Holy Places his direct confrontation with the spiritual leaves him dry and unmoved. Perhaps it is no coincidence that this is precisely how his work leaves the reader whenever Gogol' attempts to provide a direct and unqualified portrayal of positive values. Herein lies the crux of his tragedy. Throughout his life he sought to realize those values, but the nearer he comes to the normative reality whose absence from the world at large appalled him, the more like Khlestakov he becomes; whereas the more he describes the negative, diabolic aspects of his vision, the more his writing comes to life. There is a contrast, a perpetual tension between his need for the good, the true and the beautiful that he constantly tries to realize in his work, and a certain aesthetic fascination with their opposites. The more he seeks to describe positive values directly, the deader his work becomes: it is only when he writes of the *ne to* of dead souls that it comes alive. The nature of his predicament now emerges. We have seen that the one consistent element of reality in his work has been the reality of language itself, his acceptance that to whatever extent the reality of the world he moved in was undermined, he had, like Akaky, the reality of his written word in which to place his trust. Could it be that

[1] Ibid., p. 192.

GOGOL'

what drove him, in 1852, to destroy the work of twelve years, and allow himself to die some weeks later in the most appalling and undignified circumstances, was the tragic realization that he could only write about evil, that the theme of *ne to* was the very basis of his creative drive and had undermined the reality of language itself, so that he, as the creator of that language, was the deadest soul of all?

SELECT BIBLIOGRAPHY

Annensky, I., 'Estetika *Mertvykh dush* i ee nasled'e', *Apollon*, 1911, No. 8, pp. 51–8.
Bazhenov, N., *Bolezn' i smert' Gogolya*, Moscow, 1902.
Belinskiy o Gogole, ed. S. Mashinsky, Moscow, 1949.
Bely, A., 'Gogol'', *Vesy*, 1909, No. 4, pp. 10–83.
　　Masterstvo Gogolya, Moscow-Leningrad, 1934.
Bowman, H., 'The Nose', *Slavonic and East European Review*, Vol. 31, 1952, No. 76, pp. 204–11.
Bryusov, V., 'Ispepelennyy', *Vesy*, 1909, No. 4, pp. 98–120.
Čiževskij, D., 'Zur Komposition von Gogol''s *Mantel'*, *Zeitschrift für Slavische Philologie*, Vol. 14, 1937, pp. 63–94.
　　'Neizvestnyy Gogol'', *Novyy zhurnal*, Vol. 27, 1951, pp. 126–58.
Driessen, F., *Gogol as a Short-story Writer*, The Hague, 1965.
Eykhenbaum, B., 'Gogol' i delo literatury', *Moy vremennik*, Leningrad, 1929, pp. 89 sq.
　　'Illyuziya skaza', *Skvoz' literaturu*, Leningrad, 1924, pp. 152–6.
　　'Kak sdelana *Shinel'* Gogolya', *Poetika. Sborniki po teorii poeticheskogo yazyka*, Petrograd, 1919, pp. 151–65; and *Skvoz' literaturu*, Leningrad, 1924, pp. 171–95.
　　'The Structure of Gogol's *Overcoat'*, *Russian Review*, Vol. 22, 1963, No. 4, pp. 377–99.
Erlich, V., 'Gogol' and Kafka: Note on 'Realism' and 'Surrealism', *For Roman Jakobson*, ed. M. Halle, The Hague, 1956, pp. 100–8.
Ermakov, I., *Ocherki po analizu tvorchestva N. V. Gogolya*, Moscow-Petrograd, 1924.
Ermilov, V., *Geniy Gogolya*, Moscow, 1959.
Evdokimov, P., *Gogol et Dostoievsky ou la descente aux enfers*, Bruges, 1961.
Friedman, P., 'The Nose', *The American Imago*, 1951, No. 7, pp. 337–50.
Gippius, V., *Gogol'*, Leningrad, 1924.
Gourfinkel, N., *Nicholas Gogol dramaturge*, Paris, 1956.
Gukovsky, G., *Realizm Gogolya*, Moscow-Leningrad, 1959.
Khrapchenko, M., *Tvorchestvo Gogolya*, Moscow, 1956.
Letters of Nikolai Gogol, ed. C. Proffer, Ann Arbor, 1967.
Magarshack, D., *Gogol*, London, 1957.

GOGOL'

Mandel'shtam, I., *O kharaktere gogolevskogo stilya*, Helsingfors, 1902.

Mashinsky, S., *Gogol'*, Moscow, 1951.

   Khudozhestvennyy mir Gogolya, Moscow, 1971.

Merezhkovsky, D., *Gogol' i chort*, Moscow, 1906.

Nabokov, V., *Nikolai Gogol*, New York, 1961.

Ovsyaniko-Kulikovsky, D., *Gogol'*, Moscow, 1902.

Poggioli, R., 'Gogol's *Old-fashioned Landowners:* an Inverted Eclogue', *Indiana Slavic Studies*, Vol. 3, 1963, pp. 54–72.

Proffer, C., *The Simile and Gogol's 'Dead Souls'*, The Hague, 1967.

Rozanov, V., 'Neskol'ko slov o Gogole', *Legenda o velikom inkvizitore Dostoevskogo*, 2nd ed., SPb, 1902.

Seeman, K., 'Eine Heiligenlegende als Vorbild von Gogol's *Mantel'*, *Zeitschrift für Slavische Philologie*, Vol. 33, 1967, pp. 7–21.

Setchkarev, V., *Gogol: His Life and Works*, New York, 1965.

Shklovsky, V., *O teorii prozy*, Moscow, 1929.

Slonimsky, A., *Tekhnika komicheskogo u Gogolya*, Petrograd, 1923.

Spycher, P., 'N. V. Gogol's *The Nose*: A Satirical Comic Fantasy Born of an Impotence Complex' *Slavic and East European Journal*, Vol. 7, 1963, No. 4, pp. 361–74.

Stilman, L., 'Gogol's *Overcoat*: Thematic Pattern and Origins', *American Slavic and East European Review*, Vol. 11, 1952, No. 2, pp. 138–48.

Strong, R., 'The Soviet Interpretation of Gogol', *American Slavic and East European Review*, Vol. 14, 1955, No. 4, pp. 528–39.

Ul'yanov, N., 'Arabesk ili apokalipsis', *Novyy zhurnal*, Vol. 57, 1959 pp. 116–31.

Vinogradov, V., *Etyudy o stile Gogolya*, Leningrad, 1926.

Weber, J.-P., *Thématiques*, Paris, 1966.

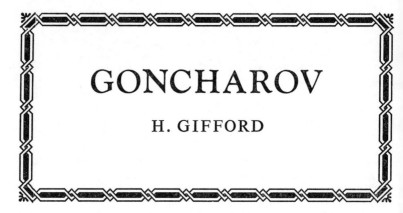

GONCHAROV

H. GIFFORD

OUTSIDE RUSSIA IVAN ALEKSANDROVICH GONCHAROV (1812–91) is known as the author of one classic novel published in 1859, *Oblomov*. In Russia too his reputation depends principally on this work; but he always insisted that it formed part of a trilogy, with *A Common Story* (*Obyknovennaya istoriya*) (1847), and the long-delayed successor to *Oblomov*, *The Precipice* (*Obryv*) (1869). Three periods of Russian life were meant to find their reflection in these novels 'as in a drop of water'.[1] It is certainly true that the images for *The Precipice* were taking shape while he was still at the beginning of *Oblomov*,[2] and the same patient, even tranquil imagination shows in all three works. Goncharov, once having found his manner, developed into the mature novelist of *Oblomov*. Thereafter he was, like Krylov in an earlier day, one of the rare static figures on the Russian literary scene.

He began to write prose fiction at a propitious time, when Turgenev and Dostoevsky were also publishing their first work, and when the influential critic Belinsky was on the look-out for new talent.[3] Goncharov took his place in what Belinsky defined as the 'natural school' (*natural'naya shkola*), proclaiming its members as the successors to Gogol'. But from the beginning Goncharov stood somewhat apart. Belinsky compared *A Common Story* with Herzen's novel *Who is to Blame?* (*Kto vinovat?*)—both had made their

---

[1] *Sobr. soch.*, vol. 8, p. 69. Note that all quotations are from the 1952–5 edition.
[2] Ibid., p. 79.
[3] See below 'Turgenev', pp. 143 sq.

appearance in the journal where Belinsky now published his criticism, *The Contemporary (Sovremennik)*. Herzen was for Belinsky the thinker, the publicist; Goncharov 'a poet, an artist—and nothing more', unique among his contemporaries in approaching 'the ideal of pure art', and without love or hatred for his characters.[1] Goncharov was not so dispassionate as Belinsky thought; but otherwise the observation is just. Goncharov did not work primarily with ideas like Herzen. He liked to repeat Belinsky's formula: 'the artist thinks through images'.[2] The way of his imagination was first to discern a living character, and then to devise scenes in which this character interacted with others. The connection between the scenes, the full significance of the figure he had first glimpsed, would slowly dawn upon him.[3] Goncharov searched for the typical and the permanent. He created a world of solid realities: it was his talent, as another critic, Dobrolyubov, later explained, 'to halt the fleeting phenomenon of life, in all its fulness and freshness, and to hold it before him until it becomes the entire possession of the artist'.[4]

1

A Common Story is overshadowed for the reader today by *Oblomov* and by the achievements of Russian prose fiction in the next three or four decades. Apart from its technical interest,[5] it has some distinct merits. The insight into character—and not least female character as Belinsky noted—is remarkably sure; the familiarity with life below stairs, as in the account of the relations between Evsey and Agrafena (I, i), seems unforced and its tone uncondescending; descriptions of places are evocative and exact. (Take for instance the scene in a country church at vespers (II, vi) where a dozen details show Goncharov's close observation—the light catching ikon frames and the 'dark and severe faces of the saints'; the breeze ruffling the priest's grey hair, fluttering his book, extinguishing his candle; the echoing steps and dismal voices of priest and reader; and overhead

[1] Belinsky, *PSS*, vol. 10, pp. 326–7.
[2] e.g. *Sobr. soch.*, vol. 8, pp. 69, 211.
[3] Ibid., pp. 70–1.
[4] Dobrolyubov, *SS*, vol. 4, p. 310.
[5] On which see *Istoriya russkogo romana*, vol. 1, p. 521.

in the cupola the noise and movement of jackdaws and sparrows.) Goncharov has the fullest possession of his subject. The book, though less saturated than its two successors, is like them concerned with the typical—the historical truth of a given moment and place.

The story contrasts a naive, somewhat old fashioned dilettante with his worldly and successful uncle. The younger Aduev derives, as Belinsky saw, from the poet Lensky in *Evgeny Onegin*; he is 'a triple romantic, by nature, by education, and by the circumstances of his life'.[1] His uncle represents a wholly new type: the high bureaucrat who is also a factory owner. Three love affairs disillusion the youth under his uncle's merciless eye. Finally he returns with a somewhat stale Byronic world-weariness to his mother in the country. The Epilogue makes a too neat reversal when, four years later, Aduev has become the replica of his uncle, while the latter, whose mordant self-sufficiency has brought his wife to a breakdown, suddenly retires. Belinsky thought the nephew would more predictably have 'vegetated in remote rural apathy and idleness'.[2] There are indeed hints of Oblomov and his servant Zakhar in the scene where Aduev tells the muttering Evsey not to interrupt his reveries which he refers to as 'work' (I, v); on another occasion we learn from Evsey that his master, Oblomov-fashion, is lying on a divan: 'At first I thought the gentleman was sleeping, but his eyes were open; it pleased him to watch the ceiling' (II, iv).

Goncharov's realism is directed somewhat like Flaubert's against a romanticism from which he had not been immune himself—the verses of the younger Aduev were based on Goncharov's own early efforts.[3] It comes out very clearly when he describes the country estate to which Aduev has retreated (II, vi). The young man is dwelling fondly on recollections of childhood. His mother encourages him to thoughts of natural piety when she tells how his father planted the limetrees just before he was born. Then she recalls how Agashka the nurse once hurt the little boy, and his father flogged her and could hardly be made to desist. Goncharov's novel shows a critical and balanced intelligence—one that really *thinks* through images.

---

[1] Belinsky, op. cit., p. 332.
[2] Op. cit., p. 343.
[3] The poems '*Otkol' poroy toska i gore* . . .' (I, ii) and '*Vesny pora prekrasnaya minula* . . .' (II, ii) had been his (*Istoriya russkogo romana*, Vol. 1, p. 529, n. 28).

He needed time for his personal experience to sink unconsciously into the mind until its image was lodged there 'as in a mirror is reflected the landscape outside the window, or sometimes in a small pond is reflected the vastness around (*gromadnaya obstanovka*)...'[1] Thus *Oblomov* required a whole decade in which to mature. While nursing it Goncharov made his celebrated—and uncharacteristic— voyage to Japan (1852–3) on the *Pallas*, as secretary to the admiral commanding a Russian expedition. His account *The Frigate Pallas* (*Fregat Pallada*) (1858) bears comparison with Darwin's work of twenty years earlier, *A Naturalist's Voyage Round the World in H.M.S. 'Beagle'* (1839). Goncharov was no scientist, but he too wrote up his observations with a meticulous care, and pondered everything he had seen. There is a mass of carefully recorded evidence in this book, which furnishes an excellent report on Cape Colony, Singapore, Hong Kong and Japan, at the beginnings of imperialist expansion. Goncharov had worked in the Department of Overseas Trade; he felt sympathy with the business and scientific interests of Aduev's uncle; and often, seeing the ubiquitous British merchant, writes in this book about the need to carry trade and civilization into the East. Mediaeval Nagasaki appears to him in a vision as another Hong Kong.

These thoughts may be surprising from the creator of Oblomov. The speculative colonialist and the sedentary dreamer take their turns in writing *The Frigate Pallas*. Goncharov more characteristically perhaps has recorded the images of lethargy—the grand peace of a tropical sunset, Manilla harbour with boats 'crawling over the huge bay ... like summer flies', the dead calm at sea which reminds him of noontide heat in a steppe village.

Such ambivalence, a hovering between reverie and the exhortation to work, constitutes the richness of *Oblomov*. Goncharov's deepest inclinations were towards what Wordsworth once called 'majestic indolence'; to offset this, he was driven to invent the exemplary Stolz (Shtol'ts), a German and a Victorian, who would speak for the practical virtues. On principle Goncharov was ready to cast down the old order, which as a disciple of Belinsky he knew to be wasteful

[1] *Sobr. soch.*, vol. 8, p. 72.

and despotic. Meanwhile the 'unprincipled heart'[1] still yearned for Oblomovka and the vision of an eternal innocence. The first part of *Oblomov* to be published—its 'overture'[2]—was the chapter relating the hero's dream (I, ix). He returns to the world of his childhood, a world inhabited by grotesques who belong there with the summer flies, the heavy furniture and the heavy food. We are taken through a *skazka* or fairy tale as irresistible as any told by the boy's nurse. The whole land lies under a spell; the weather, the regimen, the rituals and delights of Oblomovka are settled for always. A dull and procrastinating tribe surfeit and will never grow up. Thus Il'ya Il'ich acquires his fatal character which allows him the dignity of self-acceptance. The ideal order for him is Oblomovka regained, and when he speaks about it Stolz calls him a poet (II, iv). (Somewhat mischievously, Oblomov in answer is made to appropriate a maxim of Belinsky, that life is poetry.) He has an immutable purity of heart: even at the last stage of his downfall, this saves him from condemnation.

The novel contrives to honour this poetry of Oblomov while exposing its negativeness. Mrs Gould in Conrad's *Nostromo* reflects that the idea is degraded by 'the necessities of successful action'.[3] With Oblomov it stays immaculate, since he never takes the field. In the opening part his unworldliness is a rebuke to the vain and acquisitive. Goncharov knew very well the lures of inertia; but *Oblomov* is not an escapist novel. The author's veracity—his regard for the circumstantial—makes the story of Il'ya Il'ich a complete human experience: not merely the archetypal dream of a divine passivity, but the record of something lived and suffered, a *zhitie* or chronicle of perfection.

The social interpretation set out by Dobrolyubov in 'What is Oblomovism'? (*Chto takoe oblomovshchina?*[4]) does not tell the complete truth about this novel—though it greatly pleased Goncharov.[5] Dobrolyubov's essay revealed brilliantly how a new work of art, as T. S. Eliot has said, alters the 'relations, proportions, values' of the works that preceded it.[6] He traced a continuity between Oblomov

---

[1] *Doctor Zhivago*, tr. M. Hayward and M. Harari, 1958, p. 226.
[2] *Sobr. soch.*, vol. 8, p. 76.   [3] *Nostromo*, III, xi.
[4] *Sovremennik*, 5, 1859., *SS*, vol. 4, pp. 307 sq.   [5] *Sobr. soch.*, vol. 8, p. 323.
[6] Eliot, *Selected Essays*, 1951, p. 15.

and the 'superfluous men' before him, from Onegin downwards. With the appearance of Il'ya Il'ich, all the intelligent and frustrated young men described by Pushkin, Lermontov, Herzen and Turgenev took on a new aspect. These 'heroes of their time' were unmasked as Oblomovs. To the impatient activists of Alexander II's Russia Dobrolyubov disclosed in *Oblomov* a political meaning which Goncharov did not reject. At the outset his novel had made it plain that the institution of serfdom must be held responsible for Il'ya Il'ich. Without those revenues from beyond the Volga, and without the grumbling but absolute devotion of Zakhar, such perfect idleness could not have existed. A strain of social criticism, though not prominent, lies in the novel, and Goncharov felt no violence had been done by Dobrolyubov in stressing this. Oblomov was an appropriate symbol for the landowning class in decline, when serfdom had patently become inefficient as well as unjust.

This view of *Oblomov* cannot, however, account for its hold on the imagination of readers who know little about the historical setting. *Oblomov* originates from some deeper level of the mind than is suggested by Dobrolyubov. Unmistakably a novelist's work in its care for specific detail and its fidelity to social fact, it yet has the character of a mythic creation, not unlike *Dead Souls*. Zakhar can be recognized as a study after Gogol'; and some traits of Oblomov—his capacity for the grandiose dream and his notions of domestic bliss or ideal friendship—show him akin to Manilov, though he is far more reticent. Sometimes an image or tone in Goncharov's novel will seem the purest Gogol'. There are effects reminiscent of Gogol' on the first page, where Oblomov's thought wanders 'like a bird at large over his face', and insouciance passes into 'the very folds of his dressing gown'. Gogol''s humour can be recognized in the pathetic outburst to Zakhar: 'Perhaps you think when sometimes you see me with my head right under the blanket that I'm sleeping like a log. No, I'm not sleeping but I'm thinking with all my might so the peasants may want for nothing . . .' (I, viii). In temperament and attitudes Goncharov and Gogol' are vastly different (though Goncharov has more satire than one might suppose). But like Shakespeare and Molière and Gogol', all questions of stature apart, Goncharov can take up in Oblomov an extravagant idea—as they do the metaphysical entity that is Falstaff, Tartuffe, Chichikov—and impart to it wholly credible laws of being. Oblomov embodies a principle that is almost unimpeded by contingency. The suffocation of the man enables an absolute to triumph: as he declares, in lines thought afterwards by Goncharov too explicit,[1] his life was lived 'in order to express the possibility of an ideally tranquil side to human existence' (IV, ix).

Oblomov, unlike the complex novels of Tolstoy and Dostoevsky in the next decades, follows a single line of development: with Il'ya Il'ich it begins and ends. After he has died Stolz and the author are left to consider *oblomovshchina*, the immortal part of Oblomov. The circle is complete as Stolz prepares to narrate the story we have just read. Goncharov's design is extremely simple. In a few hectic weeks at Marienbad he bound together long-meditated images and scenes, using a frame of four sections. Just as the opening paragraphs set out to describe and place Oblomov, so these four sections reveal him in depth. It is done through the unfolding of three main relationships— with his friend and self-appointed director Stolz; with Ol'ga who tries to reform him through love; and with Pshenitsyna who mothers him on his relapse into an untroubled infancy. A fourth relationship with his servant Zakhar remains static. Both take it for granted; and once Oblomov is dead Zakhar has no place in the world. The first section is introductory: Oblomov receives visitors from a society that has become almost meaningless to him. One, Tarant'ev, plots his undoing, in a worldly sense—that final retreat to the Vyborg side. The last visitor is Stolz with the hope of regeneration. The second and third sections form the central episode—Oblomov's romance with Ol'ga. 'Romance' it is, collapsing before the obligations of marriage. For a brief while it has taken Oblomov out of himself, and brought some genuine moments of shock and self-discovery. But he cannot give up the poetry of a love without responsibilities (III, ii): Ol'ga has to abandon him. (The pattern of the inadequate hero and the disappointed heroine who deserves so much more is familiar in Russian fiction from *Evgeny Onegin* onwards.) With scarcely a reproach to Oblomov, Ol'ga turns in the end to the good but limited Stolz, and Il'ya Il'ich bows to his destiny, in the form of Pshenitsyna who kills by kindness. He has found the substitute for Oblomovka, a means to escape from time.

The theme of inevitability is further enforced by recurrent symbolism: the lilac that must fade, the midsummer heat turning to August rains

[1] *Sobr. soch.*, vol. 8, p. 78–9.

and finally, as their love ends, to obliterating snow; the landlady's twinkling elbows which fascinate Oblomov, the dressing gown Zakhar has kept by for his relapse. Ol'ga and Stolz had tried vainly to separate Oblomov from his true self. With something between irony and admiration the author conducts Oblomov to his final repose. Stolz's tribute to his innocence and incorruptibility is sincere (IV, ix). Such weakness in the flesh comes paradoxically to represent almost a spiritual triumph.

After Oblomov himself the most fully realized character in the novel is Ol'ga. Goncharov insisted that all the achievements of Russian literature began with Pushkin, whom he saw as his master (to a very much greater extent than Gogol' was).[1] The two opposed feminine types in *Evgeny Onegin*—Tat'yana and her sister—seemed to comprise all womanhood, and other portraits would be modifications of these. And just as Pushkin's young women were true to their time, so Naden'ka of *A Common Story* and Ol'ga (really the same character at different moments) answered each to hers.[2] Ol'ga is made vividly present: Goncharov has studied the smallest irregularity of her features. Dobrolyubov saw in her, far more than in Stolz, a hope for new life in Russia. Stolz indeed on Goncharov's own admission[3] is too much a cardboard figure, like Tushin who exemplifies the same qualities in *The Precipice*.

Oblomov may be called a great comic novel, though rather in the sense that *The Cherry Orchard* is a great comedy. It is poetic like Chekhov's play, amused and ironical; and it too catches a period in Russian life and creates a symbol. Goncharov was never again to achieve a work so perfect and individual. It takes its place among the dozen or so novels which make Russian literature the most important of nineteenth-century Europe. Its movement to the inexorable close is singularly fine—one might think of it as a tone poem, almost a communion of Goncharov's brooding mind with itself, but alive in its detail, having all the particularity and prosaic subsoil we demand from a novel. Ultimately *Oblomov* becomes a myth, in the manner of *Don Quixote* or *The Pickwick Papers*, and its hero, as theirs do, lives on independently to represent one of the potentialities in human nature.

[1] *Sobr. soch.*, vol. 8, p. 77.
[2] Ibid., pp. 77–8.
[3] Ibid., p. 8.

3

The third novel in Goncharov's trilogy, *The Precipice (Obryv)*,[1] is nearly as long as the other two combined. He once compared it with 'a clumsy omnibus heavily lurching along a bumpy causeway'.[2] Twenty years of gestation, the last three spent in feverish activity, produced a very uneven work which had in certain respects turned back on its own course. By 1869—in the period following the Emancipation—the tone of literary criticism had become more embattled; old alliances were breaking up; liberals like Turgenev and Goncharov found themselves on the defensive against the radical thought of a new generation and class—the *raznochintsy* or plebeians who followed Chernyshevsky. At the outset Goncharov had intended to make the dilettante Raysky, an 'awakened Oblomov', the hero of a novel to be called *The Artist*. The first section of *The Precipice*, in St Petersburg where Raysky plays Chatsky to his cousin Belovodova, seems to promise that he will dominate the story, but no sooner has he returned to the Volga estate administered for him by his 'grand-mother' (strictly great aunt) than the interest changes. Raysky remains an indispensable link, and Goncharov uses him, as an aspiring novelist and painter, to make us aware of the artist's eye and of his problems.[3] Meanwhile what most engages Goncharov is the struggle for Vera's soul between the 'grandmother', Tat'yana Markovna (aided by Tushin who represents the 'true party of action'[4]) and Mark Volokhov the nihilist. In the end Tushin speaks up for 'grandmother's morality' and denounces Volokhov who disappears from the scene (V, xvi–xvii).

Both Tat'yana Markovna and Volokhov acquired new significance as the novel grew in its author's mind. Tat'yana Markovna is first depicted as an autocrat, taking a rough way with inferiors (I, vii). She has some characteristics in common with the formidably selfish Arina Rodionovna of Shchedrin's *The Golovlev Family (Gospoda Golovlevy)* (1875–80), a novel which Goncharov was to admire. Her interests are bound up entirely with the estate; she 'never wanted to

[1] Note the Russian titles of all three begin with *Ob-*.

[2] *Sobr. soch.*, vol. 8, p. 397.

[3] For various comments see e.g. I, v; I, xvii (end); II, iv; II, xii; II, xiii; II, xx; IV, vii; V, vii; V, xxiii.

[4] *Sobr. soch.*, vol. 8, p. 101.

hear about the general good' (I, ix). But Goncharov turns increasingly
to her for sentimental support against the evil of nihilism. Limited and
obstinate though she is, more and more he identifies her with a kind of
traditional wisdom and goodness. Raysky's final vision is of three
figures beckoning to him—Vera the heroine, her sister Marfin'ka,
and Tat'yana Markovna. Behind these stands another gigantic
'grandmother'—Russia herself.

The innocuous Marfin'ka and her husband obey Tat'yana Markovna without question. Only Vera is led astray. 'Grandmother's
failing' had been the neglect to warn Vera against a lapse like her own,
years before; and Goncharov later interpreted this as the failure of old
Russian society to understand the younger generation's needs and to
guide it properly.[1] So Vera had gone down that symbolic precipice
to Mark Volokhov; but Tushin will bear her across it in safety
(V, xx). Volokhov, originally a more sympathetic character,[2] turned
into a travesty of Bazarov, the nihilist in Turgenev's *Fathers and
Children* (1862). Goncharov like other liberals felt deeply hostile
to Rakhmetov, the revolutionary hero of Chernyshevsky's *What Is To
Be Done? (Chto delat'?)* (1863). In Volokhov he exposes a creed
which he considered to be a plague to society like cholera or typhus.[3]
He had in his capacity as censor been forced to study many expressions
of this creed and it stirred him to indignation.[4] The opening portrait
of Mark (II, xiv) emphasizes the hardness and brutality in his character.
He seems made of metal; he has an insolent face, and the wary posture
of a sleeping dog; later he is compared with a wolf. Mark is utterly
selfish and cynical. In creating this nihilist as a supposed figure of
pre-reform days Goncharov had, of course, committed an anachronism.

He found it difficult to present the contemporary world. Everything was in ferment, and only 'in the mirror of satire or a light
sketch' could he treat the new types still forming.[5] If Volokhov
belongs to crude satire or invective, then in Tushin—as Goncharov
owned—we have the lightest, most insubstantial of sketches. Again
the didactic purpose has interfered. Goncharov wanted to produce
a great salutary work in which Russia might recognize the dangers

[1] *Sobr. soch.*, vol. 8, p. 97.   [2] Piksanov, *Roman Goncharova 'Obryv'*, pp. 56–9.
[3] *Sobr. soch.*, vol. 8, p. 95.   [4] Piksanov, op. cit., pp. 49 sq.
[5] *Sobr. soch.*, vol. 8, p. 80.

besetting her and the safeguards that remained. However, his whole conception was too provincial. Volokhov is after all a small town revolutionary; Vera never knows the life of the capital; Marfin'ka sees herself as inseparable from the sand and grass along her native Volga (II, xiii); while of Tat'yana Markovna it is said that 'her horizon ended on one side with the fields, on another with the Volga and its hills, on a third with the town, and on a fourth with the road leading to the world which was no concern of hers' (II, x). Goncharov does not repudiate these attitudes. His local piety might be admirable if it did not turn away so resolutely from the wider scene.

Critical opinion has not on the whole been favourable to *The Precipice*. Korolenko in 1912 found Vera 'more intelligible, lively and individual than Turgenev's Elena' (of *On The Eve*).[1] Turgenev however complained of the first part that it was 'musty and false in its bookishness'.[2] (Though we should recall that relations were strained between him and Goncharov, who had accused Turgenev of plagiarizing from the still unwritten *Precipice* in *A Nest of Gentlefolk* and *On the Eve*). But, as Turgenev recognized, there were some excellences: the two wanton women, the servant Marina (II, xii) and the wife of the schoolmaster Leonty.[3] Also he found 'beauties of the second order' in the provincial scenes.[4] And indeed the setting beside the Volga—whose 'pensive current' and 'broad overflows' (II, iii) recall the workings of Goncharov's imagination—conveys a sense of limitless horizons and open sky. These are at odds with the intellectual temper of the novel, yet something of this spaciousness has at least been imparted to Vera.

Goncharov would have liked to see *The Precipice* acclaimed as his master work. That title by general consent goes to *Oblomov*, which so exactly fitted his genius. There we can observe in serene interplay the best qualities of Goncharov—a steady attention to life, an almost epic inclusiveness, fantasy united with realism, delicacy of touch with firmness of outline, and a style marked by its genial and complete adequacy.

[1] Korolenko, *SS*, vol. 8, p. 260.
[2] *PSSP, Pis'ma*, vol. 7, p. 278.
[3] *PSSP, Pis'ma*, vol. 7, p. 299.
[4] *PSSP, Pis'ma*, vol. 7, p. 278.

GONCHAROV

SELECT BIBLIOGRAPHY

EDITIONS :

Sobranie sochineniy, Moscow, 1952–5, 8 vols.
Sobranie sochineniy, Moscow, 1952, 8 vols.
Sobranie sochineniy, Moscow, 1959–60, 6 vols.
Neobykovennaya istoriya (*Istinnye sobytiya*), *Sbornik Rossiyskoy publichnoy biblioteki*, ed. D. Abramovich, Vol. 2, Brokgauz-Efron, Petrograd, 1924.
Putevye pis'ma I. A. Goncharova iz krugosvetnogo plavaniya, *Literaturnoe nasledstvo*, ed. B. Engel'gardt. Vols. 22–4, Moscow, 1935.

BIBLIOGRAPHIES:

Alekseev, A., *Bibliografiya I. A. Goncharova. Goncharov v pechati. Pechat' o Goncharove.* (1832–1964), Leningrad, 1968.
Istoriya russkoy literatury XIX veka. Bibliograficheskiy ukazatal', ed. K. Muratova, Leningrad, 1962.

CRITICAL AND BIOGRAPHICAL WORKS:

Alekseev, A., *Letopis' zhizni i tvorchestva I. A. Goncharova*, Moscow–Leningrad, 1960.
Belinsky, V. 'Vzglyad na russkuyu literaturu 1847 goda. Stat'ya vtoraya i poslednyaya' (1848), *Polnoe sobranie sochineniy* (1953–1959) (*PSS*), Vol. 10, Moscow.
Dobrolyubov,N.,'Chto takoe oblomovshchina?'(1859),*Sobranie sochineniy* (1961–1964) (*SS*), Vol. 4, Moscow.
Goncharov v russkoy kritike. Sbornik statey, ed. M. Polyakov, Moscow, 1958.
Istoriya russkogo romana, Moscow, 1962–4, Vol. 1, pp. 514–59; Vol. 2, pp. 173–92.
Istoriya russkoy literatury, Moscow–Leningrad, Vol. 8, Part 1 (1956), pp. 400–61.
Korolenko, V., 'I. A. Goncharov i "molodoe pokolenie"' (1912), *Sobranie sochineniy (SS)*, Vol. 8, Moscow, 1955.
Lavrin, J., *Goncharov*, Cambridge, 1954 (Studies in Modern European Literature and Thought).
Lyatsky, E., *Goncharov. Zhizn', lichnost', tvorchestvo. Kritiko-bibliograficheskie ocherki*, Stockholm, 3rd edn., 1920.
    Roman i zhizn'. Razvitie tvorcheskoy lichnosti Goncharova. Zhizn' i byt. 1812–1857, Prague, 1925.
Mazon, A., *Un maître du roman russe. Ivan Gontcharov, 1812–1891*, Paris, 1914.

GONCHAROV

Piksanov, N., *Roman Goncharova 'Obryv' v svete sotsial'noy istorii*, Leningrad, 1968.

Pisarev, D., 'Pisemskiy, Turgenev i Goncharov' (1861), *Sochineniya*, Vol. I, Moscow, 1955.

    'Zhenskie tipy v romanakh i povestyakh Pisemskogo, Turgeneva i Goncharova' (1861), op. cit.

Poggioli, R., 'On Goncharov and his *Oblomov*', *The Phoenix and the Spider*, Cambridge, Mass., 1957.

Pritchett, V., 'The Great Absentee', *The Living Novel*, London, 1946.

Prutskov, N., *Masterstvo Goncharova—romanista*, Moscow–Leningrad, 1962.

Rapp, H., 'The Art of Ivan Goncharov', *Slavonic and East European Review*, Vol. 36, 1958, No. 87, pp. 370–95.

Rybasov, A., *I. A. Goncharov*, Moscow, 1957.

    I. A. Goncharov, Moscow, 1962.

Shchedrin, N., (M. E. Saltykov), 'Ulichnaya filosofiya', *Polnoe sobranie sochineniy*, Vol. 8, Moscow, 1937.

Shklovsky, V., 'I. A. Goncharov kak avtor *Fregata "Pallada"*', *Zametki o proze russkikh klassikov*, 2nd edn., Moscow, 1955.

Tseytlin, A., *I. A. Goncharov*, Moscow, 1950.

Zakharkin, A., *Roman I. A. Goncharova 'Oblomov'*, Moscow, 1965.

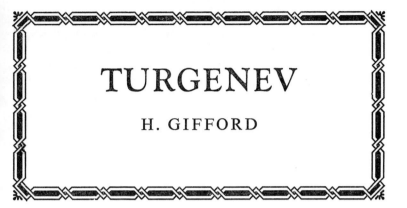

TURGENEV

H. GIFFORD

His intimacy, at different stages in life, with Belinsky and Flaubert helps to characterize Ivan Sergeevich Turgenev (1818–83). A western critic is more likely to be interested in the latter association, noting how Turgenev gained an unusual acceptance among French literary men, and how he often made it his concern to translate Russian experience into familiar terms: *A Hamlet of Shchigry District* (*Gamlet Shchigrovskogo uezda*), *A Lear of the Steppes* (*Stepnoy korol' Lir*). Turgenev was the first Russian novelist to achieve European celebrity, and became a great intermediary between Russia and the West. However, what sustained him as a novelist, and what confers his true distinction, was a deep and continuous involvement with Russian life, even when he had chosen to settle abroad. Turgenev's political awareness, his sensitivity to the least social change at home, never deserted him. The example of Belinsky, whom he once playfully addressed in a letter as 'father and captain',[1] ensured that he would combine artistic dedication with responsibility as a citizen.

Belinsky, when Turgenev first became acquainted with him in the 1840s, held extraordinary influence over a generation which he taught to view Russian life and institutions in the critical spirit of modern Europe. Through talk to his friends, among whom Turgenev soon became one of the foremost, and through impassioned articles which were mutilated by the censor, Belinsky spread the ideas of a secular liberalism that rejected serfdom and the autocracy. He was a literary critic with a gift for discerning new talent and guiding its direction.

[1] *PSSP, Pis'ma*, vol. 1, p. 264.

Turgenev's verse tale *Parasha* (1843) had caught his interest, and when this was later followed by prose sketches he recognised in Turgenev an artist whose essential qualities he proceeded to define. Turgenev was in Belinsky's opinion a writer strongly dependent on what he had himself seen and noted, one who 'must always hold the ground of actuality'.[1] The description did not displease Turgenev: he accepted it as true, and years later, when commenting on *Fathers and Children* (*Ottsy i deti*), acknowledged his need for 'a given ground on which I could walk sure-footedly'.[2] At Salzbrunn in 1847 they were together when Belinsky composed his famous denunciatory letter to Gogol'; and the ideas so eloquently expressed in it, with their appeal to the standards of 'civilization, enlightenment, humanity', remained fresh for Turgenev long after Belinsky's death. He felt for Belinsky the strongest personal affection, admiring his completely selfless pursuit of ideals. Turgenev was more complicated, irresolute, fond of his ease and worldly. But the image of Belinsky, and of those spirits very like him in their essential innocence, Granovsky and Stankevich, continued to haunt Turgenev. More than once he presented this type in his fiction: the hero of *Yakov Pasynkov* (1855) has the physical appearance and many traits of Belinsky; the poor student Pokorsky in *Rudin* (1856) recalls Stankevich; so does Mikhalevich in *A Nest of Gentlefolk* (*Dvoryanskoe gnezdo*) (1859). When Turgenev paid tribute to Pushkin at the Moscow celebrations in 1880, he deliberately invoked the name of Belinsky. From an early age serfdom (the evils of which he had seen at first hand in his own family) seemed to him the great blight on Russia. Belinsky must have added cogency to his protest.

1

Turgenev's reputation was founded on *A Sportsman's Sketches* (*Zapiski okhotnika*) (1847–52)—one of the seminal works in nineteenth-century Russian literature. The *Sketches* began with *Khor and Kalinych* written for *The Contemporary* (*Sovremennik*), the journal which Belinsky had helped to re-establish; and as they multiplied it became clear that Turgenev had discovered his natural form. ('Whatever I write', he once complained to Goncharov, 'it

[1] *Turgenev v russkoy kritike*, p. 103.
[2] 'Po povodu *Ottsov i detey*,' *PSSP, Soch.*, vol. 14, p. 97.

comes out as a series of sketches.')[1] Eventually the collection ran to twenty-two items, and three more were added in the 1870s. When Turgenev began *A Sportsman's Sketches*, he had sensed, with a fine instinct, the theme of the hour: throughout Europe, he afterwards recalled, an interest was developing in the peasantry as a subject for literature.[2] George Sand in France, Auerbach in Germany, Grigorovich, Herzen and the poet Nekrasov in Russia were all occupied with it. However, none of the last three did for Russian literature what Turgenev achieved with *A Sportsman's Sketches*. Years later, Shchedrin saluted the book as having given rise to 'a whole literature concerned with the people and its need'.[3] Belinsky may be seen as the political mentor of Turgenev while he was working on *A Sportsman's Sketches*. One of the most denunciatory among them, *The Bailiff* (*Burmistr*), was written at the same time as Belinsky's letter-manifesto to Gogol'.

The *Sketches* have been described as a kind of sequel to Gogol''s *Dead Souls*:[4] they present scenes of Russian life encountered by a roaming observer. Turgenev wrote in *The Singers* (*Pevtsy*): 'I suppose not many of my readers have had occasion to glance into village taverns (*kabaki*); but our friend the sportsman, where does he not drop in?' The sportsman is free of the whole Orel region, forest and steppe, marsh and meadow; he notes with the eye of a naturalist and an ethnographer the habits of birds and men, their haunts and peculiarities. One proven merit of the *Sketches* is their documentary exactness: not only were many characters taken from life, but the descriptions of places were accurate, their names unaltered;[5] and the book abounds in reliable information, about economic and social conditions, for instance, as in the opening paragraph of *Khor and Kalinych* or extensively in *Odnodvorets Ovsyanikov*.[6] Turgenev uses local terms and annotates them; Aksakov and Belinsky complained there was too much Orel dialect in the book.[7] It is the more remarkable that nearly

[1] *PSSP, Pis'ma*, vol. 3, p. 290. [2] *Sobr. soch.*, vol. 11, p. 349.
[3] *Turgenev v russkoy kritike*, p. 399. [4] Byaly, *Turgenev*, p. 18.
[5] See the article by B. V. Bogdanov in '*Zapiski okhotnika*' *I.S. Turgeneva*, pp. 281–95.
[6] *Odnodvortsy*—an intermediate class between landowners and peasants mainly to be found in four provinces of Central Russia, among them Orel (v. *Bol'shaya sovetskaya entsiklopediya*).
[7] Petrov, *Turgenev* (1961), p. 118.

all this precise evocation was the work of a man writing not in Russia but in France.

Reviewing another book of sketches by a sportsman, Sergey Aksakov, Turgenev praised its delicate and truthful observation of nature, which would have delighted Audubon.[1] His own writing is rich in field-lore—take, for instance, the exquisite notation of a spring twilight, with the birds falling silent in their carefully observed order, at the beginning of *Ermolay and the Miller's Wife* (*Ermolay i mel'nichikha*). Turgenev realized the central Russian landscape in its nuances as no writer before him had. The descriptions of *Bezhin Meadow* (*Bezhin lug*), *Raspberry Water* (*Malinovaya voda*), *Kas'yan from Krasivaya Mech'*, and of the final piece which anticipates the *Poems in Prose*, *Forest and Steppe* (*Les i step'*), have never perhaps been surpassed, even by Tolstoy. And with equal skill he can depict the cottage of the prosperous Khor, the hut of the forester Biryuk, or an estate office in the story named after it *Kontora* (*The Office*). It is easy to understand the appeal of Turgenev's book to foreign—and Russian—readers[2] who could study the whole region in such delightful amplitude.

But there was another motive to the *Sketches* than topography. Turgenev had seen too much of the evils inherent in serfdom at first hand—his mother's behaviour towards her serfs was often atrocious—ever to acquiesce in the system. He felt it an obligation to expose serfdom. *A Sportsman's Sketches* do this with extraordinary tact. 'Never, surely', noted Henry James, 'was a work with a polemic bearing more consistently low in tone, as painters say.'[3] The *Sketches* do not need a Simon Legree to make their point; instead there is what James called 'the cumulative testimony of a multitude of fine touches' —some indeed deeply incisive (Lenin liked to quote from *The Bailiff* that incident when a landowner has his man-servant seen to for not warming the wine: 'About Fyodor . . . see to it'). The *Sketches* do in effect contain a mass of evidence indicting serfdom; but the actual indictment is never spelt out.

He pleads his case rather by a consistently romantic treatment of the peasants, who are often revealed as naturally poetic people,

---

[1] *PSSP, Soch.*, vol. 5, p. 417.

[2] The first English translation (1855) was entitled *Russian Life in the Interior or the Experiences of a Sportsman.*

[3] *French Poets and Novelists*, p. 221.

with warm sympathies and a silent dignity. Khor is admired, among other things, because talking with him the author 'heard for the first time the simple, intelligent speech of the Russian peasant'. The boys tending their horses in *Bezhin Meadow* are seen as interesting and serious, and at least one of them, Pavlusha, as 'a splendid lad'. The Russian peasant—often in these pages a solitary and a misfit, like Ermolay—is shown to have sensibility, charm, and the courage to face disaster. Although not in agreement with the Slavophils, Turgenev shared their view of the national character as exhibited by the peasant.[1] He testifies to the unused energies of the people in a story that celebrates Russian spontaneity and feeling, *The Singers*. Yakov's victorious song is broad like the steppe, 'receding to an infinite distance': it flows out in irrepressible energy, and Yakov becomes the traditional *bogatyr'*, the folk-hero who prevails by daring and strength.

In these *Sketches* much of Turgenev's later work had its beginning. Several stories turn back to the brutal recent past, when a landlord ignored any will but his own (*Odnodvorets Ovsyanikov, Raspberry Water*). Already Turgenev was drawing upon traditions of his maternal family, the Lutovinovs; and he would write, in the year in which the *Sketches* were published as a volume, *Mumu* which narrates one of the darkest incidents from his mother's household. In *A Hamlet of Shchigry District* the 'superfluous man' first appears. The mood of *Forest and Steppe* for the first time reveals that sense of man's insignificance in the depth of nature, to be given full expression in *A Journey to Poles'e* (*Poezdka v Poles'e*) (1857). Turgenev had found his identity as an artist, and achieved something almost like perfection. 'I have been reading Turgenev's *A Sportsman's Sketches*', Tolstoy recorded in 1853, 'and it seems hard to write afterwards.'[2]

2

Turgenev too had to contend with his own success. There would always be those like Goncharov who insisted that *A Sportsman's Sketches* had marked his limit. In the 1850s he began to feel the necessity for trying a major form. His attempt at a properly epic

[1] Granjard, *Ivan Tourguénev* (1966), pp. 190–2.
[2] *Diary*, 27th July, 1853.

novel, *Two Generations* (*Dva pokoleniya*), came to nothing,[1] and he was driven back to a shorter form, the tale or *povest'*. In Sergey Aksakov's *A Family Chronicle* (*Semeynaya khronika*) (1856) Turgenev could discern 'the promise of a future Russian novel',[2] and the same breadth was evident in Herzen's memoirs, *My Past and Thoughts* (*Byloe i dumy*), which began publication in the same year. Anything however on the scale of either book in fiction was not possible for Turgenev. He was to achieve a good deal in this decade: *Rudin* (1856), *A Nest of Gentlefolk* (*Dvoryanskoe gnezdo*) (1859), and some very accomplished shorter tales, including *Faust* (1856) and *Asya* (1858). Yet the whole period was one of doubt and difficulty for Turgenev. Granjard speaks of it as a continuing crisis which beset him in various ways.[3] After the rout of European liberalism in 1848, his own political faith became less confident. He could no longer share the optimism of his old teachers, Granovsky and Stankevich. For a while he felt some sympathy with the Slavophils, but his claim for the rights of the individual conscience separated him from them.[4] Nor could he recognize, as they did, the hand of providence in an institution like the village commune. The Slavophils all too easily overlooked the tragic side of peasant life, well known to Turgenev and attested by the very songs that the people sang.[5] While not a religious man, he felt a keen sense of human limitations, and became reconciled to a view of man's place in nature which he would later find supported by Schopenhauer.[6] *A Journey to Poles'e* expresses the thought inspired by the primeval forest where the passer-by 'feels that the last of his brothers could vanish from the face of the earth—and not one needle would shiver on these branches; he feels his solitude, his weakness, his fortuitousness—and in a flurry of secret alarm turns to the petty cares and labours of life . . .'[7] Turgenev's vision of nature's awesome indifference brings him very close to the poet whose work he edited in this decade, Tyutchev.[8]

His doubts even extended to the question whether he should continue as a writer. After the appearance of *Boyhood* (*Otrochestvo*), by a

---

[1] For the plan of this work, see *PSSP, Soch.*, vol. 6, pp. 379–88, and the notes on pp. 594–605 for an account of it.

[2] *PSSP, Pis'ma*, vol. 2, p. 335. [3] Op. cit., pp. 201–2.

[4] *PSSP, Pis'ma*, vol. 2, p. 356. [5] *PSSP, Pis'ma*, vol. 2, p. 108.

[6] First ref. from 1862, according to Granjard, op. cit., p. 250. But for derivations in 1861, see *Turgenevskiy sbornik*, 3, pp. 123–5.

[7] *PSSP, Soch.*, vol. 7, p. 51. [8] *Stikhotvoreniya F. Tyutcheva*, Spb., 1854.

newcomer Lev Tolstoy, Turgenev was convinced that the first place in contemporary Russian literature waited for Tolstoy to claim it.[1] And yet these were the very years when Turgenev established his own position as a writer of unique importance. With *Rudin* he found his appropriate form—the short novel growing out of the longish tale that described a single episode. This form was to serve him for all his major projects. The novel as written by Turgenev seldom runs to more than two hundred printed pages (*Virgin Soil* (*Nov'*) with three hundred is the exception); it involves perhaps ten or a dozen characters in all; the plot is extremely simple and free from intrigue. Uniting a love story with political interest, the method develops from Pushkin's *Evgeny Onegin*, though the author with his commentary is missing from it. Turgenev liked to start with 'not an idea but a living person' and then to discover the relations that would elicit that person's quality.[2] The characters must all be representative: he had learned from Pushkin and Belinsky 'to strike through the play of contingencies to types',[3] placing these firmly in a historical context, and using the art of fiction as a means to discovering the nature and direction of social change. The action is rendered through brief dramatic scenes, alternating with documentary passages which explain the characters and narrate their past lives. Everything has been sifted for its relevance; Turgenev selects no more than he can use. (Of Tolstoy's *Polikushka* he said 'painfully much material had been wasted')[4]. His novel requires a steady though not strained attention, such as is appropriate to a well-devised play like his own *A Month in the Country* (*Mesyats v derevne*) (1850). We are to note small gestures, the tone of voices, silences; and to expect that changes of season and weather will rhyme with the action and mood of the characters.

3

Rudin, written at the height of the Crimean war, examines through its hero the generation and class to which Turgenev belonged. Here is the idealist of the 1830s, in middle age—and what does he add

---

[1] *PSSP, Pis'ma*, vol. 2, p. 247.
[2] *PSSP, Soch.*, vol. 14, p. 97.; James, *The Art of the Novel*, pp. 42–3.
[3] *PSSP, Pis'ma*, vol. 11, p. 280.
[4] *PSSP, Pis'ma*, vol. 5, p. 216.

up to? In Dmitry Rudin, Turgenev perfects his study of the 'super-fluous man', so called from a story he had written in 1850.[1] On this brilliant stranger whose ideas so fascinate the seventeen-year-old Natal'ya, and whose conduct proves so wretchedly irresponsible, the novel is centred. He cannot act on his professed love for her: 'I shall die', he predicts in his farewell letter, 'without having achieved anything worthy of my powers' (XI). A first epilogue added after the Crimean defeat puts him in a more sympathetic light; a second, of 1860, allows him a heroic though futile death on a Parisian barricade, waving his 'crooked and blunt sword'. However, by the time he has revealed his final weakness to Natal'ya at the dried pond (IX), it seems too late for Rudin's character to be restored. The points against him have been scored relentlessly, from love of empty rhetoric to a poor ear for Russian speech (in contrast with Natal'ya herself whose genuine Russian feeling is attested by the fact that she knows the whole of Pushkin). Even Rudin's voice and his moist, bright eye and incapacity for laughter disqualify him as a man in whom to trust as Natal'ya has trusted him. Like the hero of *Asya*, taken by Chernyshev-sky as representing all those enlightened gentry whose usefulness to Russia in his view had ended,[2] Rudin was to furnish a text for radical critics prompt to note his inadequacy, and Turgenev himself—though relenting a little in the epilogues—offered no complete defence of him.

Natal'ya represents all that Rudin should have been—a generous idealist as he was, but one who differs from him in her willingness to exchange rhetoric for action. She is very far from unique in Turgenev's work; she has a counterpart also in Goncharov's Ol'ga, the heroine of *Oblomov* (1859); and all such self-reliant and deeply sincere girls, who normally find the man of their choice when it comes to the test unworthy of them, derive from Pushkin's Tat'yana. Inevitably in Turgenev's novel more attention goes to Rudin, because his scope for activity so far exceeds that of Natal'ya. But she owns the moral strength which provides the standard by which to judge him.

A Nest of Gentlefolk, the novel that followed *Rudin*, is the least political work in Turgenev's major fiction, though it does not fail to have some bearing on the dilemma of the 'superfluous man'. Lavretsky, whose mother had been a serf girl, learns, as none of his predecessors

---

[1] *The Diary of a Superfluous Man* (*Dnevnik lishnego cheloveka*).
[2] 'Russkiy chelovek na rendez-vous'.

ever did, to become a practical landlord of benefit to his peasants. This step is taken after the return of his wife, presumed dead, has prevented him from marrying Liza. It is, like *Faust*, a story of renunciation, though Turgenev has carefully stressed the tendency to self-mortification in the deeply religious Liza. (She steels herself not to avoid Lavretsky's wife 'in punishment of what she called her criminal hopes').[1] Irving Howe suggests that, 'by the most exquisite indirection', Turgenev would have us see in Lavretsky's forfeiture of happiness with Liza a judgement on his earlier wrong thinking which had led him away from simple Russian truths to a cosmopolitan wife who chatters French.[2] When at last he recognizes those simple Russian truths in Liza, it is too late: the past rises to imprison him. Certainly after the failure of his marriage Lavretsky is reunited like a prodigal to the immemorial Russia of his paternal home (XX). The book shows a distinctly Slavophil current of feeling, which may have helped win it approval in such a wide circle of readers.

The tone throughout is elegiac rather than tragic. By the Epilogue indeed many of its people are dead; Lavretsky has suffered a cruel blow, and Liza, if not destroyed physically, has buried herself in a convent. (Turgenev seems to share the old aunt's horror at her wilful decision). Lavretsky bids farewell to his youth—he is not yet forty-three. The story has been distanced in time, so that the opening paragraph, when one returns to it, seems to catch at a moment of tranquil beauty which must soon be swallowed up: 'The bright spring day inclined towards evening; small rosy clouds stood high in the clear heaven and seemed not to float past but to sink into the very depth of the azure. Before the open windows of a handsome house, in one of the outlying streets of the provincial town O . . . (this happened in 1842) sat two women . . .' There are images like 'stills' that arrest a brief, illusory happiness, of which two may be cited here: Liza fishing beside Lavretsky, in her white dress with a straw hat dangled from her arm, while 'the shadow of the neighbouring lime tree fell upon them both'[3] (XXVI); Lemm the old music master playing his 'marvellous piece'—afterwards to be lost—in honour of Lavretsky's love, a majestic figure in his creative pride: 'the light of the risen moon fell slantingly through the windows; the responsive

---

[1] Chap. XXXIX.   [2] *Politics and the Novel*, pp. 125–6.
[3] The last detail was added in revision.

air trembled loudly; the little poor room seemed a shrine, and lofty and inspired there rose up in the silvery gloom the old man's head' (XXXIV).[1] It is obvious that such evocations are very near being sentimental; and *A Nest of Gentlefolk*, with its slender, dark-eyed, interesting heroine, its nightingales and summer garden, and kindly old Lemm, and the self-willed but no less kindly Marfa Timofeevna, might seem too much a charming idyll. That element is there; but the underlying conception reveals a tougher mind than one might suppose; the writing is not self-indulgent and it often has asperity. The morning after Lemm's celebration, brutal coincidence brings back the unscrupulous wife of Lavretsky—and he at once notices a physical change: she is paler and fatter (XXXVI). Turgenev misses nothing of the absurdity in the grand reconciliation scene planned by Mar'ya Dmitrievna, after which she feels there has been too little display of 'sensibility': 'Varvara Pavlovna, she considered, ought to have flung herself at her husband's feet' (XLIII). Throughout he keeps his eye on the object—especially when the object repels him, like the French governess dispatched in one sentence: 'a tiny wrinkled creature with a bird's ways and a bird's little mind' (XXXV).

4

By 1858, at the age of forty, Turgenev like Lavretsky felt that he belonged to the past. In the previous year he had confided to an old friend: 'As a writer with tendencies I shall be replaced by Mr Shchedrin (the public now need coarse and spicy things), while poetic and full natures like Tolstoy will complete and present fully what I only hinted at.'[2] He no longer felt at ease with the editorial board of *The Contemporary* where his voice had formerly been so much respected. The newcomers Chernyshevsky and Dobrolyubov shared his veneration for Belinsky, but the veneration was not extended by Dobrolyubov to Turgenev himself. These plebeian democrats, in the period of crisis following the Crimean fiasco, were sharply critical of the generation that had produced Rudins and Oblomovs. They wanted art to accept commitment: their demand was for positive heroes and a literature of militant ideas. Turgenev was shocked and angry when Dobrolyubov drew some outspoken conclusions in a review of his

[1] Inserted in revision.   [2] *PSSP, Pis'ma*, vol. 3, p. 92.

next novel *On the Eve* (*Nakanune*) (1859). He broke with *The Contemporary*—on the whole to his own loss. As Shchedrin wrote long afterwards, the irritants there had been good for him—they compelled Turgenev to think and change.[1]

He had been meditating for some years on what he took to be the two basic types of humanity, and now published at the same time as *On the Eve* his lecture *Hamlet and Don Quixote* (*Gamlet i Don-Kikhot*). In Quixote he saw the selfless idealist, such as Belinsky or Garibaldi, who finds his truth outside himself; in Hamlet—a Hamlet interpreted on German-Romantic lines—the hesitant and self-regarding sceptic. Hamlet's doubts destroy for him the appeal of any cause; he is 'preoccupied not with his duty but with his situation', though continuing to 'war relentlessly against falsehood'. The principles behind Don Quixote and Hamlet are, in Schopenhauerian terms, the centrifugal and the centripetal. Turgenev, by nature an irremediable Hamlet, was drawn to the Quixotic kind. He sought in his new novel to proclaim 'the necessity of *consciously* heroic natures'.[2]

Elena, the intense, awkward, questing heroine of *On the Eve*, rejects an artist, an academic and a bureaucrat in favour of the Bulgarian freedom-fighter Insarov. By her choice she affirms the highest values known to her: not 'love as happiness', the ideal set forth by Shubin and disputed by Bersenev (I), but 'love as sacrifice', Bersenev's own aim, a uniting not a divisive principle. She lacks the inept diffidence of Bersenev: her disregard of anything but Insarov's need makes her the equal to the Decembrists' heroic wives, to be celebrated in a well-known poem by Nekrasov,[3] and points forward to the nihilist saint in Turgenev's own late prose-poem 'The Threshold' (*Porog*).[4] Turgenev is a little dismayed by her type, but he approves Elena's selflessness. Insarov, as Dobrolyubov remarked,[5] is made up of negations—to be admired for his freedom from the weakness, venality, lack of candour and so on of which Turgenev accused his own countrymen. He remains the picture of resolution, allowing few glimpses into his mind—a figure whom Chernyshevsky was to recall in the Rakhmetov of *What Is To Be*

---

[1] Byaly, op. cit., p. 154.   [2] *PSSP, Pis'ma*, vol. 3, p. 368. Turgenev's italics.
[3] '*Russkie zhenshchiny* (*Dekabristki*)', 1871–2.
[4] Cf. another of the same year, 1878, '*Pamyati Yu. P. Vrevskoy*'.
[5] '*Kogda zhe pridet nastoyashchiy den'?*', (*Sovremennik*, 3, 1860). *SS*, vol. 6, pp. 96–140.

Done? Turgenev knows too little about his Bulgarian: he respects him but has no intuitive understanding. The novel seemed to at least one sensitive critic, Leont'ev, too evident an allegory.[1] The author is most profoundly engaged when he comes to the final scene: Elena and the now stricken Insarov find themselves in Venice, and Turgenev responds eloquently to the pathos of love at the mercy of an unheeding fate, which Elena feels she may have hastened on. This final episode was a *donnée* of the autobiographical sketch that had been entrusted to Turgenev by a young man going off to the Crimean war, and out of which he fashioned his novel. It accorded perfectly with his instincts as an artist, and the result was a fine *bravura* piece, dominated by the theme *morir si giovane* which rings out through a Venice also consigned to death.

5

Fathers and Children (1862) is unquestionably Turgenev's finest novel —the work most people associate with his name after *A Sportsman's Sketches*, and the one in which he accepted the greatest challenge to his beliefs. With Rudin or Insarov some detachment was possible; but the new hero Bazarov makes a frontal attack on the class and the culture with which Turgenev identified himself. *Fathers and Children* reflects the antagonism between the Old and the New Left;[2] it is a study of the conflict between generations as the title promises, but a conflict seen in social and—by implication—political terms. There was nothing here for Freud to analyse, no rivalry between father and son for the same woman[3]—Bazarov's duel with Pavel Petrovich over Fenichka has no significance other than one that is broadly ideological. The book owes its continuing appeal to the honesty and humane feeling with which it presents a crisis of values. Turgenev brings his own generation to trial; and, as many of them felt, he is dangerously candid about their failings. All the energy and most of the truth are to be found on Bazarov's side.

The values at issue become clear through Bazarov's various brushes with Pavel Petrovich and subsequently with Arkady himself.

---

[1] *SS*, (1912), vol. 8, p. 6.
[2] For a full account see Lampert, *Sons against Fathers* (1965).
[3] This had been present in *First Love* (*Pervaya lyubov'*), (1860).

These disagreements hardly achieve the status of debates, however Pavel Petrovich may flatter himself; they are expressed rather through tone and gesture—Bazarov's harsh interjection 'What is this, a cross-questioning?' (VI), the 'strangely quiet voice' in which Pavel Petrovich says 'So that's what it is' after having heard the definition of nihilism (X), the way in which Bazarov extends 'his long and hard fingers' as if to throttle Arkady in their dispute on the haystack (XXI). What interests Turgenev is the situation of his protagonists. Bazarov did not turn out to be merely another Rudin, as the Russian friend on the Isle of Wight to whom Turgenev disclosed his idea had supposed;[1] but he is rendered by the same process. Once again, an alien and disturbing force is introduced into a community with set ways; once again, the ripples run out in every direction, breaking the surface of life; then the intruder retires from the scene, and soon the old patterns are forming again, while Katya dares only whisper a toast to Bazarov's memory at her wedding breakfast (XXVIII). But the reader is not allowed to forget him, any more than he can Rudin: indisputably, Bazarov has dominated the novel.

This was a remarkable tribute to Turgenev's opponents. The ideas that Pavel Petrovich defends so ineffectually were those of Granovsky and Turgenev's own generation in the 1830s. They are exposed as sterile by the ineptitude and affectation of Pavel Petrovich, as harmlessly sentimental by the well-meaning incompetence of his brother. Bazarov is objectionable, crude in speech and thought, egotistical, and, until he meets Odintsova, unwarrantably self-assured. Yet his hard integrity and brutal candour even with himself make Bazarov a real man among conventional shadows. None of the others—even Odintsova with her freedom from prejudices and her claim to be a kindred spirit (XXVI)—ever appear his equals. Bazarov is worsted by two great and impersonal arbiters of human destiny, as Turgenev saw them—passion and death. No human being ever defeats him: Odintsova merely draws back in fear not unmixed by a sense of guilt when he offers his love (XIX). Rudin had been rejected as unworthy by Natal'ya; but here the position is reversed.

So far the impression may have been given that Bazarov has the author's whole-hearted sympathy. This is not so: however much Turgenev may appreciate the justice of Bazarov's position, he cannot

[1] *PSSP, Soch.*, vol. 14, p. 98.

deny his own prejudices. On the grounds of logic he could accept
Bazarov; but sentiment spoke otherwise. He would protest later that
all Bazarov's opinions were his too—except on art.[1] And over this
exception, a very important one for Turgenev, he takes issue with his
nihilist, obliquely, throughout the novel. Art for Chernyshevsky was
no more than 'a surrogate for reality' and therefore, so it seemed to
the outraged Turgenev, a serious matter 'only for immature people'.[2]
Bazarov quite often voices ideas from Chernyshevsky or Dobrolyubov.
He and Nikolay Petrovich hold utterly opposing views of nature. This
is delicately conveyed at the very beginning of the book when Arkady,
still the obedient disciple of Bazarov, sees the spring landscape in
terms of its poverty and dereliction—the willows beside the road
remind him of beggars, and everywhere they meet ragged peasants and
starving cattle. Arkady judges the scene much as Bazarov will, who
the next morning remarks 'The little place isn't much to look at' (V).
The clear social emphasis—'changes must be made'—places this
description in the line of Gogol' and of the protest literature that
stemmed from him. But then suddenly 'the spring came into its own':
Arkady in spite of himself responds to the gleaming verdure, the soft
breeze and the bird song. In a moment his father is quoting Pushkin
on springtime and love. Immediately, however, the poetry is checked
by Bazarov's voice from the other carriage, demanding a light. And
this kind of counterpoint between two sensibilities occurs more obviously when Arkady, at Bazarov's prompting, confiscates the Pushkin
his father is caught with and replaces it by a textbook on physics (X).
The sequel is instructive. Nikolay Petrovich alone in his summerhouse
concedes that his son's generation are superior to his own: they have
less of the *barin* in them. And yet—how can he renounce poetry and
nature as they do? Turgenev has already referred to Nikolay Petrovich's weakness for playing the 'cello (IX); and the flawless evocation
of a summer nightfall that now follows, inviting him to reveries about
his dead wife as a girl, has the effect of a slow movement on the 'cello
vibrant with tender feeling. Thus Turgenev solicits the reader's
sympathy for this representative of the fathers. The weaknesses in
Nikolay Petrovich are not disguised, but Turgenev cannot refrain from
sympathizing with him—as well he might since 'N.P. is myself,

[1] *PSSP, Soch.*, vol. 14, p. 100.
[2] *PSSP, Pis'ma*, vol. 2, p. 300.

Ogarev, and thousands of others.'[1] He makes the relationship with Fenichka altogether charming and a little pathetic in the innocence of both partners. Not for nothing was Arkady so named; he belongs, after all, to an Arcadian world.

Bazarov meets also with another kind of resistance from his creator. Katkov, who edited *The Russian Messenger* (*Russkiy vestnik*) in which the novel originally appeared, thought Turgenev had been too deferential to the nihilist Bazarov. Accordingly modifications were put in.[2] Bazarov had failed to win the approval of the Kirsanovs' aged butler who on revision describes him with those sidewhiskers as 'a real hog in the bush' (X). Though he inspired Fenichka with confidence in his whole personality, and got on easily with the village boys, now it seems that the peasants on his father's estate regard him as a buffoon (XXVII). Turgenev also emphasises the 'wolfish' element in Bazarov, his 'almost bestial' face (XVIII), his arrogance in expecting others to step out of his path (XXI), and the unkindness with which he taunts his old father (XXI). Not all the changes, however, told against Bazarov: an interpolation has the father say that he never sponged on his parents (XXI). Turgenev yielded here and there to the insistence of alarmed friends; but he left Bazarov with the same heroic stature in death. Until Bazarov has met Odintsova (and surprised Arkady by his embarrassment) the reader has little insight into his feelings. The final episode however makes him fully and stirringly human. No more humbled by his fate than Dante's Farinata or Brunetto Latini, the man whom Russia does not need remains his own master. Like a dying tragic hero he is allowed to articulate the sense of his own situation. The last words from Bazarov—'Now . . . darkness'—recall those of Hamlet: 'The rest is silence.' There had been in this character an essential Hamlet, which made him accessible to Turgenev's imagination.

The dispute over Bazarov was long and bitter. Neither party in Russia approved of what Turgenev had done. His reply to a lost letter thanks Dostoevsky for understanding what he was about;[3] and the critic Pisarev became an unexpected champion of Turgenev's nihilist. 'If he is called a nihilist', Turgenev told one correspondent, 'you

---

[1] *PSSP, Pis'ma*, vol. 4, p. 380.
[2] See *PSSP, Soch.*, vol. 8, pp. 446 sq. for variants of *Ottsy i deti*; changes in the presentation of Bazarov are discussed there on pp. 577–83.
[3] *PSSP, Pis'ma*, vol. 4, p. 385.

must read "revolutionary".[1] But Bazarov in this light did not commend himself to genuine revolutionaries; and Chernyshevsky set up in opposition Rakhmetov, the hero of *What Is To Be Done?* (*Chto delat'?*) (1863). Pisarev, however, did not believe in the imminence of a peasant Revolution, and eagerly accepted Bazarov and his 'style' as a model for other young 'realists'.[2]

With extraordinary divination Turgenev had seized on a type which was to be taken up by many novelists in the ensuing period, and would acquire new dimensions under the hand of Dostoevsky. *Fathers and Children* was the first work in fiction to notice and give an account of the Russian nihilist. The account is limited, and the foreclosure of death saved Turgenev from questions about Bazarov's future role. It is nonetheless a novel of high distinction, bringing together the representative figures of two periods—and even of a third, because Bazarov's father and mother belong to a much older Russia, with the era of Catherine in its foreground and the middle ages stretching behind Arina Vlas'evna and her primitive superstitions (XX). The novel was dedicated to the memory of Belinsky, who would have seen much to commend in it, especially the accurate and complete delineation of types (down to the emancipated woman Kukshina) and its essential justice.

6

In the 1860s Turgenev entered what was to be the final phase of his career—isolated, no longer living in Russia except on occasional visits, and increasingly subject to adverse criticism as being no longer in touch with the contemporary world. He wrote two further novels *Smoke* (*Dym*) (1867) and *Virgin Soil* (*Nov'*) (1877). Their symbolic titles indicate something different from *Rudin* or *A Nest of Gentlefolk*: in those novels he had chosen a representative figure or a typical scene; in *Fathers and Children* he had a specific conflict of ideas and attitudes to describe. But *Smoke* implies a greater abstraction, and *Virgin Soil* the attempt to deal with an unknown quantity. Both novels are frankly tendentious. *Smoke* unites a love intrigue of some psychological force with satire both on revolutionaries (not the most serious kind) and on reactionary young

---

[1] *PSSP, Pis'ma*, vol. 4, p. 380.
[2] See his comments in *Turgenev v russkoy kritike*, pp. 273–396.

generals. The latter come off worse. Turgenev upset the design of his novel in order to reaffirm a salutary principle. 'I rejoice', he told Pisarev, 'that it should be my part now to display the word "civilization" on my banner.'[1] The hero Litvinov is ousted by Potugin, Turgenev's spokesman, who waves that banner vigorously. His long tirade on Russia's need for civilization (V) is a good example of what Turgenev could do as a publicist; but in earlier times he would have been more scrupulous to avoid such interpolations. The novel (in spite of Potugin) seems more nihilistic than Turgenev may really have wished.

Virgin Soil caused him a lot of difficulty. 'It is impossible', he complained, 'to depict Russian life when one is abroad . . .'[2] Like Goncharov in his last work, *The Precipice*, Turgenev felt dissatisfied with his characterization of the practical man—Solomin, who was to provide an alternative to revolution. Neither Solomin nor his factotum Pavel were persons 'adequately studied on the spot'.[3] Similarly, with the peasants he felt unsure of himself, as he would perhaps never have done at the time of *A Sportsman's Sketches* (though these deal with peasants mainly as single figures, not in the mass). The whole business of 'going to the people' and the revolutionary mood impelling it had to be divined or pieced together from enquiries (Lavrov the populist in exile was sought out by Turgenev). He had the satisfaction of finding his guesswork confirmed when the 'trial of the fifty' took place early in 1877. The writer Garshin was impressed with Turgenev's ability, from a distance, 'to *divine* all this with such genius'.[4] But the novel did not meet with much sympathy anywhere. Henry James could find in it 'the deepest reality of substance . . . with the most imaginative, most poetic, touches'.[5] Nearly all Russian readers were dissatisfied.

It has been noted that Turgenev in *Virgin Soil* made recourse to the modes of contemporary writers. Fomushka and Fimushka (XIX) suggest Leskov who depicted a similar couple in *Cathedral Folk* (*Soboryane*) (1872); and Shchedrin, Ostrovsky and Dostoevsky all appear to have guided his treatment of particular passages.[6] One

[1] *PSSP, Pis'ma*, vol. 6, p. 261.   [2] *PSSP, Pis'ma*, vol. 10, p. 81.
[3] *PSSP, Pis'ma*, vol. 10, p. 49.   [4] *PSSP, Soch.*, vol. 12, p. 535. Garshin's italics.
[5] *Literary Reviews and Essays* (1957), pp. 190 sq.
[6] Byaly, op. cit., p. 232.

should not conclude, however, that in these latter years Turgenev's was a failing talent. He could still achieve excellent shorter works—for instance *A Lear of the Steppes* (*Stepnoy korol' Lir*) (1870) and *Spring Torrents* (*Veshnie vody*) (1872). But it is true that the absence from Russia was telling on him. He resorted now to the past, to his childhood or to family traditions: *Punin and Baburin* (1874), *Living Relics* (*Zhivye moshchi*) (1874), *Old Portraits* (*Starye portrety*) (1881). Or he explored the supernatural, in *Phantoms* (*Prizraki*) (1864), *The Dog* (*Sobaka*) (1866), and other stories. Or else he wrote elaborate fantasies like *Enough!* (*Dovol'no*) (1865) or *The Song of Triumphant Love* (*Pesn' torzhestvuyushchey lyubvi*) (1881) which escape from present-day reality. They seem alien to his genius, although the last story was much admired at the time.

Turgenev's final achievement was the *Poems in Prose* (*Stikhotvoreniya v proze*) (1882).[1] He had anticipated these more than once in passages of meditation, such as begin and close *A Journey to Poles'e*, or the twenty-sixth chapter of *Smoke* in which Litvinov watching the smoke from his train takes it as symbolic of 'everything, his own life, Russian life'. Comparisons have been made with similar essays in the genre by Tolstoy, and a prototype found in the poetic 'interludes' of *Dead Souls*.[2] Baudelaire had already published his *Petits poèmes en prose* (1869). The governing ideas of the series by Turgenev are often derived from Schopenhauer,[3] whose cosmic pessimism (like that of Leopardi) has deep affinities with Turgenev's own view. Mention of Leopardi points the limitation inherent in the genre, which as Mazon admits 'is slightly artificial'. A sustained poem like *La ginestra* has the dignity of a major statement, where the famous *Nature* (*Priroda*) seems by contrast a little mannered and didactic. It lacks the splendour and energy of Tyutchev's not dissimilar poem 'Spring' (*Vesna*) (1838). For all their accomplishment, their ability to distil the essence of Turgenev, the *Poems in Prose* seem in their majority faintly Parnassian.

7

The series of *Poems in Prose* published in Turgenev's lifetime concluded with one that has become very famous, 'The Russian Language'

[1] Thirty-three further poems were published in 1930 by André Mazon.
[2] See Mazon's Introduction to Ivan Turgenev, *Poems in Prose* (1951).
[3] See Walicki, 'Turgenev and Schopenhauer', pp. 10 sq.

(*Russkiy yazyk*). Only a few months before his death, Turgenev reaffirmed his belief in the virtues of that tongue which by its very existence seemed to ensure the greatness of the people who had formed it. Turgenev in his Pushkin speech of 1880 made reference to the comment by Mérimée that 'Russian poetry seeks truth before everything'.[1] The language itself is called truthful in this prose poem. Turgenev learned to cooperate with the genius of the language by studying Pushkin. Like others who had admired the once-fashionable Marlinsky he needed to cure himself of Romantic excess. 'One thing I beg of you', Bazarov says to Arkady who has just delivered a minor 'poem in prose' about the resemblance between a falling leaf and a butterfly, 'no fine talk (*ne govori krasivo*)!' By careful application Turgenev had conquered in himself the tendency to 'fine talk'.

André Mazon first made it possible to watch this in process when he published the Parisian manuscripts. The new Soviet edition prints all the variants—together with notes and plans where these exist—for every tale. Turgenev habitually submitted his first draft to a jury consisting of Annenkov, Botkin and others. At their suggestion he might insert an explanatory chapter (like the thirty-fifth in *A Nest of Gentlefolk* which recounts the childhood of Liza), or he would rework the details of a character or a scene. In the main his revisions aimed at greater exactitude. He knew how to extract value from small details. Thus, in the scene describing Lavretsky's declaration of love for Liza (XXXIV) a very slight change after 'He bent his head a little', from 'and sought her lips' to 'and touched her pale lips', suddenly gives the relationship in all its tentative hope on the one side and half-smothered uneasiness on the other. Invariably it is the minutiae that reveal Turgenev's discipline. In *Asya*—a story that could lend itself to facile Romanticism—he wanted to describe the effect of the moon rising above the summer Rhine. His first attempts were too rhetorical—'the bright magnificence of night not yielding to the bright magnificence of day', or 'there reigned over sky and earth—every-where—the solemn night'. Such phrases had at least a tinge of Marlinsky. In the final version one single evocative epithet—'myster-ious'—is admitted, but it gains validity from the close observation of detail: 'everything grew bright, grew dark, changed, even the wine

[1] *PSSP, Soch.*, vol. 15, p. 70.

in our cut glasses shone with a mysterious gleam'.[1] Often by his revisions he will seek to convey a livelier dramatic sense of an episode, as in the farewell scene between Bazarov and Odintsova at the latter's home:[2]

'What do you advise me?' asked Anna Sergeevna [continuing to laugh].
'Well, I think' [answered Bazarov with a laugh, though he was not at all gay and did not want to laugh any more than she did, 'I think] the young people should have your blessing . . .'
[Odintsova walked about the room. Her face by turns flushed and went pale.]
. . . ['Goodbye', he said again after a short silence]. 'I should wish you to round off the business in the pleasantest way; and I shall rejoice from a distance'.
[Odintsova turned quickly towards him.]

Turgenev's art, like that of his friend Flaubert, expends a minute care on the verbal texture. The effect, however, is more open and fluid. His translations of *La Légende de Saint-Julien L'Hospitalier* and *Hérodias*, both made in 1877, lack the intricate harmonies of Flaubert. Yet his own style has often been singled out for its music: this can be heard notably in *A Nest of Gentlefolk* (where it also happens that playing or listening to music is significant in the design).[3] Turgenev likes to impose a melodious pattern on his sentences, and there are set pieces of description in the earlier writing (such as the introductory paragraphs of *Bezhin Meadow*) which have a complex lyrical flow that might almost be Gogol''s. But the tendency of his style is towards neatness and compression. Tolstoy said of his art in describing a landscape: 'two or three strokes and you can smell it.'[4] Language with Turgenev does not parade its beauties; and he admits roughness or discord when these are effective.

The range of his linguistic interest was wide. He could render popular speech accurately, with a fine ear for peculiarities; he could catch the intonations of a village priest, as in *Father Aleksey's Tale* (*Rasskaz ottsa Alekseya*) (1877), or the jargon of belated idealists

---

[1] *Turgenevskiy sbornik*, 4, p. 17; discussed in *PSSP, Soch.*, vol. 7, pp. 431–2.
[2] *Fathers and Children*, Chap. XXVI. Revisions in square brackets.
[3] *PSSP, Soch.*, vol. 7, p. 486.   [4] *Istoriya russkogo romana*, vol. 2, p. 166.

from the 1830s (Mikhalevich in *A Nest of Gentlefolk*) or small-town intellectuals (Kukshina in *Fathers and Children*). His own voice in the novels and tales is never one assumed for ironic purposes, as with Pushkin's Belkin, or Gogol', or Dostoevsky. The author is present throughout in the expression of certain attitudes through certain tones. Turgenev once declared 'I have written for that class of the public to which I belong'[1]—the landed aristocracy. After Pushkin he is the most sensitive exponent of their ideal in manners, that frankness and ease which characterized Tatyana's drawing room.[2] Turgenev is not an exuberant writer; he does not become frenzied; and often he gains his effect by the implications of a gesture as when Natal'ya in *Rudin* quietly touches chords on the piano and lays her forehead on the cold keys (VII).

8

Compared with Tolstoy or Dostoevsky, as in the end he must be, Turgenev obviously lacks their greatness. Who today would echo Henry James's tribute—'he understands so much that we almost wonder he can express anything'?[3] Or Conrad's—'the incomparable artist of humanity . . . the clearest mind, the warmest heart, the largest sympathy—and all that in perfect measure'?[4] Readers today are more conscious of his shortcomings, which Turgenev himself freely acknowledged. In one respect he does patently inherit the tradition of Pushkin, always his master.[5] Pushkin's clarity and good sense, his grace and his openness of mind are also Turgenev's. But more essentially it was Tolstoy, with his bolder and more original procedures, who continued the work of Pushkin. Nothing that Turgenev achieved could not have been foretold by a critic familiar, as Belinsky was, with Pushkin—and Gogol'. He made no revolutionary break, but perfectly adapted the perceptions and methods of Russian literature to contemporary needs. In the 1850s these were wonderfully adequate. Thereafter Tolstoy and Dostoevsky struck out in unforeseen directions and the limits of Turgenev's art became more apparent.

[1] *PSSP, Pis'ma*, vol. 5, p. 120.   [2] *Evgeny Onegin*, chap. VIII.
[3] D. Davie, *Russian Literature and English Fiction*, 1965, p. 52.
[4] *Notes on Life and Letters*, p. 46.   [5] *PSSP, Pis'ma*, vol. 13, ii, p. 118.

His two great contemporaries wrote from a much more profound understanding of human nature. They have the Shakespearian energy of the truly creative novelist—to be found also in Balzac and Dickens. Turgenev, without the poet's originating power, does not belong to their company. He has some inestimable gifts: the capacity to observe manners and social currents with an almost prophetic insight; a fine critical intelligence; a sometimes miraculous touch with language (as shown in his letters and memoirs as well as in his fiction). But humane and sensitive though he is, an accomplished artist, the conscience it might be argued of a whole generation, Turgenev does not speak urgently to the present day.

Even for Chekhov in 1893 he was beginning to date—most of his female characters, whether middle-aged or young maidens, seeming 'intolerably artificial', the famous landscapes no longer in fashion.[1] After the 1917 revolution Blok complained of his 'antimusical' nature (his deafness to elemental voices) and found in him a 'want of sonority' (*nepolnozvuchnost'*). It tormented Blok that a 'great artist' should also be a 'flabby, idle-rich (*barstvuyushchiy*) liberal-constitutionalist'.[2] Both Chekhov and Blok are complaining that in certain ways Turgenev did not get through to realities. He only seldom achieves the rawness of great art—the shocking quality that appears for example in Bazarov's death scene.

There is nothing avid in Turgenev's curiosity about human beings. Compassion and rage do not storm through his novels; he does not press hard into the recesses of the mind in an effort to catch, like Tolstoy, the irrationalities behind thought; he never exerts on his characters the fearful pressures of Dostoevsky, under which identity comes near to collapse. For him the moral world admits nothing arbitrary except the passion of love—a large exception, one might insist, bearing as it does on Turgenev's view of human life in a universe with its own overriding purposes. Yet the man whom love drives out of his course (as in *Smoke* or *Spring Torrents*) totters back after the experience to become his rational self. Turgenev is aware that destructive forces can overwhelm the individual; he forgets neither our weakness nor our mortality; but he still holds to a belief in the paramountcy of reason, and for him civilization seems both attainable and necessary.

[1] *Turgenev v russkoy kritike*, p. 526.
[2] Blok, *Sobranie sochineniy*, 1960–3, vol. 7, p. 359.

TURGENEV

He does not ignore the cold and silent spaces that look down on the human comedy, but continues to advocate social responsibility, tolerance, and disinterestedness.

Turgenev is more than 'the novelists' novelist'—anyway, writers of fiction turn elsewhere in our time for technical guidance—and more than the chronicler of a vanished society. He represents at its finest that sympathy with western ideas which characterized many among his generation. Lawrence once declared, in an essay on Shestov, that 'European culture is a rootless thing in the Russians.'[1] Against such a half-truth Turgenev—and Pushkin—rise in protest. The roots may have been delicate but they went deep into an imaginative soil that could nourish them. Turgenev would have his value in any literature, but his significance on the Russian scene is that he seldom allows himself to exaggerate. 'The Greeks', he once reminded the Russian public, 'used to say that the last and greatest gift of the gods was a sense of proportion.'[2] Outwardly in the form of Turgenev's stories proportion is very evident. It exists too as a quality of his mind, issuing in balanced judgment not unmixed with sympathy, and in a firm sense of truth.[3]

SELECT BIBLIOGRAPHY

EDITIONS:

Sobranie sochineniy, Moscow, 1953–8, 12 vols.
Polnoe sobranie sochineniy i pisem (PSSP), Moscow–Leningrad: *Sochinenya*, 1960–8, 15 vols., *Pis'ma*, 1961–8, 13 vols.
Turgenevskiy sbornik. Materialy k polnomu sobraniyu sochineniy i pisem I. S. Turgeneva, Moscow–Leningrad: Vol. 1, 1964; Vol. 2, 1966; Vol. 3, 1967; Vol. 4, 1968; Vol. 5, 1969.
Manuscrits parisiens d'Ivan Tourguénev. Notices et extraits, ed. A. Mazon, Paris, 1930.
Parizhskie rukopisi I. S. Turgeneva, ed. A. Mazon, Moscow–Leningrad, 1931.
Poems in Prose, ed., A. Mazon, Oxford, 1951.
Spring Torrents, translated and edited by L. Schapiro, London, 1971.

[1] *Phoenix* (1957), p. 213.
[2] *PSSP, Soch.*, vol. 14, p. 20.
[3] Cf. Tolstoy's comment: 'The chief thing about him was his truthfulness', *Turgenev v russkoy kritike*, p. 524.

TURGENEV

V. I. Botkin i I. S. Turgenev: neizdannaya perepiska 1851–1869, ed. N. L. Brodsky, Moscow–Leningrad, 1930.

Nouvelle Correspondance Inédite, ed. A. Zviguilsky. Vol. 1, Paris, 1971. Vol. 2, 1972.

Literaturnoe nasledstvo, Vol. 73 (2 parts), *Iz parizhskogo arkhiva I. S. Turgeneva*, Moscow, 1964.

    Vol. 76, *I. S. Turgenev: novye materialy i issledovaniya*, Moscow, 1967.

Istoriya russkoy literatury XIX veka. Bibliograficheskiy ukazatel', ed. K. Muratova, Leningrad, 1962.

CRITICAL AND BIOGRAPHICAL WORKS:

Annenkov, P., *Literaturnye vospominaniya*, Moscow, 1960.

Belinsky, V. '*Parasha*. Rasskaz v stikhakh' (1843), *Polnoe sobranie sochineniy* (1953–59), Vol. 7, Moscow.

    'Vzglyad na russkuyu literaturu 1847 goda. Stat'ya vtoraya i poslednyaya' (1848), ibid, Vol. 10.

Byaly, G., *Turgenev i russkiy realizm*, Moscow–Leningrad, 1962.

Chernyshevsky, N., 'Russkiy chelovek na rendezvous' (1858) *Polnoe sobranie sochineniy* (1939–53), vol. 5, Moscow.

Conrad, Joseph, 'Turgenev' (1917), *Notes on Life and Letters*, London, 1926.

Dobrolyubov, N., 'Kogda zhe pridet nastoyashchiy den'?' (1860), *Sobranie sochineniy* (1961–4), Vol. 6, Moscow.

Efimova, E., *I. S. Turgenev. Seminariy*, Leningrad, 1958 (useful bibliographies).

Freeborn, R., *Turgenev: The Novelist's Novelist. A Study*, London, 1960.

Gershenzon, M., *Mechta i mysl' I. S. Turgeneva*, Moscow, 1919.

Granjard, Henri, *Ivan Tourguénev et les courants politiques et sociaux de son temps*, Paris, 2nd edn., 1966.

    Ivan Tourguénev, la Comtesse Lambert, et 'Nid de Seigneurs', Paris, 1960.

Irving Howe, *Politics and the Novel*, London, 1961.

Istoriya russkogo romana, Moscow, 1962–4, Vol. 1, pp. 455–513, Vol. 2, pp. 149–73.

I. S. Turgenev (1818–1883—1958). Stat'i i materialy, ed. M. Alekseev, Orel, 1960.

James, Henry, 'Ivan Turgenev's *Virgin Soil*' (1877), *Literary Reviews and Essays*, ed. Albert Mordell, New York, 1957.

    'Ivan Turgénieff', *French Poets and Novelists*, London, 1884.

    'Ivan Turgénieff' (1884). *Partial Portraits*, London, 1888.

    'Ivan Turgénieff (1818–1883)' (1897), *Russian Literature and Modern English Fiction*, ed. Donald Davie, Chicago and London, 1965.

    'Turgenev and Tolstoy' (1897), *The House of Fiction*, ed. Leon Edel, London, 1957.

TURGENEV

Preface to *The Portrait of a Lady, The Art of the Novel*, ed. Richard P. Blackmur, New York, 1934.

Kleman, M., *Letopis' zhizni i tvorchestva I. S. Turgeneva*, Moscow–Leningrad, 1934.

Ivan Sergeevich Turgenev: ocherk zhizni i tvorchestva, Leningrad, 1936.

Lampert, E., *Sons Against Fathers*, Oxford, 1965.

Leont'ev, K., 'Pis'mo provintsiala k g. Turgenevu' (1860), *Sobranie sochineniy*, Moscow, 1912.

Petrov, S., *I. S. Turgenev—tvorcheskiy put'*, Moscow, 1961.

    I. S. Turgenev: zhizn' i tvorchestvo, Moscow, 2nd edn., 1968.

Phelps, Gilbert, *The Russian Novel in English Fiction*, London, 1956.

Pisarev, D., 'Pisemskiy, Turgenev i Goncharov' (1861), *Sochineniya*, Vol. 1, Moscow, 1955.

    'Zhenskie tipy v romanakh i povestyakh Pisemskogo, Turgeneva i Goncharova' (1861), op. cit.

    'Bazarov' (1862), op. cit., Vol. 2.

Pritchett, V., 'The Russian Day', *The Living Novel*, London, 1946.

Pustosvoyt, P., *Roman I. S. Turgeneva 'Ottsy i deti' i ideynaya bor'ba 60-kh godov XIX veka*, Moscow, 1965.

Shklovsky, V., *Zametki o proze russkikh klassikov*, Moscow, 2nd edn., 1955.

Tseytlin, A., *Masterstvo Turgeneva—romanista*, Moscow, 1958.

Turgenev i krug 'Sovremennika'. Neizdannye materialy, 1847–61, Moscow–Leningrad, 1930.

Turgenev i teatr, ed. G. Berdnikov, Moscow, 1953.

Turgenev's Literary Reminiscences and Autobiographical Fragments, translated by D. Magarshack, London, 1959.

Turgenev v russkoy kritike, Sbornik statey, ed. K. Bonetsky, Moscow, 1953.

Tvorchestvo I. S. Turgeneva, ed. S. Petrov, Moscow, 1959.

Walicki, A., 'Turgenev and Schopenhauer', *Oxford Slavonic Papers*, Vol. 10, 1962, pp. 1–17.

Wilson, Edmund, 'Turgenev and the Life-Giving Drop', *Turgenev's Literary Reminiscences and Autobiographical Fragments*, translated by D. Magarshack, London, 1959.

Woolf, Virginia, 'The Novels of Turgenev', *The Captain's Deathbed and Other Essays*, London, 1950.

Yarmolinsky, A., *Turgenev: The Man, His Art and His Age*, New York, 1959.

'Zapiski okhotnika' I. S. Turgeneva (1852–1952). Stat'i i materialy, Orel, 1955.

Zaytsev, B., *Zhizn' Turgeneva*, Paris, 2nd edn., 1949.

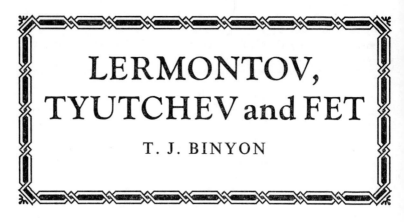

LERMONTOV, TYUTCHEV and FET

T. J. BINYON

INTRODUCTION

In 1837, with the death of Pushkin, the golden age of Russian poetry came to an end. In the 1890s, with the first volumes of the symbolist poets, its silver age began. The literature of the intervening years was dominated by the great Russian novelists: during this period there appeared *Dead Souls* (1842), *Oblomov* (1859), *Fathers and Children* (1862), *War and Peace* (1865–9), *Crime and Punishment* (1866), *Anna Karenina* (1875–7), *The Golovlev Family* (1876–80) and *The Brothers Karamazov* (1879–80). The poets of this epoch have inevitably been overshadowed, not only by these immense contemporary achievements, but also by their predecessors and successors. Nevertheless, they are more interesting and variegated than they appear at first sight.

They can be divided, perhaps somewhat schematically, into four groups. The first of these can conveniently be termed Romantic, and includes the poets M. Yu. Lermontov (1814–41), F. I. Tyutchev (1803–73) and A. A. Grigor'ev (1822–64). They all employ the Romantic mood and idiom in different ways; however, they have more in common with each other than with any of their contemporaries.

The middle years of the epoch were the scene of a conflict between two groups of writers and their attendant critics; groups holding widely differing views on the nature and function of art. On the one hand stood the Parnassians, believers in the doctrine of 'art for art's sake', on the other, the 'civic' poets, whose views were summed up in Nekrasov's well-known lines:

> Поэтом можешь ты не быть,
> Но гражданином быть обязан.

It is possible for one not to be a poet, | But one is obliged to be a citizen.

To the former group belonged the poets A. A. Fet (1820–92), A. N. Maykov (1821–97), L. A. Mey (1822–62), Ya. P. Polonsky (1819–98) and also, though less closely identified with the views of this group, A. K. Tolstoy (1817–75) and Karolina Pavlova (1807–93).

Their opponents, the 'civic' poets, were headed by N. A. Nekrasov (1821–77), and included I. S. Nikitin (1824–61), N. P. Ogarev (1813–77), A. N. Pleshcheev (1825–93) and, in the 1880s, S. Ya. Nadson (1862–87).

Finally, in the latter years of the period, a fourth group can be distinguished, consisting of poets such as A. N. Apukhtin (1840–93), K. M. Fofanov (1862–1911), K. K. Sluchevsky (1837–1904) and A. A. Golenishchev-Kutuzov (1848–1913), whose work, in mood and tone, adumbrates the symbolist verse of the 1890s and 1900s.

Of all these poets three names obviously stand out above all others: those of Lermontov, Tyutchev and Fet. One is tempted to add to these three a fourth, that of Nekrasov. But though Nekrasov's work is undeniably important from a literary historical point of view, his poetry, even in his best work, *Moroz krasnyy nos* (*Frost the Red-Nosed*) (1863), cannot stand comparison with that of the other three poets. And since a literary historical approach, within the confines of this chapter, would lead to an extremely general treatment, Nekrasov has been excluded.

The following short essays do not in any way purport to give an overall, synoptic view of the work of the poets concerned; nor do they set out to trace their artistic or ideological development. The aim is rather to examine, in some reasonable detail, one or two aspects of their work which seem to cast some light on their main creative preoccupations.

LERMONTOV

In 1844, Belinsky, in a general article on contemporary Russian literature, drew a comparison between Lermontov and Pushkin. 'With Lermontov', he wrote, 'Russian poetry, which in Pushkin's period reached its extreme development *as art*, took a decisive step forward as the expression of contemporary life, as the living organ of the ideas, the ailments, the most sublime strivings of the age.' He amplified this elsewhere, when he noted that: 'For Lermontov verse was only the means for the expression of his ideas—deep and at the same time simple in their pitiless truth—and he thus did not place a very high value on it.'[1] There can be no doubt that here Belinsky has hit upon an essential difference between the two poets: whereas for Pushkin the emotion is always subordinated to the demands of poetry, for Lermontov the feeling, the mood, the passion take precedence over the form which embodies them. And it is this basic quality of Lermontov's work which illuminates certain of its particular characteristics.

For example, Lermontov shows little concern for the stylistic unity of his poems, borrowing voraciously: in his early work from his predecessors—Pushkin, Kozlov, Dmitriev, Batyushkov, Bestuzhev-Marlinsky and others—and in later poems from his own earlier work. These lines from Bestuzhev-Marlinsky's poem *Andrey, Prince of Pereyaslavl'* (*Andrey, knyaz' Pereyaslavskiy*) (1827–8):

> Хребта Карпатского вершины
> Пронзали синеву небес,
> И оперял дремучий лес
> Его зубчатые вершины.
> Обложен степенями гор,
> Расцвел узорчатый ковер...

The summits of the Carpathian chain | Pierced the blue of the skies, | And the dense forest feathered | Its jagged summits. | Edged by the rising mountains, | The patterned carpet bloomed.

are, with the adjective in the first line changed from 'Carpathian' to

[1] *M. Yu. Lermontov v russkoy kritike*, pp. 212, 207.

'Caucasian', included in Lermontov's *A Prisoner of the Caucasus* (*Kavkazskiy plennik*) (1828). The description of a snake in the final section of *The Demon* (*Demon*) (1841):

> И осторожная змея
> Из темной щели выползает
> На плиту старого крыльца,
> То вдруг совьется в три кольца,
> То ляжет длинной полосою
> И блещет, как булатный меч,
> Забытый в поле давних сеч,
> Ненужный падшему герою!..

And the cautious snake, | Crawling out of a dark crack | On to a flagstone of the old porch, | Will sometimes coil himself suddenly in three rings, | Sometimes lie stretched out at length | And glitter, like a Damascene sword, | Forgotten on the field of ancient battles, | Useless to the fallen hero!..

is a rephrasing of lines from Lermontov's earlier poem *Izmail-Bey* (1832); another variant of the same description occurs in *The Novice* (*Mtsyri*) (1839). A final example, which illustrates strikingly how Lermontov can employ the same material in different contexts, is the description, in *The Demon*, of the dead Tamara:

> И были все ее черты
> Исполнены той красоты,
> Как мрамор, чуждой выраженья,
> Лишенной чувства и ума,
> Таинственной, как смерть сама.

And all her traits | Were filled with that beauty, | Like marble, empty of expression, | Without feelings or thoughts, | Mysterious, like death itself.

This repeats, with one additional line, the description of the dead Orsha in the poem *The Boyar Orsha* (*Boyarin Orsha*) (1835–6). Yet in one poem Lermontov is describing a young, innocent girl; in the other an old stern warrior.

Lermontov's lack of interest in the purely poetic qualities of his work is betrayed too by his failure, especially in the earlier long poems, to maintain a consistent standard of verse. He lapses all too often into rhymed prose, as in this extract from *Julio* (*Dzhyulio*) (1830):

> Вожатому подарок я вручил.
> Но, признаюсь, меня он удивил,
> Когда не принял денег. Я не мог
> Понять зачем, и снова в кошелек
> Не смел их положить... Его черты
> (Развалины минувшей красоты,
> Хоть не являли старости оне),
> Казалося, знакомы были мне.

I handed the guide a gift. | But, I must admit, he surprised me, | When he did not accept the money. I could not | Understand why, and back in my purse | Did not dare to put it... His features | (Ruins of former beauty, | Although they did not display age), | Were, it seemed, familiar to me.

Yet though Lermontov seems incapable—with the exception of some of the mature short poems—of a sustained poetic effort, his work is full of striking individual lines and short passages. Indeed, it seems that a feature of his artistic method is to concentrate the force of a poem into a few lines, which stand out vividly from the rest. Such lines often take an almost aphoristic form and, like his descriptions, are repeated in poem after poem. An example occurs in this short poem, written in 1831:

> Я не люблю тебя; страстей
> И мук умчался прежний сон;
> Но образ твой в душе моей
> Всё жив, хотя бессилен он;
> Другим предавшися мечтам,
> Я всё забыть его не мог;
> Так храм оставленный — всё храм,
> Кумир поверженный — всё бог!

I do not love you; the former dream | Of passions and torments has passed by; | But your image in my soul | Is still alive, although it is powerless; | Although I abandon myself to other dreams, | I still cannot forget it; | So an abandoned temple is still a temple, | A dethroned idol—still a god!

The last two lines are repeated without alteration in *We have parted,
but your portrait...* (*Rasstalis' my, no tvoy portret...*) (1837), and the
same image, compressed into a single line, occurs in *The Confession*
(*Ispoved'*) (1830), *The Boyar Orsha* and *The Demon*, where the demon,
addressing Tamara, cries:

> Что без тебя мне эта вечность?
> Моих владений бесконечность?
> Пустые звучные слова,
> Обширный храм — без божества!

*What is this eternity to me without you? | What is the infinity of
my domains? | Empty ringing words, | A spacious temple—with-
out a divinity!*

Striking lines of this type are especially frequent, as might be
expected, in the longer poems. In *The Demon* and *The Novice* almost
each section ends with an example. From *The Demon:*

> И всё, что пред собой он видел,
> Он презирал иль ненавидел.

And everything that he saw before him | He despised or hated.

Or:

> Забыть? — забвенья не дал Бог,
> Да он и не взял бы забвенья!..

*To forget? God has not given forgetfulness, | And he would not
have accepted it.*

and from *The Novice:*

> И я, как жил, в земле чужой
> Умру рабом и сиротой.

And I, as I lived, in an alien land | Will die a slave and an orphan.

This feature of Lermontov's method has an effect on his use of
language: the search for terse, aphoristic formulations occasionally
brings about a blurring of semantic values when the meaning of a

word becomes secondary to the effect which it produces in its context. Thus the demon describes his condition to Tamara with the line:

Всегда жалеть и не желать,

Always to regret and never to desire,

where the structure of the line, with the opposition heightened by the use of almost identical verbs, leads one to expect a similar opposition between the concepts. In fact, this does not exist, and the sense of the line is somewhat unclear. An example of a slightly different kind is the first line of the same poem:

Печальный Демон, дух изгнанья

The melancholy Demon, the spirit of exile

—an obvious imitation of Pushkin's line:

Дух отрицанья, дух сомненья

Spirit of negation, spirit of doubt

in the poem *Angel*. But whereas Pushkin's meaning is clear, Lermontov's, through the change in quality of the noun in the genitive, is ambiguous, even not readily comprehensible. A similar obscurity of meaning occurs occasionally, especially in Lermontov's more rhetorical poems, when the poet heightens the emotion of individual lines. His famous poem on Pushkin's death, *The Poet's Death* (*Smert' poeta*) (1837), provides an example:

А вы, надменные потомки
Известной подлостью прославленных отцов,
Пятою рабскою поправшие обломки
Игрою счастия обиженных родов!

And you, the arrogant descendants | Of fathers, famed for their well-known baseness, | You, who have spurned with your slavish heel the debris | Of families insulted by the fickleness of fortune!

Here the actual sense of the lines is obscured by the sheer weight of the invective concentrated in them.

When one turns from Lermontov's poetic method to an examination of the content of his works, it soon becomes apparent that the poet is employing a very narrow range of ideas and emotions; he is constantly reworking the same material, striving to express it in a more finished, more convincing form. It is this characteristic which leads to the repetition of certain images and descriptions. And the subject of Lermontov's verse, almost without exception, is the personality of the poet himself. As Eykhenbaum puts it in his excellent work on Lermontov, the poet's method leads to 'the transformation of the lyric into a pathetic confession, the heightening and intensification of the personal element, the creation of a special "I", which regards the whole universe from the point of view of its own fate, and makes of its fate a universal problem.'[1]

The prevailing mood of Lermontov's verse is one of disillusion, melancholy, world-weariness. Indeed, it often seems that only death can provide him with an escape from the agony of existence:

> Оборвана цепь жизни молодой,
> Окончен путь, бил час, пора домой,
> Пора туда, где будущего нет,
> Ни прошлого, ни вечности, ни лет;
> Где нет ни ожиданий, ни страстей,
> Ни горьких слез, ни славы, ни честей;
> Где воспоминанье спит глубоким сном
> И сердце в тесном доме гробовом
> Не чувствует, что червь его грызет.

The chain of young life is broken, | The journey is ended, the hour has struck, it is time to leave, | Time to go where there is no future, | No past, no eternity, no years; | Where there are no expectations, no passions, | No bitter tears, no fame, no honour; | Where memory sleeps deeply | And the heart in its narrow coffin home | Does not feel the worm gnawing it. (Death: Smert', 1830 or 1831)

The problem which obsesses the poet, the cause of his pessimism, is the sense of his own isolation, his alienation from society. The basic pattern of his verse is antithetical: on the one hand stands the poet, or lyric hero; on the other society, the rest of mankind. And it is by a

---

[1] Eykhenbaum, *Lermontov*, p. 61.

study of the way in which Lermontov treats these two subjects that one can, perhaps, best arrive at an understanding of his work.

> ...человек, сей царь над общим злом,
> С коварным сердцем, с ложным языком...

...man, this ruler over general evil, | With a perfidious heart, with a lying tongue...

In these two lines from an early poem, *The Cemetery* (*Kladbishche*) (1830), Lermontov expresses a view of man and society which is to be constantly repeated. Certain key words and phrases recur time and again. Man is *kovarnyy* [perfidious]; his words are *kleveta* [slander, calumny]. A poem addressed to the memory of the Decembrist poet A. I. Odoevsky contains the lines:

> Пускай забудет свет
> Столь чуждое ему существованье:
> Зачем тебе венцы его вниманья
> И терния пустых его клевет?
> Ты не служил ему. Ты с юных лет
> Коварные его отвергнул цепи...

Let society forget | An existence which was so alien to it: | What good to you are the wreaths of its attention | And the thorns of its empty slanders? | You have not served it. From your youth you | Rejected its perfidious chains... (*In Memory of A. I. O.: Pamyati A. I. O.*, 1839)

Society is superficial, worthless, and, above all, false:

> ...этот свет,
> Где носит всё печать проклятья,
> Где полны ядом все объятья,
> Где счастья без обмана нет.

...this society, | Where everything bears the stamp of damnation, | Where all embraces are full of poison, | Where there is no happiness without deceit. (*January 1831: 1831-go yanvarya, 1831*)

176

The poet's vision enables him to:

> Невольно узнавать повсюду
> Под гордой важностью лица
> В мужчине глупого льстеца
> И в каждой женщине — Иуду.

Involuntarily recognize everywhere | Beneath a face's proud importance | In a man a stupid flatterer | And in every woman—a Judas. (What is the point of living!: Chto tolku zhit'!, 1832)

Lermontov's indignation with society is primarily a moral one:

> В очах людей читаю я
> Страницы злобы и порока,

In people's eyes I read | Pages of malice and sin.

he writes in *The Prophet* (*Prorok*) (1841), and, in a poem written ten years earlier, contrasts the evil of man with the innocence of nature in the lines:

> ...этот снег, летучий, серебристый
> И для страны порочной слишком чистый...

...this snow, flying, silvery | And too pure for a sinful land... (Fair are you, fields of my native land: Prekrasny vy, polya zemli rodnoy..., 1831)

He views society, civilization, even man in general terms, not only as corrupt, but also as inevitably corrupting. In a series of allegorical poems—*The Three Palm-trees* (*Tri pal'my*) (1839), *The Sea Princess* (*Morskaya tsarevna*) (1841), *The Quarrel* (*Spor*) (1841)—he shows how man's activity must lead to the destruction of the beauties of nature, and sums up his views on the contrast between nature and man in the thoughts of a Russian soldier after an engagement in the Caucasus:

> Окрестный лес, как бы в тумане,
> Синел в дыму пороховом.
> А там вдали грядой нестройной,
> Но вечно гордой и спокойной,
> Тянулись горы — и Казбек
> Сверкал главой остроконечной.

И с грустью тайной и сердечной
Я думал: 'Жалкий человек.
Чего он хочет!.. небо ясно,
Под небом места много всем,
Но беспрестанно и напрасно
Один враждует он — зачем?'

The surrounding forest, as though in a mist, | Was blue in the powder smoke. | But there, far off, in a disordered ridge, | Which was yet eternally proud and calm, | Stretched the mountains— and Kazbek | Gleamed with its sharp peak. | And with secret, heartfelt sorrow | I thought: 'Pitiable man. | What does he want! The sky is clear, | Beneath it there is much room for all, | But constantly and vainly | He alone wages war—why?' (I am writing to you... Ya k vam pishu..., 1840)

In opposition to society stands the figure of the lyric hero, the poet himself, constantly represented—explicitly or implicitly—in terms which emphasize his isolation.

He sees himself as a boat, or a sailor, cast away on a furious sea, a prey to the storms of fate; as a lonely tree over an abyss:

Я одинок над пропастью стою,
Где всё мое подавлено судьбою;
Так куст растет над бездною морскою,
И лист, грозой оборванный, плывет
По произволу странствующих вод.

I stand alone above the abyss, | Where everything that is mine has been crushed by fate; | So a tree grows over the abyss of the sea, | And a leaf, torn off by a storm, floats | At the mercy of the wandering waves. (Give me your hand, lean on the poet's breast: Day ruku mne, sklonis' k grudi poeta, 1830 or 1831)

or as a cliff, proudly indifferent to the rest of mankind:

Укор невежд, укор людей
Души высокой не печалит;
Пускай шумит волна морей,
Утес гранитный не повалит...

The reproaches of the ignorant or of men | Do not grieve the lofty soul; | Let the sea wave roar, | It will not bring down the granite cliff. (I do not wish the world to know...: Ya ne khochu, chtob svet uznal..., 1837)

The figure of Napoleon occurs with some frequency in Lermontov's verse—from the early poem *Napoleon* (1829) to *The Last House-warming (Poslednee novosel'e)* (1841). And it is obvious that the poet regards him as an ideal, another symbol for his own existence. Though he believes that his own fame will equal Napoleon's:

> Я рожден, чтоб целый мир был зритель
> Торжества иль гибели моей...

I was born, so that the whole world could be a spectator | Of my triumph or my doom... (Fate brought us together by chance...: My sluchayno svedeny sud'boyu..., 1832)

for him the emperor is primarily a man who, like himself, has been rejected and betrayed by his fellow-countrymen. He reproaches the French bitterly:

> Как женщина, ему вы изменили
> И, как рабы, вы предали его!

Like a woman, you were unfaithful to him | And, like slaves, you betrayed him! (The Last House-warming: Poslednee novosel'e, 1841)

and in another poem he writes:

> Порочная страна не заслужила,
> Чтобы великий жизнь окончил в ней,

The sinful land did not deserve, | That the great man should end his life in it. (St. Helena: Sv. Elena, 1831)

echoing the condemnation of Russia quoted earlier:

> ...этот снег, летучий, серебристый
> И для страны порочной слишком чистый...

...this snow, flying, silvery | And too pure for a sinful land... (Fair are you, fields of my native land...: Prekrasny vy, polya zemli rodnoy..., 1831)

179

In Lermontov's verse Napoleon is never the triumphant emperor, he is always the 'gloomy exile' of St. Helena:

> Изгнанник мрачный, жертва вероломства
> И рока прихоти слепой,
> Погиб как жил — без предков и потомства,
> Хоть побежденный, но герой!

The gloomy exile, a victim of treachery | And the blind caprice of fate, | Perished as he lived—without ancestors or descendants, | Conquered, but a hero! (St. Helena: Sv. Elena, 1831)

he writes, and repeats the image in *The Last House-warming*, written on the occasion of the return of Napoleon's body to France, where he refers to the:

> ...хладный прах
> Погибшего давно среди немых страданий
> В изгнаньи мрачном и цепях...

...the cold ashes | Of him who perished long ago in silent suffering, | In gloomy exile and in chains...

It is this concept of exile which perhaps expresses most forcibly the poet's sense of alienation from the rest of society. He constantly describes himself, or his hero, as an exile, cast out by society, or voluntarily fleeing its deceit and falsity.

> Коварной жизнью недовольный,
> Обманут низкой клеветой,
> Летел изгнанник самовольный
> В страну Италии златой.

Dissatisfied with the perfidious life, | Deceived by base slanders, | The voluntary exile flew | Into the golden land of Italy. (Romance: Romans, 1829)

he writes on the departure of the poet Shevyrev from Russia. The words *izgnannik* [exile], *izgnanie* [banishment, exile], recur time and again:

> Как жалок тот...
> Кто рано свет узнал — и с страшной пустотой,
> Как я, оставил брег земли своей родной
> Для добровольного изгнанья!

180

How pitiable is he... | Who became acquainted early with society—and with a terrible void, | Left, like I, the shores of his native land | For voluntary exile! (*Elegy: Elegiya, 1830*)

or:

> Послушай! вспомни обо мне,
> Когда, законом осужденный,
> В чужой я буду стороне —
> Изгнанник мрачный и презренный...

Listen! Remember me, | When, condemned by law, | I will be in a strange country— | A gloomy and despised exile... (*Listen! Remember me...: Poslushay! Vspomni obo mne...*, 1831)

And here, with the phrase 'gloomy exile', the poet identifies his fate with that of Napoleon.

The heroes of Lermontov's longer poems are almost without exception exiles, outcasts from society. The robber-hero of *The Criminal* (*Prestupnik*) (1829) describes himself, like Lermontov, as a *izgnannik svoevol'nyy* [a voluntary exile];

> И здесь, в сей бездне, в северных горах,
> Зароют мой изгнаннический прах,

And here, in this abyss, in the northern mountains, | They will bury my exile's ashes. (*Julio: Dzhyulio, 1830*)

laments Julio; Vadim (*The Last Son of Freedom* (*Posledniy syn vol'nosti*), 1830 or 31) is an exile from his native Novgorod; the hero of *The Novice* an exile from his native village; Izmail-Bey, in the poem of the same name (1832), is rejected both by the Russian society he adopts and by his Caucasian fellow-tribesmen; and, finally, Lermontov's demon, the *dukh izgnan'ya* [spirit of exile], cast out from heaven and despising humanity, is doomed to an eternal existence *mezhdu nebom i zemley* [between heaven and earth].

Lermontov himself was exiled twice, in 1837 and 1841; but his fascination, indeed his obsession with the concept of exile, which he employs again and again, as theme and image in his work, long predates his experience of it, while references to his own physical exile are far outnumbered by those to an imaginary spiritual one.

Confronted by a society which rejects him, and which he despises, the poet rejects it in his turn; he retires within himself, refusing even

181

his verse to mankind, for he knows that its message will inevitably be distorted:

> К чему толпы неблагодарной
> Мне злость и ненависть навлечь,
> Чтоб бранью назвали коварной
> Мою пророческую речь?

Why should I attract the ungrateful crowd's | Anger and hatred, | In order that they might give the name of perfidious abuse | To my prophetic words? (The Journalist, the Reader and the Writer: Zhurnalist, chitatel' i pisatel', 1840)

But society is not only false and superficial in itself, its corruption has also tainted the poet: in contact with it he has lost his former innocence and ideals:

> Готов лобзать уста друзей был я,
> Не посмотрев, не скрыта ль в них змея.
> Но в общество иное я вступил,
> Узнал людей и дружеский обман,
> Стал подозрителен и погубил
> Беспечности душевной талисман.

I was ready to kiss the mouths of my friends, | Without looking to see whether a snake was concealed in them. | But I entered another society, | Became acquainted with people and the deceit of friends, | Became suspicious and destroyed | The talisman of spiritual carelessness. (1830. 15 July: 1830 god. Iyulya 15-go, 1830)

His denunciations of it are thus doubly vehement, for it is doubly guilty; and his exile too, like that of his demon, is a double one: he can neither accept his present state, nor return to his former one.

It is from this view of his progress through life that there springs that sense of irredeemable loss, of irrevocable exile which pervades Lermontov's work.

> К чему творец меня готовил,
> Зачем так грозно прекословил
> Надеждам юности моей?..

For what did the creator prepare me, | Why did he so terribly contradict | The hopes of my youth?... (My future is in darkness...: Moe gryadushchee v tumane..., 1837) he asks, and, seeking his lost youth, turns constantly to the past, away from the present, which can only be a pale reflection of his former life:

> Нет, не тебя так пылко я люблю,
> Не для меня красы твоей блистанье:
> Люблю в тебе я прошлое страданье
> И молодость погибшую мою.

No, it is not you I love so ardently, | The glitter of your beauty is not for me: | I love in you my past suffering | And my perished youth. (No, it is not you I love so ardently...: Net, ne tebya tak pylko ya lyublyu..., 1841)

His heroes strive unceasingly to escape their condition, to regain the paradise from which they have fallen:

> Хочу я с небом примириться,
> Хочу любить, хочу молиться,
> Хочу я веровать добру.

I want to reconcile myself with heaven, | I want to love, I want to pray, | I want to believe in good.

cries the demon. But he cannot deny his nature: his kiss is poisonous, and Tamara dies, leaving him:

> Один, как прежде, во вселенной
> Без упованья и любви!..

Alone, as before, in the universe | Without hope and without love!..

Similarly, the hero of *The Novice* discovers that his monastic up-bringing has made it impossible for him to lead the primitive, innocent life of his kinsmen, those Caucasian tribesmen whom he hopes to find after his flight from the monastery:

> Напрасно грудь
> Полна желаньем и тоской:
> То жар бессильный и пустой,
> Игра мечты, болезнь ума.
> На мне печать свою тюрьма
> Оставила... Таков цветок

Темничный: вырос одинок
И бледен он меж плит сырых,
И долго листьев молодых
Не распускал, всё ждал лучей
Живительных. И много дней
Прошло, и добрая рука
Печалью тронулась цветка,
И был он в сад перенесен,
В соседство роз. Со всех сторон
Дышала сладость бытия...
Но что ж? Едва взошла заря,
Палящий луч ее обжег
В тюрьме воспитанный цветок...

In vain my breast | Is full of desire and longing: | This is a power-less, empty fervour, | A freakish dream, a sickness of the mind. | On me its imprint prison | Has left...Such is a flower | In a dungeon: it grew lonely | And pale between damp flagstones, | And for a long time young leaves | Did not grow, it continually awaited invigorating rays. | And many days | Passed, and a kind hand | Touched with pity the flower, | And it was moved into the garden, | Into the neighbourhood of roses. From every side | Breathed the sweetness of existence... | But what happened? Scarcely had the dawn arisen | When its fiery ray burnt | The flower brought up in prison.

And Lermontov himself, though finding, at times, momentary consolation in nature or in his art, is forced to realize that it is only momentary. Society has left as deep an imprint on him as the monastery has on the novice. All attempts to escape his fate are in vain: he can never recover what he has lost. Scorched, like his hero, by the pitiless sun, he can hope for a new life only in death:

Земле я отдал дань земную
Любви, надежд, добра и зла;
Начать готов я жизнь другую,
Молчу и жду: пора пришла;
Я в мире не оставлю брата,
И тьмой и холодом объята

184

Душа усталая моя;
Как ранний плод, лишенный сока,
Она увяла в бурях рока
Под знойным солнцем бытия.

To the earth I gave the earthly tribute | Of love, hopes, good and evil; | I am ready to begin another life, | I am silent and wait: the time has come; | I shall leave no brother in this world, | And dark and cold embrace | My tired soul; | Like a premature fruit, deprived of sap, | It withered in the storms of fate | Under the burning sun of existence. (I look upon the future with fear...: Glyazhu na budushchnost' s boyazn'yu..., 1838)

TYUTCHEV

Tyutchev has been called: 'a union of two opposites: romanticism and baroque',[1] and it is true that, from a formal point of view, his verse often seems to have more in common with that of his eighteenth-century predecessors—and especially Derzhavin—than with that of his contemporaries of the nineteenth century. His poems are full of lexical archaisms, such as: *vvyspr'* [upwards], *tolikiy* [such], *dnes'* [today], *podnes'* [to this day], *ogn'* [fire], *bregi* [banks], *zrak* [vision], *dobliy* [brave], *dkhnoven'e* [breath]. Occasionally, as Tynyanov points out,[2] he will make use of an archaism humorously, with comic intent, as in a poem on the opening of the Suez canal in 1869, where the festivities in Turkey are described in a parody of an eighteenth-century ode:

Пушек гром и *мусикия*!
Здесь Европы всей привал,
Здесь все силы мировые
Свой справляют карнавал.

Thunder of cannon and music! | Here is a concourse of all Europe, | Here all the world powers | Are celebrating their carnival. (Contemporary: Sovremennoe, 1869)

[1] Pumpyansky, 'Poeziya F. I. Tyutcheva', *Uraniya. Tyutchevskiy al'manakh*, p. 57.
[2] Tynyanov, 'Vopros o Tyutcheve', p. 379.

but in another context will employ a related form in a mood of high seriousness:

> Певучесть есть в морских волнах,
> Гармония в стихийных спорах,
> И стройный *мусикийский* шорох
> Струится в зыбких камышах.

There is melody in the sea waves, | Harmony in the strife of elements, | And a graceful musical rustle | Flows through the swaying reeds. (There is melody in the sea waves...: Pevuchest' est' v morskikh volnakh..., 1865)

And it is this latter use which is more typical of Tyutchev's verse: his archaisms are not an affectation, but come to him naturally and unforcedly. He often employs a sustained, rhetorical high style, as in the poem *Day and Night (Den' i noch')* (1839):

> День — сей блистательный покров —
> День, земнородных оживленье,
> Души болящей исцеленье,
> Друг человеков и богов!

Day is this shining cover | Day, the quickener of the earthborn, | The healer of the ailing soul, | The friend of men and gods.

One might note in this stanza the typically eighteenth-century use of metonymy (*zemnorodnykh ozhivlen'e*—quickener of the earth-born), a device Tyutchev uses with some frequency in his verse: *Pernatykh pesn' po roshche razdalasya* [The song of the feathered [birds] resounded in the grove]; *Vysokyy dub, perunami srazhennyy* [The tall oak, struck by gods of lightning]; *Metalla golos pogrebal'nyy* [The funereal voice of metal] (compare Derzhavin's *Glagol vremen! metalla zvon!*—Word of time! Sound of metal!—which also refers to a bell).

Tyutchev's word order, too, exhibits archaic traits: a noun is often placed between two dependent adjectives, as in *Prestupnyy lepet i shal'noy* [Criminal prattle and crazy]; *Vselenskiy den' i pravoslavnyy* [A universal day and orthodox]; *Zheleznyy mir i dyshashchiy | Veleniem odnim* [An iron world and breathing / With one command].

The extension of this device to the sentence, when a word or phrase is removed from its normal position and placed between grammatically connected elements, gives the poet's style a Latinate flavour and, occasionally, leads to obscurities of meaning as in:

> Есть некий час в ночи всемирного молчанья...

There is a certain hour of universal silence in the night...

or:

> И осененный опочил / Хоругвью горести народной...

And he rested, shaded by the banner of popular grief...

or:

> Лишь Музы девственную душу / В пророческих тре-
> вожат боги снах!

Only the virginal soul of the Muse / Do the gods disturb with prophetic dreams!

Perhaps the most obvious characteristic of Tyutchev's style, however, and one which emphasizes his debt to eighteenth-century verse, is his use of compound and composite adjectives.

He employs a number of archaic compound adjectives: *iskrometnyy* [spark-throwing], *gromokipyashchiy* [thunder-seething], *ognetsvetnyy* [fiery-coloured], *zhivotrepetnyy* [live-quivering], *zlatotkanyy* [gold-embroidered], *shirokokrylyy* [wide-winged], *pyshnostruynyy* [luxurious-streaming], *edinokrovnyy* [consanguineous] etc. His predilection for this form is well illustrated when he chooses to translate the lines from Schiller's poem 'Das Siegesfest':

> Pallas, die die Städte gründet
> Und zertrümmert, ruft er an,

as:

> Градозиждущей Палладе,
> Градорушащей молясь...

Pallas, who founds cities / And destroys them, he invokes. (The Funeral Feast: Pominki, 1851)

Tyutchev's use of composite adjectives is more individual. If one examines composite adjectives in the work of an eighteenth-century writer such as Derzhavin, an obvious influence on the later poet, it can be seen that the most frequent type is that in which two colour adjectives are combined, as in: *krasno-rozovyy* [red-pink], *srebro-rozovyy* [silver-pink], *cherno-ognennyy* [black-fiery], *safiro-svetlyy* [sapphire-radiant], *sizo-yantarnyy* [gray-amber] etc. A much smaller group is formed by those composite adjectives which unite non-colour epithets. Examples of this type, again from Derzhavin's poems, are: *nezhno-strastnyy* [tender-passionate], *svyashchenno-vdokhnovennyy* [sacred-inspired], *zhelezno-kamennyy* [iron-stone].

In Tyutchev's work, however, the proportions are reversed: composite colour adjectives are far outnumbered by those of the second type, and, furthermore, Tyutchev's coinages, in both types, tend to differ radically from those of his predecessor.

Derzhavin, in combining two adjectives, almost always chooses them from the same semantic group: *krasno-rozovyy*, *nezhno-strastnyy*. His aim is to define a particular shade of colour, to specify an object or an emotion by detailing it more exactly. And although composite adjectives of this kind are met with in Tyutchev's work, those which are most characteristic of his style are of a very different kind.

He combines adjectives from different semantic groups, and describes by contrast, rather than similarity. His colour adjectives are far more impressionistic than those met with in Derzhavin's verse: Tyutchev strives to convey the effect of the colour on the poet, the emotion it arouses within him. Simple combinations of two colours are replaced by composite adjectives such as: *tusklo-rdyanyy* [dull-red], *pyshno-zolotoy* [luxurious-golden], *pasmurno-bagrovyy* [cloudy-purple], *tumanisto-belyy* [misty-white] etc.

In the other, and by far the larger, group of composite adjectives, Tyutchev, although he sometimes employs conventional combinations—*mladencheski-zhivoy* [childish-lively], *mladencheski-bespechnyy* [childish-carefree], *nezabvenno-dorogoy* [unforgettable-dear]—more often and more typically unites seemingly disparate adjectives to produce not only a striking and, at times, almost paradoxical effect, but also, as it were, a synthesis of the two concepts rather than a refinement of one of them. Some examples are: *pritvorno-bespechnyy* [feigned-carefree], *prorocheski-proshchal'nyy* [prophetic-valedictory], *prorocheski-slepoy* [prophetic-blind], *nezrimo-rokovoy* [unseen-fatal], *blazhenno-rokovoy* [blessed-fatal], *blazhenno-ravnodushnyy* [blessed-indifferent], *volshebno-nemoy* [magic-dumb], *plamenno-chudesnyy* [ardent-miraculous], *tselomudrenno-svobodnyy* [chaste-free], *udushlivo-zemnoy* [stifling-earthly], *usypitel'no-bezmolvnyy* [soporific-silent], *gordo-boyazlivyy* [proud-timid].

The mode of thought implicit in this stylistic device seems central to Tyutchev's work as a whole. In a number of poems he, as it were, expands the device over the complete work. An example is *The Fountain* (*Fontan*) (1836):

> Смотри, как облаком живым
> Фонтан сияющий клубится;
> Как пламенеет, как дробится
> Его на солнце влажный дым.
> Лучом поднявшись к небу, он
> Коснулся высоты заветной —
> И снова пылью огнецветной
> Ниспасть на землю осужден.
>
> О смертной мысли водомет,
> О водомет неистощимый!
> Какой закон непостижимый
> Тебя стремит, тебя мятет?
> Как жадно к небу рвешься ты!..
> Но длань незримо-роковая,
> Твой луч упорный преломляя,
> Свергает в брызгах с высоты.

Look, how—a living cloud— | The shining fountain swirls; | How flames and scatters | Its moist smoke in the sun. | Having risen like a ray to heaven, it | Has touched the sacred height— | And again in fiery-coloured dust | Is fated to fall back to earth.
O fountain of mortal thought, | O inexhaustible fountain! | What incomprehensible law | Drives you, crushes you? | How thirstily you strive towards heaven!... | But an unseen fatal hand, | Refracting your stubborn ray, | Hurls it down in spray from the height.

Here once again two disparate concepts, each of which defines the other, have been linked together, but have been developed from adjectives into stanzas.

In addition, we find this same approach expressed not only as hitherto, formally, but also thematically in that series of contrasts, oppositions and dichotomies which give Tyutchev's thought its profoundly dualistic nature.

As many critics have pointed out, Tyutchev views life as split between, on the one hand, the dark primordial forces of chaos and disorder, and, on the other, the realm of light, harmony and order. These two worlds are often symbolized by the alternation of day and night, as in the poems *Day and Night* (*Den' i noch'*) (1839) and *Holy night has risen into the sky...* (*Svyataya noch' na nebosklon vzoshla...*) (1850). Both poems make use of the same imagery: day is visualized as a woven cloth of gold which temporarily conceals the dark, mysterious and unknowable abysses of the night:

> На мир таинственный духов,
> Над этой бездной безымянной,
> Покров наброшен златотканый
> Высокой волею богов.

Over the mysterious world of spirits, | Over this nameless abyss | A gold-embroidered veil has been thrown | By the exalted will of the gods. (*Den' i noch'*)

and:

> Святая ночь на небосклон взошла,
> И день отрадный, день любезный
> Как золотой покров она свила,
> Покров, накинутый над бездной.
> И, как виденье, внешний мир ушел...
> И человек, как сирота бездомный,
> Стоит теперь, и немощен и гол,
> Лицом к лицу пред пропастию темной.

Holy night has risen into the sky, | And comforting day, kind day | It has rolled up like a golden cloth, | A cloth, thrown over the abyss. | And, like an apparition, the outer world has departed... | And man, like a homeless orphan, | Now stands, powerless and naked, | Face to face with the dark abyss.

In opposition to the world of chaos stands the ordered cosmos: the harmony and beauty of nature. But its existence is a precarious one;

the day is not necessarily sacrosanct; even here the dark and disruptive forces can break in, as in the poem *Mal'aria* (1830), in which the same image is employed again, in slightly different form. Here the beauty of Rome, the purity and clarity of nature are revealed to be but a screen masking the inevitable approach of death:

> Как ведать, может быть, и есть в природе звуки,
> Благоухания, цвета и голоса,
> Предвестники для нас последнего часа́
> И усладители последней нашей муки.
> И ими-то Судеб посланник роковой,
> Когда сынов Земли из жизни вызывает,
> Как тканью легкою свой образ прикрывает,
> Да утаит от них приход ужасный свой!

Who knows, perhaps there are sounds in nature, | Fragrances, colours and voices, | Heralds for us of the final hour | And sweeteners of our final torture. | And by means of them the fatal messenger of Fate, | When he summons the sons of Earth from life, | Covers his image as with a light veil, | In order to conceal from them his terrible arrival!

In *The Italian Villa* (*Ital'yanskaya villa*) (1837) the beauty and tranquillity of the day are again shattered by the incursion of an alien force, but here the contagion, the *tainstvennoe Zlo* [mysterious Evil] of the other poem has been personified as the *zlaya zhizn'* [evil life] of the guilty lovers, whose arrival disturbs the peace of the abandoned villa, once constructed by man, but now taken over by nature and absorbed into its harmony:

> И мы вошли...всё было так спокойно!
> Так всё от века мирно и темно!..
> Фонтан журчал... Недвижимо и стройно
> Соседний кипарис глядел в окно.
>
> Вдруг всё смутилось: судорожный трепет
> По ветвям кипарисным пробежал, —
> Фонтан замолк — и некий чудный лепет,
> Как бы сквозь сон, невнятно прошептал.

Что это, друг? Иль злая жизнь недаром,
Та жизнь, — увы! — что в нас тогда текла,
Та злая жизнь, с ее мятежным жаром,
Через порог заветный перешла?

And we entered…everything was so tranquil! | So peaceful and dark was everything from time!… | The fountain murmured… Immobile and graceful | The neighbouring cypress looked in at the window.

Suddenly everything was agitated: a convulsive shudder | Ran along the cypress branches,— | The fountain fell silent—and some strange babble, | As if through sleep, whispered incoherently.

What is it, friend? Could it be that not for nothing has the evil life, | That life,—alas!—which then flowed in us, | That evil life, with its turbulent heat, | Has crossed the sacred threshold?

For Tyutchev man, like the universe, is split between the forces of light and those of darkness; his spiritual strivings align him with the former; his passions, his sensuality with the latter:

> Пускай страдальческую грудь
> Волнуют страсти роковые —
> Душа готова, как Мария,
> К ногам Христа навек прильнуть.

Though my suffering breast | Is excited by fatal passions— | My soul is ready, like Mary, | To cleave forever to the feet of Christ. (O my prophetic soul!..: O veshchaya dusha moya!.., 1855)

he writes, and this rift in his personality is often symbolized by another contrast: that between the valley and the heights, as in the following poem written in 1861:

> Хоть я и свил гнездо в долине,
> Но чувствую порой и я,
> Как животворно на вершине
> Бежит воздушная струя, —
> Как рвется из густого слоя,
> Как жаждет горних наша грудь,
> Как всё удушливо-земное
> Она хотела б оттолкнуть!

Although I too wove my nest in the valley, | *Sometimes I also feel* | *How invigoratingly on the summit* | *Rushes the airy stream,—* | *How our breast strains to escape from this thick layer,* | *How it thirsts for the heights,* | *How all that is suffocatingly earthly* | *It would like to spurn!* (*Although I too wove my nest...; Khot' ya i svil gnezdo...*)

He experiences in agonizing fashion this conflict between the Dionysian and the Apollonian within himself, and envies those who have never known this lack of inner unity, writing, for example, in memory of the poet Zhukovsky:

> В нем не было ни лжи, ни раздвоенья —
> Он всё в себе мирил и совмещал.

In him there was no lie, no duality— | *He reconciled and combined all within himself.* (*In Memory of V. A. Zhukovsky: Pamyati V. A. Zhukovskogo, 1852*)

At times he feels the fatal attraction of the abyss, is drawn reluctantly towards night and chaos:

> О, страшных песен сих не пой
> Про древний хаос, про родимый!
> Как жадно мир души ночной
> Внимает повести любимой!
> Из смертной рвется он груди,
> Он с беспредельным жаждет слиться!..
> О, бурь заснувших не буди —
> Под ними хаос шевелится!..

O, do not sing those terrible songs | *About ancient, native chaos!* | *How avidly the world of the night soul* | *Listens to the loved story!* | *It longs to burst out of the mortal breast,* | *It thirsts to merge with the unbounded!..* | *O, do not awaken sleeping storms—* | *Under them chaos is stirring!* (*Of what do you wail, wind of the night?..: O chem ty voesh', vetr nochnoy?.., 1836*)

More often, however, the poet turns in the other direction,

towards the order and harmony of nature, the cosmos, which he views
pantheistically, as a manifestation of the divine:

> Не то, что мните вы, природа:
> Не слепок, не бездушный лик —
> В ней есть душа, в ней есть свобода,
> В ней есть любовь, в ней есть язык...

*Nature is not what you think: | Not a mould, not a soulless
image— | In her there is a soul, in her there is freedom, | In her
there is love, in her there is a tongue... (Nature is not what you
think...: Ne to, chto mnite vy, priroda..., 1836)*

He longs to submerge himself in it, to heal the rift within himself by
becoming part of a higher unity:

> Игра и жертва жизни частной!
> Приди ж, отвергни чувств обман
> И ринься, бодрый, самовластный,
> В сей животворный океан!
> Приди, струей его эфирной
> Омой страдальческую грудь —
> И жизни божеско-всемирной
> Хотя на миг причастен будь!

*Plaything and victim of private life! | Come, throw off the deceit
of feelings | And throw yourself, brisk and self-possessed, | Into
this revivifying ocean! | Come, with its ethereal stream | Lave
your suffering breast— | And with the divine-universal life |
Commune, if only for a moment! (Spring: Vesna, 1838)*

But the point of this quotation lies in the last line: the experience of
unity, if at all possible, can only be momentary; the poet can never
attain to full possession of this other existence, never become part of
the *zhizn' bozhesko-vsemirnaya* [divine-universal life], as he recognizes elsewhere, when he writes:

> ...не дано ничтожной пыли
> Дышать божественным огнем.

*...it is not given to the insignificant dust | To breathe the divine
fire. (The Gleam: Problesk, 1825)*

The limitation placed on man's aspirations is, in fact, a recurrent theme in Tyutchev's verse. It is the subject of *The Fountain*, quoted earlier, and of the poem *A buzzard has risen from the glade...* (*S polyany korshun podnyalsya...*) (1836), which can also be seen as an example of the same formal pattern:

> С поляны коршун поднялся,
> Высоко к небу он взвился;
> Всё выше, дале вьется он,
> И вот ушел за небосклон.
>
> Природа-мать ему дала
> Два мощных, два живых крыла —
> А я здесь в поте и в пыли,
> Я, царь земли, прирос к земли!..

A buzzard has risen from the glade, | High into the sky it has soared; | Ever higher and further it circles, | And has vanished beyond the horizon.
Mother nature gave it | Two powerful, living wings— | But I lie here in sweat and dust, | I, the emperor of the earth, am rooted to the earth!..

And here the contrast between earthbound man, ironically described as the *tsar' zemli* [emperor of the earth] and the soaring bird leads us on to another aspect of Tyutchev's view of the relationship between man and nature.

More often than not the poet is aware of himself, not as a part of the natural order, but rather as a discordant element within it, a view expressed most clearly in the poem *There is melody in the sea waves...* (*Pevuchest' est' v morskikh volnakh...*) (1865):

> Певучесть есть в морских волнах,
> Гармония в стихийных спорах,
> И стройный мусикийский шорох
> Струится в зыбких камышах.
>
> Невозмутимый строй во всем,
> Созвучье полное в природе, —
> Лишь в нашей призрачной свободе
> Разлад мы с нею сознаем.

Откуда, как разлад возник?
И отчего же в общем хоре
Душа не то поет, что море,
И ропщет мыслящий тростник?

There is melody in the sea waves, | Harmony in the strife of elements, | And a graceful musical rustle | Flows through the swaying reeds.
An imperturbable order in everything, | A full consonance in nature,— | Only in our phantom freedom | Are we conscious of discord with it.
Whence, and how did this discord arise? | And why in the general chorus | Does the soul not sing as the sea does, | And why does the thinking reed complain?

The answer to the poet's despairing question is given in the last line of the poem by the Pascalian image of man as *un roseau pensant*. It is man's capability for thought, his consciousness, that very quality which enables him to perceive himself as a dissonant chord in the harmony of nature, which is the cause of his inability to become part of it. For nature herself is sublimely unconscious of her own existence, and in this lies the essential difference between her and man. This concept is a key one in Tyutchev's thought: he returns to it again and again, amplifying and developing it.

Since the poet, man, is aware of his own existence, he strives to preserve and maintain it against the pressure of external forces, the strongest of which is time. For man lives in time, as well as in space. Indeed, his life only has significance in the past or the future, in the achieved or the potential, in what he was, or what he will be: he can never know the present. Nature, on the other hand, simply is, in the present; past and future have no meaning for her. Tyutchev draws the contrast in *Spring (Vesna)* (1838):

Не о былом вздыхают розы
И соловей в ночи поет;
Благоухающие слезы
Не о былом Аврора льет, —
И страх кончины неизбежной
Не свеет с древа ни листа:

196

Их жизнь, как океан безбрежный,
Вся в настоящем разлита.

Not of the past the roses sigh | Nor the nightingale sings in the night; | Fragrant tears | Aurora sheds not for the past,— | And the fear of the inevitable end | Does not blow a single leaf from the tree: | Their life, like the boundless ocean, | Is completely diffused in the present.

and, again, in two lines from the poem *From the life, that once raged here... (Ot zhizni toy, chto bushevala zdes')* (1871):

Природа знать не знает о былом,
Ей чужды наши призрачные годы...

Nature knows nothing of the past, | Our phantom years are alien to her...

The epithet *prizrachnyy* [phantom] in the second line introduces an image which often occurs in this context. The passing of time emphasizes the fragile, transient quality of man's life; it makes of it something insubstantial and wraithlike. We endeavour desperately to cling to our past:

Минувшее, как *призрак* друга,
Прижать к груди своей хотим...

The past, like the phantom of a friend, | We try to clasp to our bosom... (The Gleam: Problesk, 1825)

but the poet realizes how impossible of fulfilment this attempt is when he apostrophizes his former happiness in the lines:

О бедный *призрак*, немощный и смутный,
Забытого, загадочного счастья!..

O, poor phantom, powerless and dim, | Of forgotten, mysterious happiness!.. (So again I see you...: Itak, opyat' uvidelsya ya s vami..., 1849)

He knows that his physical existence must come to an end with death; but it is far more bitter to contemplate the thought that the very essence of his personality—his memories of the past—is doomed to oblivion and extinction:

> Как ни тяжел последний час —
> Та непонятная для нас
> Истома смертного страданья, —
> Но для души еще страшней
> Следить, как вымирают в ней
> Все лучшие воспоминанья...

However heavy the final hour may be— | That incomprehensible to us | Weariness of mortal suffering,— | For the soul it is yet more terrible | To trace, how in itself are dying out | All the best memories... (However heavy the final hour may be...: Kak ni tyazhel posledniy chas..., 1867)

Only nature is eternal: man cannot hope to preserve his individuality in the face of time, and will, eventually, leave no trace behind:

> Бесследно всё — и так легко не быть!
> При мне иль без меня — что нужды в том?
> Всё будет то ж — и вьюга так же выть,
> И тот же мрак, и та же степь кругом.

Nothing leaves a trace—and not to have been is so simple! | With me or without me—what is the difference? | Everything will be the same—the blizzard will howl in the same way, | The same dark, the same steppe on every side. (Brother, who accompanied me for so many years...: Brat, stol'ko let soputstvovavshiy mne..., 1870)

he writes, journeying back to St. Petersburg after the funeral, in Moscow, of his brother Nikolay, and he repeats this conclusion in *Look, how on the river expanse... (Smotri, kak na rechnom prostore...)* (1851):

> Смотри, как на речном просторе,
> По склону вновь оживших вод,
> Во всеобъемлющее море
> За льдиной льдина вслед плывет.

На солнце ль радужно блистая,
Иль ночью в поздней темноте,
Но все, неизбежимо тая,
Они плывут к одной мете.

Все вместе — малые, большие,
Утратив прежний образ свой,
Все — безразличны, как стихия, —
Сольются с бездной роковой!..

О нашей мысли обольщенье,
Ты, человеческое Я,
Не таково ль твое значенье,
Не такова ль судьба твоя?

Look, how on the river expanse, | Down the incline of the revived waters, | Into the all-embracing sea | Ice-floe follows ice-floe. Whether shining radiantly in the sun, | Or at night in the late darkness, | They all, inevitably melting, | Float towards one goal. All together—small, large, | Losing their previous form, | All—indifferent as the element,— | Will merge with the fatal abyss!... O delusion of our thought, | You, the human I, | Is not such your significance, | Is not such your fate?

And here, with the image of the all-engulfing *bezdna rokovaya* [fatal abyss], we return to the chaotic forces of the dark side of the universe.

For Tyutchev, however, time has a double significance. It is not only a force which obliterates the individual's consciousness of his past, and hence his own existence, but also one which makes him aware of the fact that he is but a part of the eternal cycle of death and renewal:

Как грустно полусонной тенью,
С изнеможением в кости,
Навстречу солнцу и движенью
За новым племенем брести!..

How sad it is as a sleepy shadow, | With exhaustion in one's bones, | Towards the sun and movement | To wander following a new generation!... (Like a little bird at early dawn...: Kak ptichka, ranneyu zarey..., 1836)

199

he writes, and brings the two concepts together in *Insomnia* (*Bessonnitsa*) (1829), in which the image of man's life as a wraith, *prizrak*, returns:

> И наша жизнь стоит пред нами,
> Как призрак, на краю земли,
> И с нашим веком и друзьями
> Бледнеет в сумрачной дали;
>
> И новое, младое племя
> Меж тем на солнце расцвело,
> А нас, друзья, и наше время
> Давно забвеньем занесло!

And our life stands before us, | *Like a phantom, on the edge of the earth,* | *And with our age and friends* | *Pales in the dusky distance; And a new young generation* | *Has since blossomed in the sun,* | *And we, friends, and our times* | *Have long been covered by oblivion!*

And in *I sit thoughtful and alone...* (*Sizhu zadumchiv i odin...*) (1836) he draws the parallel between man and his natural surroundings: generation follows generation, as crop follows crop:

> За годом год, за веком век...
> Что ж негодует человек,
>   Сей злак земной!..
> Он быстро, быстро вянет — так,
> Но с новым летом новый злак
>   И лист иной.

Year after year, century after century... | *Why does man rage,* | *This earthly crop!...* | *He quickly, quickly withers —so,* | *But with a new summer there is a new crop* | *And another leaf.*

One can, digressively, note that the image of this stanza illustrates both Tyutchev's closeness to Derzhavin, who writes:

> Едва увидел я сей свет,
> Уже зубами смерть скрежещет,
> Как молнией, косою блещет
> И дни мои, как злак, сечет.

Scarcely have I glimpsed this world, | Yet death already grinds his teeth, | Flashes his scythe like lightning, | And mows my days like a crop. (*On the Death of Prince Meshchersky: Na smert' knyazya Meshcherskogo, 1779*)

and at the same time, in the progress from simile to metaphor, the difference between the two poets.

Chto zh negoduet chelovek? [Why does man rage?] the poet asks. Why can he, realizing as he does the inevitability of his fate, not submit peacefully to it? The answer is, in essence, that given to the earlier question:

> ... отчего же в общем хоре
> Душа не то поет, что море,
> И ропщет мыслящий тростник?

...why in the general chorus | Does the soul not sing as the sea does, | And why does the thinking reed complain?

The parallel with the natural world is only partially true; it conceals a deeper contrast: because man, unlike nature, exists only through his consciousness of himself, he cannot accept without a struggle that his life should vanish without trace and he himself be succeeded by a new generation. *O vremya, pogodi!* [O Time, wait!] he cries in *So, there are moments in life... (Tak, v zhizni est' mgnoveniya...)* (1855): time must stop, the fleeting moment of life, symbolized by the ephemeral rainbow, must be held fast:

> Оно дано нам на мгновенье,
> Лови его — лови скорей!
> Смотри — оно уж побледнело,
> Еще минута, две — и что ж?
> Ушло, как то уйдет всецело,
> Чем ты и дышишь и живешь.

It is given us for a moment, | Catch it—catch it quickly! | Look— it has already faded, | Another minute or two—and what is there? | It has vanished, as all that will completely vanish, | By which you breathe and live.

he writes in *How unexpectedly and brightly... (Kak neozhidanno i yarko*...) (1865)—another poem with a structure similar to that of *The Fountain* and *A buzzard has risen from the glade*...

In this context the poet's longing to become one with nature, expressed in *Spring:*

> ...ринься, бодрый, самовластный,
> В сей животворный океан!

...throw yourself, brisk and self-possessed, | Into this revivifying ocean!

takes on an additional meaning: his divided self will be healed in the higher unity of the divine, and at the same time he will conquer the tyranny of time by becoming part of that life which:

> ...как океан безбрежный,
> Вся в настоящем разлита.

...like the boundless ocean, | Is completely diffused in the present.

Yet the attempt must always be in vain; his yearning for a higher existence is always checked, like the fountain's spray, by the *dlan' nezrimo-rokovaya* [unseen fatal hand].

Where the poet fails, however, the poem can succeed. The very cry of anguish in which he announces the impossibility of his attempt denies its own meaning through its existence as a work of art. And the form of many of Tyutchev's poems—brief, abrupt, almost interjectional, which begin *in medias res*, as though continuing an idea or train of thought:

> И распростясь с тревогою житейской...

And bidding farewell to the cares of life...

> Еще томлюсь тоской желаний...

Still I pine with yearnings of desire...

> Итак, опять увиделся я с вами...;

So, again I see you...

as exclamations:

> О вещая душа моя!..

O my prophetic soul!...

О, как на склоне наших лет...;

O, how as our years decline...

or as aphorisms:

Есть некий час в ночи всемирного молчанья...

There is a certain hour of universal silence in the night...

Две силы есть — две роковые силы...;

There are two forces—two fatal forces...

gives them the quality of fragments of emotion or thought which have escaped the flux of time.

Poetry can achieve this paradoxical triumph of form over content because, like nature, it is unaware of its own existence. To the poet, however, his own life must always appear evanescent and insubstantial. It is only when he turns his attention away from himself, towards the world which surrounds him, that he can fulfil his boast that:

Поэт всесилен, как стихия...

The poet is omnipotent, like an element... (*Do not believe the poet, maiden...: Ne ver', ne ver' poetu, deva..., 1839*)

and eternalize the present moment, as he does in his landscapes, those descriptions of the cold North, or hot, languid South, in which the earth's motion seems to be stopped, arrested by slumber:

Здесь, где так вяло свод небесный
На землю тощую глядит, —
Здесь, погрузившись в сон железный,
Усталая природа спит...

Here, where the vault of heaven so inertly | Gazes on the meagre land,— | Here, sunk in iron slumber, | Tired nature sleeps... (*Here, where the vault of heaven so inertly...: Zdes', gde tak vyalo svod nebesnyy..., 1830*)

Here life is frozen into immobility, while in *Noon* (*Polden'*) (1827–30)

203

the same effect is achieved, the instant prolonged to eternity, by the drowsy heat of the summer midday:

> Лениво дышит полдень мглистый;
> Лениво катится река;
> И в тверди пламенной и чистой
> Лениво тают облака.
>
> И всю природу, как туман,
> Дремота жаркая объемлет;
> И сам теперь великий Пан
> В пещере нимф покойно дремлет.

Lazily breathes the misty noon; | Lazily flows the river; | And in the fiery and pure firmament | Lazily melt the clouds.
And all nature, as if with a mist, | Is embraced in a warm drowsiness; | And now great Pan himself | Peacefully slumbers in the nymphs' cave.

The final triumph over time has been achieved: the god himself has been lulled to sleep by the poem.

FET

Fet has never been a very popular poet, nor one, indeed, who has received much critical attention. His work appeared in an age dominated by prose writers, while the aesthetic philosophy it embodied—with its complete and, as Fet himself put it, 'deplorable lack of civic grief',[1] of any social or political commitment—found no favour with the radical critics of the 1850s and 60s. Their views were crudely summed up by Pisarev in 1863, when he wrote: 'In time...Fet's work will be sold by weight for wallpapering rooms or wrapping up tallow candles...in this way it will, for the first time, serve some small practical use.'[2] The mainstream of Russian critical thought since has broadly followed the same line, with the result that Fet has been to a large extent ignored.

However, Fet has always been appreciated by poets, and especially

---

[1] Quoted in Eykhenbaum, *O poezii*, p. 396.
[2] Quoted in Fet, *Polnoe sobranie stikhotvoreniy*, p. 19.

by those who might be considered his immediate successors—the symbolists of the early twentieth century, on whom he exerted an influence comparable to that of no other writer.

Three symbolists in particular—Bal'mont (1867–1942), Bryusov (1873–1924) and Blok (1880–1921)—have affinities with Fet, but in each of them the legacy of the earlier poet takes on a different form.

For Bal'mont the attraction of Fet's verse lay in its verbal instrumentation, its alliteration and assonance. The effects obtained by Fet in poems such as *Storm in the evening sky... (Burya na nebe vechernem...)* (1842):

> Буря на небе вечернем,
> Моря сердитого шум —
> Буря на море и думы,
> Много мучительных дум —
> Буря на море и думы,
> Хор возрастающих дум —
> Черная туча за тучей,
> Моря сердитого шум.

Storm in the evening sky, | Sound of the angry sea— | Storm on the sea and thoughts, | Many torturing thoughts— | Storm on the sea and thoughts, | A chorus of rising thoughts— | Black cloud after cloud, | Sound of the angry sea.

were developed—even, occasionally, exaggerated—by Bal'mont in his own verse, as the following stanzas, written in the late 1890s, demonstrate:

> Я вольный ветер, я вечно вею,
> Волную волны, ласкаю ивы,
> В ветвях вздыхаю, вздохнув, немею,
> Лелею травы, лелею нивы.
>
> Весною светлой, как вестник мая,
> Целую ландыш, в мечту влюбленный,
> И внемлет ветру лазурь немая, —
> Я вею, млею, воздушный, сонный...

*I am the free wind, I blow eternally, | I ruffle the waves, I caress
the willows, | I sigh in the branches, and sighing fall silent, | I
cherish the grasses, cherish the cornfields.*
*In bright spring, like a herald of May, | In love with a dream, I kiss
the lily-of-the-valley, | And the speechless azure hears the
wind,— | I blow, I languish, airy, sleepy...*

Bal'mont himself emphasized the connection between his verse and
that of Fet when he wrote: 'This enchanter, this magician of verse was
Fet, whose name is like a spring garden, filled with the cries of joyful
birds. I exalt this radiant name as that of the herald of those phonetic
explorations and discoveries in verse which some decades later were
incarnated in the collections *Tishina* [*Calm*], *Goryashchie zdaniya*
[*Burning Buildings*], *Budem kak solntse* [*Let us be like the Sun*], and
which will continue in *Zarevo zor'* [*The Glow of Dawns*]'[1]—the titles
being those of four of his own works.

The verse of Valery Bryusov, on the other hand, except perhaps for
the interest it shows in technical experimentation, has very little in
common with that of Fet. It is true that contemporary critics such as
Vladimir Solov'ev claimed that Bryusov's earliest poems, which
purported to be written in the manner of French symbolist verse, in
fact owed much more to Fet and Heine. But the assertion was a
polemical one, and certainly cannot be made about Bryusov's later
verse.

Bryusov was drawn to Fet because he saw in him a poet who
believed, as he did, that art was an activity superior to all others, even
to life itself; and, consequently, that it should never be made the
instrument of any ideology.

> Быть может, всё в жизни лишь средство
> Для ярко-певучих стихов.

*Perhaps, everything in life is only a means | For brightly-singing
verses.* (*To the Poet: Poetu, 1907*)

he wrote. Further, he interpreted Fet's view of the poet's task as he
conceived it for himself: the poet should strive to incarnate those

[1] Bal'mont, *Poeziya kak volshebstvo*, Moscow, 1915, p. 85.

timeless moments of revelation, suprasensible intuition, which the human spirit most often achieves through love.

Since Bryusov is primarily interested in the philosophy he finds in Fet's work, those few verbal parallels which exist between the verse of the two poets occur, as might be expected, in poems of philosophical content. In *Tortured by life, by the deceit of hope...* (*Izmuchen zhizn'yu, kovarstvom nadezhdy...*) (1864?), for example, Fet writes:

И так прозрачна огней бесконечность,
И так доступна вся бездна эфира,
Что прямо *смотрю я из времени в вечность*
И пламя твое узнаю, солнце мира.

And the infinity of lights is so transparent, | And the whole abyss of the ether so accessible, | That I look *straight* out of time into eternity | *And recognize your flame, sun of the universe.*

This can be compared with the following lines from a poem by Bryusov, the subject of which is St John's revelations on Patmos:

Единый раз свершилось чудо:
Порвалась связь в волнах времен.
Он был меж нами и отсюда
Смотрел из мира в вечность он.

Once a miracle occurred: | The connection in the waves of time was broken. | He was among us and from there | He looked out of the world into eternity. (*Patmos, 1904*)

An identical mode of expression conveys an identical theme: both poems seek to describe a revelation, an escape from 'time into eternity' experienced by the poet and the prophet.

In this context it might also be noted that Bryusov, in his critical and theoretical writings, often uses phrases culled from Fet's poems as synonyms for his philosophical concepts. One such which occurs repeatedly is *golubaya tyur'ma* [the blue prison], an expression taken from Fet's poem *In Memory of N. Ya. Danilevsky (Pamyati N. Ya. Danilevskogo)* (1886):

Отдаваяся мысли широкой, доступной всему,
Ты успел оглядеть, полюбить голубую тюрьму.

Giving yourself to a broad idea, which all could attain, | You managed to examine, to love this blue prison.

and which in Bryusov's terminology is a metaphor for the world of
appearances, of phenomena as opposed to noumena.

Bryusov's view of Fet is one-sided, even, perhaps, distorted;
furthermore it reveals much more about his own personality and his
own verse than it does about Fet's. For once Bryusov is not the
objective critic he shows himself to be elsewhere. His attitude to Fet
is a deeply emotional one, which transcends, too, the relationship
implied when one speaks of the 'influence' of one writer upon
another. From Fet and his work Bryusov created an ideal image of the
poet and his task, an image which he strove to embody himself, in
his own work. It is no accident that, in a speech he made at the celebrations which marked his fiftieth birthday, after summing up the
achievements of his life, he chose to end with Fet's lines:

> Покуда на груди земной
> Хотя с трудом дышать я буду,
> Весь трепет жизни молодой
> Мне будет внятен отовсюду.

*Whilst on the earth's bosom | I still breathe, if with difficulty, | All
the tremors of young life | Will be audible to me from everywhere.
(I still love, still languish…: Eshche lyublyu, eshche tomlyus'…,
1890)*

While both Bal'mont and Bryusov were interested primarily in only
one aspect of Fet's work—Bal'mont in its euphonic qualities,
Bryusov in the philosophy he believed it expressed, in Blok's case the
links between his verse and that of his predecessor are more manifold
and various. 'Fet's work was once for me a guiding star', he wrote in
1919.[1]

Occasionally in Blok's earlier work one comes across a poem which
seems to be a variation on a theme first stated by Fet. An example is
*In a slow succession the autumn day descends… (Medlitel'noy chredoy
niskhodit den' osenniy…)* (1900):

> Медлительной чредой нисходит день осенний,
> Медлительно крутится желтый лист,
> И день прозрачно свеж, и воздух дивно чист —
> Душа не избежит невидимого тленья.

[1] Blok, *Sobranie sochineniy*, vol. 1, Moscow–Leningrad, 1960, p. 332.

Так, каждый день стареется она,
И каждый год, как желтый лист кружится,
Всё кажется, и помнится, и мнится,
Что осень прошлых лет была не так грустна.

*In a slow succession the autumn day descends, | Slowly revolves
the yellow leaf, | And the day is transparently cool, and the air is
miraculously pure— | The soul will not escape the unseen decay.
So, each day she grows older, | And each year, as the yellow leaf
descends, | It seems to her, she remembers, and thinks, | That the
autumn of past years was not so sad.*

This can be compared with the first stanza of Fet's poem *The fallen
leaf trembles from our movement*... (*Opavshiy list drozhit ot nashego
dvizhen'ya*...) (1891):

Опавший лист дрожит от нашего движенья,
Но зелени еще свежа над нами тень,
А что-то говорит средь радости сближенья,
Что этот желтый лист — наш следующий день.

*The fallen leaf trembles from our movement, | But the green
shade above us is still fresh, | And something tells us amidst the
joy of meeting, | That this yellow leaf is our next day.*

Blok's poem echoes Fet's in subject, image and metre (although he
introduces a variation characteristic of his verse: lines 1, 3, 4 and 8
have six feet, the remainder only five); he has developed what is in
fact a subsidiary theme in Fet's poem into a work in its own right.
More often the connection is less tangible: Fet's lines:

Я ждал. Невестою-царицей
Опять на землю ты сошла.
И утро блещет багряницей,
И всё ты воздаешь сторицей,
Что осень скудная взяла.

*I waited. As a bride and tsaritsa | You descended again to earth. |
And the morning shines with a purple robe, | And you give back a
hundredfold all, | That barren autumn took away. (I waited. As a
bride and tsaritsa...: Ya zhdal. Nevestoyu-tsaritsey..., 1860?)*

14   209

irresistibly point forward to Blok's *Verses about the Beautiful Lady*
(*Stikhi o Prekrasnoy Dame*), though not, perhaps, to any particular
poem of this cycle. And, as Bukhshtab has pointed out, certain
concepts which have a symbolic meaning for Fet, such as: *metel'*
[blizzard], *v'yuga* [snowstorm], *noch'* [night], *sumrak* [twilight], *zarya*
[dawn], *mgla* [mist], *vesna* [spring], are used by Blok in a very similar
fashion.[1]

The stanza quoted above illustrates the links between Blok and Fet
in another way. It exemplifies a structural pattern often employed by
Fet in the opening of a poem: the stanza is sub-divided into three
elements, which progressively increase in length. Here the relative
lengths are a quarter of a line; one and three-quarter lines; three
lines. The pattern is in fact met with far more often in four-line
stanzas, when the proportions are usually $\frac{1}{2}:1\frac{1}{2}:2$. Examples, from
Fet and Blok respectively, are:

> Ты вся в огнях. / Твоих зарниц
> И я сверканьями украшен; /
> Под сенью ласковых ресниц
> Огонь небесный мне не страшен.

*You are all in fires. Your summer lightnings | Deck me also with
glitter; | In the shadow of tender eyelashes | The heavenly fire does
not terrify me. (You are all in fires. Your summer lightnings...:
Ty vsya v ognyakh. Tvoikh zarnits..., 1886)*

> Уходит день. / В пыли дорожной
> Горят последние лучи. /
> Их красный отблеск непреложно
> Слился с огнем моей свечи.

*The day departs. In the dust of the road | The last rays burn. |
Their red reflection has irrevocably | Merged with the light of my
candle. (The day departs. In the dust of the road...: Ukhodit den'.
V pyli dorozhnoy..., 1902)*

The pattern occurs frequently in Blok's earlier work, but is more
rarely met with in later poems.

Perhaps the most interesting similarity between Fet and Blok can
be found in their creative method, the way in which they both move,

---

[1] Bukhshtab, 'A. A. Fet', p. 74.

in the course of a poem, between the literal and the figurative planes, between concrete and metaphorical situations.

An example of this technique in Fet's verse is the poem *Forgive me! In the mists of memory…* (*Prosti! vo mgle vospominan'ya…*) (1888):

> Прости! во мгле воспоминанья
> Всё вечер помню я один, —
> Тебя одну среди молчанья
> И твой пылающий камин.
>
> Глядя в огонь, я забывался,
> Волшебный круг меня томил,
> И чем-то горьким отзывался
> Избыток счастия и сил.
>
> Что за раздумие у цели?
> Куда безумство завлекло?
> В какие дебри и метели
> Я уносил твое тепло?
>
> Где ты? Ужель, ошеломленный,
> Кругом не видя ничего,
> Застывший, вьюгой убеленный,
> Стучусь у сердца твоего?..

Forgive me! In the mists of memory | I keep on remembering one evening,— | You alone in the silence | And your blazing fireplace. Looking into the flame, I lost myself in thought, | The magic circle wearied me, | And there was some kind of bitter taste | From the excess of joy and energy.
Why this meditation at the goal? | Where has madness lured me? | Into what forests and snowstorms | Have I carried your warmth? Where are you? Can it be that, stunned, | Seeing nothing around, | Stiff with cold, whitened by the blizzard, | I am knocking at your heart?…

In the first stanza the poet remains on the level of reality. He remembers an evening in the past, when he had visited his beloved and thay had sat together in front of the fire. In the second stanza metaphor begins to be introduced: he remembers, too, how, lost in thought, he felt the oppressive nature of the 'magic circle' of domestic bliss, and how his youthful energies demanded an escape from it: *chem-to gor'-kim otzyvalsya/Izbytok schastiya i sil* [there was some kind of bitter taste/From the excess of joy and energy]. In the third stanza we move, through a series of gradually heightened questions, entirely into metaphor. *Razdumie* [meditation] refers back to *zabyvalsya* [I lost myself in thought], the thoughts of the second stanza, but the poet now realizes these to have been madness, *bezumstvo*. The contrast between past and present is emphasized by the phonetic similarity (razdum*ie*:bezum*stvo*). *Bezumstvo* also begins the transition into metaphor: it was madness that lured him away from what he realizes should have been his goal, the *volshebnyy krug* [magic circle], symbolized in the first stanza by the *pylayushchiy kamin* [blazing fireplace]. In lines 11 and 12 this *pylayushchiy kamin*, the fire in the woman's home, gives rise to two metaphors: on the one hand it becomes the warmth, the love of the woman; and on the other, by contrast, it conjures up the forest and snowstorms outside—the undomestic, cold environment in which the poet has moved since leaving this woman.

Finally, in the last stanza, metaphor has taken over completely: the poet, stunned by the storm and the recognition of his madness; seeing nothing around him (*krugom*), as he has failed to see where his happiness lay (in the *volshebnyy krug*); physically frozen, as he was earlier emotionally; whitened by snow, as he is now by time, calls out in vain to his lost love: *Gde ty?* [Where are you?], echoing *Prosti!* [Forgive me!] in the first line—his plea to be forgiven for abandoning her—as he knocks at her heart: the door of the house in which he had sat.

A poem by Blok with a similar compositional technique is: *Your storm rushed me away...(Tvoya groza menya umchala...)* (1906):

> Твоя гроза меня умчала
> И опрокинула меня.
> И надо мною тихо встала
> Синь умирающего дня.
>
> Я на земле грозою смятый
> И опрокинутый лежу.
> И слышу дальние раскаты,
> И вижу радуги межу.

LERMONTOV, TYUTCHEV AND FET

Взойду по ней, по семицветной
И незапятнанной стезе —
С улыбкой тихой и приветной
Смотреть в глаза твоей грозе.

*Your storm rushed me away | And overturned me. | And above me
quietly rose | The blue of the dying day.*
*On the ground, crumpled by the storm | And overturned I lie. |
And hear the distant thunders, | And see the rainbow's boundary.*
*I will rise along it, along the seven-coloured | And unsullied
path— | With a quiet and affectionate smile | To look into the
eyes of your storm.*

Rebuffed by a woman, the poet is depressed and distraught. He
leaves her and retires within himself. But after a period of isolation he
finds peace again, decides to see her once more and meet her anger
with calm affection.

Unlike Fet, who begins in reality and gradually glides into metaphor, Blok opens with a metaphor: the woman's anger is a storm,
tvoya groza, which rushes the poet, possibly visualized as a leaf, away
from her and overturns him. In the third line, however, we begin to
move on to a different level of metaphor. The storm becomes a real
one, rather in the manner of Fet's forest and blizzards, and gives rise
to a description of other natural phenomena. The storm itself passes
on, and is replaced by the clear blue of the evening sky, but its distant
thunders (*dal'nie raskaty*) can still be heard and a rainbow forms. The
two planes of metaphor are linked together by the verbs *umchala...
oprokinula* [rushed...overturned] in lines 1 and 2 and the participles
smyatyy...oprokinutyy [crumpled...overturned] in lines 5 and 6, one
of which repeats the previous verb, while both occur in identical
positions in the line. At the same time the change from active
verb to passive participle emphasizes the movement from one
plane to another: the first is dynamic, the second static—the
period of quiet isolation; and this mood is reinforced by the
quality of the verbs in this stanza: *lezhu* [I lie], *slyshu* [I hear], *vizhu*
[I see].

In the third stanza we move back again into the metaphor of the
first: the mood reverts to action: *vzoydu* [I will rise]. The link is the

rainbow, which loses its real existence to become a metaphor for the poet's radiant and pure love, the path by which he will return to his mistress: *Vzoydu po ney, po semitsvetnoy | I nezapyatnannoy steze* [I will rise along it, along the seven-coloured / And unsullied path]. A subsidiary connection is provided with *S ulybkoy* tikhoy [With a *quiet* smile], which catches up the earlier: *nado mnoyu* tikho *vstala| Sin' umirayushchego dnya* [Above me *quietly* rose / The blue of the dying day] and emphasizes that it is the contemplation, the communion with nature that has achieved the change in the poet's mood. The last line returns to the initial metaphor: *Tvoya groza...tvoey groze* [Your storm...your storm] and rounds off the poem through the change in position from the beginning to the end of the line. But there is a final twist. *Smotret' v glaza tvoey groze* [To look into the *eyes* of your storm]: the storm is given human attributes, metaphor is piled on metaphor. Yet, paradoxically, the effect is to bring us closer to reality: the person of the loved one; the introduction of her eyes provides a key to what has gone before.

These two poems move between the real and the metaphorical along very different paths. Fet goes from reality into gradually thickening metaphor. Blok begins with a metaphor for reality, moves into reality in metaphor, and returns. Nevertheless, the method by which these results are achieved is essentially the same: metaphor breeds metaphor, engendering a reality of its own.

This method of creation through a chain of metaphors or images is one of the most obvious and individual characteristics of Fet's work. An interesting poem from this point of view is *Lying back in my armchair, I gaze at the ceiling...* (*Na kresle otvalyas', glyazhu na potolok...*) (1890). In it Fet presents us not with a result—reality transformed through the poet's imagination, as in *Forgive me! In the mists of memory...*, but with a process—he demonstrates how this transformation takes place.

> На кресле отвалясь, гляжу на потолок,
>   Где, на задор воображенью,
> Над лампой тихою подвешенный кружок
>   Вертится призрачною тенью.

Зари осенней след в мерцаньи этом есть:
    Над кровлей, кажется, и садом,
Не в силах улететь и не решаясь сесть,
    Грачи кружатся темным стадом...

Нет, то не крыльев шум, то кони у крыльца!
    Я слышу трепетные руки...
Как бледность холодна прекрасного лица!
    Как шепот горестен разлуки!..

Молчу, потерянный, на дальний путь глядя
    Из-за темнеющего сада, —
И кружится еще, приюта не найдя,
    Грачей встревоженное стадо.

Lying back in my armchair, I gaze at the ceiling, | Where, a challenge to my imagination, | The suspended circle over the quiet lamp | Revolves with a wraith-like shadow.
There is the trace of an autumn sunset in that flickering: | Above the roof, it seems, and garden, | Unable to fly away and not deciding to roost, | The rooks circle in a dark flock...
No, that is not the sound of wings, that is horses at the porch! | I feel your trembling hands... | How cold is the paleness of your beautiful face! | How sad the whisper of separation!...
I am silent, lost, looking at the distant road | From the darkening garden,— | And there still circles, finding no shelter, | The disturbed flock of rooks.

Beginning with the shadow cast on the ceiling by the lampshade, which offers a challenge to his imagination, the poet moves through a series of interconnected images in a full circle, as the shadow revolves on the ceiling. Each image in the chain appeals to a different sense: sight—the circling flock of rooks; hearing—the sound of their wings, then re-interpreted as horses' hoofs; touch—the hands and cold face of his beloved. One cannot pass on without commenting on the elegance with which, through two puns, these last transitions are accomplished. *Net, to ne* kryl'ev *shum, to koni u* kryl'tsa [No, that is not the sound of wings, that is horses at the porch]: the mistake in recognizing the nature of the sound is underlined by the presence of these two almost identical words, which, however, differ importantly in stress. And *Ya* slyshu *trepetnye ruki* [I feel your trembling hands]: when taken in conjunction with the previous line this seems to mean: 'I hear'; but in conjunction with the following line, which introduces sensation—the coldness of the face—it must be read as: 'I feel'.[1] In this third stanza the poet has gone back in time to the final parting with his now dead love and has summoned up her insubstantial shade from the past—a climax adumbrated at the beginning of the poem in the words: *Vertitsya prizrachnoyu ten'yu* [Revolves with a wraith-like shadow]. The imagination has replied to the challenge it was offered, and, in doing so, has involved the poet's emotions. He returns in the last stanza to the present, but his mood has been changed to one of melancholy by the realization that he is irrevocably severed from his past, and the final image of the disturbed flock of rooks, which *kruzhitsya eshche, priyuta ne naydya* [still circles, finding no shelter], seems to symbolise those memories he has disturbed in the course of the poem.

By revealing the workings of poetic creation in this way, Fet has written a poem the subject of which is its own composition. This is not an isolated example—he has other poems which comment, as this does, on the way in which their genesis has occurred. An example is the well-known: *I have come to you with a greeting...* (*Ya prishel k tebe s privetom...*) (1843):

> Я пришел к тебе с приветом,
> Рассказать, что солнце встало,
> Что оно горячим светом
> По листам затрепетало;

---

[1] Fet used the same phrase, with the same ambiguity, in a poem written eight years earlier, *To Chopin* (*Shopenu*) (1882):

> Ты мелькнула, ты предстала,
> Снова сердце задрожало,
> Под чарующие звуки
> То же счастье, те же муки,
> Слышу трепетные руки —
>   Ты еще со мной!

You appeared for a moment before me, | *Again my heart quivered,* | *To the accompaniment of the enchanting sounds* | *The same happiness, the same torments,* | *I feel your trembling hands—* | *You are still with me!*

Рассказать, что лес проснулся,
Весь проснулся, веткой каждой,
Каждой птицей встрепенулся
И весенней полон жаждой;

Рассказать, что с той же страстью,
Как вчера, пришел я снова,
Что душа всё так же счастью
И тебе служить готова;

Рассказать, что отовсюду
На меня весельем веет,
Что не знаю сам, что́ буду
Петь, — но только песня зреет.

*I have come to you with a greeting, | To tell you that the sun
has risen, | That its burning light | Has begun to quiver along the
leaves;*

*To tell you that the forest has awakened, | Awakened completely,
with every branch, | Has fluttered with every bird | And is full of
spring thirst;*

*To tell you that with the same passion, | As yesterday, I have
come again, | That my soul is still as ready | To serve happiness
and you;*

*To tell you that from everywhere | The air brings joy to me, | That
I myself do not know what I will | Sing, but only that a song is
ripening.*

Here again it can be seen how, in the second stanza, one metaphor
grows out of another in the manner typical of Fet.

The poem as a whole, however, works in a very different manner
from *Lying back in my armchair, I gaze at the ceiling...* In the latter
the poet is always conscious of what he is doing: reacting to the
challenge the revolving shadow poses his imagination. In *I have come
to you with a greeting...* the stimulus is much more general and
diffused: the emotions called forth by the sights and sounds of
spring. And the poem itself is consequently far more spontaneous and
unconscious. It is only in the last lines: *ne znayu sam, chto budu |
Pet',—no tol'ko pesnya zreet* [I myself do not know what I will / Sing,
but only that a song is ripening] that the poet—and reader—realize
that the ripening song has blossomed into the poem itself.

Poems such as these illustrate an important aspect of Fet's work: the original impulse for a poem and the end-product which results are for him really less important than the process through which one is transmuted into the other. This is one of the reasons for the significance which metaphorical description has in his verse. For metaphors are the instruments through which this transformation is achieved; in them the dynamic force of the work is concentrated.

In Fet's poems, therefore, the metaphor is all-important, and he employs it with a boldness and density which mark off his work from that of any of his predecessors or contemporaries. It is this characteristic which caused some nineteenth-century critics to dismiss as incomprehensible lines such as:

> Устало всё кругом: устал и цвет небес...

Everything around is tired: tired too the colour of the skies... (1889)

> ...сонных лип тревожа лист,
> Порхают гаснущие звуки.

...Disturbing the leaf of sleepy limes | Dying sounds flutter about. (Into the forests of the uninhabited land...: V lesa bezlyudnoy storony..., 1856?)

or:

> Зачем же за тающей скрипкой
> Так сердце в груди встрепенулось,
> Как будто знакомой улыбкой
> Минувшее вдруг улыбнулось?

Why to the sound of the melting violin | Does my heart so flutter in my breast, | As though with a well-known smile | The past had suddenly greeted me? (A smile of deadly boredom...: Ulybka tomitel'noy skuki..., 1844)

—in which a statement containing a metaphor calls forth a comparison which is itself another metaphor.

Occasionally Fet's imagination leaps abruptly from the literal to the figurative to produce a sudden and startling effect. An example occurs in the poem: *Rocking, the stars blinked their rays...(Kachayasya, zvezdy migali luchami...)* (1891). The poet and his beloved, on a ship in the Mediterranean, together admire the lights reflected in the sea, which seem to be rushing past them. The poem continues:

> В каком-то забвеньи, немом и целебном,
> Смотрел я в тот блеск, отдаваяся неге;
> Казалось, рулем управляя волшебным,
> Глубоко ты грудь мне взрезаешь в побеге.

In some kind of oblivion, silent and healing, | I gazed at this brightness, abandoning myself to bliss; | It seemed as if, controlling the magic helm, | You were cutting deeply into my breast in your flight.

The shock this image produces seems due to a number of factors: the sudden change in the verbal subject, from the poet to the woman, who indeed here appears for the first time as a separate person; the accompanying change in their physical situation—they no longer stand together, but are opposed as the ship and the sea; the apparent reversal of sexual roles—the woman as ship, the man as sea; and, finally, the violence of the image: *Gluboko ty grud' mne vzrezaesh' v pobege* [You were cutting deeply into my breast in your flight], contrasted with the languorous reverie of the first two lines. All these changes take place without any warning: it is as if, between the two halves of the stanza, a link has been omitted which would show that the poet's thoughts were gradually moving towards the woman.

More often, however, Fet glides almost imperceptibly from one plane to the other, as in *At the Window* (*U okna*) (1871):

> К окну приникнув головой,
> Я поджидал с тоскою нежной,
> Чтоб ты явилась — и с тобой
> Помчаться по равнине снежной.
>
> Но в блеск сокрылась ты лесов,
> Под листья яркие банана,
> За серебро пустынных мхов
> И пыль жемчужную фонтана.
>
> Я видел горный поворот,
> Где снег стопой твоей встревожен,
> Я рассмотрел хрустальный грот,
> Куда мне доступ невозможен.

Вдруг ты вошла — я всё узнал —
Смех на устах, в глазах угроза.
О, как всё верно подсказал
Мне на стекле узор мороза!

Leaning my head against the window, | I waited with tender longing | For you to appear—and with you | To dash across the snowy plain.

But you hid yourself in the glitter of the forests, | Under the bright leaves of the banana, | Beyond the silver of the deserted mosses | And the pearly dust of the fountain.

I saw the mountain turning, | Where the snow was disturbed by your tread, | I discerned the crystal grotto, | To which I could have no access.

Suddenly you entered—I saw everything— | Laughter on your lips, a threat in your eyes. | O, how everything was truly predicted | To me by the frost pattern on the glass.

Here the transition from the real snow scene outside to the imaginary one fashioned by the poet from the frost patterns on his window goes almost unnoticed. The first hint that something strange is happening occurs in the line: *Pod list'ya yarkie banana* [Under the bright leaves of the banana], but the puzzle this horticultural incongruity poses is not resolved until the final stanza, when the woman's entrance brings the poem back to reality as the poet turns away from the window.

This kind of concealed movement from one level to another is often brought about by ambiguities. One example has already been noted above (*Ya slyshu trepetnye ruki* [I feel your trembling hands]), where the transition is from image to image. The first stanza of the poem: *The fire burns in the forest like a bright sun…* (*Yarkim solntsem v lesu plameneet koster…*) (1859) offers another example, but here the movement is from the literal to the figurative:

Ярким солнцем в лесу пламенеет костер,
И, сжимаясь, трещит можжевельник;
Точно пьяных гигантов столпившийся хор,
Раскрасневшись, шатается ельник.

The fire burns in the forest like a bright sun, | And, contracting, the juniper crackles; | Like a crowded chorus of drunken giants, | Blushing, the fir-grove sways.

The stanza consists of three statements, each of which has the form: image—verb—subject. The first two verbs: *plameneet* [burns], *treshchit* [crackles] describe concrete actions. Because of the parallel nature of the statements, we tend also to ascribe a concrete action to the third verb—*shataetsya* [sways]—and to interpret it as referring to the fir-grove swaying in the wind. The poem continues, however, with a description of how the fire will die down during the day:

> И лениво и скупо мерцающий день
> Ничего не укажет в тумане;
> У холодной золы изогнувшийся пень
> Прочернеет один на поляне.

And lazily and sparsely the flickering day | Will reveal nothing in the mist; | Only a twisted stump by the cold ashes | Will show black on the glade.

and ends with a variation on the first stanza:

> Но нахмурится ночь — разгорится костер,
> И, виясь, затрещит можжевельник,
> И, как пьяных гигантов столпившийся хор,
> Покраснев, зашатается ельник.

But as soon as night frowns—the fire will flame up, | And, curling, the juniper will begin to crackle, | And, like a crowded chorus of drunken giants, | Flushed, the fir-grove will sway.

Here the three parallel verbs occur again, but in the future perfective, and a causal connection is expressly made between the approach of night and the commencement of the actions they describe. That is, the trees are not swaying in reality; it is the moving lights and shadows cast on them by the fire that give this impression.

This last example illustrates that impressionistic technique which forms the basis of Fet's creative method. He describes objects not as they are, but as they appear to be at that moment when they impinge on his senses. Reality is thus restructured through the poet's perception of it, as can be seen most clearly perhaps in those instances where his vision inverts the normal relationship between two objects:

> Весеннее небо глядится
> Сквозь ветви мне в очи случайно...

The spring sky is looking | Through the branches accidentally into my eyes... (1844)

...там затопленный навстречу лес летел...

...there the submerged forest flew towards us...(On the Dnepr at Flood-time: Na Dnepre v polovod'e, 1853)

По каналам посребренным
Опрокинулись дворцы...

Along the silvery canals | The palaces were overturned... (Venice by Night: Venetsiya noch'yu, 1847)

This last image, of reflections in water, occurs constantly in Fet's work; and in most cases the inversion is present: the water does not reflect the object, the object is overturned in the water:

Солнце, с прозрачных сияя небес,
В тихих струях опрокинуло лес.

The sun, shining from the transparent skies, | Overturned the forest in the quiet streams. (The clamorous herons flew off from their nests...: S gnezd zamakhali kriklivye tsapli... 1883?)

Свод небесный, в воде опрокинут,
Испещряет румянцем залив.

The heavenly vault, overturned in the water, | Mottles the bay with blushes. (How beautiful in the barely shimmering morning...: Kak khorosh chut' mertsayushchim utrom..., 1857?)

Над озером лебедь в тростник протянул,
В воде опрокинулся лес,
Зубцами вершин он в заре потонул,
Меж двух изгибаясь небес.

The swan stretched over the lake into the reeds, | The forest overturned in the water, | Its jagged treetops sank in the sunset, | Curving between two skies. (The swan stretched over the lake into the reeds...: Nad ozerom lebed' v trostnik protyanul..., 1854)

In this quotation Fet employs an image similar to that used in *The fire burns in the forest like a bright sun...* The first statement: *lebed'...*

protyanul [the swan stretched] influences our understanding of the two following verbs—*oprokinulsya* [overturned], *potonul* [sank]—with the result that these appear to be describing actions, rather than states, and in this way the momentary nature of the vision is emphasized.

Fet is an impressionist. There is no objective reality in his verse; it is a record of transient impressions: the external world as refracted through the poet's perception. And this explains, from a different point of view, his constant and original use of metaphor. Through metaphor the poet expresses his peculiar, individual and immediate apprehension of his surroundings.

SELECT BIBLIOGRAPHY

There are numerous collections of Lermontov's verse; Tyutchev and Fet have been published less frequently. For all three poets, however, one of the best, and certainly one of the most convenient editions is that in the *Biblioteka poeta* series. These are:

Lermontov, M. Yu., *Izbrannye proizvedeniya v dvukh tomakh*, Moscow-Leningrad, 1964.
Tyutchev, F. I., *Polnoe sobranie stikhotvoreniy*, Leningrad, 1957.
Fet, A. A., *Polnoe sobranie stikhotvoreniy*, Leningrad, 1959.

The following works, which deal with nineteenth-century Russian poetry in general, or with these poets in particular, are recommended:

GENERAL

Bukhshtab, B., *Russkie poety*, Leningrad, 1970.
Eykhenbaum, B., *Melodika russkogo liricheskogo stikha*, Petrograd, 1922.
Eykhenbaum, B., *O poezii*, Leningrad, 1969. (includes *Melodika russkogo liricheskogo stikha*)
Istoriya russkoy poezii, ed. B. Gorodetsky, 2 vols., Leningrad, 1968-9.

LERMONTOV

Duchesne, E., *Lermontov, sa vie et ses oeuvres*, Paris, 1910.
Eykhenbaum, B., *Lermontov: opyt istoriko-literaturnoy otsenki*, Leningrad, 1924. (reprinted Munich, 1967.)

LERMONTOV, TYUTCHEV AND FET

Fedorov, A., *Lermontov i literatura ego vremeni*, Leningrad, 1967.
Lavrin, J., *Lermontov*, London, 1959.
Maksimov, D., *Poeziya Lermontova*, Leningrad, 1964.
Merezhkovsky, D., *M. Yu. Lermontov, poet sverkhchelovechestva*, St. Petersburg, 1909.
M. Yu. Lermontov v russkoy kritike, Moscow, 1952.
Ovsyaniko-Kulikovsky, D., *M. Yu. Lermontov*, St. Petersburg, 1914.

TYUTCHEV

Bryusov, V., 'F. I. Tyutchev' in Bryusov, *Izbrannye sochineniya*, Moscow, 1955, Vol. 2, pp. 210–25.
Bukhshtab, B., 'F. I. Tyutchev' in Tyutchev, *Polnoe sobranie stikhotvoreniy*, Leningrad, 1957.
Gregg, R., *Fedor Tiutchev. The Evolution of a Poet*, Columbia University Press, 1965.
Gudzy, N., 'Tyutchev v poeticheskoy kul'ture russkogo simvolizma', *Izvestiya po russkomu yazyku i slovesnosti*, 1930, 3, i, pp. 465–549.
Pigarev, K., *Zhizn' i tvorchestvo Tyutcheva*, Moscow, 1962.
Tynyanov, Yu., 'Vopros o Tyutcheve' in Tynyanov, *Arkhaisty i novatory*, Leningrad, 1929.
Uraniya. Tyutchevskiy al'manakh. 1803–1929, Leningrad, 1928.

FET

Bryusov, V., 'A. A. Fet. Iskusstvo ili zhizn'' in Bryusov, *Dalekie i blizkie*, Moscow, 1912, pp. 18–26.
Bukhshtab, B., 'A. A. Fet' in Fet, *Polnoe sobranie stikhotvoreniy*, Leningrad, 1959.
Gustafson, R., *The Imagination of Spring; the Poetry of Afanasy Fet*, Yale University Press, 1966.

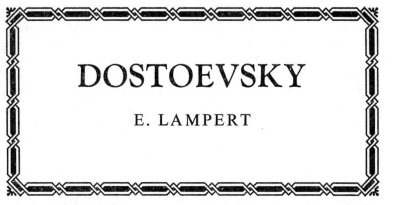

DOSTOEVSKY

E. LAMPERT

THERE IS A SENSE IN WHICH TO PAY A REAL TRIBUTE TO DOSTOEVSKY is to resist the biographical spell, to withstand the temptation to react to his work as one might react—in simultaneous revulsion and fascination—to his character. The spell is irresistible. The reminder of the gap between the life and work of a writer seems irrelevant, not because, as with Tolstoy, the two are naturally inseparable, but because Dostoevsky was an autobiographical writer who makes himself the chief character of his novels, while appearing to speak not at all of himself but of others, or even of opposites of himself.[1]

As a person Dostoevsky is the most frightening of all Russian novelists. His life is a charmless story of unchecked passion in all its vicissitudes, in its obsessions, its morbidities, its guilts, its jealousies, and its moments of illumination. First there is Dostoevsky as a scared child growing up in a family that could provide a case-study of morbid pathology, with an insanely despotic, drunken father and a gentle, down-trodden mother, whose meekness alternated with hysteria. Then came the student days in the uncongenial surroundings of a Military Engineering School, where he spent his time in voracious reading rather than in the study of engineering, and surrendered to introspection, fantasies and romantic dreams of grandeur. The mood

---

[1] Unless otherwise stated, all quotations from Dostoevsky's works refer to *Polnoe sobranie khudozhestvennykh proizvedeniy*, indicating volume and page numbers. The quotations from his correspondence (similarly indicated) are from the Dolinin edition of *Pis'ma*. For a more detailed description of both editions as well as for a list of biographical and critical works, see the select bibliography at the end of this chapter.

was transposed by Dostoevsky into the ambiguously autobiographical stories *White Nights* (*Belye nochi*) and *The Landlady* (*Khozyayka*) (both published in 1848).

These dreams and fantasies came to a crude and abrupt end when he discovered that the serfs on his father's small, insolvent estate had murdered him in revenge for the brutalities he inflicted on them. For nearly forty years Dostoevsky kept this incident and the traumatic effect it had on him a secret. The experience seems to have resulted in the first attack of epilepsy. According to Dostoevsky's daughter, he 'never ceased brooding over the causes of this terrible death',[1] and he finally came out with a grim obituary of his father in the Karamazov drama of vice, corruption and crime.

A short period of compulsory military service was followed by an equally short-lived literary success with the publication of *Poor Folk* (*Bednye lyudi*) (1845), which was rapturously reviewed by Belinsky and earned Dostoevsky the reputation of 'a new Gogol". Dostoevsky himself revelled exaggeratedly in his celebrity and went out of his way to make it known to others. He craved for acceptance and acclaim more than any other Russian writer, while at the same time feeling humiliated by his need for them.

The first literary success coincided with Dostoevsky's participation in the secret socialist circle of Petrashevsky. This activity culminated in imprisonment, in the celebrated mock-execution enacted by the government in order to terrorize the prisoners, and the nightmare years of penal servitude in Siberia. Dostoevsky left a record of this in *Notes from the House of the Dead* (*Zapiski iz mertvogo doma*) (1860)— a House of the Dead in which, as he found, the dead were more alive than the living. It is the greatest and most harrowing testimony in the long history of Russian prison literature.

The involvement with the Petrashevskists left an indelible mark on Dostoevsky's mind: paradoxically, he remained a socialist during the Siberian deportation when his radicalism underwent a change towards political reaction. There is some evidence that the change itself was caused by the desire, part-expiatory, part-masochistic, to make up for his injury by becoming a willing victim.[2] It did not affect his basic conviction, except by making it more tortuous and tormenting.

---

[1] Aimée Dostoevsky, *Fyodor Dostoevsky*, p. 37.
[2] See Grossman, *Dostoevskiy*, p. 174.

Dostoevsky's socialism was like a futuristic vision to him. 'Reality', he wrote in his Notebooks, 'is not reducible to the existant; a great part of it is contained in the shape of a latent, as yet unuttered future.'[1] He saw a new earth and wanted total reconciliation, the whole bounty of the earth for all people. 'The golden age', he wrote in 1867 in the *Diary of a Writer* (*Dnevnik pisatelya*), 'is the most improbable dream. Yet for it men gave their lives and all their powers. For it prophets died and were stoned. Without it peoples do not want to live and cannot even die.' Similar attitudes are expressed by a number of characters in Dostoevsky's novels: the 'dream' of Raskol'nikov, the 'dream' of Versilov, the 'dream' of the Ridiculous Man, the 'dream' of Mitya Karamazov, and Dostoevsky's own and final dream as expressed in his speech on the occasion of the unveiling of the Pushkin monument in 1880. In this as in other things his triumph and misery arose from an almost tragi-comic indifference to the dividing line between dream and reality. He was an optimist, but a stricken, desperate one.

After Siberia, or rather towards the end of the Siberian exile, it was the turn of women to plague Dostoevsky and be plagued by him: particularly the consumptive, over-wrought Maria Isaeva and the mesmerizing, 'infernal' Apollinaria Suslova. His sombre, sado-masochistic relations with women were interrupted by attempts to flee from oppressive penury and remorseless creditors, by frenzied and disastrous gambling sessions in German holiday resorts and still greater running up of debts, by epileptic fits, by trivial and not-so-trivial family and politico-literary quarrels, and by compulsive writing which led to the genesis of the great novels, and the final calmer years under the protective shadow of his devoted, shrewd, genteel stenographer and wife Anna Snitkina.

There is a kind of hideous rhythm in this pattern of life, if anything so disrupted can be termed a rhythm at all. It is like the unremitting movement of a murky whirlpool. Dostoevsky was not a 'nice' man. Like his own creation, the Man from the Underground, he was 'sick and spiteful'. He lacked all serenity and repose. He was insolent yet cringing, flagrant yet secretive, confiding yet mistrustful, perverse yet innocent, humble yet proud of his humility, obstinate in harbouring enmities yet longing for forgiveness. He sought out enemies to abuse them and then fawned on them. This is the impression conveyed by his

---

[1] *Zapisnye tetradi*, p. 179.

personal relations, in his correspondence and in the recollections of such varied writers as Annenkov, Grigorovich, Turgenev, Chernyshevsky, Strakhov, even in the comments of such a touchingly devoted friend and admirer as Vsevolod Solov'ev. Dostoevsky's inner life was made up of a savage combination of intellectual insight, audacity, prejudice, venom, vulnerability, and an untrammelled imagination that fed partly on Gothic terrors, partly on hilarious fantasy. Everything about him was unrelenting, poignant and intense, even though often he inflated himself—or inflated himself through his fictional characters—in order all the more effectively to deflate himself in a kind of pressure-relieving, self-exorcising fashion. It is hard to understand how blinding imaginative and spiritual exhilaration, as of the heavens taken by storm, could conceal such oppressiveness of character, peevish egotism, irritability, even pettiness in personal dealings and a sordidly humdrum existence of a literary hack.

What is remarkable is that, victim though he was of all these conflicting traits and stresses, Dostoevsky saw deeply into them, turning all the turmoil and disorder within himself into imaginative facts and people. In a sense, he was as much concerned with disorder itself as with the portrayal of disorder, being himself drawn to it by evoking it, exciting himself with excitement, tormenting himself with torment.

What is equally remarkable is Dostoevsky's awareness that the disorder and the imaginative projections of what happened to him in the flesh involved him in the drama of his time, in the 'pitchy hell of senseless and unmerciful life' (vol. 13, p. 350), as he observed apropos of one of his early novels, *The Humiliated and Offended* (*Unizhennye i oskorblennye*) (1857). He stood at the point where the inner nature of the age in which he lived and in which we are still living was felt most deeply. There was in this respect something almost mediumistic about Dostoevsky. No Russian writer paid such a price for encompassing his time by living out all its confusions and discord. In a conjunction of agonized acceptance and refusal, Dostoevsky gives us the central perplexity of man as he emerged from the social and moral conflicts of post-Reform Russia and as he had already emerged in contemporary Europe.

Dostoevsky has been described as the poet of modern city life. Even where he writes about life in provincial backwaters (as, e.g. in *The*

Devils (*Besy*) (1871–72), and *The Brothers Karamazov* (*Brat'ya Karamazovy*) (1880)) he gives it the peculiar mental climate derived from grim, inhospitable, scrambling megalopolitan existence. Dostoevsky was himself a plebeian, a *raznochinets*, in conflict with the land-owing tradition, which, he stated, 'has said all it had to say' and 'had outlived its time' (*Pis'ma*, vol. 2, p. 359), although he harboured a half-covetous half-contemptuous feeling about the advantages it afforded to such fellow-writers of his as Turgenev (whom he despised) or Tolstoy (whom he admired but resented). He was as far from Turgenev's cultivated manorial idyll as he was from Turgenev's antiseptic liberalism, from Turgenev's posture of eminent by-stander, registering polite astonishment and turning the perfect phrase. He was equally far from Tolstoy's pastoral simplicity, however threatened it may have proved in the end, from Tolstoy's unspoiled animal curiosity and sense that the world begins anew every morning.

Dostoevsky is both the product and the poet of life at its most dis-rupted in the modern capitalist metropolis, and into his work he gathered its hallucinations. Like Balzac and Dickens who depicted the descending Dantesque circles of the new hell of Paris and London, Dostoevsky was overshadowed by the spectre of St. Petersburg, which Tolstoy, in imagination as in life, refused to have anything to do with. It was to Dostoevsky a city of anonymous citizens, of restive, prodigal strangers, a city of undescribable beauty but also of nightmares, of 'forsaken holes', of 'narrow dead-ends' and 'slummy cellular tenements', a city enveloped in mists that drifted from time to time to reveal terrifying images of man's loneliness and revolt. The city was not merely a setting to fertilize Dostoevsky's imagination. He was involved in the human condition epitomized in this kind of environ-ment and inescapably bounded by it, and he created from its centre. None of his predecessors had penetrated so deeply into the psycho-logical structure and origin of hostile, frenzied, greedy, mammon-ridden society, where 'all is chaos, all is confusion' (vol. 13, p. 21). He provides, ironically perhaps, one of the most telling if partial confirmations of the validity of Marx's idea. Money as the symbol of man's state in an irrational, deranged society pervades Dostoevsky's novels with the insistence of Greek deities in seventeenth-century tragedy. None more than Dostoevsky felt so dramatically what this society did to man, how feverishly it entered him, conditioning him and being conditioned by him. Generally, he sensed the environment not as some objective setting or an observer's actuality, but as a symbol of man or, even more, as an extension of him. Almost every sentence Dostoevsky wrote reflects the intense, hectic, breathless atmosphere which suffuses modern society and invades man. In this sense, his language may be said to be the *lingua communis* for the age, the means whereby, as Middleton Murry puts it in his somewhat turgid study of the Russian writer, Dostoevsky 'penetrated into a new consciousness ... inevitable for mankind'.[1]

Basically, it is the consciousness peculiar to man's disinherited, homeless, proletarian existence—the emanation of an atomized world whose anonymous forces have dissolved the old one into a whirlpool of molecules, destroying in its wake human relationships and leading to man's increasing estrangement from reality and from himself. Dostoevsky's experience of strangeness, of the menacing otherness of human beings reveals a situation in which man has been cheated of the fulness of life. It is significant that 'alienation' and its synonyms (*'otchuzhdenie'*, *'otchudilsya'*, *'vse eto stalo ne moe'*, etc.) are among the most frequently recurring words in Dostoevsky's novels. And undoubtedly it is the 'alienated', uprooted social beings, even the aristocrats among them—Svidrigaylov in *Crime and Punishment* (*Prestuplenie i nakazanie*) (1866) or Versilov in *The Raw Youth* (*Podrostok*) (1875)—who are properly alive, whereas such rooted, self-assured characters as Val'kovsky in *The Humiliated and Offended* are not.

The alienation however could be seen as the beginning of liberation. Indeed, it is the 'freest' as well as the most unprotected and vulnerable condition—free to the point of absurdity. The 'man from the under-ground', the 'wanderer' (*skitalets*), the 'idiot', the proletarian are free because they have nothing to lose but their chains and their conscious-ness. Dostoevsky possessed in an eminent measure the gift of such consciousness, which, in its fierce concentration, at times seemed to reach the proportions of insanity, or which he worked up, in full knowledge of what he was doing, into a state of insanity so as to watch its extreme consequences. 'I swear to you, gentlemen, that to be too conscious (*slishkom soznavat'*) is a disease, a real, a total disease' (vol. 4, p. 111). D. H. Lawrence considered this to be 'the foulest

[1] Murry, *Fyodor Dostoevsky*, p. 96.

thing' about Dostoevsky. 'The whole point of Dostoevsky', he observed, 'lies in the fact of his fixed will that the individual ego, the achieved I, the conscious I, shall be infinite, God-like, absolved from all relations.'[1]

In point of fact, Dostoevsky never did absolve himself from 'all relations', although 'relation' for him differed from the intestinal flow advocated by Lawrence. Dostoevsky's intense self-awareness, solipsism, sense of solitude induced a longing for contact, for a path to 'the other' which would reveal self-consciousness for what it is, namely a consciousness of ourselves in relation to what is not ourselves, and which would make man lose his unbearable opaqueness. Hence Dostoevsky's dream of an all-embracing, collective, mysterious whole behind and beyond existing reality, and of the people rising again from the Medean cauldron of social fragments.

It was this which made Dostoevsky join the *pochvenniki* (from *pochva*, soil: adherents of the soil). The *pochvenniki* made a significant contribution to the intellectual and literary debate in Russia in the latter half of the nineteenth century and they helped in the upsurge of national self-consciousness of their day. Dostoevsky became their most vociferous spokesman, devoting the greater part of his journalistic activity to the propagation of their doctrine (in contributions to his own journals *Time* (*Vremya*) and *Epoch* (*Epokha*), to Meshchersky's extreme reactionary *The Citizen* (*Grazhdanin*), of which he became the editor, and in his later *Diary of a Writer*).

The *pochvenniki* were belated but unquiet Slavophils who lamented what Dostoevsky called the Slavophil 'aristocratic satiety' (*aristokraticheskaya sytost'*) and yet sought Slavophil salvation in a recovery of the severed link with the sacred motherland. Anything that led to separation from it was a modern sin, a source of death and destruction. The individualistic, self-reliant western European, the cosmopolitan citizen, the rootless industrial worker, the *déclassé* of the radical intelligentsia, the revolutionary were, therefore, fallen men guilty of hate of the Great Mother and of Russia. This fallen state is contrasted with the meekness of the humiliated and offended, the forgiving who accept the piercing sword into their soul and are at one with the earth and with God. In addition, because the fate of being Russian was such

---

[1] D. H. Lawrence, *Selected Literary Criticism*, ed. Anthony Beal, London, 1967, p. 230.

a difficult and complex matter, or because they suffered from an exaggerated pride in being humble, the *pochvenniki*, together with the Slavophils—and Dostoevsky more than either—were indefatigable national soul-searchers, always worrying about what was happening to their national way of life, always reconstituting their national identity. It is Dostoevsky who is largely responsible for the discovery of the 'Russian soul'—that curious, irrational, but not altogether preposterous notion that salvation, spiritual as well as temporal, comes from Russia. Russia is in fact the secret and at times the declared presence that looms large over his whole life and work. There was a mundane angle to this: the belief that Russia's world mission was to replace the decadent civilization of the West and that she had the sacred right to occupy Constantinople.

It is true, Dostoevsky admitted that his beloved was not without blemish. Love of Russia was like an anguish to him—a characteristic whose reverse side showed a mindless patriotism. It was Dostoevsky's worst fantasy and, typically enough, he made inconsequent moves to refute it—for instance in *The Devils*. After Shatov's frantic eulogy of the Russian people, 'the only God-bearing people', Stavrogin asks coldly:

> "'I only wanted to know, do you believe in God, yourself?"
> "I believe in Russia . . . I believe in her Orthodoxy . . . I believe in the body of Christ . . . I believe that the new advent will take place in Russia . . .
> I believe . . ." Shatov muttered.
> "And in God? In God?"
> "I . . . I will believe in God."' (Part Two , Ch, 1, vii)

In the end, Dostoevsky could only be associated with political reaction by those who did not understand that nothing for him was self-contained and that he was continually moving to the opposite of whatever was his case. This quality made him an unreliable ally of such *éminences grises* of the tsarist order as Pobedonostsev and Katkov, whose uneasy protection he both enjoyed and resented. He propagated the idea of the suffering God-bearing Russian turning the other cheek and healing the wounds of discord. But, at the same time, he fostered an awareness of those threatening rebels who defy all divine and human sanctions for the more atrocious dispensations of history. He extolled the 'Russian wanderers', the natural crossers of frontiers, who carry within them the restless spirit of their age, who are driven by the 'urge to negation', who, far from perpetuating the familiar, the customary and earthbound, invest life with the fierce element of destruction. Lunacharsky said that Dostoevsky 'cast the spell of revolution on Russia'.[1]

Still, Dostoevsky's quarrel with society sprang from his identity with it no less than from his alienation, for the horror of alienation lent force to the need for unity, for removing the boundaries between individual and social life. Not unlike Tolstoy, but with greater or more anticipant, restive awareness of living at a moment in history when enormous tensions were created by the accelerated dissolution of the old, 'organic' world and the extension to all areas of the new, divisive social forces, Dostoevsky groped impatiently for the lost paradise. While having the future in his bones, he yearned to be re-absorbed in a prehistoric, unified and unifying 'folk-soul', to speak and pledge himself for it, and at times to cover its nakedness with the sham clothes of a romantic 'Russian socialism'. He continually moved backwards and forwards as the situation became more menacing and his forebodings more intense. He was a traditionalist who believed in revolution, or a revolutionary who sought a foothold in tradition amidst the uncertainties and anxieties of revolutionary experience.

Human action for Dostoevsky occurred between these kinds of extremes and he found it neither expedient nor inexpedient, neither fortunate nor unfortunate, neither commendable nor condemnable, but innocent and guilty, good and evil, divine and human, or all these things together.

God was Dostoevsky's misadventure and for this reason perhaps he was a religious man, that is, he did not expect to get anything but conflict and pain out of religion. 'I will tell you regarding myself', he wrote to the wife of the Decembrist Fonvizin, 'that I am a child of unbelief and doubt, up till now and even (I know it) until my coffin closes' (*Pis'ma*, vol. 1, p. 142). And Dostoevsky's reply, often quoted,

---

[1] *Dostoevskiy v russkoy kritike*, p. 434. An early Soviet critic wrote: 'Merezhkovsky entitled one of his studies on Dostoevsky "The Prophet of Revolution". Prophet or not, it is an incontestable fact that Dostoevsky understood deeply the psychological element (*stikhiya*) of revolution, that even before the revolution he clearly saw in it what many—not only in his time but even at the time of the revolution itself—did not guess.' (Pereverzev, *Tvorchestvo Dostoevskogo*, p. 3.)

to the critics' verdict on *The Brothers Karamazov* was: ' . . . these thickheads did not dream of such a powerful negation of God as that put in "the (Grand) Inquisitor" and in the preceding chapters . . . I do not believe like a fool (a fanatic). And they wished to tease me, and laughed over my backwardness! But their stupid natures did not dream of such powerful negation as I have lived through.' (Ibid., vol. 3, p. 368.)

It is this kind of experience, recorded in Dostoevsky's private statements and expressed even more ambivalently in the oscillations of his fictional characters, which enabled him to understand the process of believing and disbelieving as it breaks down the unity of man's personality. Here as elsewhere Dostoevsky showed his propensity for turning into the opposite of himself. A schizophrenic has two contradictory personalities which operate at different times, in the manner of Dr. Jekyll and Mr. Hyde, but the double rôles in Dostoevsky operated simultaneously: love and hate, pride and abasement, cruelty and tenderness, belief and unbelief did not succeed each other, nor were they mingled, but appeared incongruously together.

This incongruity was an overwhelming advantage to Dostoevsky as a didactic writer, for it took the dead-weight out of his teaching and launched his message on the confusing and changing currents of human existence. Divine revelation for him was not a shadowy parallel world into which one might escape and which could serve as an explanation of otherwise unmotivated actions. It was a way of seeing human life in depth and finding it torn by opposing forces. His statements about God are really statements about man. This may explain Dostoevsky's enigmatic admission that 'even if somebody proved to me that Christ was outside truth, and it *really* were true that the truth was outside Christ, then I would rather remain with Christ than with truth' (*Pis'ma*, vol. 1, p. 142). Son of God or Son of Man. The ambiguity of the situation is summed up in the dialogue between Kirillov and Stavrogin in *The Devils*. Kirillov says:

> '"He who teaches that all are good will end the world."
> "He who taught it was crucified."
> "He will come, and his name will be man-god."
> "The God-man?"
> "The man-god. That's the difference."

"Surely it wasn't you who lighted the lamp under the icon?"

"Yes, I lighted it."

"Did you do it believing?"

"The old woman likes to have the lamp and she hadn't time to do it today", muttered Kirillov.

"You don't say prayers yourself?"

"I pray to everything. You see the spider crawling on the wall, I look at it and thank it for crawling."

... Stavrogin frowned and watched him disdainfully, but there was no mockery in his eyes.

"I'll bet that when I come next time you'll be believing in God too", he said ...

"Why?" ...

"If you were to find out that you believe in God, then you'd believe in him; but since you don't know that you believe in him, then you don't believe in him", laughed Nikolay Vsevolodovich ...'
(Part Two, Ch. 1, v.)

Rozanov wrote in his commentary on the Legend of the Grand Inquisitor that 'when Dostoevsky died he did not carry the secret of his soul to the grave with him. Before his death he left us, as if by some instinct revealing his soul, an astonishing scene by which we can see that the words of Alesha [Karamazov] to Ivan "And you are with him [the Grand Inquisitor]" can be definitely applied to the author himself, who so clearly [?] is on Ivan's side.'[1] One believes in Dostoevsky's believing because he did not believe, because, at any rate, the less he inclined to resolve his dilemmas the more believable he was.

Theologians and philosophers may argue about the validity and meaning of such a position, but it is this which allowed Dostoevsky to use—at least in his novels—the currency of Christian symbolism with hardly any trace of falseness or preciosity—something which only a Dante, a Milton or a Blake could achieve to the same degree. It distinguishes his religious avowals alike from academic pleas in favour of a theistic interpretation of the universe and from the monolithic certainties, the handy solutions and privileged insights which religious commentators of his work have attributed to him.[2]

---

[1] Rozanov, *Legenda o Velikom inkvizitore*, pp. 167 sq.

[2] Cases in point are Lossky, *Dostoevskiy i ego khristianskoe miroponimanie*, and V. Zenkovsky, *Istoriya russkoy filosofii*, 2 vols., Paris, 1948, vol. 1, pp. 414–37.

'I have my special view of reality (in art)', Dostoevsky wrote to Strakhov in 1869, 'and what people call almost fantastic and exceptional constitutes for me sometimes the very essence of the real. The commonplace appearance of things and the stock views of them are short of being realism and are even contrary to it' (*Pis'ma*, vol. 2, p. 169). Later he stated again that 'events, depicted as they occur in all their uniqueness, nearly always assume a fantastic, almost improbable character' (vol. 10, p. 83). Facts, it seems to be accepted, are more incredible than fiction. Paradoxically, they are more real than life because our own view of life, as ordinary people, is less real than life itself. Dostoevsky brings in things which a complacent cult of realism banishes: intrigue, complication, masquerade, dissimulation—not in order to make a show of them or as a literary entertainment, but as a way of discovering where the secret of life lies. He breaks the rules of 'realism' by portraying as entirely natural facts the 'fantastic', the 'improbable', the anomalous and forbidden, and by revealing such facts where none were suspected by others. This is his great device, and he used it with a resourcefulness which enabled him not only to observe the quirks and oddities streaking our normality, but to scoop out hidden potentialities, to demonstrate man's ability to become or do almost anything, to melt down the 'given', to dissolve 'being' into 'becoming'. Dostoevsky is the novelist of man's limiting situations. He knew his characters by their manias.

The effect was to alter not only a literary tradition but the very quality of perception. What were once celebrated or dismissed as grotesque impossibilities are seen by Dostoevsky as literal truths, when they accumulate to concentrated nightmares. It is indicative that words like 'idiot', 'delirium' (*bred*), 'madman' (*sumasshedshiy*), 'funny' (*smeshnoy*) acquire for him a meaning opposite to the dictionary one: 'idiotic' can mean 'uncorrupted', 'delirious' can mean 'acutely aware', 'mad' can mean 'wise', and 'funny'—'common'. To see, for instance, that a situation is funny rather than just ordinary required a more than normal apprehension of reality and its contradictions. But then even clowns at times sport a darker shade of melancholy, frustration and sadness than is expected of them.

In claiming to render reality truthfully and significantly by showing its distortions, its dislocations and intensifications, Dostoevsky was in

DOSTOEVSKY

a sense continuing the tradition of Gogol', for whom the image of man represented more often than not a grimace, a disfiguration of humanity. Gor'ky, who battled against what he called Dostoevsky's 'slave ethics', told young writers to study and cherish 'that horrible Dostoevskian grimace' because it could not have been conceived apart from the relevance it had already acquired in their own historical experience.[1] According to a statement attributed to Dostoevsky, 'we have all come out of Gogol''s *Overcoat*'.[2] This applies to Dostoevsky himself, but with a difference.

Devushkin in *Poor Folk* recognizes himself in the scarecrow image of Gogol''s crushed little civil servant Akaky Akakievich who, like Devushkin, is as much entitled to his tragedy as the big men of old. But Devushkin loathes the image. He is a more tangibly humanized Akaky Akakievich. He presents the revolt of the absurd individual struggling against uncontrollable powers in an alien world and longing for some form of community. In fact, while harking back to Gogol', Dostoevsky already in this early work looks forward to Kafka. The estrangement, the solitude, the private hurt, the malign pressures, and not least the grim hilarity of his world are Kafkaesque: in Kafka they found their allegorist, in Dostoevsky their progenitor. Dostoevsky, moreover, discovered the pressures beyond private fantasy (as shown by Kafka)—in a realm where they drive the world to catastrophe or to salvation.

Devushkin is the first in the gallery of Dostoevsky's characters who, when they are not meek and acquiescent, assert their humanity by incessant questioning and by rebellion against the world in which they live. It is by probing their consciousness that Dostoevsky discovers the fantasies of their lives and the inconsistency and irrationality of their behaviour. Whether on the level of '*nadryv*', of moral and emotional 'cracks', of the propensity to self-hurt for purposes of hurting others, which many of Dostoevsky's male and most of his female characters share, or on the level of ultimate moral choices, where individual conflicts show a vision of life as a whole, Dostoevsky's characters tend to remain claustrophobically self-centred. They

[1] M. Gor'ky, *O literature. Stat'i i rechi*, 1928–35, Moscow, 1935, p. 263.
[2] As far as is known, the first to make the attribution was Melchior de Vogüé, who in turn refers to a Russian 'très mêlé à l'histoire des quarante dernières années' (*Le Roman russe*, Paris, 1897, p. 96). The 'Russian' in question, however, is untraceable.

237

keep shutting themselves up into 'corners': 'to live I needed a corner, literally a corner' (*dlya zhitya moego mne nuzhen byl ugol, ugol bukval'no*); 'I grew up in a corner' (*ya vyros v uglu*); 'I will bottle myself up even more into a corner' (*ya zakuporyus' eshche bol'she v ugol*); 'my idea is a corner' (*moya ideya—ugol*). They are self-centred even when they turn themselves inside out, abandon all restraint, mobilize all their resources, become intensely gregarious, noisy and loquacious (as on the occasion of the 'stupid funeral feast' for the departed Marmeladov in *Crime and Punishment* (Part Two, Ch. 2) or of the invasion of Nastas'ya Filippovna's flat by the 'Rogozhin gang' in *The Idiot* (1868) (Part One, Ch. 15). No writer has a greater sense than Dostoevsky of situations that will drive man the more into himself through being driven out of himself.

Dostoevsky's world has a Gothic extremism. It is a world where extremes of degradation and of exultation are inevitable and where those potentially most virtuous are the most extreme. It contains few averagely cheerful individuals, and when they are endowed with divine innocence, like Prince Myshkin and Alesha Karamazov, their very innocence draws them to disaster, or involves them in disaster. The permanent inhabitants tend to be extravagant or preposterous or monstrous. At any rate, in the inimitable words of Stefan Trofimovich Verkhovensky (*The Devils*), '*tous les hommes de génie et de progrès en Russia étaient, sont et seront toujours des* gamblers (*igroki*) *et des* drunkards (*p'yanitsy*) *qui boivent* in outbreaks (*zapoem*)' (Part One, Ch. 2, v). What is more, in the peculiar Dostoevskian fashion, characters switch rôles with greater or lesser torment, or have discordant characteristics and motives at one and the same time. Even primary impulses turn out to be ambivalent and the emotions of love and hatred in any pure, unmixed form are seen to be an artificial and precarious development of them: an intense desire to preserve the object of emotion is linked with an impulse to destroy it, an intense desire to please with the impulse to hurt. ' "Why [Raskol'nikov asks himself], with what object did I go to her [Sonya] just now? I told her—on business; on what business? I had no sort of business! To tell her I was *going*; but there was no need. Do I love her? No, no, I drove her away just now like a dog. Did I want her crosses? Oh, how low I have sunk! No, I wanted her tears, I wanted to see her terror, to see how her heart ached! I had to have something to cling to, something to delay me, some friendly face to see. . . ." ' (*Crime and Punishment*, Part Six, Ch. 8). Men not only seek pleasure and self-preservation but, at the same time, they seek pain and self-destruction. ' "When I do leap into the pit [Dmitry Karamazov says to Alesha], I go headlong with my heels up, and am pleased to be falling in that degrading attitude, and pride myself on it. And in the very depth of degradation I begin a hymn of praise. Let me be accursed. Let me be vile and base, only let me kiss the hem of the veil in which my God is shrouded" ' (*The Brothers Karamazov*, Part One, Book 3, Ch. 3). In probing such strange, illogical states, Dostoevsky shows every twist and turn and exposes a kind of dancing madness in its intimations of human nature.

When all is strange, it would seem, nothing escapes the imputation of banality. Yet Dostoevsky hardly ever yields to the temptation which affects many writers dealing with tormented characters: that of making them stranger or more incredible than they are. To judge from his notebooks (the work on *The Devils* is particularly revealing in this respect), the temptation was real enough, and Dostoevsky struggled against it by selecting, changing, re-changing and exchanging his plots and characters to make them plausible both in the context of what happens to them in the novels and even apart from this, as independent human beings, recognizable in their own right and living out the consequences of their inner nature.[1]

The characters may be absurd, especially when placed in trouble-stirring situations, when scandal and catastrophe are ripe (as, for instance, the money-burning scene in *The Idiot*, or the Karamazov family gathering in *starets* Zosima's monastic cell, or, with swelling intensity, throughout *The Devils*). They and their relationships may produce an uncontrolled mixture of tragi-comedy, of farce and total, sometimes omen-charged, seriousness. But even then the material is held in check by its reference to real events and is, in fact, drawn from recorded evidence, indicating, as Dostoevsky said, 'a society without foundations', a social order in the process of dissolution. A whole dimension of Dostoevsky's work would be lost if one were to fail to take into account the concrete social events and circumstances, the

---

[1] See *Zapisnye tetradi*, pp. 14–52. The only constant elements throughout the work on *The Devils* appear to be Stavrogin, Verkhovensky-father, Stavrogin's mother, and one or two other minor characters.

ordinary occurrences which provide its term of reference. He was, as he himself remarked, a writer 'obsessed with a longing for current life' (*oderzhim toskoy po tekushchemu*). Dostoevsky converts this 'current life'—as he converts personal heart- and mind-searchings—into vivid people. He transmits, as it were, the one to the other, and it is not always possible to say which is the current incident, the situation, the 'given' and which is a matter of personal meaning, of belief, of fantasy or delirium. Many of his plots are a re-hash of facts reported in newspapers, which he absorbed as avidly as he read Pushkin, Gogol', Balzac, Cervantes, or Dickens. His own journalism was a compulsion with him, even though the dynamics of his fictional characters are often determined by forces other than those which inform Dostoevsky the journalist, or are in conflict with them.

In someone who like Dostoevsky was subject to such internal and external strains, and who leads his characters such a dance and keeps them under such pressure, the sense of realism, however 'unreal' at times, of psychological justness and inevitability, is a measure of his integrity as a writer. Some critics, admittedly, have found Dostoevsky indigestible or artistically offensive just because they miss in him the quality of selectiveness. Henry James described his, and, incidentally, Tolstoy's (although not, of course Turgenev's) novels as 'fluid puddings' or 'baggy monsters'.[1] But this may mean no more than that they have a fullness, an intensity, an air of being true to the open texture of life for the lack of which more rigorously selective novels dry up. In Dostoevsky's work, particularly, the undoubted gaps, the occasional rambling and looseness are ultimately more like experience than the most coherent and urbane Jamesian novel which has none of the untied and untidy ends of life and is stuck in an historical limbo. And yet Dostoevsky was extremely and cunningly inventive as a novelist. He always marked out his course, hatched his plots, even when they originated in reported incidents in life. 'I am a novelist', he said, 'so that I can invent.' This marks an important contrast to Tolstoy, for whom embroilment, complexity, invention ('it's all invented') were terms of literary disparagement.

Poor Folk could be considered a novel in the 'sentimental' manner.

---

[1] Henry James, *Selected Letters*, London, 1956, p. 202; and 'The Tragic Muse', reprinted in *The Art of the Novel*, ed. by R. Blackmur, London, 1934, p. 84.

Its hero illustrates the 'philanthropic' conviction which persists throughout Dostoevsky's whole work and which might seem tautologous if it were not one of the most difficult things in the world to accept as true, namely that 'the humblest person is also a man'. Devushkin is a lovable failure, even if the failure is commingled with self-consciousness. *Notes from the Underground* (*Zapiski iz podpol'ya*) (1864), intended as a counterblast to Chernyshevsky's socialist novel *What Is to Be Done?* (*Chto delat'?*), is first in addressing itself to the exploration of the vagaries of consciousness in the raw, at its most diseased. The book is a strange combination of the imaginary narrator's philosophical monologue, veering towards a dialogue with someone else, and weird anecdotes reflecting the twists of his wilful nature crushed underground and out of contact with 'living life' (one of many typically Dostoevskian pleonasms). His 'acute consciousness' urges him to defy the accepted norms and procedures of thinking and acting. He sets his face against established truths and indeed against truth itself. He is a liar, although not yet to the same degree of gratified, euphoric perfection as some other and later Dostoevskian characters are (Ivolgin in *The Idiot*, for instance). He is a liar by choice, rather than from necessity, for to be truthful would imply conforming to rules and restricting one's non-liability, one's privilege to do as one pleases. He lies, but his lies become truths to him. 'I swear to you', he says, 'there is not one thing, not one word of what I have written, that I really believe. That is to say, I believe it perhaps, but at the same time I feel, I suspect that I am lying like a cobbler.' (Part Two, Ch. 10.) He repudiates what others (especially Chernyshevsky) consider reasonable and of benefit and advantage to all. He is ready to blow up the world as long as he can have his tea whenever he wishes. He gluttonously gives and takes offence. He records an occasion on which a dignified gentleman was thrown out of a window during a fight in a billiardroom and how he himself was filled with envy and went in to see what he could do to be thrown out too. 'I came to the point of feeling', he says, 'a sort of secret, abnormal, mean enjoyment in returning home to my corner on some most foul Petersburg night and of being acutely aware that now, even today, I had again committed a repulsive deed, that that which has been done, can never again be reversed, and inwardly, secretly, gnawing, gnawing myself for this with my teeth, plaguing

16   241

and consuming myself to the point when bitterness would be turned, at last, into a kind of shameful, accursed sweetness, and, finally, into a decisive, serious pleasure! Yes into pleasure, I insist on that!' (Part One, Ch. 2.)

The Man from the Underground is intent on making a virtue of not knowing what he means, because he does not wish to be 'defined'. He is in no need of logic or any abstract intelligibility or existence, because logic soothes and intelligibility gives confidence. 'Twice two is four, after all, is a truly insufferable thing . . . Twice two is four, why this, in my opinion, is simply an affront, Sir. Twice two is four looks like a fop, blocks the way, arms akimbo and spits. I am agreed that twice two is four is an excellent thing—but if we are to give everything else its due, then twice two is five is also sometimes a very charming little thing.' (Part One, Ch. 9.) He asserts his right to personal peevishness, to 'sticking [his] tongue out', to complaint, to gloom and disappointment, because these things rise from the irredeemable and dreaming prodigal inside man, and because they allow him to gamble on his freedom. He is free, even though freedom may lead to chaos, and even if there is nothing but itself that makes it desirable.

Whether tragic or malicious, whether terrifying or merely aiming to show man's panicky fear of being ridiculous, Dostoevsky took a new step in placing this kind of character at the centre of his imaginative universe and declaring that the incongruous, deviant, problematic human condition could no longer be fenced about. 'Such persons as the author of these Notes,' Dostoevsky commented, 'not only can, but even must exist in our society, taking into account those circumstances in which our society has been formed . . . [He] only carries to an extreme [what others] have not dared to carry through half-way.' (Part Two, Ch. 10.)

Actually, Dostoevsky's subsequent work carries 'what others dare carry through only half-way' to even further extremes. Raskol'nikov in *Crime and Punishment* is also at strife with all things outside. Initially, impressed as he was from time to time by foreign writers, Dostoevsky envisaged Raskol'nikov as another Rastignac in Balzac's *Père Goriot*. Like Rastignac, who discusses the moral right to kill an unknown Chinese mandarin to gain a million francs for it, Raskol'nikov wants to murder an old woman as an act of benefaction and 'practical usefulness'. But in the course of working on the novel, Rastignac is replaced by 'Napoleon' and Raskol'nikov finds himself involved with the consequences of a deed done by a 'strong personality' in order to 'prove an idea', to 'overstep the boundaries', and live beyond good and evil.

Dostoevsky did not assume, in the manner of Balzac, that the wicked inevitably exploit the good, or that the good are inevitably silly; nor did he divide people, again in the manner of Balzac, into 'black' and 'white'—the result of a habit of envisaging moral qualities before the characters themselves. Dostoevsky is primarily concerned with the internal logic of his characters' moral and psychological development and most of all with the forces which impel their reasoning. The logic of Raskol'nikov's fate appears to be that, in asserting his freedom to the very end, he makes himself by his isolation not more but less human. The super-man turns out to be sub-man, and Raskol'nikov 'experiences a moral need' for repentance, which would make him once more a man by breaking down the isolation that separates him from other men.

But this indicates only approximately the direction of the novel. Dostoevsky liked to think that there were human beings who by their untrammelled will could acquire power over humanity, or even over life and death. The suicide of Kirillov (in *The Devils*) is shown as an exalted deed because to die was passive, but to kill oneself was to turn passivity into action, into total possession of oneself, to become, as he says, man–god, beyond all gropings after ideals, all qualms and guessings that enfeeble the mind. But Dostoevsky had too much compassion to be at ease in a posture of Byronic hubris. Compassion shows his characters, in their ceaseless fabrications, to be urged by a cruel need to reassure themselves of their humanity against the nothingness of life, rather than by the attractions of a glittering fallen angel. *Crime and Punishment*, therefore, is not about romantic satisfaction derived from a Promethean desire for omnipotence; nor does Dostoevsky merely use Raskol'nikov's fate to show that to assert one's freedom is a presumptuous and self-defeating thing to do. Rather, as in *Notes from the Underground*, Dostoevsky examines Raskol'nikov's mental and moral experiment with himself, which assumes its own relentless force and allows him to test his freedom as an act of choice lying beyond the familiar world of cause, effect, and solid obstacle. The word 'test', 'testing' (*proba, isprobovat'*, *ispytat'*) is continuously on Raskol'nikov's lips. 'I had to endure all the agony of that battle of ideas [he says to Sonya Marmeladova], and I longed to throw it off: I wanted to murder without casuistry, to murder for my own sake, for myself alone! I didn't want to lie about it even to myself. It wasn't to help my mother I did the murder—that's nonsense—I didn't do the murder to gain wealth and power and to become a benefactor of mankind. Nonsense! I simply did it; I did the murder for myself, for myself alone, and whether I became a benefactor to others, or spent my life like a spider catching men in my web and sucking the life out of men, I couldn't have cared at that moment . . . And it was not the money I wanted, Sonya, when I did it. It was not so much the money I wanted, but something else . . . I know it all now . . . Understand me! Perhaps I would never have committed a murder again. I wanted to find out something else; it was something else which led me on. I wanted to find out then and quickly whether I was a louse like everybody else or a man. Whether I can step over barriers or not, whether I dare stoop to pick up or not, whether I am a trembling creature or whether I have the *right* . . . Listen: when I went then to the old woman's I only went to *test* . . . You may be sure of that!' (Part Five, Ch. 4.)

Could Raskol'nikov endure the 'overstepping of the boundaries'? He could not because he had reached a threshold beyond which what man does is done by someone else; because he had to choose for others and the choice was made by others for him. He is put in a position from which it is impossible to go on, except by breaking down the isolation which separates him from other men. But, at the same time, in escaping from his solitude, Raskol'nikov discovers that he is never more closely in touch with his fellow-men than in the apparent isolation of his crime, of his moment of revolt, since it was to assert his right to be human that he was rebellious. This, it appears, is the true condition of man.[1]

Raskol'nikov does not in fact repent, and he does not 'rise to a new life', but his crime is significant as a revelation of human potentiality for debasement and nobility. In the end, it is not only man's fate but

---

[1] It could be said that J.-P. Sartre's theme of 'ways of freedom' (*les chemins de la liberté*) echoes the auto-experimentation of Dostoevsky's characters. Indeed, it is just another, imitative version of what those characters are involved in.

his obligation to lose innocence. This involves taking all the risks of freedom, making the damning as well as the saving choice, and thus revealing the supreme importance of the human act. D. H. Lawrence called this derisively 'Dostoevsky's sinning his way to Jesus'—the humble recognition of one's impurity and the excuse for going on being impure. *Ne sogreshish' ne pokaesh'sya* ('if you don't sin you won't repent'), as the Russian saying goes. What Lawrence failed to see is Dostoevsky's notion, which received full imaginative expression in *The Brothers Karamazov*, that man was driven out of paradise, but paradise itself was not destroyed; that man's exile was in a sense a fortunate thing, for had he not been driven out, paradise would have been destroyed, or, in the words of the Gospel, which serve as an epigraph to the novel, 'unless a grain of wheat falls into the earth and dies, it remains a single grain; but if it dies, it bears rich fruit'.

The significance of human action as an experiment in freedom at its most macabre is summed up by Stavrogin (*The Devils*) in his letter to Dasha Shatova shortly before his suicide: 'I tried my strength everywhere. You advised me to do this so as to learn "to know myself" ... But what to apply my strength to—that's what I have never seen and don't see now ... I can still wish to do something good, as I always could, and that gives me a feeling of pleasure too ... My desires are not strong enough, they cannot guide me. You can cross a river on a log but not on a chip of wood.' (Part Three Ch. 8.)

Stavrogin is the most enigmatic of Dostoevsky's characters and he passes through the novel with the unapproachable disdain of a visiting Lucifer. The desire to gauge the measure of his own strength, the pride, the disgust, the relentless self-interrogation, the degradation are the familiar traits of other Dostoevskian characters, whether they be sinners or saintly fools, evil-doers or holy men, hysterical women or guiltless children, revolutionaries or intoxicated die-hards. But Stavrogin has none of the 'miracle-working force of life' which sustains a Raskol'nikov or an Ivan Karamazov. Nothing any longer can give him a sensation and he goes from depravity to depravity in search of something, anything, by which to prove himself still capable of feeling. Systematic dissimulation, pointless conspiracies and abductions, and senseless murder fail to mean anything to him, even where he is responsible for them. It all sounds satanic to the point of ludicrousness. Indeed, the novel tends towards melodrama.[1] But, on one level at least, it is a realistic political tragedy, and it is interspersed with comic scenes which enhance the link with reality. Even Stavrogin's 'nightmare' turns comically realistic with the appearance of the devil in the shape of a 'nasty little, scrofulous imp, with a cold in his head, one of the unsuccessful ones' (Part Two, Ch. 3, iv; cf. the similar situation in *The Brothers Karamazov* where Ivan's devil is described as having the appearance of 'gentility on straitened means', wearing 'a tortoise-shell lorgnette on a black ribbon' and 'a massive gold ring with a cheap opal stone in it on the middle finger of his right hand', Part Four, Book 11, Ch. 9). *The Devils* has a factual basis in the Nechaev affair and in the real-life prototypes of Granovsky (Stefan Trofimovich Verkhovensky), Turgenev (Karmazinov), Bakunin or Speshnev (Stavrogin), the murdered Ivanov (Shatov), Zaytsev (Shigalev), Nechaev himself (Petr Verkhovensky), and so on. Yet all this is woven into a story of angels and demons clothing their abnormal passion for political violence with idealism.

When it came to politics Dostoevsky, like Stendhal and Proust before and after him, could do no more than fail with distinction—maybe because in their kind of society politics could only remain a subject for satire and farce, not a subject of realism, Dostoevskian or otherwise. As a political farce or fantasy, *The Devils* is terrifying indeed. But Saltykov-Shchedrin, Dostoevsky's most hated enemy and detractor, was probably right to argue that the terror on which Dostoevsky raises the curtain should have been traced not to revolution but to counter-revolution. With characteristic ambiloquy, Dostoevsky implied as much himself in *The Raw Youth*, in which the revolutionary 'devils' who have settled in the herd of swine are replaced by millenarian dreamers and belated idealistic Petrashevskists (the 'Dolgushintsy').

---

[1] Elsewhere, too, Dostoevsky displays melodramatic tendencies, where his skill becomes almost the same thing as bad taste, even if it is at times good bad taste. Alesha's utterances at Ilyusha's funeral (*The Brothers Karamazov*, Epilogue, Ch. 3), could be taken as an illustration of the latter and Dunya Raskol'nikova's encounter with Svidrigaylov illustrates the former ('Dunya raised the revolver and, deadly pale, gazed at him, measuring the distance and awaiting the first movement on his part. Her lower lip was white and quivering and her big black eyes flashed like fire. He had never seen her so handsome, the fire glowing in her eyes at the moment she raised the revolver seemed to kindle him and there was a pang of anguish in his heart . . .' Part Six, Ch. 5).

Stavrogin himself is a dead-end as a revolutionary or a 'nihilist'—the last survivor of the Byronic ideal. Yet even he acquires in Dostoevskian hands a human dimension, partly because he has a grim, all-too-human *alter ego* in Petr Verkhovensky who cuts loose the romantic threads and attaches 'nihilism' to a pragmatic cause; and mainly because Stavrogin seeks forgiveness. Somewhere the awful line of diabolic descent must be broken and forgiveness offered and accepted. This is what Stavrogin learns to do, or almost learns to do, in his confrontation with Tikhon.[1] Obsessed by a passion for exploring the darkest situations, Dostoevsky made his case that even these situations could be enfolded within forgiveness, that to elicit the pathways of man's freedom one must understand his degradation.

The curse of degradation as the lowermost experience in the world which opens up the highest constitutes the principal theme of *The Brothers Karamazov* and it accounts for the novel's extraordinarily wide-ranging quality: it spans the whole extent of man's spiritual universe as well as embodies all the intellectual, psychological and social preoccupations of Dostoevsky's previous work. It achieves the effect of a vision of life that is greater than any particular experience or any actions and motives of particular characters and yet reveals the characters as all the more themselves for being 'eccentric', for revealing more life than they contain within their narrow selves and being pressed by violence, catastrophe and joy into an existence beyond their individuality.

The climax of *The Brothers Karamazov* gives special weight to this wide-ranging, divergent feature of the novel. Dostoevsky is a superb, if at times diffuse, story-teller and plot-designer, whose eyes and sympathies are open to the surprising in events, who knew how to put people in the most exposed situations, how to make the most of scandal and calamity, and how to create suspense. Often this is achieved by keeping dark, or merely alluding to, facts and experiences which explain the actions and relationships of his characters, as in the unresolved mystery of the murder of old Karamazov, or in the studied silence about the past life of Myshkin, Rogozhin and Natas'ya Filippovna in *The Idiot*. Since the plot of *The Brothers Karamazov*,

[1] *'U Tikhona'*, Ch. 3 (vol. 7, pp. 580 sq.), where this is brought out with particular poignancy. *'U. Tikhona'* was suppressed in Russia and restored to its proper place in post-revolutionary editions of the novel.

as of many other novels of Dostoevsky, is centred round a murder, one would have expected it to culminate in the detection of the crime, in the apprehension and confession of the criminal, or in his trial and conviction. But, though the interest and ingenuity of *The Brothers Karamazov* as a detective novel is considerable, its real focus lies elsewhere. It is to be found in the fifth and sixth Books, called '*Pro* and *Contra*' and 'The Russian Monk', and more particularly in the section entitled 'Rebellion', which describes Ivan's confrontation with Alesha and his 'confession', together with the chapter 'The Grand Inquisitor'. Dostoevsky himself intended these to be the 'culminating' statement of 'extreme blasphemy'—'the essence of the destructive ideas of our times'—and 'along with the blasphemy . . . the refutation in the words of the dying *starets* Zosima [Part Two, Book 6]' (*Pis'ma*, vol. 4, p. 53).

There is a structural justification for narrowing down the novel to these sections. It follows the pattern of Dostoevsky's other novels which are built on the principle not of a gradually unfolding development, but of centring the drama on certain focal component scenes that carry the germ of the whole action. '*Pro* and *Contra*' is such a centre. Its meaning could be summarized in the proposition (implied in the title itself) that all experiences are finally interrelated, and, equally, that no experience is complete until it has been related to its opposite. Characters, their feelings, ideas and actions take life and a peculiar dramatic quality in situations of such 'dialectical' interdependence, where polarity reveals unexpected correspondence. When we say that life is both defeat and victory, or that man both wins and loses his wager, or that he retains his freedom in the act of losing it, then the pattern of our thought contains two equally valid but contradictory ideas. This is to think in the tradition of Blake, of Hegel, of Marx. The term 'dialectic' is perhaps the only word available, although it may not express precisely the imaginative complexity that is peculiar to such an interplay of opposites.

This accounts for the recurring theme of *double identity* in Dostoevsky's characters. Sometimes the image of the double aims merely at a comic effect, similar to that achieved by Gogol''s 'twins' Bobchinsky and Dobchinsky, Ivan Ivanovich and Ivan Nikiforovich, Kifa Mokievich and Moky Kifovich: 'Svidrigaylov was particularly drawn to these clerks (*svyazalsya s etimi pisarashkami*) by the fact that they both had crooked noses, one bent to the left and the other to the right.' (Part Six, Ch. 6.) But usually the image has deeper and more dramatic implications—whether embodied in the form of a personified *alter ego*, of another self, a *Doppelgänger*, or, not less dramatically, in the form of emanations of the self, of hypertrophied divided consciousness poised between two equally valid moral, spiritual, or intellectual opposites: Ivan Karamazov and the devil, Ivan Karamazov and Smerdyakov, Ivan Karamazov and Alesha, Ivan Karamazov between Christ and Anti-Christ, and so on.[1]

No modern writer, except perhaps Baudelaire, is so aware of the entwined relation between damnation and salvation as the author of *The Brothers Karamazov*. But whereas for Baudelaire to be damned in the nineteenth century implied the only significant option in a bourgeois society where it was impossible to be saved, damnation for Dostoevsky is an extension of light into the darkest places in the universe where, paradoxically, its presence is felt more than in the supposedly lighter ones, or where darkness denies itself. 'I want to tell you now', Dmitry Karamazov says to Alesha, 'about the insects to whom God gave "sensual lust" . . . I am such an insect, brother, and it is said of me specially. All we Karamazovs are such insects, and angel as you are, that insect lives in you, too, and will stir up a tempest in your blood. Tempests, because sensual lust is a tempest—worse than a tempest! Beauty is a terrible and awful thing! It is terrible because it has not been fathomed and never can be fathomed, for God sets us nothing but riddles. Here the boundaries meet and all contradictions exist side by side . . . It's terrible what mysteries there are! Too many riddles weigh men down on earth. We must solve them as we can, and try to keep our skin dry. Beauty! I can't endure the thought that a man of lofty mind and heart begins with the ideal of the Madonna and ends with the ideal of Sodom. What's still more awful is that a man with the ideal of Sodom in his soul does not renounce

---

[1] Most Dostoevskian novels contain such 'doubles'. Raskol'nikov and Svidrigagaylov (in *Crime and Punishment*), Stavrogin and Petr Verkhovensky amongst others (in *The Devils*), Myshkin and Rogozhin (in *The Idiot*), seeking each other out in their interlocking struggle, are the most dramatic instances, to say nothing of the more obvious case of Golyadkin (in *The Double* (*Dvoynik*) (1846)) trapped between two Golyadkins who mirror his inner conflicts. 'Where people used to see one thought', Bakhtin observes, 'Dostoevsky was able to discover and scent two thoughts—a bifurcation. Where people used to see one quality, he uncovered in man the presence of another, opposite quality.' (*Problemy poetiki Dostoevskogo*, p. 41.)

the ideal of the Madonna, and his heart may be on fire with that ideal, genuinely on fire, just as in his days of youth and innocence. Yes, man is broad, too broad, indeed. I'd have him narrower. The devil only knows what to make of it . . . Is there beauty in Sodom? Believe me, for the immense mass of mankind beauty is found in Sodom. Did you know that secret? The awful thing is that beauty is mysterious as well as terrible. God and the devil are fighting there and the battlefield is the heart of man . . .' (Part One, Book 3, Ch. 3.)

In the face of such polarized forces there are no easy escapes, not even into a world of apocalyptic meaning, no religious rescue squads, no moral profit out of misfortune. Dostoevsky does not of course concern himself with theological doctrines. He does not deal in absolutes. He seeks to represent a human situation, rather than to indicate the ultimate reality behind it; and he explores situations, without either conceding light to them or withholding it from them. His vision comes about, in suspense, through unpredictable experience, in which the conflicting forces are so closely interlocked that it is not possible to say until the last moment which way victory will go. Thus Ivan Karamazov's experience of the death or diminution of God at the sound of cracking human bones, of men's feeble shrill voices and mad rebellious gestures, turns into a hymn to life. It is only by taking the measure of Ivan's involvement in this kind of 'dialectic' that one can understand the significance of *starets* Zosima's oracular pronouncement: 'Everyone is really responsible to all men for all men and all things.' (Part Two, Book 6, iii(g).) The point is not that 'to understand all is to forgive all'—which implies the privileged position of the onlooker who justifies evil. In Ivan's logic, who but the injured can forgive an injury; and injury to an innocent (a child, for instance) cannot be forgiven because the innocent cannot forgive what they do not understand as an injury. Rather, the point is to bear the suffering of others as one's own by breaking out of the circles of private experience in which men are immured, to yield some of one's separate identity and become merged with others. This way lies, for Dostoevsky, the affirmation of belief in life.

Dostoevsky is not the first nor the last novelist to find joy and illumination more difficult to portray than the wish for them. His 'positive' characters, though never priggish, boring or solemn, are more credible when their virtue is darkened by the counsels of madness or is turned to ridicule by some untoward calamity—as with Myshkin, the 'idiot', who is both Christ-like and comic in his ill-fated innocence and his unsusceptibility to the perversities of social life as he knows it.[1] Zosima, on the other hand, is not free from pious starch and only just avoids setting one's teeth on edge. And yet his statement quoted above succeeds in conveying a wisdom of great depth and simplicity, with the weight of the whole heaven and hell loading the words. In a way, this brings the dilemma to one way out: the way of suffering. Suffering is chosen not because it may purge man, but because it is a 'trial', a way of freedom in which man ultimately finds the unifying link with his fellow man. To many of Dostoevsky's critics (Dobrolyubov, Pisarev, Gor'ky) this view seemed like an evasion, a call to humility addressed to the already humiliated and insulted. For such critics the characters of those who suffered were not cured but distorted by suffering; and they could scarcely think otherwise because their concern was not with their own suffering, but with that of others. Yet Dostoevsky too sought to discover meaning through closeness to the perplexity and the hope of his time, through shouldering and enduring the enormity of the grief of others as one's own—not through the acquisition and possession of an unassailable truth. What drew Dostoevsky and draws his characters irresistibly to the Russian people is its long and rich experience of suffering: suffering even convinces his characters that only by fathoming the suffering of others could salvation be found, for everything that suffered, everything that hung on the cross, was divine.

The emphasis in the preceding discussion has been on Dostoevsky's and his characters' mental attitudes, ideas and convictions—an approach which, in certain professional circles, is liable to be distrusted as an unwarranted substitution of ideology for literary analysis.

[1] This is what Dostoevsky wrote to his niece (S. Ivanova): 'The principal idea of the novel [*The Idiot*] is to represent a positively flawless person (*polozhitel'no prekrasnogo cheloveka*). There is nothing more difficult than this in the world, especially now . . . The most complete flawless character in Christian literature is Don Quixote. But he is flawless only because he is also ridiculous. Dickens' Pickwick (an infinitely weaker image than Don Quixote, but still enormous) is also ridiculous, but he only gains by this. There is evocation of compassion in the reader for the mocked, and for selfless goodness. The mystery of humour lies in the evocation of this kind of compassion . . .' (*Pis'ma*, vol. 2, p. 71.)

Since it cannot reasonably be denied that Dostoevsky put his genius at the service of his message (however this may be defined), some have suggested that, in this respect, he should be considered at best a deplorable ideologue and at worst a windbag, whilst critics should get down to 'essentials' by concentrating on Dostoevsky 'the artist', Dostoevsky 'the craftsman', Dostoevsky 'the master narrator', Dostoevsky 'the ironist', Dostoevsky 'the romanticist', and so on. This is not the proper occasion for discussing the dichotomy between 'artist' and 'thinker' which is implied in this admonition and which easily dwindles into literary trivialities and parochialism. Nor is it opportune to dwell on the familiar fact that heart-searchings, conflicts of conscience, and spiritual struggle were a dominant impulse in Russian writers, and in Dostoevsky almost as much as in Tolstoy; that indeed so severe has the struggle been that literature has been often a scourge to these writers rather than a profession, let alone an aesthetic self-gratification.

But there are other, more specific reasons why the consideration of Dostoevsky's 'ideas' must be a central part of any relevant discussion of his work. Nothing in human experience can satisfactorily explain the motives and actions of the Man from the Underground or Raskol'nikov, of Ippolit Terent'ev or Nikolay Stavrogin, of Kirillov or Ivan Karamazov, and many others, unless it be the ideas which these characters profess or, rather, with which and by which they are identified.

In a sense, Dostoevsky's theme is *anti*-intellectualism: he was committed to this by his *pochvennik* beliefs. But at the same time he was a uniquely conscious writer who not only, knowingly and directly, evoked the most pressing issues of his day, but in whose experience ideas acquired a reality, a potentiality for good and evil, as great as flesh-and-blood men and women. The conjunction of a powerful imagination and a passionate concern for conveying intellectual and moral concepts is rare among philosophers and even rarer among novelists. Dostoevsky achieved it in a remarkable degree. The nearest to him in this respect was, surprisingly perhaps, Plato, whose ideomania and almost religious madness for 'form' were, no doubt, one of the greatest evidences of the 'Greek soul', so different from the 'Russian soul' of Dostoevsky. But Dostoevsky did not 'propound' ideas, any more than Plato did; neither are his characters, any more than the characters in the Platonic Dialogues, mere proponents of the author's ideas. His ideas are not separable from experience: they are one and the same thing. Ideas conveyed in literature appear more often than not cut off from their sources in experience (Turgenev's novels are cases in point): Dostoevsky reconnects them and tests out in his art their human and imaginative consequences. His characters did not illustrate or represent ideas: they *are* his ideas or, what is especially revealing, ideas *opposite* to his, but still his own. With Dostoevsky to be in contact with an idea is to touch his deepest experience and his most living creation. The Romantics told us what it felt like to feel; Dostoevsky tells us what it feels like to think; and in fact he makes us feel human pain, solitude, rebellion, illumination, joy, exultation with our intellect. Hence the abundance in his novels of such expressions as 'the thought made me drunk' (*mysl' p'yanila menya*), 'my mind and imagination jumped off the thread' (*um i voobrazhenie soskochili s nitki*), 'all my mental perplexities came together into distress' (*sgrustilis' vse umstvennye nedoumeniya moi*). The idea is summed up by Versilov in *The Raw Youth:* 'The artist learns the face by guessing the main thought of the face' (*Khudozhnik izuchaet litso, ugadyvaya glavnuyu mysl' litsa*, Part Three, Ch. 1, ii.)

Thomas Hobbes spoke of the 'lust of the mind' which 'by a perseverance of delight in the continuall and indefatigable generation of knowledge exceedeth the short vehemence of any carnall Pleasure'. Dostoevsky shared the 'lust of the mind', but it did not 'exceed' carnal pleasure: the two were coterminous for him. He was as much interested in the body as it affects the mind as in the mind as it affects the body. As early as 1838 Dostoevsky wrote to his brother of 'intelligence as a material capacity: the soul, or spirit, lives by thought whispered to it by the heart . . . Thought arises in the soul. The mind is a tool, a machine moved by spiritual fire.' (*Pis'ma*, vol. 1, p. 50.) It is this kind of commutation of mind and body, of idea and imagination, which enabled him to conjure up such grotesquely ill-shaped figures as Svidrigaylov, Rogozhin, and particularly the appallingly corrupt Fedor Pavlovich Karamazov, who yet stand out with the force of frightening authenticity in their disembodied bodily or embodied bodiless lust.

To move away from Dostoevsky's ideas—not as 'emblems', or 'mouthpieces', or 'representations' but as creative acts, as molten images, as mental forces with their underworld of feeling and persistent assumption of human faces—is therefore effectively to deprive oneself of the major key to the understanding of his work.

The essentially *ideological* nature of Dostoevsky's imagination accounts for the fact that it depends predominantly on dialogue for its expression and thus turns his novels into dramatizations of intellectual discourse. Only playwrights of Shakespeare's genius have achieved such feats of individualization through dialogue as Dostoevsky. One can often visualize him better on the stage than in the novels, and their production by the Moscow Art Theatre proves how dramatically effective they are. Bernard Shaw's dialogue, wonderful though it is, is a parade of views by comparison, while Oscar Wilde's is a mere exercise in verbal ingenuity and repartee. It is the speech of Dostoevsky's characters which constitutes their exact particularity and real presence. A few words 'on his favourite topic' brings the essential old Karamazov to life: 'Ah, you boys! You children, little sucking-pigs, to my thinking . . . I never thought a woman ugly in my life—that's been my rule! Can you understand that? How could you understand it? You've milk in your veins, not blood. You're not out of your shells yet. My rule has been that you can always find something devilishly interesting in every woman that you wouldn't find in any other. Only, one must know how to find it, that's the point! That's talent! To my mind there are no ugly women. The very fact that she is a woman is half the battle . . . but how could you understand that? Even in *vieilles filles*, even in them you may discover something that makes you simply wonder that men have been such fools as to let them grow old without noticing them. Barefooted girls or unattractive ones, you must take by surprise. Didn't you know that? You must astound them till they're fascinated, upset, ashamed that such a gentleman should fall for such a little slut. It's a jolly good thing that there always are and will be masters and slaves in the world, so there will always be a little maid-of-all work and her master, and you know, that's all that's needed for happiness . . .' (*The Brothers Karamazov*, Part One, Book 3, Ch. 8.)[1]

---

[1] Эх вы, ребята! Деточки, поросяточки вы маленькие, для меня...даже во всю мою жизнь не было безобразной женщины, вот мое правило! Можете вы это понять? Да где же вам это понять: у вас еще вместо крови молоко течет, не вылупились! По моему правилу, во всякой женщине

DOSTOEVSKY

One cannot fail to hear the difference between the inimitable staccato of Kirillov and the jumps and jerks in the verbal flood of his fellow-'devil' Petr Verkhovensky. Nothing lays bare the character, and indeed prefigures the fate, of Dmitry Karamazov more than his impetuous, breathless, feverish 'confessions of a burning heart' (ibid. Ch. 3–5). Dostoevsky dramatizes speech and thought, revealing rather than, as with Tolstoy, concealing the inner life of man in his words and enacting through them the fabulous visions or the heinous dissimulations of the human mind. Merezhkovsky, in his critical study of Tolstoy and Dostoevsky observed—but, as usual for him, over-rationalized his case—that with Tolstoy we 'hear' because we 'see', whereas with Dostoevsky we 'see' because we 'hear'.[1] Dostoevsky's genius is made of words. He is also the most verbose of the Russian prose writers, which is saying a great deal considering the logorrhoea of Gogol'.

The language of Dostoevsky is however peculiarly suited to express his tense, discordant, intrusively urgent sense of life. The pages of his writings are studded with such heightened words as 'suddenly' (*vdrug, vnezapno*), 'instantaneously' (*mgnovenno*), 'unexpected' (*neozhidannyy*), 'extraordinary' (*chrezvychaynyy*), 'staggering'(*potryasayushchiy*); and with such equally heightened expressions—some deliberately comic, others in deep earnest—as 'I jumped up and dashed away' (*ya vskochil i kinulsya*), 'I flew, I nearly ran' (*ya poletel, ya pochti bezhal*); or 'he understood to the highest degree the word "student"' (*on v vysshey stepeni ponyal slovo student*), 'she knew how to listen in a terrible way' (*one uzhasno umela slushat'*), 'the most ferocious possible dreaminess' (*samaya yarostneyshaya mechtatel'-nost'*), 'I choked from some feeling of an infinitely aggravated haughti-

можно найти чрезвычайно, черт возьми, иитересное, чего ни у которой другой не найдешь, — только надобно уметь находить, вот где штука! Это талант! Для меня мовешек не существовало: уж одно то, что она женщина, уж это одно половина всего...да где вам это понять! Даже вьельфильки, и в тех иногда отыщешь такое, что только диву дашься на прочих дураков, как это ей состариться дали и до сих пор не заметили! Босоножку и мовешку надо сперва-на-перво удивить — вот как надо за нее браться. А ты не знал? Удивить ее надо до восхищения, до пронзения, до стыда, что в такую чернявку, как она, такой барин влюбился. Истинно славно, что всегда есть и будут хамы да баре на свете; всегда тогда будет такая поломоечка и всегда ее господин, а ведь того только и надо для счастья жизни!...'

[1] *Tolstoy i Dostoevskiy*, p. 235.

ness and defiance' (*ya zadykhalsya ot kakogo-to chuvstva bezkonechno preuvelichennoy nadmennosti i vyzova*), 'I cherished in my soul the highest ideal side by side with the greatest baseness' (*ya leleyal v dushe vysochayshiy ideal ryadom s velichayshey podlost'yu*).

A comparison between two passages from *The Brothers Karamazov* and from Tolstoy's *War and Peace*, describing analogous experiences will help to bring out Dostoevsky's verbal expansiveness in contrast to Tolstoy's plainness.

'Alesha [on leaving the dead body of his *starets*] did not stop on the steps . . ., but went quickly down—his soul, overflowing with rapture; he yearned for freedom, space, openness. The vault of heaven, full of soft, shining stars, stretched vast and fathomless above him. The Milky Way ran in two pale streams from the zenith to the horizon. The fresh, motionless, still night enfolded the earth. The white towers and golden domes of the cathedral gleamed out against the sapphire sky. The gorgeous autumn flowers, in the beds round the house, were slumbering till morning. The silence of earth seemed to melt into the silence of the heavens. The mystery of earth was one with the mystery of the stars . . . Alesha stood, gazed, and suddenly threw himself down on the earth. He did not know why he embraced it. He could not have told why he longed so irresistibly to kiss it, to kiss it all. But he kissed it weeping, sobbing and watering it with his tears, and vowed passionately to love it, to love it for ever and ever.' (Part Three, Book 7, Ch. 4.)

'[Andrey Bolkonsky lying wounded on the battlefield at Austerlitz] opened his eyes, hoping to see the end of the struggle of the French with the artillery men, and wishing to know whether the red-haired artillerist was killed, and whether the cannon was taken or saved. But he saw nothing. Above him there was nothing but the heaven, the high heaven, not clear, but still immeasurably high, with grey clouds softly creeping over it.

'"How quiet, calm, and solemn! It is different from what it was when I was running", thought Prince Andrey, "different from what it was when the Frenchman and the artillerist were pulling at the linstock with infuriated and frightened faces; quite differently the clouds creep over this high, endless heaven. How is it I did not see this high heaven before? How happy I am that at last I know it. Yes, everything is vanity, everything deception, except this endless heaven. There is nothing, nothing but the heaven. But even the heaven is not, there is nothing but quiet and calm. Thank God".' (*War and Peace*, Book Three, Ch. 16.)

And yet from Dostoevsky's impulsive, tossing verbal torrents there appear magnificent images of vivid, unrepeatable life. It may be asked whether he has succeeded in endorsing by his creative imagination the vision of the transfigured universe as witnessed by Alesha Karamazov. Which sounds truer: the recorded experience of 'the mystery of earth at one with the mystery of the stars' or the case for the opposite—Dostoevsky's savage and apparently total negations? Or, maybe, illumination and negation are no longer seen as alternatives but are a matter of the one and the other, of 'Hell' which is meaningless without 'Paradise', of 'Light that shines in the Darkness'? It is this configuration perhaps which shows the truly human identity of Dostoevsky's characters and carries their resemblance to the extremes of human variety.

The reader of Dostoevsky's novels is, indeed, overwhelmed by the veritable Babylon—or is it a pentecostal Jerusalem?—of tongues which they conjure up. Dostoevsky himself claimed, with reference to *The Raw Youth*, that 'every personage speaks his own language in [by] his own notions' (*svoimi ponyatiyami, Pis'ma*, vol. 3, p. 197), since 'notions' for him can be as individualized as the manner of speech or tone of voice. Bakhtin, who coined the term 'polyphonic' to describe the highly diversified, many-voiced quality of Dostoevsky's artistic universe, says that it is not even 'a matter of a single author-artist writing novels and stories, but of a whole series of philosophical statements by *several* author-thinkers—by Raskol'nikov, Myshkin, Stavrogin, Ivan Karamazov, the Grand Inquisitor, and many others'.[1] This is not always or immediately apparent because Dostoevsky frequently intervenes into the language of his characters, whether in the shape of a 'chronicler', or 'gossiper', or even of one or other among the protagonists (notably in *The Devils*, where the commentator appears under the guise of a distinct character who plays a part in the events themselves). Yet 'the words of a character', Bakhtin explains, 'do not serve as an expression of the author's own ideological position (as for instance in Byron). The consciousness of the character is given as his [Dostoevsky's] other, *alien* consciousness:

[1] *Problemy poetiki Dostoevskogo*, p. 5.

DOSTOEVSKY

but, at the same time, it is not reified, it is not closed up, it does not turn into a mere object of the author's consciousness'.[1] In other words, the author himself thinks in terms of his characters' discordant voices. He does not present or argue his case but contrasts a great variety of attitudes all of which are and are not his own. Thus it remains a puzzle where Dostoevsky himself stands in stating the highly and dramatically conflicting positions of Ivan Karamazov, of the Grand Inquisitor, of Christ, and of Alesha.

Bakhtin's interpretation points to Dostoevsky's essential conception of character and to his peculiar way of bringing his characters to life: the way of division into contrary voices, which mark the author's own 'multiplicity of consciousness' and his own propensity for turning into opposing selfs. The voices, the characters remain part of the highly inflected and inflated world of the author. They appear, in spite of or in consequence of their intensity, to be shadows projected on the material world by the author, whose counterparts or doubles they are. But in containing them all and struggling with them all, Dostoevsky lets them assume their separate identity. It is this shifting of the focus from the author who thinks and feels to the thoughts and feelings as forces on their own, this looking outside of himself while looking into himself, this entanglement of self-consciousness with the real order of things and dramatic enactment of mental imaginings in the human variety, which gave Dostoevsky his peculiar insight into the underworld of experience—an insight by comparison with which all 'objective', sober-faced accounts of the observable facts seem *jejune*. Without this insight we would not know what man really is.

SELECT BIBLIOGRAPHY

EDITIONS

Pis'ma, ed. A. Dolinin, 4 vols., Moscow, 1928–59.
Polnoe sobranie khudozhestvennykh proizvedeniy, ed. B. Tomashevsky and K. Khalavaev, 13 vols., Moscow–Leningrad, 1926–30.
Sobranie sochineniy, ed. L. Grossman and others, 10 vols., Moscow, 1856–8.
Polnoe sobranie sochineniy, ed. V. Bazanov, G. Fridlender, and others, 30 vols., Leningrad, 1972– (only 3 vols. of this complete edition of Dostoevsky's works have appeared at the time of printing).

[1] Problemy poetiki Dostoevskogo, p. 7, also pp. 43 sq.

258

DOSTOEVSKY

The Notebooks for 'The Possessed', ed. E. Wasiolek, translated by V. Terras, Chicago and London, 1968.

Zapisnye tetradi F. M. Dostoevskogo, ed. N. Ignatova and E. Konshina, Moscow–Leningrad, 1935.

, The major fictional works are available in English in 'Everyman's Library' and some in 'Penguin Classics'. There is also an English translation of Dostoevsky's *Diary of a Writer* by B. Brasol (3 vols., London, 1949), and a selection of his journalistic work in *Occasional Writings* by D. Magarshak (Oxford, 1961).

CRITICAL AND BIOGRAPHICAL WORKS

Bakhtin, M., *Problemy poetiki Dostoevskogo*, Moscow, 1963.

Berdyaev, N., *Mirosozertsanie Dostoevskogo*, Paris, 1923 (English translation: *Dostoevsky*, London, 1957).

Carr, E. H., *Dostoevsky (1821–1881). A New Biography*, London, 1930.

Chicherin, A., *Idei i stil'*, Moscow, 1968.

Dostoevsky. A Collection of Critical Essays, ed. R. Wellek, New Jersey, 1962.

Dostoevsky, Aimée, *Fyodor Dostoevsky. A Study*, London, 1921.

F. M. Dostoevskiy, Bibliografiya, 1917–1965, ed. A. Belkin, A. Dolinin, and V. Kozhinov, Moscow, 1968.

F. M. Dostoevskiy v russkoy kritike, ed. A. Belkin, Moscow, 1956.

F. M. Dostoevskiy v vospominaniyakh sovremennikov (Seriya literaturnykh memuarov), 2 vols., Moscow, 1964.

Gide, A., *Dostoevsky* (English translation), London, 1952.

Grossman, L., *Dostoevskiy*, Moscow, 1962.

    Poetika Dostoevskogo, Moscow, 1925.

    Put' Dostoevskogo, Leningrad, 1924.

    Zhizn' i trudy F. M. Dostoevskogo, biografiya v datakh i dokumentakh, Moscow–Leningrad, 1955.

Gus, M., *Idei i obrazy F. M. Dostoevskogo*, Moscow, 1962.

Hingley, R., *The Undiscovered Dostoevsky*, London, 1962.

Ivanov, V., *Freedom and the Tragic Life. A Study in Dostoevsky*, London, 1916.

Kaus, O., *Dostoevski und sein Schicksal*, Berlin, 1923.

Kirpotin, V., *F. M. Dostoevskiy*, Moscow, 1960.

    Molodoy Dostoevskiy, Moscow, 1947.

Kozhinov, V., *'Prestuplenie i nakazanie* F. M. Dostoevskogo' in *Tri shedevra russkoy klassiki*, Moscow, 1971.

Lossky, N., *Dostoevskiy i ego khristianskoe miroponimanie*, New York, 1953.

Magarshak, D., *Dostoevsky*, London, 1961.

Merezhkovsky, D., *Tolstoy i Dostoevskiy. Zhizn' i tvorchestvo*, 4th ed., St. Petersburg, 1909.

DOSTOEVSKY

Mochul'sky, K., *Dostoevskiy. Zhizn' i tvorchestvo*, Paris, 1947 (English translation, Princeton, 1967).

Murry, J. M., *Fyodor Dostoevsky. A Critical Study*, London, 1916.

O Dostoevskom, ed. A. Bem, 3 vols., Prague, 1929–36.

O Dostoevskom. Stat'i, Brown University Slavic Reprint IV, 1966.

Peace, R., *Dostoevsky. An Examination of the Major Novels*, Cambridge, 1971.

Pereverzev, V., *Tvorchestvo Dostoevskogo*, Moscow, 1922.

Rozanov, V., *Legenda o Velikom inkvizitore F. M. Dostoevskogo*, St. Petersburg, 1906.

Russian Literature and Modern English Fiction. A Collection of Critical Essays, ed. D. Davie, Chicago, 1965.

Seduro, V., *Dostoevsky in Russian Criticism*, Columbia–Oxford, 1957.

Shklovsky, V., *Za i protiv. Zametki o Dostoevskom*, Moscow, 1957.

Steiner, G., *Tolstoy or Dostoevsky. An Essay in Contrast*, London, 1959.

Troyat, H., *Firebrand: The Life of Dostoevsky* (English translation), London, 1946.

Tvorcheskiy put' Dostoevskogo, ed. N. Brodsky, Leningrad, 1924.

Tvorchestvo F. M. Dostoevskogo, ed. N. Stepanov, Moscow, 1959.

Wasiolek, W., *Dostoevsky. The Major Fiction*, Cambridge, Mass., 1964.

Yakushin, N., *Dostoevskiy v Sibiri; ocherk zhizni i tvorchestva*, Kemerevo, 1960.

Yarmolinsky, A., *Dostoevsky. His Life and Art*, New York, 1957.

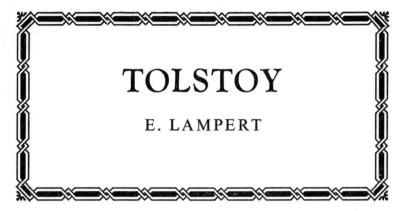

TOLSTOY

E. LAMPERT

MORE IS KNOWN ABOUT TOLSTOY THAN ABOUT ANY OTHER RUSSIAN writer. His own and his wife's frantic diary-keeping, the merciless confessions, the numerous reminiscences of his family and friends and of the many people who knew him, to say nothing of the vast number of biographies, seem like a screen between ourselves and his work.[1] But Tolstoy forces us to react to his achievement as a writer in terms of his person. Indeed, this is the measure he himself chose to apply to literature. 'The main interest [of a literary work]', he wrote in the early 1850s, 'lies in the character of the author who expresses himself in his work.' (vol. 46, p. 182.)

Tolstoy's own art provides an exhaustive revelation of his character, just as his character presents an extraordinary work of art. His earliest writings, as well as the major novels of the middle years and the late imaginative work, are a direct reflection of the drama of his life and continue or anticipate his personal preoccupations. The common features between Tolstoy's own mind-searchings in *A Confession* (*Ispoved'*, 1879–82) and Levin's in *Anna Karenina*, between

---

[1] Of the ninety volumes of the Jubilee Edition of Tolstoy's works forty-five are filled with diaries, letters, reflections and notes. In the text that follows all quotations from Tolstoy refer to the Jubilee Edition.

Among the extensive biographical works on Tolstoy the following are the most important: Gusev, *Lev Nikolaevich Tolstoy*; Biryukov, *Lev Nikolaevich Tolstoy* (there is a French and an abbreviated English version of this basic biography); Eykhenbaum, *Molodoy Tolstoy* and *Lev Tolstoy;* cf. also the collection of reminiscences of Tolstoy, *L. N. Tolstoy v vospominaniyakh sovremennikov.* The best and most talented recent biography is Shklovsky's *Lev Tolstoy.* The most useful biographies in English are by Simmons (*Leo Tolstoy*) and Troyat (*Tolstoy*).

his own experience of death and that of Andrey Bolkonsky on the eve of Borodino or of Golovin in *The Death of Ivan Il'ich* (*Smert' Ivana Il'icha*, 1886), between his own aesthetic views as formulated in *What is Art?* (*Chto takoe iskusstvo?*, 1897) and Natasha Rostova watching an opera performance, are cases in point. *Resurrection* (*Voskresenie*, 1899), written in old age, is an outstanding example of a novel whose 'main interest lies in the character of the author' and which transforms the raw material of recorded moral, social and intellectual experience into art. At the same time, Tolstoy was so instinctively an artist that, unconsciously, he fashioned his life and even the lives of those around him into a superb comedy and, at times, a tragedy, and developed his character in a life of eighty-two years into a masterpiece of the sublime and the ironic. The importance of his work for us, therefore, could be said to derive from the kind of human being he is.

Almost the first thing that impressed everyone who came into contact with Tolstoy was the gigantic scale of the man, the weight and depth of his nature—not an agreeable nature by any means, but just nature. It made, and still makes, most men look flimsy in comparison. Lenin was one of the first to comment on this: 'What hugeness!', he said to Gor'ky, 'what a primaeval chunk of a man (*materyy chelovechishche*)! Here is a real artist . . . And, you know, what is astonishing also? Before this Count there has not been a genuine peasant in literature.'[1] The monumental individuality of Tolstoy, his enormous creative energy, and the physical and moral passion which informed it, had a way of crushing people as much as they were brought to life in his novels. Avowedly and unashamedly, he ground a huge axe, mostly a huge moral axe. Whether as a promiscuous, gambling officer, or a quarrelsome lion of the literary world, or the grand old man from Yasnaya Polyana, sitting on the right hand of God and looking up the backfiles of the recording angel, or as a companion of tramps and workmen (though least of all in this capacity), he was overbearing, proud and magnificently self-sufficient, even while engaging in ruthless self-criticism and avoiding like the plague praise for qualities and virtues he did

---

[1] Gor'ky, *Sobranie sochineniy*, 30 vols., Moscow 1952, vol. 17, p. 39. Cf. Chekhov's remark: '*Tolstoy-to, Tolstoy! Eto, po nyneshnim vremenam, ne chelovek, a chelovechishche.*'

not possess. 'I, at any rate,' he wrote in 1874, 'whatever I do, am convinced that *du haut de ces pyramides 40 siècles me contemplent* and that the whole world will perish if I come to a halt' (vol. 62, p.130). Gor'ky, who in his wonderfully vivid portrait of Tolstoy describes his enormous egotism, was repelled and fascinated by it at one and the same time, just as Gor'ky's rude, bitter humanity repelled and fascinated Tolstoy.[1] He seemed to Gor'ky like a rock, like a piece of nature, or a huge animal barking out coarsely, rather than a human individual. Gor'ky also had the sensation that Tolstoy saw and knew all there is to see and know, that it was as he saw and knew it, and that he saw and knew it to be good. Even death appeared as part of the flow of life; and if he feared it, as he did with increasing terror, it was because his flesh, in his own words, 'demanded immortality'.

This stature of a giant and cosmic vision of the Almighty Tolstoy combined with the most delicate sensitiveness and imagination, compared with which the hypersensitivity of a Proust seems mere touchiness and refinement. At times one seems to be in the presence not of one man's imagination but of the imagination of humanity itself. His perception had the directness and simplicity of someone discovering the world and other human beings for the first time; yet he possessed a remorselessly analytical and rationally developed mind.[2] And neither the discriminating intelligence nor the imaginative insight had a trace of the self-conscious and literary. No great modern writer had less of the smell of 'literature' about him and was more naturally himself than Tolstoy. He did not even like to be thought of as a professional man of letters (which, as a wealthy landowner, he could perhaps afford not to like). After a brief interlude, on his return from the Crimean War, of somewhat haughty hob-nobbing with the Moscow and St. Petersburg literary society, he became alternatively irritated and bored by what he considered to be its pretentious and self-conscious air and withdrew to Yasnaya Polyana. Nothing was further from Tolstoy than the doctrine of art as a special calling and of the artist as a new kind of aristocrat,

[1] See *Tolstoy v vospominanyakh sovremennikov*, vol. 2, pp. 429, 436, 438.

[2] Stanislavsky said of Tolstoy's eyes that 'they pierced the soul, intent to fathom it. They were now sharp and cutting now tender and luminous. When Tolstoy watched someone he became motionless, recollected and searchingly probed into him as though drawing out what was hidden, both good and bad.' Ibid., vol. 1, p. 552.

defying the revolt of the masses. His own unashamed aristocratism explains in some measure his rejection of the kind of aristocratic idealism whereby the writer places himself beyond the human condition or uses art as a metaphysical salvation for the gifted and isolated individual. In this respect, he was the opposite of Turgenev, whom he suspected of disingenuousness and who in turn accused Tolstoy of 'betraying literature' by infusing his work with an inordinate concern for solving the riddle of existence. Turgenev—the cultivated, self-protective, evasive literary man *par excellence*—was the last to understand that Tolstoy and his moral passion and Tolstoy and his art, Tolstoy in pursuit of personal salvation and Tolstoy in pursuit of social redemption are inseparable: that Tolstoy could not be a Turgenev.

But the totality of experience, the simplicity peculiar to Tolstoy was by no means of a piece, although it is important to see him 'whole' before one can get at the 'parts'. His was a deeply perplexed, disrupted and unhappy life, from which he escaped only to die, literally, by the wayside, in a setting that suggests the death of a modern Lear, or the madness of a modern Quixote broken on what is stupid and dull in life. It was not only a case of fleeing from the intolerable contradictions in his domestic relations or from being married to the wrong woman, who may have had her own share of trials but whose grim conventionality, avarice, and narrow-mindedness made her hysterically resistant to moral enquiry: what family, however accommodating, could have accommodated a Tolstoy, and where in the wide world was the right woman for such a man? Rather, it was a case of escaping from a unique combination in one's mind and character of every human contradiction. Somehow or other Tolstoy embodied all the moral and social incompatibles that have plagued and tortured humanity and that plagued and tortured him more than anyone else.

One of the most remarkable contradictions in Tolstoy was that though he devoted himself more and more to God, his relations with God were, as Gor'ky says, 'suspicious', like those between 'two bears in one den'. 'The thought which noticeably gnaws at him more than any other', Gor'ky remarked, 'is the thought of God. Sometimes it does not even seem to be a thought, but an intense resistance to a thing whose presence he feels, which overshadows him. He is more reticent about it than he would like to be, but he never stops thinking about it. This cannot be a mere sign of old age, a presentiment of death. No, it comes from his magnificent human pride. And a little from the outrage, for it is outrageous that he, Lev Tolstoy, should become a victim of some streptococcus.'[1]

In any case Tolstoy's God had nothing in common with that enshrined in any known theological notions, which he himself came to regard as masks for idolatry and servility to the established order, or a mumbo-jumbo invented by clerics and obfuscators. His religious teaching and his interpretation of the Gospel, which he buttressed with a formidable array of somewhat capricious learning, demonstrates that Christ was in certain respects—not very many—by anticipation a Tolstoyan. Religion for Tolstoy was—depending on the moment and the angle of vision—in part, like the primitive response to night and day; in part, or perhaps in the main, an answer to his own moral nature, a means of sharpening his conscience and sustaining his search for the meaning of life. There never was a man who was so deeply involved in moral experience and who yet succeeded in persuading himself that life and death could be exorcised by non-smoking, vegetarianism and abstention from sex and gluttony; a man congenitally unable to resist the sense of delight in woman's beauty, in wit and experience and impatient of all that is arid, frugal and slanted, who yet thought life could be improved by chopping off its limbs; a man who, in pursuit of an unaesthetic aesthetic and a maximalist morality, erased from literature most of his own artistic work, who yet could hardly compose a moral tract or religious fable without leaving the signature of a consummate artist; a man who sought truth with such unswerving fidelity and believed he had found it, who yet failed so completely to be set free by it.

These and similar conflicts within Tolstoy reflected the inner nature of the age and society in which he lived. Indeed, it is this—the fact that Tolstoy gathered into his life and work so much of the central experience of his time—which constitutes his greatness. His spiritual search, it is true, began as an inner dialogue with himself, a desire to live in peace with God and with himself. But he could not detach himself from his surroundings, even, and especially, at moments of most

[1] Ibid., vol. 2, p. 413.

intense resistance to it. He tried to shape life to his own purpose and denied or condemned whatever was not amenable to it. He appealed to self-improvement. He thought the problem of evil would be solved, quite simply, when we are drastically pure in private life, and preached that only a change of heart (and head) could save men from disaster. He believed that man would be reasonable and good once he realized the evil consequence of behaving irrationally and badly. Like Rousseau, he identified the difference between good and evil with the difference between original and pure natural feeling and the corrupt social forms which distort it. Yet his roots remained in an order not of his making. A member of his class, an inheritor of traditions and loyalties, harbouring an aristocratic contempt for the conventional and the pretentious and claiming a feudal nobleman's sense of affinity with the peasants, he tried but could not remove the imprint of this pattern on his life and his moral and intellectual experience. Gor'ky rightly perceived the *barin* in the old man cutting logs in the clothes of a peasant.

Against this background there was no apparent cause for alarm, no reason for a sense of frustration and disillusionment of the kind which affects writers in an alienated society. No one seems further from having been a misfit than Tolstoy, living as he still did, or imagined himself to live, in a society ostensibly barren of strains and stresses and untouched by the disrupting, frenzied spirit peculiar to the bourgeois world, and indeed of its very nature. And yet he wrote (in *A Confession*) that life had 'turned sinister'. A hiatus formed, a chink appeared in things and disabused him of the idea that they were held together. 'The force that drew me away from life was stronger, fuller, and more universal than any wish: it was a force like that of my previous attachment to life, only in a contrary direction' (vol. 23, p. 12). A sense of loneliness took hold of him. Decay, death, from being a moment in nature itself, a necessary wearing away of life, or a means for enquiring into it, turned into 'the agony that overwhelms us', 'threatening life' and 'tearing the soul to rags', as Tolstoy says in the unfinished *Notes of a Madman* (*Zapiski sumasshedshego*, 1884) (vol. 26, p. 470). There was horrified fascination in this for Tolstoy: his alarming gift for scraping white-wash off sepulchres, for exposing cant in politics and religion, and insincerity behind men's ostensible transactions acquired a macabre endorsement in the experience of death—the final remover of all shams and pretences and the destroyer of all illusions, leaving no escape from reality.[1]

In the end Tolstoy's most hidden experience involved him in the predicament of modern man on whom the gates of Eden have closed and who is brought face to face with the reality of his stricken existence. This involvement grew in proportion as Tolstoy realized his own share in the responsibility for the breakdown of human relations, the conflicts in his society, and the chaos in the world. It made him—sometimes shrewdly, sometimes terrifyingly—aware of the sign of the times. It brought home to him that evil and injustice were not born merely of the wickedness and stupidity of men, but of the tyranny of society and events, that men have raised spirits and the spirits have become their masters.

A new situation had arisen in Russia with the abolition of serfdom in 1861: it could not but undermine Tolstoy's sense of the passing of life untouched by the pressure of events and liable only to the force of natural cohesion peculiar to the patriarchal, pre-industrial way of life. Feudal society was breaking up, and with this human relations became externalized, materialized and subjected to the law of competition. Most landowners still tried to do their duty by keeping up their estates, which, it was believed, was what landowners were for. Most peasants were still starved, degraded, treated worse than animals, which, it was believed, was what peasants were for. Tolstoy, alarmingly *grand seigneur* though he was, began to doubt the former belief and rejected the latter, aware that he was tied by loyalties to a world of values which he could no longer share. At the same time, he looked with revulsion and scorn at the new development in which bourgeois relations and habits were breaking in

---

[1] In *A Confession* Tolstoy records that the despair which overcame him in the middle 1870s and preceded his 'conversion' reflected his state of mind many years before, after the death of his brother Nikolay or even earlier. But while all that time the happiness of married life provided a remedy against despair, later he realized that the remedy was not more than an anodyne, a temporary protection against confusion and catastrophe. To divide Tolstoy's mental and emotional development into two or more separate parts is, therefore, misleading: there are continuities as well as discontinuities. Even the dissonance—logical and chronological —between the artist and the moralist will be found less pronounced than many critics seem to assume, if one is caught up in the current of Tolstoy's thought.

on Russia and a thrusting class of vulgarians was coming into its own, with its acquisitiveness, its obtuse ambitions, its spleen, its obsession with meaningless words and worship of lunatic ideals. The situation arising from the clash and the fusion of these trends could not be 'improved': it could be changed only by radically changing the scale of human values. Tolstoy believed it could be changed by atavistically retreating into the collective, common mind of the peasant, into the lost golden age, or by issuing a challenge so senseless as to draw attention to the senselessness of the world which he inhabited. This was the doctrine of anarchism and pacifism. It seemed infinitely scandalous and utopian to Tolstoy's contemporaries, but the contrast with reality made it all the more attractive to him. He preached the impossible. It is an old story that the highest form of belief is the belief in the impossible. Men's noble visions turn into visions of what cannot be in this world. For Tolstoy they had to come true because they were true. This could spell or did spell monstrous fanaticism, at any rate in the eyes of those who sought to reduce his vision down to a size which was less of a challenge to them. But that is how manna tasted to Tolstoy. The rest reeked of the fleshpots of Egypt.

It was a surprisingly irrational conclusion to reach for someone who had followed reason with unbounded confidence and tenacity. But in his surroundings Tolstoy could no longer believe in the triumph of reason. Reason was declining—a decline at the end of which the monsters surged up in Russia in the shape of the irresistible *embourgeoisement* of society and the 'white terror' following the revolution of 1905. While disclaiming the revolution, Tolstoy could not disclaim its significance or its judgement on the world. He could not but feel the world's burden as his own and the crisis of Russian society as the crisis of his own life and work—not least because he lived and died in the tension, but not in the dichotomy, between public and private self.

In an explanatory account of what he intended and what he did not intend to do in producing *War and Peace* (*Voyna i mir*) (1863–69), Tolstoy said that his readers should not expect 'either a beginning or an end', either a traditionally happy ending or a traditionally unhappy one; that he could not 'set any limits to [his] characters', and that, altogether, he repudiated 'the common literary language and literary methods', the received notions about novel-writing, realistic or other-wise (vol. 13, p. 54 sq.). The observations are interesting not least because Tolstoy made them at a time when European as well as Russian 'realism' was at its height and when Tolstoy himself was identified by contemporaries with its essential direction.[1]

Through its association with the French novelists and, to some extent, with the Russian writers of the so-called 'natural school', realism attempted not only to bring into literature aspects—the baser and more vulgar aspects—of nature and life previously ignored by the rule-makers, but to support the impossible aim of producing a fac-simile of reality. It derived from, and was sustained by, a belief in the poetry of literalness and the importance of the prosaic representation of existence, of people concretely given and imagined. Tolstoy shared this belief in a large measure. The style and language of his work, as well as his underlying attitude to life, serve to enforce what is direct and human and real as against the allusive, the abstract and the fanciful. He can be detected making his sentence deliberately inelegant in order to avoid the well-turned, the contrived and unsubstantial, which won him Turgenev's rebuke that 'the fear of phrases has driven him into the most desperate phrases.'[2]

---

[1] Even a remotely adequate list of books on Tolstoy's works would require an extensive bibliographical section. Apart from the studies cited in this chapter, the following general monographs can be mentioned as particularly important: Aldanov, *Zagadka Tolstogo*; Bilinkis, *O tvorchestve L. N. Tolstogo*; Bychkov, *L. N. Tolstoy*; Gudzy, *Lev Tolstoy*; Pryanishnikov, *Proza L'va Tolstogo*. To these must be added the invaluable notes and commentaries by various authors in the Jubilee Edition of Tolstoy's works, and the comments by Chernyshevsky on *Detstvo i otrochestvo* (*Polnoe sobranie sochineniy*, vol. 3, Moscow, 1947), Dostoevsky (*Dnevnik pisatelya za 1877, 1880 i 1881 gody*, Moscow–Leningrad, 1929) and Lenin ('Lev Tolstoy kak zerkalo russkoy revolyutsii', *Polnoe sobranie sochineniy*, 5th ed., vol. 17). Studies in English are also very numerous. The following books and essays are of special interest: Bayley, *Tolstoy and the Novel*; *Russian Literature and Modern English Fiction* (ed. Davie); Christian, *Tolstoy's 'War and Peace' and Tolstoy*; Lubbock, *The Craft of Fiction* (containing two essays on Tolstoy); Lukacs, *Studies in European Realism* (containing a section on Tolstoy originally published in Russian); Thomas Mann, *Essays of Three Decades*; *Tolstoy. A Collection of Critical Essays* (ed. Matlaw); Steiner, *Tolstoy or Dosto-evsky*.

[2] Two passages from *War and Peace* of Tolstoy at his floutingly most unlovely will illustrate the point:

'Он попросил Ростова рассказать о том, как и где он получил рану. Ростову это было приятно, и он начал рассказывать, во время рассказа все более и более одушевляясь. Он рассказал им свое Шанграбенское дело

TOLSTOY

It is as though the very act of putting into words becomes insincere, as does the use of metre, of poetic form, convention, imagery. Even

совершенно так, как обыкновенно рассказывают про сражения участвовавшие в них, то есть так, как им хотелось бы, чтоб оно было, так, как они слыхали от других рассказчиков, так как красивее было рассказывать, но совершенно не так, как оно было. Ростов был правдивый молодой человек, он ни за что умышленно не сказал бы неправды. Он начал рассказывать с намерением рассказать все, как оно точно было, но незаметно, невольно и неизбежно для себя перешел в неправду. Ежели бы он рассказал правду, слушатели, которые, как и он сам, слышали уже много раз рассказы об атаках и составили себе определенное понятие о том, что такое атака, и ожидали точно такого же рассказа, — или бы они не поверили ему, или, что еще хуже, подумали бы, что Ростов сам был виноват в том, что с ним не случнлось того, что случается обыкновенно с рассказчиками кавалерийских атак...'

'He asked Rostov to tell them how and when he had received his wound. Rostov was only too glad to tell about it, and while he was telling the story he grew ever more animated. He told them his part in the action at Schöngraben precisely as those who have taken part in an engagement always tell about it, that is, in such a way as they wish that it had happened, as they have heard it from other story tellers, as it is more beautiful to tell, and not at all as it has happened. Rostov was a truthful young man, who would not for anything have told an untruth on purpose. He began with the intention of telling everything as it had really happened, but imperceptibly, involuntarily, and unavoidably to himself he passed to the untruth. If he had told the truth to his listeners, who, like himself, had a great number of times heard stories of attacks, and who had formed a definite idea about what an attack was, and who, consequently, expected just such a story, they either would not have believed him or, what is still worse, they would have believed that it was Rostov's fault if nothing happened to him of the kind that generally happens to all the other narrators of cavalry attacks...' (Book 3, Ch. 7).

'Как переносил граф болезнь своей любимой дочери, ежели бы он не знал, что ему стоила тысячи рублей болезнь Наташи и что он не жалеет еще тысяч, чтобы сделать ей пользу; ежели бы он знал, что ежели она не поправится, то он не пожалеет еще и повезет ее за границу и там сделает консилиумы... Чтобы сделала Соня, ежели бы у ней не было радостного сознания того, что она первое время не раздевалась три ночи для того, чтобы быть наготове исполнить в точности все предписания доктора, и что она теперь не спит ночи для того, чтобы не пропустить часы, в которые надо давать маловредные пилюли из золотой коробочки...'

'How would the count have borne the illness of his beloved daughter, if he had not known that Natasha's illness cost him one thousand roubles and that he would not grudge another thousand in order to be useful to her; if he had not known that, if she did not get better, he would not grudge more and would take her abroad and there arrange for consultations?... What would Sonia have done if she had not had the joyful consciousness that in the beginning she had not been undressing for three nights in order to be ready to carry out the precise injunctions of the doctor, and that now she did not sleep nights in order not to miss the hours in which it was necessary to give her the harmless pills from the gilt box?' (Book 9, Ch. 16).

the wish to be sincere seemed to Tolstoy, at any rate in his later 'post-conversion' period, inevitably to burden the artist with a new self-consciousness and thus to serve as a subtle source of insincerity. Hence the completely bare, plain, simple manner of his fables and folk-tales. Generally speaking, there is no 'style' in Tolstoy's writings, in the sense in which one describes a work of art as having style, cleverness, intricacy, grace; neither is there humour or playful fancy, although he could not resist producing polished epigrams and statements of incisive wit ('All happy families are alike, but each unhappy family is unhappy in its own way'; 'He never chooses an opinion; he just wears whatever happens to be in style'; 'He will do almost anything for the poor, except get off their back', and so on). Tolstoy aimed at being true to life: and literal truth, *prima facie* at least, was better than contrivance. From this came the extraordinary factual verisimilitude in Tolstoy's description of the human scene and the lavishness of physical detail. The French critic's remark that if life could speak, life would speak as Tolstoy's novels do is, therefore, much to the point. Still more 'realistically', it has been said that one can learn how to make strawberry jam from reading *Anna Karenina*.

And yet from the beginning Tolstoy deliberately set himself against those very writers who aimed at 'objectivity' and who proclaimed the eloquence of reality's direct meanings: against Pisemsky, Ostrovsky, Goncharov, Turgenev, and others. Their ways, he stated, were old-world, 'good enough in the year dot' (*khorosho bylo pri tsare Gorokhe*, vol. 60, p. 375). His reaction to Turgenev is particularly indicative, even where it turned on personal relations. In a way, it is more illuminating than the overworked contrast, real and imaginary, between Tolstoy and Dostoevsky.

Tolstoy's grunts, on the occasion of one of his many quarrels with Turgenev, directed against the latter 'waggling his democratic haunches', are perhaps a marginal affair. But he had a keen nose for literary as for any other humbug and he shrank from such pieces of preciosity, familiar from Turgenev's novels, as charming landscapes, lovely women (with 'long eye-lashes') in rural spots, and the series of *rendez-vous* in the lap of nature, leading nowhere. More significantly, Tolstoy repudiated Turgenev himself—Turgenev the author.

Mention has already been made of the importance Tolstoy

attached to the author as reflected in his work. In fact, Tolstoy is the everlasting contradiction of the widespread belief that objectivity is necessary in art, that a literary work succeeds in proportion in which the author has made his reader forget that there is one.Tolstoy watched closely—while reading Goethe, Thackeray, Gogol'—what force and interest the writer's values and methods got from the experience that leads him to hold and use them, or simply what his motives are. *Tel arbre tel fruit.* 'It is good when the author barely stands outside his topic, so that one wonders whether it is subjective or objective' (vol. 47, p. 191). The impartiality remains suspended: the author is present, however incalculably. There is no question of his substituting himself for the object with which he is engaged—as if adding something to life—but he must avoid the separate, impersonal effect, the shutting up of the object within itself. Tolstoy saw it with the penetrating eye of an animal watching in the thicket, while at the same time communicating a sense of value or 'the author's distinctive (*samobytnogo*) moral attitude to the subject', as he wrote in his introduction to the works of Maupassant in Russian translation (vol. 30, p. 19). It was not only and not so much a matter of the author's beliefs as of his feeling for life, which he makes artistically workable.

This is what Tolstoy missed in Turgenev who had adopted a detached position—a point of safety from which he could afford to resist the idea of moral choice and to regard the coexistence of contraries with equanimity. *A Nest of Gentlefolk* (*Dvoryanskoe gnezdo*) and *On the Eve* (*Nakanune*) evoked Tolstoy's comment that 'people who are in the blues and who don't know what they want from life' should not attempt to write; that the 'splenetic and dispeptic' Turgenev was no novelist at all (vol. 60, pp. 324 sq.). He made exception for *A Sportsman's Sketches* (*Zapiski okhotnika*), but generally felt 'sickened' (*pretit*) by Turgenev's 'flabbiness' (*vyalyi*), 'thinness' (*zhidkiy*), and 'vacillation' (*somnenie vo vsem*), by the languor at the source and the want of creative energy. What Tolstoy looked for in a writer was a 'firm search for truth', and he called truth 'the real hero' of his own novels. The task was not to construct a 'true', plausible picture of reality by feeding aimlessly, haphazardly on life, not only to establish truth, but to seek and to discover it, to clear the decks, to explore, to denude, to dissect, to see what happens if one takes away some element which has been considered genuine, but which may conceal the truth. The emphasis, therefore, falls on moral and psychological analysis, which constitutes the compelling 'tone' of Tolstoy's work.

This had far-reaching formal as well as material implications. For a short time, at the end of the 1850s and in the company of Druzhinin and Botkin, Tolstoy toyed with the idea of 'pure art'. But it proved completely alien to his basic artistic assumptions. These ruled out the idea of a special, autonomous realm of art which made such would-be aesthetes as Annenkov, Botkin and Druzhinin feel safe behind a protective curtain. In the end, Tolstoy disallowed any artistic criteria where wrong moral choices have been made. There was, naturally, no suggestion of anything being slanted, and Tolstoy's innumerable drafts and proof-corrections show how often he re-wrote a scene or a conversation so as to avoid 'tendentiousness'. But the final form always remained assimilated to his moral experience. 'Anyone writing a novel', he wrote in the essay on Maupassant already quoted, 'must have a clear and firm idea as to what is good and bad.' This accounts for Tolstoy's literary sympathies and anti-pathies, for his attachment to the Romantic Hugo and his aversion to Flaubert, his love for Dickens, his reservations about Thackeray and his repudiation of Shakespeare. And when later, in *What is Art?*, Tolstoy argued that art is a form of communication, his rejection of a vast number of writers was due not to the fact that they failed to communicate with him but that he repudiated their values.

Already in *Childhood* (*Detstvo*) (1852), which in some respects is closer to Turgenev's suggestive, evocative, sentimental manner, and in the sequels *Boyhood* (*Otrochestvo*) (1854) and *Youth* (*Yunost'*) (1857), human behaviour is subjected by the author to the truth-searching, analytical treatment. Actually, the trilogy comprises three authors: the narrator who brings back the living detail of experiences in childhood, boyhood and youth, recovering the continuous or sudden motion of time in his development and growth. But he is the object rather than the subject of the narrative. He is seen by the second author, himself retracing the past. Finally, the third and proper author fuses all the parts and, by informing them with his own insight, with experiences derived from other families, by building from new impressions and new ideas, gives the whole a new dimension.

The author intervenes deliberately, almost regardless of artistic effect and untrammelled by any consideration of form, to reveal the real state of affairs. He uncovers, as Chernyshevsky already noted, the 'dialectic of the human soul,' of human actions and attitudes which carry, as it were, their own defeat within themselves—a returning echo which mocks the first impulse; he detects 'thoughts born of a first sensation leading to other thoughts and exceeding themselves'.[1] Thus, in the first version of the mother's deathbed scene in *Childhood* Tolstoy writes: 'Some say that in great grief man does not think of anything but his grief. Nothing of the kind. I felt great sorrow at this minute, but I noticed all the trifles: for instance, I noticed that half-smile of *la belle Flamande* which seemed to say 'although it is a sad occasion, I am glad to see you'. I noticed how father, while looking at the face of *maman*, threw a glance at her beautiful hands, bare almost to the elbow. I am sure father, who was stricken with grief at this moment, admired those hands but thought "how can one think of such things at such a moment?"' (vol. 1, p. 205).

These observations were omitted in the final version not, as might appear, because Tolstoy wished to conceal here as elsewhere the 'omniscient author', but for economy's sake. The author is still there. Indeed, he expresses himself more strongly, if more objectively and laconically: 'vanity', we read in the published text, 'is incompatible with genuine sorrow, and yet the feeling is so deeply embedded in the nature of man that even the most profound sorrow can seldom expel it altogether . . . But Natal'ya Savishna was so utterly stricken by her unhappiness that not a single desire lingered in her soul and she went on living only from habit' (Ch. 28).

The interpretative intervention by the author is even more apparent in the Caucasus and war stories (*A Raid* (*Nabeg*) (1853), *Sebastopol in December* (*Sevastopol' v dekabre*) and *Sebastopol in May* (*Sevastopol' v mae*) (1855), *A Wood Felling* (*Rubka lesa*) (1855), *Sebastopol in August* (*Sevastopol' v avguste*) (1856)) which are, in a more direct way than *Childhood*, *Boyhood* and *Youth*, precursory to *War and Peace* and where the author's presence is recognizable in his search for truth rather than in mere skill in evoking landscapes, events, characters and situations.

[1] Chernyshevsky, *Polnoe sobranie sochineniy* (1939–53), vol. 3, p. 422.

Tolstoy deflates the romantic myth of the Caucasus to which the poets, including Pushkin and Lermontov, have lent enchantment to the point when it was difficult to envisage the reality, when reality turned into a symbol of the exotic, and the exotic, in a kind of magic circle, fed the romantic appetite. Above all, Tolstoy explodes the splendid image of war and military valour. Anticipating his later pictures of the process of dissimulated vanity, ambition, cross-purpose and misunderstanding attending the enterprise of war, he strips down the age-old pretence to essentials, and what remains is largely a lie which Tolstoy finds as inevitable in soldiers as Plato did in poets.

The procedure, as has been frequently pointed out, was a common enough device, used especially by eighteenth-century satirists, by Swift and Voltaire (whom Tolstoy admired), and latterly by Kafka: in presenting a misproportioned picture of an object or a situation, they show up the unattractive aspect behind a veneer of embellishments or a fog of mystification. Thus soldiers playing on a drum are described by Voltaire as 'murderers six foot high, clothed in scarlet and beating a distended monkey skin'. But Tolstoy's use of the procedure is not satirical, although it achieves that effect at times, when describing particularly incongruous situations (such as Pierre's declaration of love to Hélène, together with the scenes immediately preceding and following it, or his initiation into the Masonic rites in *War and Peace*): rather it is exploratory and dramatic. It often serves to show human beings undergoing crises in which they are brought face to face with their real condition, in which they suffer illusions, are disabused of their illusions, and are ensnared by new illusions. Yet the illusions are not merely mistakes and errors of fallible human beings: indirectly they often reveal, for Tolstoy, the unsuppressible healing force of life. Despite his taste for dissection, analysis and classification, he is therefore not affected by the dryness and derisiveness of the eighteenth century.[1]

---

[1] The method, which Tolstoy himself came to repudiate when he began writing straightforward narrative and tracts for edification, is characteristic of most of his early and even of some of his later work, imaginative and otherwise. The 'surgical' possibilities of the method provided Tolstoy also with an excellent instrument for exposing the spuriousness of much religious and political argument. The method is now known by the technical term *ostranenie* (making it strange, estrangement), originally coined by the distinguished Soviet critic V. Shklovsky. See his *Material*

The philosophical implication of the method of dissection, of stripping life down to essentials, is to invalidate the idea of a symbolic world, to move away from the idealized and mystical towards the ethics or ethos of actual living existence. It is to turn heavenly bread into daily bread. Characteristically, when still a young man, Tolstoy dreamed of a religion that was not otherworldly but would create heaven on earth. Characteristically, too, Tolstoy kept away from any language that served to distract, to rarify and idealize away from nature. Sometimes a single colloquial expression helped to explode such language, as when he describes in *Anna Karenina* the air of sophisticated mystification in the salon of Countess Lidia Ivanovna where 'Stefan Arkad'ich suddenly felt that his lower jaw began to twist uncontrollably into a yawn' (*zavorachivat'sya na zevok*).

In specifically moral terms, Tolstoy's demonstration of the ambivalent character of human behaviour makes the distinction between willed or voluntary and involuntary actions seem uncertain—a human pretence. It makes one think that what one has achieved not intentionally but seemingly by accident is more indicative of one's true nature, or at least of certain elements in one's true nature. The benign and motherly Countess Rostov is shown 'to have that secret ill-feeling which a mother always has towards the future conjugal happiness of her daughter'; while the cold and dry Karenin is seen in a state of unexpected emotion at the side of his gravely-ill wife. The point is not only that these impulses in the character's make-up give them a surprising dimension, but also that they are or could be true to nature. Underlying value is accorded to 'nature'. The natural is inherently more commendable than the artificial, the spontaneous is better than the cultivated, whatever object or process or attitude is so qualified. Since Tolstoy thought that this notion would not be acceptable to any sizeable or representative group of Frenchmen, he made many of his less commendable characters speak French—to underline the contrast between naturalness, truth of feeling and the affected, conventional manners of privileged society.

i stil'. In view of the misleading satirical connotation of the term (for which, however, Shklovsky is not responsible), attention may be drawn to an analogous notion—*psikhicheskoe podglyadyvanie* (psychological eavesdropping)—invented by K. Leont'ev and expressing Tolstoy's aim of probing the ambivalent nature of human behaviour. Leontiev himself criticizes the procedure in a somewhat captious vein. See his *Analiz, stil' i veyanie*.

A number of critics, beginning with Pisarev and Strakhov (Tolstoy's personal friend and exact contemporary), have suggested that 'non-intrusion' is the hall-mark of Tolstoy as a novelist. It has been claimed, with particular reference to *War and Peace*, that self-exclusion on the part of the author constitutes the epic nature of Tolstoyan realism. The impression comes from the undisputed fact that each character in the novel has his and her own wholly recognizable, self-consistent way of acting, thinking and feeling, that they react to events and to each other in a way peculiar to each one of them, so that we have not one testimony (the author's) but several. To this extent, Tolstoy may be said to identify himself with his characters. But Tolstoy is not reducible to them, in the way in which the piece-meal form and a plain intervention by a number of narrators enables Lermontov to reduce himself to all (and therefore to none) of the characters in *A Hero of Our Time*; or in the way in which inability or unwillingness to probe the inner life of his characters, and to examine the source of their actions, forces Turgenev to carry non-commitment to the limit; or in the way in which Dostoevsky inter-rupts the narrator or supplants one narrator by another and thereby achieves his 'polyphonic' effect.

Tolstoy, on the contrary, declares himself consistently, if often unobtrusively—in his language no less than in the disposition of characters, in the analysis of their actions and the structure of a work as a whole. This is shown in the close approximation between his personal, diaristic, epistolary and his fictional style. The manner of the diaries of the 1850s, '60s and '70s is directly reproduced in the novels, with the same forms of 'argument', the same epithets and comparisons, the same interior monologue; while the epistolary manner is repeated in the narrative and discursive parts of *War and Peace*.

The relationship between what Tolstoy's work is about and the way in which it is written, or the relationship between language and the quality of his vision and attitude to life, is conspicuous in his use of syntax. A quotation from *War and Peace* will serve to illustrate this: 'Bonaparte himself, not trusting his generals, moved with the whole guard to the field of battle, being afraid of missing the ready prey, while Bagration's detachment of four thousand men, having merrily started their camp-fires, were drying and warming themselves,

277

and, for the first time in three days, stewing their broth. Not one man of the detachment knew or thought of what was in store for them' (Book 2, Ch. 14). There are no obvious intrusions on the part of the author in this passage which draw attention to themselves, no emendations and elaborations. But the way in which the sentences are constructed and the tone of the narration clearly reveal the author contrasting two worlds: one spoiling for a fight, the other at peace, quiescent, even while driven to wage war—War and Peace. The connecting gerunds, with which Tolstoy's text is over-weighed and which fastidious translators do their best to obliterate, serve to emphasize the oppositions and the inevitable connections; Napoleon, mistrustful, imposing his will (*ne doveryaya svoim generalam; boyas' upustit' gotovuyu zhertvu*), and the Russian soldiery, unsuspecting, suffering the war, and pursuing their peaceful habits (*veselo raskladyvaya kostry, sushilsya, obogrevalsya, varil kashu*).

As far as characterization is concerned, the position may seem somewhat ambiguous because of Tolstoy's use of 'superfluous detail', which allows the reader to make his own inferences. For instance, where Stendhal, from whom otherwise Tolstoy learnt much, would say, as he does say apropos of Julien Sorel and his mistress, that at a particular point Anna Karenina ceased loving her husband, Tolstoy observes merely that she suddenly noticed his big ears. There is, of course, nothing new in Tolstoy's use or, as some (e.g. Leont'ev and, indeed, Tolstoy himself in later life) would have it, misuse of this procedure: it is a familiar practice of Russian novelists. His unique gift resides in a *combination* of immediacy with 'om-niscience'. In the words of a Soviet critic, Tolstoy 'describes in words not the smile itself but its contents as he sees it, its psychological equivalent', 'not the sound of a voice and the visible gesture, but directly their inner effect and meaning'.[1] Thus Kutuzov, in a con-versation with an Austrian general, 'smiled in a way that seemed to say, "You are quite at liberty not to believe me and I don't even care whether you do or not, but you have no grounds for telling me so. And that is the whole point".' (Book 2, Ch. 3.) Or Natasha, at her first grand ball, 'still out of breath, was returning to her seat when

---

[1] N. Pryanishnikov, *Proza L'va Tolstogo*, p. 38; see also the essay by A. Chicherin, '*Stil' romanov L'va Tolstogo*' (in *Idei i stil'*), which is particularly suggestive and important.

another dancer chose her. She was tired and panting and evidently thought of declining, but immediately put her hand gaily on the man's shoulder, smiling at Prince Andrey. "I'd be glad to sit beside you and rest: I am tired but you see how they keep asking me, and I'm glad of it, I'm happy and I love everybody, and you and I understand it all", and much, much more was said in her smile' (Book 6, Ch. 17).

It is in such projection of urgent, dramatic and psychologically right equivalents to human behaviour and appearance that Tolstoy is an innovator. His characters are more than portraits: they are records of the spiritual mainsprings of thought and action. We are conscious not only of an alarmingly real presence (achieved at times by almost excessive close-ups of bodily features) but even more of the underlying spiritual identity. To put it differently, Tolstoy is concerned not merely with outward manifestations, but with interior bodily events: he goes beyond the skin level, into the interior of the being, until he touches not the body but the experience of the body. It is, speaking anachronistically, the opposite of the Hemingway school of writing, with its almost total absence in characters of the mental and moral impulses in human beings. Watchfully, Tolstoy hits off an appearance, a look, a gesture that renders his characters instantly recognizable. A movement of the hand or a shrug of the shoulder may tell all. But other writers—Balzac, Gogol', Dickens—could do the same, or did it even better. Where Tolstoy is unsurpassed is in making us aware at the same time, and in enlarging our knowledge of the characters' past, of all the time and living that has moulded them, and above all of the spirit by which they act, speak, love and die. This could be conveyed only by virtue of the intensity of the author's own vision which engages the reader's consciousness with his own. The effect could not be achieved by opting out—ironically *à la* Lermontov, or Hamletically *à la* Turgenev.

The extent to which Tolstoy holds the reins, and yet does it without a surfeit of premeditation or reflection on contingencies, can be clearly seen in the central unity between the historical and the familial, the public and private levels of *War and Peace*. Strictly speaking, they do not exist as different spheres. The one passes into the other as naturally as Tolstoy's innumerable gerundial clauses enter into the principal ones. 'War' conflicts with 'Peace', yet it is not set over against it but issues from it, and intertwines with it; or, rather, war cannot impede the all-absorbing flow of life whose force asserts itself throughout all the disruptions of human existence. The characters are taken by the author straight into the centre of the great events of their time. He purposely throws them into the stream of history, which carries them until they are overwhelmed or come out on top. The particular destinies of Pierre Bezukhov, of Andrey Bolkonsky, of Natasha, of Princess Maria are unintelligible without Austerlitz and Borodino, without the burning of Moscow and the retreat of the *Grande Armée*, without the tsar's court and Kutuzov's headquarters. Even more, there is a difference between the status of Andrey's and Pierre's personal experiences and that of, say, Nekhlyudov in Tolstoy's earlier work *A Landowner's Morning* (*Utro pomeshchika*) (1856). For Nekhlyudov the solution of his personal problems depends largely on putting right the relations between landlord and peasant, whereas what is at stake for the characters in *War and Peace* is their involvement in the fate of their country and, by implication, of mankind as a whole.

In the traditional conception of the novel the paths of the characters meet and intersect, and the frequency and intensity of the meetings and intersections determines the composition of the novel; but *War and Peace*, in its final shape, is impelled by the force of history. Personal sorrow is subsumed in common adversity, and Natasha's betrayal is effaced by the ordeal of Borodino when both Andrey and Anatole are mortally wounded.

Some have described *War and Peace* as a 'family chronicle', which grew into a historic epic only in the course of Tolstoy's work on the novel.[1] Yet the drafts of the novel show clearly that the historical events were not an afterthought on the part of the author or even a scenario, a mere background to the private lives of his characters. 'What is *War and Peace*?' Tolstoy wrote in *Some Words about War and Peace* (*Neskol'ko slov po povodu knigi 'Voyna i mir'*) after the publication of the first three volumes:

'It is not a novel, even less a poem, and still less a historical chronicle. *War and Peace* is what the author wished and was able to express in the form in which it is expressed. Such a declaration of the author's

---

[1] See, for instance, Eykhenbaum, *Lev Tolstoy. Shestidesyatye gody*. Cf. Tolstoy's own letter to Fet about this, vol. 61, p. 149.

disregard for conventional form in an artistic work might seem presumptuous were it not deliberate, and were there no precedents for it. But the history of Russian literature since the time of Pushkin not only affords many examples of such departure from European forms, but does not offer a single example of the contrary. From Gogol''s *Dead Souls* to Dostoevsky's *House of the Dead*, in the recent period of Russian literature, there is not a single imaginative prose work, above any level of mediocrity, which quite fits into the form of a novel, an epic, or a tale' (vol. 16, p. 7).

Pushkin's *The Captain's Daughter* (*Kapitanskaya dochka*), however, could still be described as an epic, a family chronicle with a historical background, whereas *War and Peace* presents, in structure and content, a unity of epic and novel in which the historical and the personal and familial are fused into an all-pervading equation. But even on the narrower level of the characters' personal life their experiences do not remain shut up within themselves, and the conclusion of such a happening as Petya's death and Countess Rostova's grief over it is that 'the wound which all but killed the Countess, that same wound called Natasha to life'.

It would be wrong to infer that this had teleological implications for Tolstoy, in which two standards are applied: one by which ends and the other by which means are judged. In fact, the meaning of events in his view constitutes neither their goal nor their justification. It precludes the dissection of life into means and ends. It is to be accounted for, if any account is needed, as part of the motion of life in the events themselves and reveals itself unpredictably in a sudden flare of comprehension. It upsets our commonplace logic which, as Tolstoy says, denies 'the liability of all that is impossible and distant suddenly becoming close, possible and necessary'.

Turgenev reported to Tolstoy in 1880 that Flaubert had expressed his admiration for the first two volumes of *War and Peace*, but disapproved of the third part because of 'all the repetitions and philosophizings': 'enfin on voit le monsieur, l'auteur et le Russe, tandis que jusque là on n'avait que la Nature et l'Humanité.'[1] It is uncertain whether Flaubert was interested in 'nature' and 'humanity'

[1] I. S. Turgenev, *Polnoe sobranie sochineniy i pisem*, Leningrad, 1960–8, vol. 12 (2), p. 205.

or, rather, in the prospect of writing without any reference to human situations and with no impelling force except 'la force intérieure du style'. He could not see the significance of the author's self-revelation in *War and Peace* because he failed to see the novel's intrinsic unity. He was not alone in considering Tolstoy an outstandingly good novelist who failed as an artist by importing into his work too much of himself and of his 'ideas'. Turgenev, as has already been noted, reproved Tolstoy for the same reason, so did the epigonian populist Mikhaylovsky. Yet the thinker, 'le monsieur', happens to be present in every line he wrote, and the philosophical sections of *War and Peace* reveal the nature of the work as inevitably as the characters do. Tolstoy himself upheld the formal and the material importance of the philosophical aspects of his work as boldly as he defended life, which, as he said to Gor'ky, 'is given to us on the understanding of being so defended'. 'My view on history is not an arbitrary piece of argumentativeness . . . These thoughts are the fruit of the mental labour of my whole life and constitute an inseparable part of my outlook on life: God alone knows how much toil and suffering went into its making, and it has given me complete calm and happiness. Yet, at the same time, I knew that in my book they will praise the sentimental scenes with my young ladies, the laughter over Speransky, and such rubbish . . .'[1]

This is not the place for embarking on a discussion of the problems raised by Tolstoy's philosophy of history.[2] In any case, it cannot be a matter of extracting such portable intellectual contents as can be prised loose from his imaginative work. The 'philosophy' does not stand up on its own any more than Tolstoy's characters or their

[1] This must be borne in mind when considering Tolstoy's consent to exclude the philosophical sections from a later published version of the novel. In one of the drafts of the epilogue to *War and Peace* Tolstoy writes this in self-justification: 'It may have been better not to write these [reflections] . . . but if it had not been for [them] there would not be any narrative either.' 'I began writing a book about the past. In describing this past, I found not only that it is unknown but that what is known and said flies in the face of reality. And I felt that the pressing need to prove what I was saying and to express the views which are at the basis of what I have been writing.' vol. 15, p. 241.

[2] See Isaiah Berlin, *The Hedgehog and the Fox*. It is the first study which examines the question of the influence on Tolstoy of French romantic historiography. See also the interesting essay by Skaftymov, 'Obraz Kutuzova i filosofiya istorii v romane L. N. Tolstogo *Voyna i mir*'. Skaftymov compares Tolstoy's idea of history with Hegel's.

experiences stand up in isolation. Broadly speaking, what is peculiar to Tolstoy's view of history is a restriction of the range and validity of individual volition and individual action in the historical drama. History (meaning the course of events into which the historian enquires, rather than the enquiry itself) sets individuals to work for it and to serve its purposes, although the individuals believe themselves to be fulfilling their own personal design. Tolstoy, in concert with Schopenhauer, hated the will whether it succeeded or failed.[1]

The past for Tolstoy is a tremendous continuum of interlocking events, and it must be arbitrary if not logically impossible to draw its boundaries. The meaning he saw—in history as in life—was not the overt one but a matter of inner links or, as he says, of an 'infinite labyrinth of connections (*stsepleniya*)'. Hence the picture of war in *War and Peace*: like the battle of Waterloo as Stendhal described it in *La Chartreuse de Parme*, it is a muddle and a confusion, where participants and onlookers are more or less in the dark, where blows and counterblows are chancy and unexpected, and where the relation between the aim and the accomplishment, between the calculation and the result is tenuous and hazy. Ultimately, perhaps paradoxically, Tolstoy's history takes on the qualities of an original historical document: life caught in the act. He scorned historians who assumed, as they are no longer inclined to assume, that changes in human

---

[1] See *War and Peace*, Part Nine, Ch. 1, and Epilogue, Part Two. This idea of history is comparable with the Marxist conception of social history in which human beings enter into relations independent of their will, and liberation consists in the recognition of the necessity of those relations. Similarly, there are analogies with Hegel's *List der Vernunft*, which uses men as instruments in the attainment of universal historic aims; and, indeed, with the traditional Christian teaching of the providential order working itself out through or in spite of human individuals. It is necessary to say, however, that Marx never held the belief in history as a super-human force guiding the course of events. 'History', he stated, 'does nothing, it possesses no immense wealth, fights no battles. It is rather *man*, real living man who does everything, who possesses and fights.' So far Tolstoy might agree, but Marx goes on to say that '"History" is not some sort of person using man as a means for the realization of *its* ends. History is *nothing but* the activity of man pursuing his ends' (K. Marx and F. Engels, *Sochineniia*, Moscow, 1939, vol. 2, p. 102). This for Tolstoy would imply an improper stress on man's creative role in history. In the end, nothing but unconscious action bears fruit. The precept runs: do not eat from the tree of knowledge! If history is an arena of human and social conflict, rather than a cosmic flow, Tolstoy may be said to have had no historical sense whatever, although, paradoxically, 'history' is the principal force in *War and Peace*.

history are carried out by the godly virtues or deadly vices of single individuals (although this is precisely what Tolstoy maintained in his later moral teaching). Even more, he scorned those who, in their drive for power, give way to the illusion of the supermen, who set up majestic aims and promote coercive civilizations, who provide crisp solutions to intractable problems, and blind themselves to the natural impulses and passions of men or their trackless social and moral nature.

The attitude reveals a deeply conservative mood, however much of a radical Tolstoy may have been in other respects: a mood growing from a sense of unity and cohesion that belongs to a feudal, pre-industrial age. Tolstoy tried to 'democratize' his view of history, as he tried to democratize his life and himself. He reduced historical agents to the just proportions of 'ambitious marionettes' in whose minds and actions the motivating forces had hitherto been found. He brought in instead the role of the mass, 'the people' (*narod*). Since he did not live in an expanding society which was growing richer every year on colonies and luxurious colonial wars, and whose soul did the same in its fantasies, he could not conceive, as, for instance, English nineteenth-century novelists conceived, characters unfailingly going up in the world as they became more refined by moral struggle or, better still, brought humbly to the faith by the glamorous sight of a duke on his deathbed. On the contrary, with all his exultation in the 'aristocratic', the 'patriarchal' and the 'familial', Tolstoy celebrates the majesty of 'the people' and identifies himself with it—in the proto-Decembrist Pierre Bezukhov no less than in Platon Karataev, in Tikhon Schcherbaty and the rebellious Bogucharov peasants. Such was the order of revolutionary intention in Russia since the Decembrists who, in the words of Rostopchin, 'started a revolution so as to lose their privileges'. And such was Tolstoy's way of being at one with the people, of being a *narodnik* or a Slavophil, or both, although he never rhapsodized over 'the people', nor, for that matter, said anything in *War and Peace* of what he thought about serfdom.[1] Unhappily, it was no longer possible to relate this attitude

---

[1] 'The national spirit (*narodnost'*) of the Slavophils', Tolstoy wrote in 1872, 'and real national spirit are two things, as different as sulphuric ether and universal ether, source of heat and light. I hate all these *choral principles* and *patterns of life and commune*, and Slav brethren, the invented ones . . .' (vol. 61, p. 278).

to the surrounding scene. The situation served to increase in Tolstoy the strain between belief and reality and eventually forced him to recognize—as Nekhlyudov in *Resurrection* recognized—that in the existing world irreparable damage had been done to the wholeness of life, and that in a divided, competitive world the sense of wholeness could not survive.

However, Tolstoy does not primarily impress on us a historical or social idea but a vision of the feelings and actions of men and women in relation to that wholeness. It is this which enabled him to see the personal aspect of the historical drama and the historical aspect of personal experience, to show that the life of one individual tells us something about other individuals, about social life as a whole, about the history of the wider society in which individuals live. They cannot be confined within their personal intensity, romantically or otherwise. They are open, like the characters of *War and Peace* to whom, in Tolstoy's already quoted words, he 'could not set any limits'. They are, in an almost ingenious way, life.

'Petya's eyes began to close and he swayed a little.

The trees were dripping. Quiet talking was heard. The horses neighed and jostled one another. Some one snored.

'"*Ozheg-zheg, Ozheg-zheg . . .*" hissed the sabre against the whetstone, and suddenly Petya heard an harmonious orchestra playing some unknown . . . hymn. Petya was as musical as Natasha and more so than Nicholas, but had never learnt music or thought about it, and so the melody that unexpectedly came to his mind seemed to him particularly fresh and attractive. The music became more and more audible. The melody grew and passed from one instrument to another. And what was played was a fugue—though Petya had not the least conception of what a fugue is. Each instrument —now resembling a violin and now a horn, but better and clearer than violin and horn—played its own part, and before it had finished the melody merged with another instrument that began almost the same air, and then with a third and a fourth; and they all blended into one, and again became separate and again blended, now into solemn church music now into something dazzlingly brilliant and triumphant . . .

'[Petya] closed his eyes, and from all sides, as if from a distance,

285

sounds fluttered, grew into harmonies, separated, blended, and again all mingled into the same . . . hymn. "Oh, this is delightful! As much as I like and as I like!" said Petya to himself. He tried to conduct that enormous orchestra.

'"Now softly, softly die away!" and the sounds obeyed him. Now fuller, more joyful . . . And from an unknown depth rose increasingly triumphant sounds . . .

'With a solemn triumphal march there mingled a song, the drip from the trees, and the hissing of the sabre, "*Ozheg-zheg-zheg* . . ." and again the horses jostled one another and neighed, not disturbing the choir but joining it . . .'

The quality of 'openness', as also the author's self-revelation, is less pronounced in *Anna Karenina* (1876) than in *War and Peace*. The conflict of characters and events relating to Anna's fate seems to follow the pattern of Balzac and Stendhal. The story—the undoing of an adulterous woman—is familiar in the nineteenth-century novel. Generally, Tolstoy refrained from plot-making—an omission or a defect, if defect it is, which, *pace* Dostoevsky, is common to the nineteenth-century Russian novelists since Gogol'. He replaced it by the exploitation and the unfolding of character, as though character was a fantastic plot in itself. But *Anna Karenina* has a clearly identifiable 'story', and once Tolstoy made the decision to tell it, its shape was determined, at any rate as far as Anna herself is concerned: she seems no more able to escape her fate than Electra or Medea. Hence the more 'fictional', the tighter framework and even the tidier, neater language of the novel as compared with *War and Peace*, and a single character who provides the apparent centre as well as the title of the book.

And yet, the range of the novel is much wider than this may suggest. It is not, in fact, possible to bring even Anna's fate into a single focus. Nothing is further from Anna, and from Tolstoy himself, than the romantic notion of exclusive, high, doomed adulterous passion and *Liebestod*, or Turgenev's idea, fictionalized in *Smoke* (*Dym*), of love as a haloed altar superseding all other relations. Tolstoy persists in his dominant idea: everything is related to everything else ('*stsepleno*'), and all relationship is either harmony or discord. Passion destroys itself because of the loss of mutual awareness and an inability to share in—instead of the will to possess—the secret of the other's being. But no one in particular can be held to blame, because life as a whole answers for Anna's fate. There is not a single episode which shows her apart from relationships with the other characters and, indeed, with the society which is deeply responsible for making those relationships what they are. Anna sees this herself: 'Yes, what is it I was thinking about? It's that I can't think of a situation where life wouldn't be agony, that we are all in it, all made to suffer, and that we all know this but keep inventing means for deceiving ourselves. But when one sees the truth what is one to do?' (Part Eight, Ch. 30.)

A great deal has been said on the dissociation of plots in *Anna Karenina*—the Anna–Vronsky–Karenin plot and the Levin–Kitty and Stiva–Dolly plots. Above all, it is suggested that Levin has been coerced into existence as a retort to Anna, to enable the author himself to round against his own instinct, which became just then, on the eve of the crisis that led to his 'conversion', unbearable to him. The suggestion can hardly be sustained in the light of the composition and the content of the novel. It is true that in the first outline (1873) the Levin part did not exist at all. But this does not mean that the Levin *theme* was absent: it is merely transferred to Anna's (originally Tat'yana's) husband who embodied, in a significantly more censorious and moralistic form, some of Levin's essential features (although in one of the drafts he even appeared as a would-be 'nihilist' advocating free love). Later, the Levin theme became personified in a new and more complex character, while Karenin (originally Stavrovich) turned into the desiccated bureaucrat of the final version. Similarly, the original drafts give greater prominence to the subject of the trapped adulteress. At this stage she is much less real as a woman and much more real as a mere object of censure.

What transpires throughout the altered versions, the changed characters and plots, is the opposite of what is indicated by some commentators: that, in producing a 'double plot', Tolstoy did not seek to establish two more or less disparate worlds—the world of Anna, whom we are asked, in vain, to consider wicked and therefore doomed, and that of Levin, whose high-mindedness (or priggishness) we are meant, but cannot quite manage, to applaud. It is well known how insistent Tolstoy himself was on the novel's structural unity and singleness of design, whatever difficulty he may have experienced in achieving it. Indeed, the only real contrast—but also the essential link—between these two worlds lies in that Anna's fate leads to a dead-end, while Levin's shows a way out. The breakdown of human relationships is complete in the case of Anna and its 'bitter consequences', in Tolstoy's own words, 'stem from what Anna Karenina experiences herself';[1] whereas Levin's moral and social conflicts are ultimately resolved in the victory of life over death, in work, in self-identification with his fellow men and, hence, in self-fulfilment. Yet they do not stand against each other as a negative and a positive character. Levin, too, is 'guilty' and finds himself on the brink of suicide. The parallels and the analogy between their respective positions are maintained throughout the novel, involving, besides Anna and Levin, the lives of many of the other characters.[2] 'Vengeance is mine; I will repay' must be taken for what it is: an epigraph to the novel as a whole, relevant to Anna and Levin alike. And the relevance is shown by Tolstoy with the same simple inevitability with which he shows the interplay of 'war' and 'peace', of the historical epic and the personal romance in *War and Peace*, or even the less well-founded, circuitous interaction of the lives of Nekhlyudov and Maslova in *Resurrection*.

It is true that *Anna Karenina* presents more of a jigsaw composed of contrary elements than *War and Peace*, as though to reflect the 'disorder' and 'discord' of Russian society which haunts Levin throughout the book: '*u nas vse perevorotilos*'' (Part Three, Ch. 26.) And this is shown to be the direct and indirect consequence of social and economic conditions in Russia in the post-Reform period. Tolstoy says that he felt weary of his work on the novel and unable to fuse the different elements. Much of what looks natural gives rise to doubts about the author's strategy: about, for instance, Tolstoy's sympathy for Anna in the web of conflicting involvements which he

[1] Quoted in Eykhenbaum, *Lev Tolstoy. Semidesyatye gody*, p. 197.
[2] For fuller evidence to this effect, see Bursov, *Lev Tolstoy. Ideynye iskaniya*, and *Lev Tolstoy i russkiy roman*; for the textual problems involved, see Zhdanov's study, *Tvorcheskaya istoriya 'Anny Kareninoy'*. There is an interesting polemical discussion of the Anna–Levin situation between Henry Gifford and Raymond Williams in the collection of essays edited by D. Davie. The controversy refers in particular to D. H. Lawrence's peculiar view that Tolstoy vitiated the novel by attempting to satisfy in it his uncontrollable puritanical urge, which made him kill Anna off as a renunciation of love's sincere passion.

has devised for her, or the effect on the narrative of his views, and still more his feelings, about sex. We do not know whether to believe and rejoice in Levin's discovery of the meaning of life, and in the feelings and thoughts that led him to the discovery. This is where the question of the author's self-revelation rises again. Tolstoy makes a great point of 'impartiality', especially in regard to Anna. The brilliant, experienced, half-ironical half-relished, impressions of fashionable life come to us through the eyes of the most unexpected characters, Levin for instance. Sometimes Tolstoy seems to grope, as if he did not know what he was doing, as if he was purposely effacing himself, speaking through Oblonsky who is transparently uncongenial to him, through Vronsky's attitude to Oblonsky, through Mikhaylov's view of Vronsky's painting, through Dolly's relations with Anna and Vronsky. But in the end the 'objective', 'impersonal' angle proves unsatisfactory to Tolstoy and he begins to stress the inevitable tensions, to confront—not Levin with Anna for the purposes of her supposed moral discomfiture—but one family with another, the capitalist cosmopolitanism of St. Petersburg with the shared traditions and patriarchal habits of rural society, the ethics of Princess Betsy with the moral consciousness of Fedor and Platon Fokanych, Levin's views with Koznychev's, and, obliquely, Turgenev's meditating, lyrical, reverential with his own vigorous, committed, toiling approach to nature.

As in *War and Peace* Tolstoy cannot refrain from taking the lead, unravelling, elucidating, 'reading between the lines': '"I always sympathized with him", Aleksey Aleksandrovich [Karenin] said to himself, although this was untrue and he never sympathized.' If anything, *'ostranenie', 'podglyadyvanie'* is extended and, from being largely concerned with discovering associations that exist between inconsonant thoughts and feelings, it is now directed to the explorations of fissions and of cleavages in human relations.

There has never been so intimate a study of a woman as Anna's portrait. Many women wrote to say they recognized themselves in it. Because he was so many men and women (and even so many animals—horses, dogs), Tolstoy could get into the skin of all. But Anna's portrait is of a deeply sundered person. Loveliness, charm, spontaneity, guilelessness, moral sensibility are at war with cunning, falseness, egotism, vulgarity. Needless to say, Tolstoy had no intention of showing that beauty is the conjunction of the superb and the vulgar, that the Egyptian courtesan is all the grander for the bugs that crawled on her. Rather, he expressed his growing sense of conflict within human beings, seeing it to be the forge in which all value, all life is beaten into good or bad shape. The already mentioned sudden awakening of compassion in the stiff, arid, ossified Karenin, ('a ministerial machine') is a triumph of Tolstoy's psychological perception. So is the urge to commit the most unsuspected and desperate acts—to disregard his career, to contemplate suicide—in Vronsky of the 'gilded youth of Petersburg'; so is the recognition of the moral integrity of the prostitute Katyusha Maslova in *Resurrection*.

It is this vision of the troubled complexity of human beings, who have so many faces, which undoubtedly accounts for Dostoevsky's effusive, almost passionate welcome of *Anna Karenina*, which the Russian writers and critics of all persuasions in the 1870s tended to misread or dismiss. Though he complained of Dostoevsky's 'shapelessness', Tolstoy for his part wrote to Strakhov that Dostoevsky was 'the closest, dearest and most necessary man to me'. (vol. 63, p. 142.)

SELECT BIBLIOGRAPHY

EDITIONS

Polnoe sobranie sochineniy (Jubilee Edition), 90 vols., Moscow, 1928–58.
Sobranie sochineniy, 14 vols., Moscow, 1953.
Sobranie sochineniy, 20 vols., Moscow, 1960–5.
Works (Centenary Edition), translated by L. and A. Maude, 21 vols., Oxford, 1928–37 (some reprinted in 'The World's Classics').
    Other English translations are available in 'Everyman's Library' and in 'Penguin Classics'.

CRITICAL AND BIOGRAPHICAL WORKS

Aldanov, M., *Zagadka Tolstogo*, Berlin, 1923.
Bayley, J., *Tolstoy and the Novel*, London, 1966.
Berlin, I., *The Hedgehog and the Fox*, London, 1953.
Bibliografiya literatury o L. N. Tolstom, 1917–1958, ed. N. Shelyapina and others, Moscow, 1960.
Bilinkis, Ya., *O tvorchestve L. N. Tolstogo. Ocherki*, Moscow, 1959.

TOLSTOY

Biryukov, P., *Lev Nikolaevich Tolstoy. Biografiya*, 4 vols., Moscow, 1911–23.

Bocharev, S., '*Voyna i mir* L. N. Tolstogo' in *Tri shedevra russkoy klassiki*, Moscow, 1971.

Bursov, B., *Lev Tolstoy i russkiy roman*, Moscow–Leningrad, 1963.

    Lev Tolstoy. Ideynye iskaniya i tvorcheskiy metod, Moscow, 1960.

Bychkov, A., *L. N. Tolstoy. Ocherk tvorchestva*, Moscow, 1954.

Chicherin, A., *Idei i stil'*, Moscow, 1968.

Christian, R., *Tolstoy's 'War and Peace'*, Oxford, 1962.

    L. Tolstoy, Cambridge, 1969.

Eykhenbaum, B., *Lev Tolstoy*, 3 vols., Leningrad, 1928, Moscow, 1931 and 1960.

    Molodoy Tolstoy, Petrograd–Berlin, 1922.

Gor'ky, M., *Reminiscences of Tolstoy, Chekhov, and Andreev*, London,1934.

Gudzy, N., *Lev Tolstoy*, Moscow, 1959.

Gusev, N., *Lev Nikolaevich Tolstoy. Materialy k biografii*, 3 vols., Moscow, 1954–63.

Khrapchenko, M., *Lev Tolstoy kak khudozhnik*, Moscow, 1963.

Lavrin, J., *Tolstoy. An Approach*, London, 1944.

Lenin, V., *O Tolstom. Literaturno-kriticheskiy sbornik*, Moscow–Leningrad, 1928.

Leo Tolstoy. A Critical Anthology, ed. H. Gifford, Penguin Books, 1971.

Leont'ev, K., *Analiz, stil' i veyanie. O romanakh gr. L. N. Tolstogo*, Brown University Slavic Reprint III, 1965.

L. N. Tolstoy v russkoy kritike, ed. S. Bychkov, Moscow, 1949.

L. N. Tolstoy v vospominaniyakh sovremennikov (Seriya literaturnykh memuarov), 2 vols., Moscow, 1960.

Lubbock, P., *The Craft of Fiction*, London, 1965.

Lukacs, G., *Studies in European Realism*, London, 1964.

    The Historical Novel (translated by H. and S. Mitchell), London, 1962.

Mann, Thomas, *Essays of Three Decades*, New York, 1947.

Maude, A., *The Life of Tolstoy*, 2 vols., Oxford, 1930.

Merezhkovsky, D., *Tolstoy i Dostoevskiy. Zhizn' i tvorchestvo*, 4th ed., St. Petersburg, 1909.

Pryanishnikov, N., *Proza L'va Tolstogo*, Orenburg, 1959.

Rolland, R., *Tolstoy* (English translation), London, 1911.

Russian Literature and Modern English Fiction. A Collection of Critical Essays, ed. D. Davie, Chicago, 1965.

Saburov, A., '*Voyna i mir*' L. N. Tolstogo. Problematika i poetika*, Moscow, 1959.

Shklovsky, V., *Lev Tolstoy*, Moscow, 1963.

    Material i stil' v romane L'va Tolstogo 'Voyna i mir', Moscow, 1928.

Simmons, E., *Leo Tolstoy*, London, 1949.

TOLSTOY

Skaftymov, A., 'Obraz Kutuzova i filosofiya istorii v romane L. N. Tolstogo *Voyna i mir*', *Russkaya literatura*, 1959, No. 2.

Steiner, G., *Tolstoy or Dostoevsky. An Essay in Contrast*, London, 1959.

Strakhov, N., *Kriticheskie stat'i o Turgeneve i Tolstom*, St. Petersburg, 1895.

Tolstoy. A Collection of Critical Essays, ed. R. Matlaw, New Jersey, 1947.

Troyat, H., *Tolstoy* (English translation), London, 1968.

Wilson Knight, G., *Shakespeare and Tolstoy*, London, 1934.

Zhdanov, V., *Tvorcheskaya istoriya 'Anny Kareninoy'. Materialy i nablyudeniya*, Moscow, 1957.

Zweig, S., *Adepts in Self-Portraiture* (English translation), London, 1952.

CHEKHOV

M. H. SHOTTON

THE LITERARY CAREER OF ANTON PAVLOVICH CHEKHOV (1860–1904) bridges two centuries and two eras. Beginning, falteringly, in the 1880s beneath the titanic shadows of Tolstoy and Dostoevsky, in fragile skiffs of stories seemingly dwarfed by the dreadnoughts of the immediate past, it ended in the years spanning the turn of the century, confidently established as part of a new art and a new culture. His life and literary career were equally tales of escape and self-discovery: escape from a social heritage of serfdom and petty bourgeois mercantilism, from a bleak age of reaction in politics and epigonic stagnation in the arts, and the discovery within himself of human dignity and creative artistic genius.

The process in the man is recorded in the famous letter[1] to Suvorin (7 January 1889): 'Write a tale of a young man, the son of a serf, a former shop-boy, choir-boy, schoolboy and student, brought up to be servile, to kiss the hands of priests, and to defer to other people's ideas; thankful for every bite of bread, often whipped, going to lessons without galoshes, fighting, torturing animals, enjoying dinners with rich relations, playing the hypocrite before God and man for no reason whatsoever, except from an awareness of his own insignificance,—write of how this young man squeezes the slave out of himself, drop by drop, and, waking up one fine morning, senses that it is now not the blood of a slave, but real human blood, which courses through his veins.'

---

[1] Page references will not be given, but all works and letters referred to or quoted can be found in: Chekhov, *Polnoe sobranie sochineniy i pisem.*

The path to artistic self-assurance was harder—harder in itself, but obstructed too by a modesty, fervent at times almost to the point of injuriousness. The self-depreciatory tone is ubiquitous, but particularly intense in the early years. Apologizing, in his letter to Suvorin (25th November, 1892), for serving in his stories mere 'lemonade', rather than 'the alcohol which would intoxicate and enthral', he laments that all art is doomed to triviality in his trivial age. But there is no such open expression of the confidence finally and painfully achieved at the triumphal climax of his career. It is there, concealed, in the sureness of his advice to the numerous young writers who sought his guidance; and it leaks out when, avoiding specific reference to himself, he permits himself to generalize upon the nature of the new culture, of which he clearly saw himself as part. In a letter to Dyagilev (30th December, 1902) Chekhov asserts that the new intelligentsia has turned its back on the philosophical-religious questions which so obsessed its predecessors.

'Our present culture is the beginning of a job of work being performed in the name of a great future, work which will, perhaps, go on for tens of thousands of years, so that man at some time, no matter how far in the future, may apprehend the truth of the real God; that is, instead of hazarding guesses or searching in Dostoevsky, that he may recognize it as clearly as he has recognized that two and two make four.'

Chekhov's abandonment of the great philosophic-religious themes, the 'accursed questions' of Tolstoy and Dostoevsky, and his attempt to urge man's consciousness towards an apprehension of 'the truth of the real God' is inseparably linked with the revolution which he effected in genre—the rejection of the novel and the rehabilitation of the short story and of the drama.

Since Gogol' the short story in Russia had been in decline, tacitly considered a second-rate genre or simply a useful preparatory exercise for the apprentice novelist. Tolstoy's short early pieces, memoir, sketch and story, are all unashamed experiments in techniques and ideas which were later to be transferred to the novels; he disdains and ignores any notion of the formal specificity of the short story. In the early stories and *povesti* of Turgenev and Dostoevsky, too, one

294

constantly senses the novelist bursting to break free from their cramping confines: there is a development of technique, a profusion of ideas, a promise of themes so grand, that the novel, and the novel alone, will accommodate them. The decline of the drama also, from the glorious peak of Gogol''s *The Inspector General*, may be explained in the same way. Turgenev's flirtation with the drama produced *A Month in the Country*, a clumsy piece of theatre, whose themes, moreover, found so much finer and fuller expression in his novels. There is, of course, Ostrovsky. Yet, is not Ostrovsky's masterpiece *The Storm* marred precisely by a disparity of theme and genre? Are his three hours of dialogue and gesture adequate for the treatment, except in barest outline, of his profound and complex themes— the conflict between libido and religious-moral instinct, the dilemma of the bright spirit in the 'dark kingdom', the concept of freedom in society, within oneself, and before God? Can one really compare *The Storm* in any terms with Tolstoy's re-creation of Ostrovsky's tragedy, his comprehensive exploration of the same themes in the novel *Anna Karenina*?[1] The theatrical grotesqueries of Sukhovo-Kobylin, and the historical dramas of Alexey Tolstoy likewise seem pallid in comparison to Dostoevsky's *The Devils* and Tolstoy's *War and Peace*.

Why then was Chekhov able to assume the mantle of the great novelists, yet reject their genre? The question was often asked of him, and he may even have asked himself. External enquiries he was inclined to fob off with two equally irrelevant answers: that he lacked the talent to write a novel,[2] or that writers of his generation had nothing to say which was worthy of a novel.[3] The key lies in fact not in any deficiency of his talent or his environment. It lies, on the contrary, firstly in an instinctive awareness of the ultimate indivisibility of form and content; Chekhov says what he has to say in the way it can best, and therefore *must*, be said. In this sense, Chekhov's choice of genres was

---

[1] Tolstoy's own return to the drama and the short story towards the end of his career was, of course, no more than an attempt to fulfil the dictates of his treatise *What is Art?* The story (the parable) and the drama (the morality play) had long since been proven the two most 'infectious' literary genres, i.e. the most capable of directly transmitting to a broad audience good (Christian) feelings. In neither case did he make any lasting or significant contribution to the genre.

[2] E.g. letter to Suvorin (11th March, 1889).

[3] E.g. letter to Suvorin (25th November, 1892).

not so much a choice, as an inevitability; the short stories and sketches, which first engaged his pen for purely commercial reasons, became, in their developed form, the perfect expressive mode for his particular vision of man and the world; and this developed short story technique brought him just as naturally, even inevitably, to the drama. Secondly —and this is no more than an extension of the first reason—Chekhov's whole human and artistic personality was attuned more to the comparative reticence of his chosen genres than to the broad self-exposure of the novel. His treatment of ideas is characterized above all by laconism, deliberate ambivalence, the regular and almost exasperating withdrawal from total self-commitment. The dominant features of his style are, similarly, detachment from his characters, a cool, gaunt and economic diction, relieved only by periodic bursts of lyricism, and the substitution of nuance and symbol for statement. These features of his writing are not simply the stuff of his technique in the short story and the drama; they are a direct expression of Chekhov the man and Chekhov the artist, they spring from the character of the man, from his vision of life and from his concept of the nature and function of literature. When he died of tuberculosis in Badenweiler at the age of forty-four, his fame was worldwide; and his ghost no doubt approved the jest of fate which brought his body back to St. Petersburg in a goods wagon marked 'Oysters'. It is perhaps significant too that Chekhov was spurred to a literary career not by any craving for intellectual self-assertion, but by the simple pressures of circumstance and poverty.

CHEKHONTE AND CHEKHOV

Anton Chekhov was born in 1860, the third of six children of Pavel Chekhov, a shopkeeper of Taganrog. Pavel's father, a serf, had bought the family's freedom only forty years before. Pavel was a pious disciplinarian, but an ineffectual creature. Though ensuring a sound education for his sons at the local *gymnasium*, he blighted their young lives by subjecting them to a relentless routine of school, service at the shop-counter, and interminable nocturnal vigils at the local Orthodox church. Reduced to bankruptcy in 1876, Pavel fled to Moscow, where his two eldest sons, Aleksandr and Nikolay, were students. Anton stayed on in Taganrog to finish his schooling, but in 1879 joined the family in Moscow and enrolled in the Medical Faculty of the University. He shared with his brother Aleksandr a natural and effusive wit and a talent for clowning, which both had developed largely as a mechanism of defence against the drudgery of their childhood. It was Aleksandr who first induced Anton to help swell the family's meagre budget by writing jokes, anecdotes and short sketches for some of the multitudinous comic magazines which flourished in Moscow and Petersburg at the time. Thus ended a period of Chekhov's life, of which he himself said: 'In my childhood I had no childhood . . .'[1] It is established critical practice to divide Chekhov's literary career into two periods: the first, commonly called the '(Antosha) Chekhonte period'—after the most popular of the several frivolous pseudonyms which he then employed—extends from his debut in 1880 until approximately 1886–8, when begins the 'mature period'.

In many ways the period 1886–8 does indeed mark a turning point. Between 1880 and 1883 his output, in quantitative terms, reached prodigious proportions; he wrote with facility, and, in addition to the successful pursuance of his medical studies, was by 1883 producing over a hundred pieces a year, most of them trifling nonsense of no literary value. In 1883 he began a regular humorous gossip-column for Leykin's journal *Fragments* (*Oskolki*). In 1886 he achieved the elevated position of contributor to Suvorin's *New Times* (*Novoe vremya*), a highly respectable and conservative Petersburg newspaper. Increasing financial security, the publication of two collected editions of his stories,[2] and a letter out of the blue from the established author Grigorovich encouraging him not to waste an obvious talent, all led Chekhov to consider for the first time whether he should not take himself more seriously as a writer. The decision, that perhaps he should, induced in 1887 and 1888 a massive decrease in output and an already distinct improvement in quality. In 1886 he wrote roughly 110 items, in 1888 a mere ten.

Chekhov in later years had little to say in defence of his early literary efforts; indeed, he was known to lump them together under a

---

[1] A. P. Chekhov, 'Iz detskikh let A. P. Chekhova' in *Chekhov v vospominaniyakh*, p. 55.

[2] *Motley Stories* (*Pestrye rasskazy*), 1886, and *In the Twilight* (*V sumerkakh*), 1887.

mild obscenity. The prevalently self-depreciatory tenor of his comments even on his finest works, however, mark him out as the least reliable of his own critics. Though it would be idle to suggest that the years 1886–8 mark no significant change in the development of Chekhov's art, the change that did occur was one of temperament rather than of direction. The external pressures impelling him towards a serious literary career increased. To those already mentioned were added further pleas and persuasion from Korolenko, Pleshcheev, Suvorin and others, the steadily growing approbation of the reading public, and the award of a Pushkin Prize for Literature by the Academy of Sciences in 1888. These things combined with Chekhov's own pursuit of dignity to produce in him a new sense of artistic responsibility, a conviction that the *serious* writer is and must be answerable to his fellow men and to his art. One is constantly aware of this belief in his numerous comments on literature hereafter in correspondence and elsewhere. Jokey sketches and other trivia may be written just for the money, but to be a *real* writer is a very different thing.

The culminating point of this process of self-examination was his journey in 1890 to the penal settlement on Sakhalin Island off Russia's Pacific coast. This arduous adventure, undertaken by a man who had been spitting blood already for six years, involved a trans-Siberian journey of enormous hardship, the single-handed conduct of a census of the penal colony, and the compilation of a sociological survey which fell like a bombshell upon the Russian public and stirred even an apathetic tsarist officialdom to reform. Chekhov offered a variety of reasons for the journey, all in their way equally valid. It was a change, a chance to make some valid contribution to medical and social science, an escape from the artificial glamour of the world of letters. What it really offered him was the time and the opportunity to come to terms with himself, and to reconcile the divergent attractions of medicine and literature. It is notable that after his return, though still periodically subject to doubts about his own worth as a writer, he never again seriously questioned his literary vocation.

Over this critical intermediary period then, Chekhov was gradually forging his artistic temperament; yet much of the essence of his mature art is to be found already in dilute form in the mass of works produced during the early years.

The writings of Chekhonte, as indeed of Chekhov, are all firmly rooted in his contemporary reality. Penetrating every nook of his own society, Chekhov never strays beyond it. As a clearly delimited and comprehensive analysis, his work matches, on a grander scale, the treatise on Sakhalin. For the basic matter of his literature Chekhov neither tries, nor needs, to look beyond his own experience. Indeed, one of the marks of the transition from Chekhonte to Chekhov is the pursuit of a more perfectly realistic basis for his work, a concentration in choice of subject upon those parts of life, not which the author simply knows, but which he knows best.[1] The scrupulously realistic basis, however, for Chekhov always remains an instrument rather than an aim in itself. The meaning and intention of all Chekhov's work, and perhaps of much of Chekhonte's too, extend far out beyond the contemporary social context.

The element of simple social satire in the Chekhonte tales is inescapable: the follies of men, rooted in the particular and typical institutions and conventions of contemporary Russian society, are exposed and ridiculed. Yet the real butt of Chekhonte's joking remains the man, rather than the social phenomenon. Class, rank, privilege etc. are shown less as absurd in themselves than as the prerequisites for a display by man of the destructive absurdity to which he is always inclined. Chekhonte has nothing to say about the inherent rights or wrongs of social hierarchies; hence the total absence of sentimentality in his treatment of the 'little man', who concedes nothing in asininity to his more elevated brother. In *Fat and Thin* (*Tolstyy i tonkiy*) (1883) two former school-friends, one fat, one thin, meet by chance at a railway station. All goes well until the fat man reveals that he has risen to the rank of privy counsellor. The thin man is instantly, and in spite of the other's protestations, reduced to a stuttering

[1] Hence the ubiquitous men of medicine, from professor (*A Dreary Story* (*Skuchnaya istoriya*) (1889)) to *fel'dsher* (doctor's assistant) (*An Unpleasant Business* (*Nepriyatnost'*) (1888) and passim); the 'clinical studies' (so christened by Elton), in which he charts with textbook precision the sensations and manifestations of various mental and physical conditions, from pregnancy to megalomania (*Volodya* (1887), *Typhus* (*Tif*) (1887), *Ivanov* (1889), *The Name-day Party* (*Imeniny*) (1888), *A Dreary Story* (1889), *A Nervous Breakdown* (*Pripadok*) (1888), *The Black Monk* (*Chernyy monakh*) (1894)); the echoes of the Sakhalin adventure (*Gusev* (1890), *Peasant Women* (*Baby*) (1891), *In Exile* (*V ssylke*) (1892)), and of his short return visit to Taganrog and the Don Steppe in 1887 (*Happiness* (*Schast'e*) (1887), *The Steppe* (*Step'*) (1888), *The Beauties* (*Krasavitsy*) (1888)).

obsequiousness. *The Death of a Government Official* (*Smert' chinov-nika*) (1883) depicts a petty civil servant, Chervyakov, who worries himself literally to death after accidentally sneezing upon the bald pate of a general while sitting behind him in the theatre. Again there is no question of persecution: the general is considerably more dis-comforted by Chervyakov's persistent servile apologies than by the sneeze itself. *The Mask* (*Maska*) (1884) is in similar vein.

The impact of many tales derives from the implicit ironic contrast between eternal human values and the conventional values of contemporary man, which, though enjoying the same name, represent abhorrent distortions of the real thing. Thus 'dignity' defines nothing more than a sense of social respectability; the undignified ass who is called an ass in public must sue for slander to preserve this 'dignity' (*Out of the Frying Pan into the Fire* (*Iz ognya da v polymya*) (1884)). 'Respect' means no more than subservience to wealth or rank. 'Love' within the family is granted only to those who represent a potential bequest (*What an Idyll!* (*Idilliya—uvy i akh!*) (1882)).

Amongst the hordes of anti-men who people his pages Chekhonte occasionally produces a type in whom the process of dehumanization has taken so sinister a turn, that the reaction provoked hovers between laughter and a genuine disquietude. Hereabouts lies the borderline between Chekhonte the jester and Chekhov the satirical humanist. The tailor Merkulov, who duns a captain for payment for a coat and receives a beating for his pains, is found with a beatific smile on his face. It is an honour to be thrashed by a gentleman (*The Captain's Coat* (*Kapitanskiy mundir*) (1885)). In *The Trial* (*Sud*) (1881), Serapion, the wretched son of a brutish shopkeeper, is thrashed at his father's instigation for a theft he has not committed, but accepts the beating as reasonable.

The central figure in this group is the eponymous hero of *Corporal Prishibeev* (*Unter Prishibeev*) (1885). This former NCO, a sneak, meddler and killjoy, has appointed himself village vigilante. Convinced that decent behaviour consists of doing only what is expressly sanctioned by written statute, he applies himself to the suppression of all such 'illegalities' as singing, dancing, talking together in public, or lighting fires after dusk. 'There's no such law', he states, 'as allows for the singing of songs.' Because the effects of Prishibeev's mindless bullying extend beyond himself on to the lives of others, he was inevitably seen as a thinly veiled symbol of the forces of oppression at work in Russia. Chekhov denied the implication; but Prishibeev remains the first of a series of important symbolic characters in his work, in whom the laughable has acquired distinct overtones of evil. Prishibeev is given a month's sentence for slander and assault; but as he is taken away through a chattering crowd of villagers, he cannot resist coming rigidly to attention and bawling at them to disperse. Fools are as unchangeable as they are ubiquitous in Chekhonte's world. Yet the disillusionment verging upon misanthropy of such tales as *Corporal Prishibeev* is more than adequately counterbalanced by the humane optimism of a different group.

Chekhonte's vision of the human potential for goodness is revealed primarily through a Rousseauesque-Tolstoyan belief in the fundamental innocence of children. The idyllic gaiety and warmth of a child's world, totally devoid of artificiality, is exquisitely caught in a series of stories (*The Cook is Getting Married* (*Kukharka zhenitsya*) (1885), *An Incident* (*Sobytie*) (1886), *Boys* (*Mal'chiki*) (1887)). *A Trifle of Everyday Life* (*Zhiteyskaya meloch'*) (1886) tells of a young boy, Alesha, whose parents have separated, and whose mother is living with her lover Belyaev. Unknown to their mother, Alesha and his sister regularly meet their father in a café. Belyaev is informed of these meetings, but promises the children he will not tell their mother. When he quite cynically breaks this promise, Alesha's faith in adults is shattered: 'He trembled, stuttered and wept: for the first time in his life he had come face to face with deceit; previously he had not known that besides sweet pears, pies and expensive watches, there were many other things on this earth which had no name in a child's vocabulary.'

A Day in the Country (*Den' za gorodom*) (1886) describes the relationship between an impoverished shoemaker and two waifs. The shoemaker shares with them his knowledge of the lore of nature: his selfless affection and his revelations of nature's secrets to the wide-eyed children more than compensate for their homelessness.

The marginal sentimentality of these stories is a not uncommon failing in Chekhonte's works about children, but can probably be put down as much to his recognition, as a purely mercenary writer, that he must give his public what they enjoy, as to any lack of artistic sensibility. It is frequently present too in the second category of

301

'humane' Chekhonte tales—those in which he invites our sympathy for unhappy people. Though falling within the broad confines of the 'Chekhonte' period, these stories, dating mostly from the late 1880s, show few of the marks of the standard Chekhonte mould.

In *A Nightmare* (*Koshmar*) (1886) Kunin, a young civil servant, returns from Petersburg to his country estate. Since he has been appointed guardian of the local parish school, he summons the priest. The priest, to Kunin's astonishment, turns out to be a ragged and emaciated figure, who surreptitiously filches sugar from the table. Kunin, a lifelong wastrel, refuses financial help to the school, and in a letter to the bishop denounces the priest. Only later does he learn that the priest is poverty-stricken and half-starved, and that, moreover, the local doctor is in much the same plight.

The wretchedness of the priest may be directly attributable to social conditions: in other cases, Chekhonte/Chekhov depicts unhappiness as the accidental but inevitable outcome of human frailties. In *The Doctor* (*Doktor*) (1887) Tretkov, a country practitioner, is treating for incurable tuberculosis of the brain a young boy, whom he knows may well be his own natural son. The boy's mother, for whom Tretkov still feels a warm affection, asserts that this is so, but the doctor, plagued by the knowledge that she has in the past attributed the boy's paternity to other lovers too, ends by bullying and insulting her. There can be no resolution: the boy is left dying, while the doctor and the mother each suffer their private misery, unable to offer each other the comfort which both desperately need.

EARLY TECHNIQUE

Form in Chekhov is at all stages of his career a further expression of his view of reality. The maturing of that view over the first decade, therefore, finds its reflection in an increasing formal sophistication. The insouciance of the young Chekhonte, his voluntary self-subordination to the demands of editor and reading public, his superficial scanning of situations for the shock effect and the quick laugh moulded and defined the basic formal characteristics of his work—satirical hyperbole in the manner of Gogol' and Shchedrin, reinforced in absurdity by the dead-pan manner of its presentation, outrageous parody, verbal clowning, anecdotal structure with startling denouement, prevalence of action over motivation and caricature over characterization, together with the assorted sins of vulgarity, sentimentality and melodrama. Amongst this motley apparatus, however, Chekhonte forged some instruments of value. The iron dictates of column-space taught him concentration, driving him, as Tolstoy remarked, to the Pushkinian virtues of precision, brevity, simplicity, and, above all, '*nasyshchennost''*—the saturation of word and phrase with meaning by a process of selection and location. He learnt, again in the interests of conciseness, to employ an impressionistic method for defining the complex, particularly in the realm of psychology.

Most important, Chekhov with the years began to see these processes of reduction, practically imposed upon him in the beginning by *force majeure*, less and less as a compromise with necessity and more and more as composing a stylistic method, valid in its own right. The lulling self-sufficiency and all-explaining expansiveness of, say, Tolstoy's style in the novels was to be replaced by a manner of writing which demanded intellectual participation and imaginative response from the reader in the plane of style as well as of content.

The primitive Chekhonte sketch, of course, made little such demand; but much of the basic development of the mature Chekhovian manner took place during the Chekhonte period.

In narrative structure one detects a gradual shift from the easy anecdotal form with its 'twist' in the tail to the type of story which, in terms of external event, has no real 'ending', nor, at times, any precise narrative shape at all. The realistic artistic philosophy underlying the shift is plain: Chekhov was beginning to recognize the artificiality of literature's attempts to impose the symmetry of conventional external plot, the ordered routine of exposition, action and denouement, upon the infinitely convolute patterns of life itself. If the subject of literature is human experience, then the inner processes which shape and constitute that experience should be the stuff of realistic literature. The external actions of men and the events which those actions compose are the products of inner processes; but it is folly to suppose that inner processes and external actions are always either synchronous or symmetric. A finished inner process, a psychological denouement, may find no immediate expression in external event. Likewise, an external 'denouement' may go quite unaccompanied at the time by any proportional psychological development. To organize literature merely according to the pattern of external event is to ignore what constitutes the essence of life, and is, therefore, unrealistic.

This Chekhovian view of life and art is to be recognized first, perhaps, in those 'Chekhonte' tales which demonstrate the unchangeability of fools. *Out of the Frying Pan into the Fire, Corporal Prishibeev*, and *The Chameleon* (*Khameleon*) (1884) all have a sort of 'denouement'. Yet, consisting as it does in each case not in the discomfiture of the fool as a result of events, but in the fool's blind pursuit of his folly *in spite of* events, it becomes an anti-denouement: the focus of the story is transferred from its outcome in terms of 'plot' to the quality of the character at its centre.

In some Chekhonte tales the trappings of external plot have vanished altogether, as in the portrait of the domineering wife and down-trodden husband in *The Last of the Lady Mohicans* (*Poslednyaya mogikansha*)(1885). Gradually over the Chekhonte period the outward narrative structure of the story begins to be reshaped in accordance with this notion of realism. At the centre of the story, acting as its cohesive force and ultimate *raison d'être*, is the psychological world of the character or characters involved. The story may be static in quality, depicting a single mood or the unchanging nature of a Prishibeev; or it may be dynamic, marking the course of inner processes, the change or development of mood, emotion, outlook or temperament.

One of the most perfect examples of the former type, dating, admittedly, from the later period, is *After the Theatre* (*Posle teatra*) (1892) in which Chekhov brilliantly attempts to capture the mood of a young girl enjoying the first trembling raptures of adolescence. In its way, it is as precisely 'clinical' as the studies of medical conditions mentioned above.

Among the early stories, however, one (*The Kiss* (*Potseluy*) (1887)) stands out as a pointer to the future, demonstrating how not merely the narrative structure, but the whole style has begun to mould itself around the story's hub—the depiction of the hero's inner world. It makes a deceptively conventional start: the officers of an artillery regiment, stationed for the night in a small village, are invited for the evening to the house of the local landowner, a retired lieutenant-general. Amongst them is the round-shouldered, bespectacled captain Ryabovich, 'with side-whiskers like a lynx', whose whole appearance seems to state 'I am the most timid, modest and colourless officer in the whole brigade'. His shyness and sense of inferiority preclude his joining in the billiards, and the dancing and polite chatter with the young ladies invited along for the occasion. Ill at ease, he wanders off into the dark recesses of the house; entering by chance a darkened room, he hears the rustle of a dress. The arms of a young lady, who is clearly expecting a rendezvous with one of his comrades, entwine themselves around his neck. There is a whispered 'At last!', a warm cheek is pressed to his, and he is tenderly kissed. The moment of enchantment is brief; the girl, recognizing her mistake, cries out, and Ryabovich flees.

At this point of the story conventionality ends: contrary to expectations, the story does not pursue the relationship between Ryabovich and the girl, nor, indeed, any of the 'external' consequences of their encounter. Chekhov, from this point, narrows down his focus to the psychological effects of the kiss upon his hero. This unprecedented experience becomes for a time almost an obsession with Ryabovich: he pursues his duties as if in a daze, his mind revolving endlessly around the question of the girl's identity and the sheer wondrousness of the kiss. All his previously vague yearning for emotional experience is now multiplied to an intolerable degree. He attempts catharsis by relating the incident to his comrades, and is astounded to find that the whole tale, which has assumed such immense significance for him, is told in a minute, and quickly capped by a somewhat more salty anecdote in similar vein, told by a fellow officer. Disillusionment and the effects of time gradually bring him to the sombre realization that, really, nothing has changed. Passing through the same village on a subsequent occasion, he refuses an invitation to visit the general's house again. Once more his life seems barren, wretched and colourless . . .

During this latter part of the story the whole treatment of the narrative is conditioned by the mood and psychological experiences of Ryabovich. Sights and sounds around him acquire special qualities, are described by Chekhov in a certain way, not because, objectively, that is the way they are, but because they are impinged upon and transmuted by Ryabovich's mood.

Occasionally Chekhov is explicit, as in this episode, when the officers, making their way home after the visit to the general's house are resting awhile on the bank of a river: 'On the far bank they could see a dull red light and, for lack of anything better to do, had a long discussion as to whether it was a bonfire, a light in a window, or something else . . . Ryabovich was also looking at the light, *and it seemed to him*,[1] that the light was smiling and winking at him as though it knew about the kiss.'

Elsewhere, however, the impingement of the character's mood upon his environment is stated, without explanation, as though it were bald fact. The regiment leaves the village, which now exerts a powerful emotional attraction upon Ryabovich:

'After half a verst he looked back: the yellow church, the house, the river and the garden were bathed in light; the river, with its bright green banks reflecting in itself the blue sky and here and there glittering silver in the sunlight, was very beautiful. Ryabovich glanced for the last time at Mestechki, and felt sad as though he were parting with something very dear and close to him.

'Meanwhile before his eyes on the road ahead there lay only dreary, well-known sights . . . To right and left fields of young rye and buckwheat, with rooks hopping about; look ahead, and you see dust and the backs of people's heads, look back, and you see the same dust and faces . . .'

This process—the selection of detail, particularly descriptive detail, via the perception of the character(s) involved, and the colouring of that detail to correspond with or evoke the character's mood or emotional attitude—is the key to the Chekhovian technique commonly called '*nastroenie*' (mood).

In some cases the interaction between human mood and described environment is mutual: in two 'steppe' stories (*Happiness* (1887), *The Steppe* (1888)), written after his journey through the Don Steppe in 1887, Chekhov creates an impression of total harmony between the steppe scenery and the mood of the people in its midst. The establishment of this harmony dominates both stories, turning them into verbal tone-poems. *Happiness* has no narrative pattern, but merely describes a scene in the steppe: two shepherds and an itinerant land-agent, resting for the night, engage in a desultory conversation

[1] My italics.—MHS.

about buried treasure and human happiness. The vast expanse of the steppe about them, the sleeping flocks of sheep, the dim silhouettes of ancient tumuli, the re-echoing report of a snapping cable in a distant mine, the lazy flight of rooks through the morning mist, all reflect and reinforce the superstitious fears, and vague yearnings for wealth and happiness of the three men. *The Steppe* is a longer piece, describing a cart journey across the steppe under a sultry July sky. Egorushka, a young boy, is travelling in the company of a merchant and a priest to enter high-school in a distant town. The tale is not without incident; but the series of disjointed episodes which compose the external narrative give the story no unity. This is achieved rather by the uniformity of the process by which these incidents are presented in terms of their physical and psychological effect upon the boy—his bewilderment at leaving home, his reactions to the people he meets on the journey, particularly the peasant carters, his fears during a thunderstorm, and the physical sensations of a fever.

In both these tales the style is, as it were, controlled by the psychology of the characters; Chekhov attempts to detach himself, as author, even from decorative elements such as imagery; the image becomes primarily the product of the character's imagination and only indirectly of the author's. Hence in the simple minds of the peasants the characteristic personification of animals and natural phenomena:

'Against the grey background of dawn, already spreading across the eastern sky, here and there could be seen the silhouettes of sheep, which were not asleep: they were standing and, with lowered heads, thinking about something.' (*Happiness*.)

'To the left, as though someone had struck a match across the sky, a pale phosphorescent streak flashed and died. There was a noise as though someone far away had walked across an iron roof. Probably they walked across barefoot, because the iron gave a dull, hollow rumble.' (*The Steppe*.)

This preference for an imagery matching the artless psychological responses of his characters is clearly a deliberately innovatory element of Chekhov's style and coincides with what later emerged as a precept of Tolstoy's *What is Art?*—that art should be shorn of 'cultured' pretentious artifice. Not surprisingly, Chekhov, while admiring the literary skills and imaginative powers of the Modernists and Decadents of the nineties, is known to have deplored the mystic and often pretentious ultra-aestheticism which marred their work.[1] He had little time either for writers of the opposite extreme, who believed they could give their literature an authentic 'populist' flavour by the admixture of heavy doses of 'folk vocabulary', culled from Dal', Ostrovsky and Leskov. He did admire Mamin-Sibiryak, whose use of popular speech elements in his tales about Russian miners was patently based on genuine personal experience.

In the late 1880s Chekhov turned his hand for the first time seriously to the theatre.[2] He had been since childhood an insatiable theatregoer. Now growing confidence as a writer and the promise of considerable financial reward spurred him to attempt the drama. It was a natural step: many of the Chekhonte tales were essentially dramatic in quality—structurally anecdotal and often consisting almost exclusively of dialogue. The gift for producing typical and expressive dialogue was one of the earliest to emerge in the young Chekhov, and five of his first short pieces for the theatre: *On the High Road* (*Na bol'shoy doroge*) (1885), *Swan Song* (*Lebedinaya pesnya*) (1887), *An Unwilling Tragedian* (*Tragik ponevole*) (1889), *The Wedding* (*Svad'ba*) (1889), *The Anniversary* (*Yubiley*) (1891) were conversions for the stage of early short stories.

The majority of his work for the theatre in this period consists of short vaudeville farces: (*The Bear* (*Medved'*) (1888), *The Proposal* (*Predlozhenie*) (1888), *An Unwilling Tragedian*, *The Wedding*, *The Anniversary*), thoroughly conventional in type, but executed with a consummate professionalism, which has made them masterpieces of their genre in Russian. These farces, together with the short sketches, *On the High Road*, *Swan Song*, and *On the Harmfulness of Tobacco* (*O vrede tabaka*) (1886, rewritten 1902), fall outside the mainstream development of Chekhov's art; two long plays of the period,

---

[1] A. Serebrov (Tikhonov) records Chekhov, referring to Bryusov's one-line poem 'O, cover up your pale legs' as saying: 'Don't you believe them; their legs aren't "pale" at all, but just as hairy as everybody else's.' (*Chekhov v vospominaniyakh*, p. 560).

[2] There is a weak and bulky four-act play with no title, written, it is believed, in 1880–1. It was not published during Chekhov's life, and is sometimes called *Platonov*.

however, point forward to the future. The first, *Ivanov* (1887), represents Chekhov's first move to inject new ideas and methods into a stagnant Russian theatre. In articles and stories of the early 1880s Chekhov had conducted a campaign of ridicule against the playwrights and producers of his day. The theatre of his day was indeed in steep epigonic decline; second-rate dramatists, aping the '*bytovaya drama*' [drama of everyday life] of Ostrovsky, had reduced his full-blooded characters to anaemic stereotypes, his rich language to pallid cliché. The public, however, had through long usage become addicted. Chekhov's 'new' drama was given a hostile reception, which caused him great distress, and brought him close to a total abandonment of the theatre as a medium for his art.

Outwardly, *Ivanov* relies heavily still upon the trappings of conventional drama—the twist at the end of each act, the final climax in a melodramatic suicide. Yet, as in the stories, the essence of the drama lies not in the development and outcome of plot, but in the penetrative psychological treatment of the central characters. The amoral and ineffectual landowner Ivanov treats his Jewish wife Sarah, who is dying of tuberculosis, with appalling callousness; while she lies dying, he spends gay evenings at the house of his rich neighbour Lebedev, and flirts with Lebedev's daughter Sasha. Warned by the tediously self-righteous Dr. L'vov that the discovery of his deceit may kill his wife, Ivanov nonetheless persists. His cruelty to his wife culminates in his taunting her with being a Jewess and announcing that she does not have long to live. After Sarah's death, Sasha agrees to marry Ivanov; but before the marriage can take place, he commits suicide.

The play was a failure. Audiences were unable to accept or even understand Chekhov's intention, which was to convince them that Ivanov was more worthy of their sympathy than L'vov. Such a judgement implied a rejection of the didactic ethical system of the *bytovaya drama*, by whose criteria Ivanov's treatment of his wife was patently wicked, and L'vov's attitude correct. Chekhov was demanding a judgement in terms not of conventional ethics but of human quality. The distinction between the two protagonists was between an uneasy and reproachful self-awareness, and a smug self-satisfaction. L'vov is a sermonizing bore: Ivanov has no illusions about himself, and practically all he says has a self-castigatory ring. Recognition that he can bring only wretchedness to himself and others motivates his suicide. For all his faults, which, Chekhov suggests, are the products of forces outside his control, Ivanov has sufficient warmth of personality to retain the love of Sarah and win that of Sasha.

The distinction between complacency and critical self-awareness, and the implicit assertion that in judging men this distinction represents a higher criterion than that of moral rectitude in the conventional sense, must be seen as the central idea inspiring the play. There is a similar assault on accepted modes of judging human behaviour in the play *The Wood Demon* (*Leshiy*) (1889).[1]

The majority of the characters in *The Wood Demon* represent a degenerate system of values. The retired professor Serebryakov 'has for twenty-five years been reading and writing about art, while himself understanding absolutely nothing about art'; having achieved fame and eminence, he has shut himself off from the world behind a barrier of complacence, and indulges his taste for jealousy (of his wife) and hypochondria. His second wife Elena is beautiful, and conscious of the power of her beauty over several of the men about her, particularly Voynitsky, the brother of Serebryakov's first wife. Elena has no love for her husband, but a conventional sense of propriety checks all impulse to adultery. Fedor Orlovsky, son of a neighbouring landowner, has become totally involved in his lust for Elena. Dyadin, nicknamed 'Waffles', is an impoverished nobleman, the perpetual 'victim of fate', whose only remaining zest in life is for the pronouncement of flowery platitudes. Even Voynitsky and his niece Sonya, whose unhappiness and melancholy are the products of other people's thoughtlessness, are not entirely untainted by the atmosphere of vulgarity, pretence and stultifying indolence which dominates the play. It is a small point in Voynitsky's favour that he exposes the absurdity of Elena's cold incorruptibility: 'To deceive your husband, whom you cannot stand—that is immoral; but to try to stifle in yourself your wretched youthfulness and the feeling of life—that is not immoral. Where, for heaven's sake, is the logic in that?' (Act 1, Scene 3.)

Chekhov's own antidote to the debased concepts of intelligence, beauty and morality is incorporated in Khrushchov, a landowner and doctor. Khrushchov, a devoted medical practitioner and a lover

[1] Later rewritten and transformed into *Uncle Vanya* (1890–6). See p. 334.

of trees and forests, is a man of action, acting not from self-interest, but in the pursuance of altruistic ideals. True, Khrushchov discovers flaws within himself. When Voynitsky commits suicide as a result of his unrequited love for Elena, and of Serebryakov's decision to sell the estate, Khrushchov experiences a profound sense of guilt; it was he who unjustly reproached Voynitsky for conducting a shameless affair with Elena.

'I considered myself a humane person, a man of principle, and at the same time I could not forgive people the slightest mistakes; I believed gossip, I spread slander together with the others . . . Inside me there sits a wood demon, I am trivial, mediocre and blind.' (Act 4, Scene 9.)

In spite of this, as with Ivanov, Khrushchov's awareness of himself is a saving grace.

One's inclination to see in Khrushchov Chekhov's first transmission via imaginative literature of positive notions about the ideal man and the ideal life can only be strengthened by a non-fictional, but illuminating piece which he wrote in 1888 to mark the death of the explorer and geographer Przheval'sky. It deserves lengthy quotation:

'One Przheval'sky or one Stanley is worth a dozen institutes of learning and hundreds of good books. Their adherence to principle and nobility of ambition, based upon the honour of their country and of science, their pertinacity, their striving towards a chosen goal, impregnable against any hardship, danger or temptation of personal happiness, their wealth of knowledge and of industry, their acquired tolerance of intense heat, hunger, homesickness, and debilitating fevers, their fanatical belief in Christian civilization and science,— all these things make them, in the eyes of the people, heroic figures embodying the highest moral authority. And where this authority ceases to be an abstract idea and is embodied in one or a dozen living men, there exists a powerful school . . .

'In our sick age, when European societies are in the grip of idleness, boredom with life, and unbelief, when distaste for life and fear of death reign in strange interdependance, when even the best of men sit with arms folded, justifying their idleness and debauchery by the lack of any fixed aim in life, heroic figures are as vital as the sun.

Composing the most poetic and joyful element in society, they arouse, comfort and ennoble us.

'Their personalities are living documents which point out to society that, besides people engaged in arguments about optimism and pessimism, people writing out of boredom mediocre tales, unnecessary schemes and cheap dissertations, people indulging in debauchery in the name of a denial of life and lying for the sake of a crust of bread —that, besides sceptics, mystics, psychopaths, Jesuits, philosophers, liberals and conservatives, there exist men of a different stamp, men of heroic deeds, of faith, men with clearly avowed aims. If positive types created by literature constitute valuable educative material, then the same types produced by life itself are of inestimable value.'

In many ways this article is a lynchpin in the evolution of Chekhov's attitudes towards himself as man and writer, and towards literature in general. It certainly makes clearer the motivations behind the journey to Sakhalin and the final commitment to serious literary endeavour. Shortly before his departure for Sakhalin he wrote to Lavrov, editor of *Russian Thought* (*Russkaya mysl'*), 'I have never been a writer without principles, or, which is the same thing, a scoundrel' (10th April, 1890), and to Suvorin, 'This is a necessity for me, since I am a Ukrainian and I've started getting lazy. I must school myself.' (9th March, 1890.)

The article on Przheval'sky also indicates in Chekhov a concept of the positive hero very similar to Turgenev's—the genuine idealist who believes but, above all, acts. 'I have an infinite affection for such men as Przheval'sky', he wrote.[1]

The apparent paradox—that Przheval'sky types are rare in Chekhov's literature—is not difficult to explain. No doubt for Chekhov, the creation of a wholly virtuous character, with the attendant risk of that character being identified in some degree with the author himself, smacked of immodesty and bad literary taste. Of course, he objected strongly to any identification of characters in his work with himself.[2] On the practical level too, as we shall see, he believed that nothing was so guaranteed to destroy the effectiveness of an idea of virtue as its pretentious and dogmatic presentation in literature.

[1] Letter to E. M. Lintvareva, 27th October, 1888.
[2] *See* Letter to Suvorin, 18th October, 1889.

Hence, the majority of 'virtuous' figures or bearers of positive Che-khovian ideas in his works are flawed; being flawed, they are more real; being more real, they influence us.

Khrushchov in *The Wood Demon* illustrates the point. He retains the independence of mind and spirit which Chekhov valued so highly: 'If only you knew what a stifling, oppressive atmosphere there is amongst you! It's a place where people sidle up to a man, take a slanting glance at him and search to discover in him a populist, a psychopath or a peddler of empty words—anything you like except a human being... And when they don't understand me and don't know what label to stick on me, they blame not themselves, but me, saying, "He's a strange fellow, very strange!"'—yet finds himself infected with intolerance. Possibly the only perfectly heroic figure in Chekhov's fiction appears in *The Flibbertigibbet* (*Poprygun'ya*) (1892). The 'Flibbertigibbet' of the title is Ol'ga Ivanovna Dymova, a doctor's wife, who fritters away her time in a circle of vain and para-sitic artistic dilettantes, and eventually forms a liaison with one of them. Meanwhile her husband, a man dedicated to the cause and practice of medicine, scrapes together the money which she will squander on her idle friends. When Dymov learns of his wife's adultery, his reaction is one of embarrassment rather than anger. Shortly afterwards he catches diphtheria from a child he is treating, and dies. Ol'ga is left ruefully to contemplate her mistake.

Dymov is unflawed: but, characteristically, this honour is allowed him by Chekhov only because in the story he rarely appears, he is not psychologically revealed, and his heroic qualities are fully disclosed only after his death. Thus Chekhov avoids both the technical diffi-culties and the aesthetic dangers of presenting his own notion of flawless virtue in terms of real human psychology.

This dilution of the expression of his own positive ideas is a per-manent feature of Chekhov's work, though the methods employed to achieve it vary. Khrushchov exemplifies one, Dymov another. In other cases Chekhov deliberately dissociates a character from the apparently 'positive' ideas to which he or she gives voice, by indicating either that the character's behaviour is in some way inconsistent with his professed beliefs, or that the very profession of these 'beliefs' is no more than vacuous philosophizing.

Mention of Chekhov's 'expression of his own positive ideas', however, must bring us back to the article on Przheval'sky, and to its illustration of the author's deep-rooted suspicion of ideals in verbal form, of ideologies, systems, programmes—or, in the jargon of the day—*tendencies*. The contrast stated between, on the one hand, 'people engaged in arguments about optimism and pessimism, writing out of boredom mediocre tales, unnecessary schemes and cheap dissertations' and, on the other hand, 'men of heroic deeds' pinpoints the most delicate and perplexing problem which faced Chekhov as a writer.

THE QUESTION OF 'TENDENCY'

Chekhov lived in an age of 'tendencies'. The impenetrable conservatism of real life, organized in accordance with immutable political and religious dogmas which were established by law and protected, if necessary, by force, now denied the intellectual classes even the hope, to say nothing of the opportunity, of testing new social or political theory in practice. The great Russian intellectual movements of the middle decades of the nineteenth century had flourished only because they fed upon the optimistic belief that change was possible. Slavophilism, Westernism, Nihilism and Populism retained their vitality as systems of ideas only as long as their respective adherents saw them as being directly related to Russia's future. In the eighties and nineties practically all such hopes foundered. Even the 'emancipation' of the serfs had turned out to be a pathetic parody. The mid-century atmosphere of intellectual conflict and search had produced, at its climax, the great novels of Turgenev, Tolstoy and Dostoevsky. Chekhov rose to eminence in darker days: the great wave of intellectual energy, directed towards the spiritual and political regeneration of Russia, had stilled under the counter-pressure of reaction, oppression and censorship. The lull did indeed precede a storm, but it was a storm which Chekhov was not to see.

Meanwhile, Tolstoy, in all he wrote after *Anna Karenina*, and Dostoevsky, in his *Diary of a Writer*, had both lapsed into blatant moralizing. Intellectual activity turned in upon itself. While some locked themselves off from reality in the religious, mystic and ultra-aesthetic philosophies which now bred in profusion, others converted socio-political thought, from a means by which life itself might be changed, into an end in itself, a product of frustration, an empty

314

game divorced from life, in which the intellectual world, dividing itself into factions according to 'tendency' and 'conviction', did verbal battle in the salons and on the pages of the journals.

The utilitarian tradition in literary criticism initiated by Belinsky had reached its apogee in the writings of Dobrolyubov, Chernyshevsky, D. I. Pisarev and others, who, often with a carefree unconcern for the actual intentions of the authors concerned, had employed criticism simply as a platform for their own radical socio-political ideas. This tradition too lived on into Chekhov's age in a debased form; the critical treatment of a writer of fiction now consisted predominantly in the mere elucidation and definition of his ideological tendencies, as revealed in his literature. Even major critics such as Mikhaylovsky and Skabichevsky, therefore, were more than a little put out when they were unable to discover in the works of the new 'mature' Chekhov any specific 'tendency'.

Chekhov's responses to their strictures upon him came mainly in letters of the period, often concerning his own stories. *Lights* (*Ogni*) (1888) is devoted to a discussion between a railway engineer, Anan'ev, and his student-assistant, Von Sternberg, about mortality and pessimism. Anan'ev relates how his whole attitude to life was changed by an encounter he had with a married woman, Kisochka, whom he had known previously in his youth. After seducing her, he took the first train out of town to avoid meeting her again, but, stung by conscience, turned back and begged her forgiveness. Only a realization at the deepest level that life is more than a meaningless joke, he suggests, could have motivated this action: for if life is meaningless, then such concepts as honour, conscience and morality also have no meaning. Von Sternberg is unimpressed. Chekhov throughout the story remains totally detached from his two characters and their respective viewpoints. The narrator of the story, a doctor, who has listened to the argument, reaches the conclusion 'You can't make head or tail of anything in this world!'

When the story was inevitably fallen upon for its lack of 'tendency', Chekhov write to Suvorin (30th May, 1888):

'What you write about *Lights* is perfectly just ... You write that neither the conversation about pessimism nor the tale of Kisochka move forward, or go any way towards solving, the problem of pessimism. It seems to me that it is the business of other people than writers of literature to try to solve such questions as God, pessimism etc. The writer's business is simply to show who has spoken about God and pessimism, how, and in what circumstances. The artist should not be the judge of his characters and what they say, but only an important witness. I once heard a desultory conversation between two Russians about pessimism, in which nothing was solved, and it is my responsibility to report this conversation exactly as I heard it: any evaluation must be done by the jury—that is, my readers. It is my business simply to be talented, that is, to know how to distinguish the important evidence from the trivial, to illuminate the characters and to speak their language. Shcheglov-Leont'ev blames me for finishing my tale with the phrase "You can't make head or tail of anything in this world!" In his opinion, an artist-psychologist should be able to do precisely that. But I disagree. The time has come for people who write, and particularly for artistic writers, to admit that in this world one cannot indeed make head or tail of anything, as Socrates admitted in his time, and as Voltaire also admitted. The crowd thinks it knows and understands everything: and the more stupid it is, the broader it considers its horizons to be. If an artist, whom the crowd believes, takes it upon himself to declare that he understands nothing of what he sees, then that alone constitutes a considerable perception in the field of thought and a major step forward.'

The Name-day Party (1888) produced similar responses from the critics and, in turn, from Chekhov. The central figure of the story is Ol'ga Mikhaylovna, the pregnant wife of a *zemstvo* president, Petr Dmitrich. The mental and physical tensions of pregnancy bring her to see herself, her husband, and their life together in a much clearer light than she ever has before. During a name-day party in her honour, she is made sharply aware of her husband's faults—the arrogant snobbishness under which he conceals an essentially good nature, the display of rabid conservatism, which has alienated most of his friends and involved him in an unpleasant lawsuit with the local 'liberal' judge, and the wilful exploitation of his natural attractiveness to women. Tired by the party and infuriated by her husband, Ol'ga Mikhaylovna finally provokes a row with him, which results in her suffering a miscarriage. Her husband is suddenly appalled by his responsibility for the tragedy: Ol'ga, totally enervated, can feel only a dull indifference.

Chekhov wrote to his good friend, the poet and translator A. N. Pleshcheev (9 October 1888): 'It's true, the suspicious thing in my story is the attempt to balance out the pluses and minuses. But I'm balancing not conservatism against liberalism, which are not the main thing for me, but the falseness of the heroes against their truthfulness. Petr Dmitrich lies and acts the buffoon in court, he is dreary and hopeless, but I cannot hide the fact that by nature he is a kind and gentle man. Ol'ga Mikhaylovna lies at every step, but there is no need to conceal that this lying is painful to her.'

It is letters like these that confirm what the sensitive reader of Chekhov has always been aware of. His assertions of neutrality, his claim that the writer should be only 'an important witness', remaining uninvolved in the ideas of his work, are no more than a red herring. When Chekhov admits the absence of, and denies the need for, 'tendencies' in his work, he is clearly using the word in no more than its hackneyed conventional sense: what he feared above all was being allotted a place in any of the contemporary ideological camps.

A Dreary Story (1889) describes a professor of medicine who, in spite of his fame, popularity and achievements as scientist and teacher, finds that life has lost its taste. He has become irritable, has lost enthusiasm for his work, and can find no comfort in his family. Worst of all, he finds himself incapable of helping his beloved young ward Katya, who, after some failures in life, has herself fallen victim to melancholy and pleaded to the professor for advice. He finally attributes his misery to the fact that he lacks 'what our philosopher-friends call a general idea . . . which would bind everything into a single whole'. Chekhov, writing to Suvorin (17th October, 1889), denied, and rightly too, that the professor's problem was his also. For everything which Chekhov wrote is permeated by a sense of good and bad, right and wrong; and in the year preceding this letter to Suvorin, he had had no hesitation, in two letters to Pleshcheev, in defining the ideas against which he measured his characters and their actions: 'I am afraid of those who look between the lines for tendencies and wish to see me as an avowed liberal or conservative. I am not a liberal, not a conservative, not a gradualist, not a monk, not an indifferentist. I would like to be a free artist—and that's all . . . I consider trade-marks and labels as irrational conventions. My holy of holies is the human body, health, intelligence, talent, inspiration, love and the most absolute freedom, freedom from violence and falsehood . . .' (4th October, 1888.)

Then, writing of a novel which he attempted, but never finished: 'My aim is to kill two birds with one stone: to draw life as it is, *and at the same time to indicate to what extent this life deviates from the norm.*[1] This norm is as much an unknown quantity to me, as it is to everyone else. We all know what a dishonourable deed is, but what is honour—that we do not know. I shall keep within that framework which is closest to my heart, and which has been tested by stronger and wiser men than me. It is—the absolute freedom of man, freedom from violence, from prejudice, from ignorance, from the devil, from the passions etc.' (9th April, 1889.)

On the aesthetic question of the extent to which an author should be involved with the ideas in his work, Chekhov, in a letter to Suvorin, was equally explicit: 'Remember that the writers whom we call eternal or simply good, and who intoxicate us, have one very important thing in common: they are going somewhere and calling you there too, and you sense not with your mind, but with your whole being, that they have some aim, just like the ghost of Hamlet's father, who did not come and trouble the imagination for nothing . . . The best of them are realists and paint life as it is, but because every line is saturated with the consciousness of an aim, you get a feeling not only of life as it is, but of life as it should be, and that is what captivates you.' (25th November, 1892.)

With characteristic modesty Chekhov goes on to deny that he will ever attain such immortality. Yet the lines quoted do not only sum up Chekhov's achievement as a writer; they do it very specifically. The key phrase is 'calling you there'; for it was precisely by calling his readers, rather than driving them, by 'saturating every line with the consciousness of an aim', instead of baldly and dogmatically stating his intentions, that Chekhov distinguished his writing from the overtly tendentious literature which he abhorred. The development of his mature manner finally released him from the problem which plagued him in the late 1880s—the reconciliation of his instinctive distaste for didactic literature with an equally deep-felt need to express through his literature his own view of the human condition.

[1] My italics.—MHS.

318

The final acceptance of this artistic credo of subdued and controlled subjectivity largely explains that measure of disenchantment discernible in Chekhov's later attitudes to his great contemporary Tolstoy. For ultimately it was not so much Tolstoy's message to the world as the dogmatic manner of its delivery which Chekhov repudiated.

In 1894 Chekhov admitted: 'Tolstoyan philosophy affected me strongly and took possession of me for six or seven years: and what influenced me were not his general propositions, which I knew all about earlier, but the manner in which Tolstoy expressed himself, his reasonableness and, I suppose, a sort of hypnotism.'[1]

Soon, however, he came to see this 'hypnotism' as a potentially insidious and unartistic instrument of persuasion. In spite of his declared admiration for Tolstoy's great novels, he criticized their more dogmatic features, e.g. the treatment of Napoleon in *War and Peace*;[2] and he had little patience for many of the later Tolstoyan tracts and treatises on sex, morality and art. *What is Art?* Chekhov referred to as the typical bad-tempered moralizing of a grumpy old man.[3]

His intellectual reactions to the actual doctrines of Tolstoyism were complex. The letter to Suvorin quoted above gives a general outline: a powerful surge of early enthusiasm, then scepticism and even hostility. The Tolstoyan influence is unmistakable in many of the stories of the eighties. There are those already mentioned, which convey the Tolstoyan vision of childish innocence; *In the Courtroom* (*V sude*) (1886) exposes the evil of established systems of law; while such pieces as *Fine People* (*Khoroshie lyudi*) (1886), *Love* (*Lyubov'*) (1886), *The Cossack* (*Kazak*) (1887) and *The Beggar* (*Nishchiy*) (1887), proclaiming the virtues of charity, simplicity, humility and love, have Tolstoy's mark stamped heavily upon them. The peak is reached in a series of stories of 1888–9: *The Name-day Party* (1888), *A Nervous Breakdown* (1888), *The Shoemaker and the Devil* (*Sapozhnik i nechistaya sila*) (1888), *The Bet* (*Pari*) (1888) and *The Princess* (*Knyaginya*) (1889).

[1] Letter to Suvorin (27th March, 1894).
[2] Letter to Suvorin (25th October, 1891).
[3] Letters to A. I. Ertel' (17th April, 1897) and Suvorin (4th January, 1898).

The Name-day Party, as we have seen, implicitly pleads that man strip off the sham of conventional behaviour and follow the promptings of his better nature. *A Nervous Breakdown* describes the shattering psychological effects upon a sensitive young law-student, Vasil'ev, of a visit to a number of Moscow brothels. The trauma he undergoes effects in Vasil'ev a typically Tolstoyan 'spiritual awakening': perceiving the falsity of social values and the conspiracy of evil inherent in art and science, he is made suddenly conscious of the primacy of love for one's fellow men over all other human instincts, and realizes that only by observing the dictates of conscience and by active self-devotion to the cause of goodness can the individual hope to change the world. The remaining three stories all expose the pernicious nature of traditional values and the masks which hide the 'real' man—wealth, rank, superficial piety etc.

Nonetheless, Chekhov had never adopted a wholly uncritical approach to Tolstoy's teaching. As early as 1885 he had poked fun at the doctrine of non-resistance to evil in his article, *A Household Remedy* (*Domashnee sredstvo*), which described how to be nice to bed-bugs. By the early nineties he had perceived not only the absurdity, but in some cases the sinister implications of certain Tolstoyan precepts: 'Peasant blood runs in my veins, and you won't surprise me with peasant virtues . . . Reason and justice tell me that in electricity and steam there is more love of man than in chastity and abstinence from meat . . . War is evil and courts of law are evil, but it doesn't follow from that, that I should go about in bast shoes and sleep on the stove with the workman and his wife.'[1]

His most eloquent attacks upon Tolstoyan doctrines come in some of the finest stories of the mature period. Non-resistance to evil is ridiculed in *Ward No. 6* (*Palata No. 6*) (1892), while in two impressive studies of contemporary peasant life—*The Peasants* (*Muzhiki*) (1897) and *In the Ravine* (*V ovrage*) (1900)—Chekhov was later to reveal as patent self-deceit Tolstoy's mystic notion of the peasant as the vessel of god-like spiritual purity and moral instinct. The same two doctrines, together with Tolstoy's proposition of 'simplification' as the means by which members of a corrupt upper class might find godliness and their own true selves, are explored and implicitly rejected in *My Life* (*Moya zhizn'*) (1896).

[1] Letter to Suvorin (27th March, 1894).

Ward No. 6 is a filthy barrack, part of a squalid provincial hospital. It houses five madmen, and is guarded by the brutal Nikita, whose greatest pleasure is beating the 'patients'. Doctor Ragin, the newly arrived hospital superintendent, is fully aware of the system of squalor, corruption and cruelty he has inherited from his predecessor, but being a firm believer in the philosophy of indifference, does nothing to change it. He takes pleasure, however, in discussing such questions as non-resistance to evil with one of the lunatics, Gromov. His cultivation of this madman and his assertion that Gromov is the only truly intelligent man in town lead to rumours, a plot against him, and eventually to his being himself imprisoned in Ward No. 6. Here, a brutal beating at the hands of Nikita quickly teaches him the distinction between theory and practice. Shortly afterwards, he dies of an apoplectic fit.

In *The Peasants* Chekhov tells of Nikolay Chikil'deev, a lackey in a Moscow hotel, who returns to his native village to die, and of what befalls him and his family when they arrive. The outline story, however, is hardly more than an excuse for presenting a schematized microcosmic portrait of the life of the rural peasantry of his day. Chapter by chapter, paragraph by paragraph, Chekhov lists his data on peasant life and behaviour. Poverty, squalid housing, hunger, debt, back-breaking labour and the added enslavement of encroaching capitalism constitute the background, and the attitudes of the peasantry towards the *zemstvo*, religion, death, drink, medicine etc. are plotted one by one. Though the story ends with a somewhat rhetorical apologia for the immorality and brutality of the peasants, Chekhov makes it clear that he has as few mystic Tolstoyan illusions about the 'simple folk' as did Gor'ky.

In the Ravine, although very much a story in its own right, also has documentary qualities, illustrating the pernicious and disruptive effect of industrialization upon the rural community, and the growth of the new *kulak* class. It centres upon a typical *kulak* family, the Tsybukins. The father is a shopkeeper who deals in 'anything that comes to hand', and moneylender. His one son is deaf and stupid, the other a policeman turned forger. His daughter-in-law Aksin'ya is a vicious grasping harridan, who builds a brick factory and exploits peasant labour, and whose avarice leads her in a fit of temper to murder a child. If in *The Peasants* Chekhov's basic attitude to the peasants

21   321   .

is one of understanding and sympathy, the Tsybukin family are depicted as degenerate and vile.

My Life deals with the search for Tolstoyan simplicity of Misail, son of a thoroughly conventional and untalented architect. Misail's rejection of conventional social values and his desire for purity through simplification survive social ostracism, hardship and hunger; but he is shaken in his endeavours by the ignorance, inertia and perverse resistance to self-improvement of the peasantry on a farm which he attempts to run on Tolstoyan lines. Tolstoy's ideal 'simple man' has little in common with the farm workers, whose indolence and embezzlement of his property bring Misail to ruin. Needless to say, Misail is also a believer in non-resistance; yet, driven to desperation one night by the noise of a brawl, he separates the combatants by twice knocking one of them to the ground. He is left at the end disillusioned but unrepentant.

For all Chekhov's scepticism of Tolstoyism, however, his finest writing was modelled in two immensely significant respects on that of Tolstoy. Firstly, he inherited from Tolstoy the conviction that the essence of human affairs, and therefore of literature also, lay in the inner world of man, that the externals of life could be understood only by a penetration of the psychological processes which underlay them. Although Chekhov was to develop in the short story and drama very different techniques from Tolstoy's for the depiction of this inner world, the debt is a clear one. Concomitantly, Chekhov believed, as did Tolstoy, that the ultimate shape of human life, its good or its evil, were the products not of political and social systems, not of laws, not of conventional codes of morality, but of the state of consciousness of every individual. Both held the very un-Marxian view that consciousness determines being: both held that life would be reformed only when man rediscovered the instinctive sense of why he lives, and how he should live, which is his birthright. Here Chekhov differed essentially from Tolstoy only in his denial of the divine origins of this sense.

'If he [Tolstoy] were to die, then in my life there would appear a huge void. Firstly, I have loved no man as I have loved him; I am an unbeliever, but of all faiths it is his which I consider the closest to my heart, and the most suited to my nature.'[1]

[1] Letter to M. O. Men'shikov (28th January, 1900).

CHEKHOV

THE CENTRAL THEME

It is to a study of the state of man's consciousness that the whole of Chekhov's mature work, including the drama, is devoted; indeed, the majority of the Chekhonte stories may, in retrospect, be seen as falling within the same pattern. His subject is contemporary Russia, his meaning is universal.

This universality is indicated by a trilogy of stories written in 1898, representing a sort of programmatic key, a symbolic hub around which revolves the remainder of his work. They are *The Man in a Case* (*Chelovek v futlyare*), *Gooseberries* (*Kryzhovnik*) and *About Love* (*O lyubvi*); the device of three narrator-friends, each of whom tells one story, is used to link them.

As if to stress its broader significance, the first story and its anti-hero, Belikov, are presented less in terms of realism than of symbolic caricature. Belikov—clearly an extension of Corporal Prishibeev—is a teacher of ancient Greek, who even in the warmest weather goes out with an umbrella, in galoshes and a warm overcoat, his collar turned up, his eyes hidden by dark glasses and his ears stuffed with cotton-wool. Besides his own person, he keeps his umbrella, watch and penknife too in neat cases. These external cases, however, are no more than the outer manifestations of Belikov's mind and consciousness. Like Prishibeev, Belikov loves nothing in life so much as to prohibit things, particularly everything which smacks of pleasure or culture. He has a motto: 'Hm, yes, all very fine, but I'm afraid it may lead to trouble!'. He finally, to everyone's relief, achieves perfect self-fulfilment in those most permanent of outer and inner cases —a coffin and death.

The symbolic purport of the story does not escape the narrator and his listeners. One of them adds: 'And the fact that we live in the stifling, crowded atmosphere of the town, write unnecessary papers, play *vint*—isn't that also a "case"? Or that we spend our whole lives amidst loafers, petty litigants, stupid idle women, that we talk and listen to all manner of trivial rubbish—isn't that also a "case"?'

In the other two stories Chekhov presents, this time in perfectly realistic vein, two other classic examples of human 'cases', amplifying and further defining the symbolic value of the figure of Belikov.

Gooseberries tells of Nikolay Chimsha-Gimalaysky, a poor clerk,

323

who from his earliest days has devoted himself, body and soul, to a single aim—the purchase of a small country estate, where he may grow and enjoy his own gooseberries. By marrying a rich and ugly widow, starving her to death and inheriting her fortune, he realizes his dream. His brother, the narrator, pays him a visit, to find that the humble clerk has transformed himself into a pompous ass, braying the slogans of conservatism. When the first gooseberries are picked, Nikolay is reduced to tears of emotion: all night the narrator hears him walking his bedroom floor, eating gooseberries one by one from a plate. They are, needless to say, sour.

It is the narrator who points the morals: 'It's often said that a man needs only seven feet of ground: but really it's a corpse, not a man, that needs those seven feet . . . A man needs not seven feet of ground, not an estate, but the whole world, the whole of nature, so that in those wide open spaces he may reveal all the qualities and distinctive features of his free spirit. . .

'That night it became clear to me, how satisfied and content I was too . . . Happiness is a blessing, I used to say, it's as necessary as the air we breathe, but we must wait for it. Yes, that was what I used to say, but now I ask why should we wait? . . . You may refer to the natural order of things, to the rationality of the real world, but is there order or rationality in the fact that I, a living thinking man, stand by a ditch and wait for it to fill itself in, when perhaps I could jump over it or build a bridge across?'

The 'cases' in *Gooseberries* are materialism, complacency and narrow self-indulgence. Those encapsulating the free spirit of Alekhin, the narrator and central figure of *About Love*, are deference to an empty conventional morality, and spiritual cowardice. Alekhin relates how for years he refrained from declaring his love for Anna Luganovich, the wife of a friend, though he knew she loved him too. His motives for this self-restraint were a sense of delicacy, a reluctance to hurt Luganovich, whom he respected, or to break up his home; finally, he lacked the courage to face the consequences of such a declaration. Thus for years he poisoned his own life and Anna's. He declares himself at last, when Luganovich and his family are leaving to live in a distant province, and have already boarded the train. It is, of course, too late; and Alekhin is left to rue his cowardice: 'With a burning pain in my heart I realized how unnecessary, trivial and deceptive all those things had been, which had prevented our love. I realized that when a man is in love, then in his reasoning about that love, he must take as his starting point something higher, something more important than happiness or unhappiness, or sin or virtue in their conventional sense, or else he should not reason about it at all.'

The 'man in a case' can be taken as the central and most potent symbol in Chekhov's literature: a 'case' can be interpreted as any feature, or combination of features, of personality or outlook which confines man's consciousness, restricts his freedom of spirit, initiative and imagination, and hinders the achievement of his 'higher', 'more important' aim—the realization of his full potentialities as a human being.

Chekhov's concept of the 'man in a case' coincides to a considerable measure with Gogol''s dominant symbol—the 'dead soul'. For Gogol' also, though with mystic-religious overtones which Chekhov did not share, was concerned primarily with creatures so entirely encased in their own triviality that they have lost all semblance of humanity. Both writers see the illness as pernicious, infectious and endemic in the Russia of their day: but neither treats it in terms of social morality. Gogol''s miser, Plyushkin, is not presented as an immoral or amoral man; his miserliness has no active force left in it, even for evil. It has, rather, become the whole soul and spirit of Plyushkin, it has replaced the man; he does not consciously wield his miserliness to exploit life, but sees life only in terms of miserliness. The result is a superb irony: Plyushkin's miserliness makes him not richer, but poorer. His wealth rots in the barns, while he hoards bits of paper and feathers. 'Dead souls' and 'men in cases' are equally automata.

Both Chekhov and Gogol' discovered the inevitable elements of tragi-comedy, of 'laughter through tears', in the conflicts of interest, encounters and collisions of such types, and in their resultant antics. Like many of Chekhov's stories and plays, Gogol''s *The Inspector General* is built upon just such a series of encounters between differing automata, all totally incapable of adjusting their response either to each other or to facts which stare them in the face. In each of them the conventional pattern of behaviour has ossified and replaced the living personality. There is no basic qualitative distinction between the comic misunderstandings which occur in Khlestakov's dealings with the town officials, and the melancholy lack of understanding which characterizes the relationships of individuals in so much of Chekhov's work; there is simply a difference of emphasis. Nor need one ask further why the word *'poshlost'* [vulgarity, mediocrity] is so bandied about in critical commentaries on both writers. For is not *poshlost'* in all its forms the manifestation in real life of the Gogolian 'dead soul' or the Chekhovian 'case'?

The stories written during the last fifteen years of Chekhov's life constitute a catalogue of 'cases'.

There is religion: in *Three Years* (*Tri goda*) (1895) Chekhov re-creates in the experience of his hero Laptev his own suffering as a child, when he was forced to endure the endless, dreary and stultifying rituals of the Orthodox Church. Largely as a result of the patriarchal and fanatically religious atmosphere in which he has been brought up, Laptev remains emotionally stunted: the story relates the tragic fate of the man and of his marriage. In *The Murder* (*Ubiystvo*) (1895) rival religious fanaticisms lead a man to fratricide. Rotting in a Siberian penal colony, the murderer Yakov finally recognizes that he has been destroyed by his own intolerance and pride.

Materialism, greed, vanity, ambition, self-indulgence—these are the most commonplace forces paralysing the human spirit: Chekhov explores and analyses them in a series of further stories. *A Woman's Kingdom* (*Bab'e tsarstvo*) (1894), *In the Ravine*, *A Doctor's Visit* (*Sluchay iz praktiki*) (1898), and *Ionych* (1898) amply illustrate the soulless and soul-destroying nature of commerce and capitalism, and the power of wealth in eroding human idealism. *The Flibberti-gibbet*, *Ariadna* (1895) and *Anna on the Neck* (*Anna na shee*) (1895) expose the destructive qualities of ambition, sensuality and blind self-indulgence.

Perhaps the most typical symptom of all 'cases' is a complacent indifference to men and to the world. The narrator of *Gooseberries*, commenting upon his brother's delight at the taste of the first sour fruit, adds: 'I saw before me a happy man, whose cherished dream had so visibly come true, who had achieved his aim in life, had got what he wanted, who was satisfied with his lot and with himself. My thoughts regarding human happiness had for some reason always been tinged with sadness: but now, at the sight of this happy man, I found myself gripped by an oppressive feeling, close to despair.'

Chekhov's stories as a whole leave us in no doubt that this is spoken with his own voice. A Chekhovian formula suggests itself: positive consciousness is inversely proportionate to contentment. Abhorring the self-satisfied, Chekhov admires and defends the restless, the searchers, those who may not know what is right, but know at least that things as they are, are wrong. In *In Exile* (1892) he contrasts two exiled convicts who man a Siberian river ferry. Semen, fully reconciled to his wretched existence, comforts himself with the motto 'You'll get used to it' and finds a perverse satisfaction in his own misery. His companion, a Tatar, is restless and homesick. An occasional passenger on their ferry is an exiled nobleman, whose wife joined him in Siberia, but then abandoned him to return to European Russia with a lover. The daughter of the marriage, who remained with her father, is now dying of tuberculosis; her father frenziedly seeks out and brings back doctors from distant towns in the vain hope that she may be cured. Semen has only contempt for the nobleman's refusal to accept his fate. The Tatar turns in fury upon Semen: 'He is good . . . good, but you—are bad! You are bad! The *barin* is a good fellow, a fine fellow, but you are a beast, you are evil. The *barin* is alive, but you are dead meat. God created man that he should live, that there should be joy and yearning and grief; but you want nothing, and that means you are not a living man, but stone, clay! A stone needs nothing and you need nothing . . . You are a stone, and God does not love you, but he loves the *barin*.'

The central figure of *Big Volodya and Little Volodya* (*Volodya bol'shoy i Volodya malen'kiy*) (1893) is one Sof'ya L'vovna, who has married an aging general, partly for his money and partly to spite the young though philistine 'intellectual' whom she loves. After calling at a nearby convent to visit Ol'ga, formerly a ward of her family and now a nun, Sof'ya L'vovna is struck by the contrast between her own life, with its round of restaurants, troika rides and flirtations, and the clarity of purpose and acute awareness of herself which characterize Ol'ga. The mood, however, soon passes.

In *A Doctor's Visit* a Doctor Korolev is called to visit Liza Lyali-kova, daughter of the owners of a textile factory. He finds Liza depressed and nervous, and attributes this not to any physical disorder, but to her general despondency at being the heiress to the factory. Korolev is not surprised: the factory, the life of the workers and the owners, and the capitalist system as a whole depress him too—not because he sees in them social and economic injustices, but because the whole thing seems a drab and futile exercise, bringing advantage to no one, neither owner, worker, nor eventual buyer of the cheap cotton cloth. The only person who appears to profit from the Lyalikov enterprise is Liza's smug governess, who can indulge her taste for sturgeon and madeira. To Liza Korolev announces: 'You, as an owner of the factory and a rich heiress, are dissatisfied, you don't believe in your right to be such, and now you can't sleep. Well, that, of course, is better than if you were content, slept soundly and believed that all was well. Your insomnia is to be respected . . .'

THE 'CASE' OF PESSIMISM

A popular intellectual affectation of the eighties and nineties was a cult of pessimism, which owed its success to the ease with which it rationalized and thus alleviated the widespread feelings of intellectual frustration and ineffectuality experienced by thinking minds in a stagnant and oppressive society. From the fact of individual mortality and the transitoriness of human life the pessimists deduced a simple philosophy of despair, denying any meaning in human life and achievement. For Chekhov there could be no more noxious and outrageous intellectual 'case' than this: his response to the cult in his literature is patently hostile, and provides, incidentally, an adequate rebuttal to those who curiously insist on naming him one of its members.[1]

In his first treatment of the problem—the discussion in *Lights* (1888) —Chekhov, as mentioned above, remains detached. It is interesting, however, to note the most powerful argument used by Anan'ev against his pessimistic-minded antagonist:

'Suppose you sit down to read Darwin or Shakespeare or somebody. You've hardly read a page when the poison begins to work: your own long life, and Shakespeare, and Darwin seem a nonsense, an absurdity, because you know that you will die and that Shakespeare and Darwin also died, that their thoughts didn't save either them, or the earth,

[1] Notably Shestov.

or yourself, and that if life is thus meaningless, then all knowledge, poetry and lofty thoughts are an unnecessary pastime, the idle toy of grown-up children. And you stop reading on the second page. Now then, let's suppose people come to you, as an intelligent person, and ask your opinion about war, for instance: is war desirable or undesirable, moral or immoral? Your answer to this terrible question is merely to shrug your shoulders and utter nothing more than some platitude, because to you, with your way of thinking, it's a matter of complete indifference whether hundreds of thousands of people die a violent or a natural death; in either case the result is the same— dust and oblivion. You and I are building a railway. Why, I might ask, should we rack our brains, invent, use our imagination, be decent to our workers, steal or not steal, if we know that in two thousand years our railway will have turned to dust? And so on and so forth ... You must agree that with your wretched manner of thinking it is impossible to envisage any progress, science, art, or even thought itself.'

In a second treatment of the theme (*The Wife* (*Zhena*) (1892)) Chekhov abandons his neutral posture; there is no doubting where the author's sympathies lie. The narrator of *The Wife* is Asorin, another railway engineer, but, unlike Anan'ev, a pessimist totally engrossed in his own ineffectuality and unhappiness. On a visit to a friend, Asorin is shown a fine mahogany cupboard, the work of a peasant craftsman, Butyga. Asorin, admiring the solid workmanship of the piece, cannot but compare his own attitude to his work with Butyga's.

'I thought: what a strange distinction between Butyga and myself! Butyga, who built things soundly, to last, and saw that as the main quality of his work, attached special significance to human longevity, had no thoughts of death and probably didn't much believe in the possibility of death. But I, building my bridges of steel and stone to stand for thousands of years, could never help thinking "It won't last for ever ... It's all a waste of time." If in the future some intelligent art historian should ever come across Butyga's cupboard and my bridge, he will say "Here we have, in their own ways, two remarkable men: Butyga loved people and never allowed himself to think that they might die and turn to dust; and so, making his furniture, he saw man as immortal: but the engineer Asorin loved neither people nor life, and even in his happy moments of creativity did not shrink from

329

thoughts of death, destruction and finality; and so see how trivial, timid and pitiful are these lines of his design . . ."'

Chekhov applied the same criterion to writing literature as to making furniture; in his own works he pleads eloquently and force-fully that man should see beyond his own mortal span to the infinite continuity of human existence. The beautiful and the eternal can be created and enjoyed only by those who never doubt the beauty and permanence of life itself. Coming from a young man stricken with tuberculosis, the idea has a particular poignancy. Dr. Chekhov, in spite of his constantly cheerful protestations of good health, knew well enough the implications of his own symptoms. Was it this knowledge which inspired a third and exquisitely poetic treatment of the theme?

The story concerned is *The Lady with the Little Dog* (*Dama s sobachkoy*) (1899). Gurov, a petty philanderer on holiday in Yalta, seduces the pretty wife of a provincial bureaucrat, Anna Sergeevna, who is awaiting her husband's arrival by steamer. Though Gurov attaches no particular significance at the time to this, for him, trivial affair, it is destined to develop into a profound relationship of love, and, in doing so, to work a wondrous change in him. The first hint of the new meaning which will be brought to his life by his relationship with Anna is given when, after their first night together, Gurov and Anna drive to Oreanda and, sitting upon a cliff-top, watch the dawn rise over the sea. Gurov contemplates the scene:

'The leaves did not stir upon the trees, the cicadas called, and the dull, monotonous rumble of the sea, rising from beneath, spoke of the peace, of the eternal sleep which awaits us. The sea had rumbled down there below, before Yalta and Oreanda had even existed, it was rumbling now, and it would go on rumbling with the same dull, indifferent sound, when we too had disappeared. And in this per-manency, in this total indifference to the life and death of each of us, there lay, perhaps, the pledge of our eternal salvation, of the unbroken movement of life on earth, of the continuous process of perfection . . . it crossed Gurov's mind that actually, if one really thought about it, everything on this earth was beautiful, everything except that which we ourselves think and do, when we forget about the higher purposes of life and about our human dignity.'

Thus is Gurov—and Chekhov also—able to deduce from the awful contrast between nature's permanency and man's frailty not that confirmation of the meaninglessness of human life which the pessimist finds, but its very opposite. Nature in her unchanging beauty reminds man of the perpetuity of human kind; she reminds him that life, seen in this way, has meaning in the process of perfection, in progress. The life of the individual has meaning when, and only when, he sees his mortal span as one link in an unending chain. Man is mortal, mankind immortal.

THE INTELLIGENTSIA

For Chekhov all 'cases' were abhorrent. He deplored the hunger, poverty and disease which so circumscribed the life of the peasants as to deny them any chance of spiritual self-betterment; he deplored the avarice, narrow-mindedness, ambition and servility of merchants and officials. The intelligentsia aroused in him, however, a special dismay—special for two reasons. Firstly, in spite of occasional explosions of anger about the contemporary intelligentsia,[1] he believed they had a greater role to play than any other section of society in the achievement of progress and reform.[2] Secondly, this class, being for the most part materially secure and enjoying the gifts of intelligence and insight, had, in Chekhov's eyes, the least excuse for sharing the faults of other men.

Chekhov understood well the bases of the intellectual stagnancy of his age. Quite apart from the curbs on political and intellectual freedom imposed by an oppressive regime, the intellectual world had conspired to produce its own causes for the '*epokha bezvremen'ya*' ['the age of stagnation']. Massively influenced by its intellectual inheritance—the doctrines of Tolstoy and Dostoevsky—it had fallen victim to the extraordinary paradoxes inherent in both. For while the two great novelist-teachers had both propounded man as the potential vessel of true godliness, capable via the regeneration of his conscious- ness and soul of creating the Kingdom of Heaven on earth, each had in his own way simultaneously sown the seeds of inertia and reaction—

[1] E.g. letter to I. I. Orlov, 22nd February, 1899, in which he describes the intelligentsia as 'hypocritical, false, hysterical, ill-educated, idle . . .'
[2] Cf. *Notebooks* (*Zapisnye knizhki*, 1891–1904), p. 87, note 3: 'The strength and salvation of a people lies in its intelligentsia—or in that part of it which thinks honestly, has feelings and knows how to work.'

Tolstoy in the dogma of non-resistance to evil, and Dostoevsky in the justification of suffering. At the same time, the development of the natural sciences, particularly Darwinism and geology, had brought to the thinking mind an increased awareness of man's accidental and fragile nature, and had inclined it even further towards pessimism and resignation.

Dr. Ragin in *Ward No. 6* is a typically confused product of the age. Baffled by the contradiction between, on the one hand, man's genius and, on the other, human mortality and the impermanence even of the very earth, he has lapsed, body and mind, into total inertia. If all is doomed, then why indeed relieve suffering or resist evil? 'Given that prisons and lunatic asylums exist', he says, 'then someone has got to be put in them.'

Gromov, the lunatic, rejects this fatalism and points out that intellectuals like Ragin find it easy to accept suffering and evil, since they have never experienced either. When Ragin derides Gromov's faith in progress and a golden age on the grounds that, even were the golden age to come, neither of them would be there to see it, Gromov responds: 'In Dostoevsky or Voltaire someone says that if there were no God, man would invent one. Well, I believe deeply that if there is no immortality, then sooner or later the great human intellect will invent it.'

Gromov's dispute with Ragin clearly expresses Chekhov's impatience with all the pet theories and 'philosophies' of the contemporary intelligentsia, which, while allegedly directed towards an explanation of life and a solution of its problems, were in fact employed merely as a means of escaping all such intellectual responsibility.

Ragin reminds Gromov of the theory of Marcus Aurelius that pain is no more than a concept of pain: reject the concept, and the pain disappears. 'If you would only think about it more often,' he continues, 'you would understand how trivial are all those external things which worry you. One should strive to comprehend life, for comprehension is true bliss.' Gromov replies with a grimace, 'Comprehension . . . External, internal . . . I'm sorry, I don't understand . . . I only know that God made me of warm blood and nerves! And organic tissue, if it is viable, should react to any irritation. And I react!'

Chekhov delivered an even more explicit expression of faith on the subject of the intelligentsia, its problems and its responsibilities, in

The Black Monk (1894). Kovrin, a philosopher who is under severe mental stress, converses, like Dostoevsky's Ivan Karamazov, with his own hallucinatory *alter ego*. This projection of Kovrin's megalomania takes the form of a black monk, who praises Kovrin for devoting his life to the 'rational and the beautiful', to 'eternal truth'. Kovrin replies:

'You said: eternal truth . . . But is eternal truth attainable or necessary to man, if there is no eternal life?

—There is eternal life,—said the monk.

—Do you believe in man's immortality?

—Yes, of course. A great and shining future awaits you and all men. And the more such men as you exist, the sooner will this future be realised. Without you—men who serve the highest principle, who live consciously and freely—mankind would have no meaning: developing naturally, it would have to wait a long time for the culmination of its earthly history. But you will introduce it many thousands of years earlier into the kingdom of eternal truth, and this is your great service to man.'

Kovrin's devotion to 'the rational and the beautiful' obviously has Chekhov's sympathy: and it is interesting that, like Gogol',[1] Chekhov associates the 'conscious' character with nervous stress or insanity—cf. Liza Lyalikova in *A Doctor's Visit* and Gromov in *Ward No. 6*. In an insanely petty world the penalty for, or mark of, idealism is mental instability. Kovrin at one point ruminates 'It would seem that in all walks of life men of ideas are nervous types and stand out for their heightened sensitivity to things. Probably, that's the way it has to be.' And later the monk tells him 'My friend, only commonplace people, members of the herd, are healthy and sane.'

One final intellectual toy of the upper classes, dealt with in Chekhov's work, was the enthusiasm for *malye dela*—charitable works undertaken for the benefit of the peasantry and the urban poor. Chekhov was himself an unashamed doer of *malye dela*, particularly in the fields of medicine and education, but he had little faith in them as a really constructive answer to the problems of poverty and hardship. In *The Wife* (*Zhena*) (1892) he pointed out the absurdity of a rich class handing out charity to the poor, while still stuffing themselves with

[1] E.g. in *Nevskiy Prospekt* and *Diary of a Madman*.

333

huge meals, exploiting the labour of the peasantry, philosophizing and salving their consciences with trivial good deeds. He saw the upper classes' *malye dela* as more than anything else an escape from the stifling boredom of their lives, and as yet another intellectual 'case'. This attitude is implied in the dispute between the artist-narrator and a typical do-gooder in *The House with a Mezzanine* (*Dom s mezoninom*) (1896). Chekhov's own choice, at an earlier point in his life, of literature before medicine was perhaps his most eloquent expression of a profound belief: that an albeit unsure and indirect means of effecting some permanent improvement in the quality of human life must be preferred to a sure and direct means of effecting only temporary relief.

THE RETURN TO DRAMA

In the period 1889–1895, during which Chekhov produced nothing new for the stage, his ambition to master the drama did not wane. From 1890 onwards he worked intermittently at converting *The Wood Demon* into what was to become *Uncle Vanya*. Moreover, the whole development of his art in the short story during this period seemed to be leading him naturally and inevitably back to the stage. In the four great plays of the last period (*The Seagull* (*Chayka*) (1895–6), *Uncle Vanya*, first published 1897, *Three Sisters* (*Tri sestry*) (1900), and *The Cherry Orchard* (*Vishnevyy sad*) (1903)) the mature forms and ideas found a new and, in the view of some critics, a finer expression.

Chekhov's stories all centre upon the struggle of the human personality and soul against their environment and their own built-in self-destructive tendencies. It is a struggle for perfect awareness, for self-fulfilment as man, for liberation from the 'cases' which confine and paralyse.

In outline structure the majority fall into three broad categories: the investigatory portrait ('clinical study') of a static state, of the personality incurably encased (e.g. *Darling*, 1898), or flapping convulsively in the deadly grip of *poshlost'* (e.g. *The Teacher of Literature*, 1894); those which trace the decline of the free personality into *poshlost'* (e.g. *Ionych*, 1898); finally—the rarest—those which describe the opposite, upward movement (e.g. *The Lady with the Little Dog* and, significantly, Chekhov's last work *The Fiancée* (*Nevesta*) (1903).

Nearly all Chekhov's stories written prior to the long plays *Ivanov* and *The Wood Demon* were of the first category; and the two plays themselves are no more than complex 'clinical studies', revealing and contrasting static psychological types. They are both failures as 'Chekhovian' drama because the inner world of the protagonists is without movement. Chekhov successfully defines the qualities of Ivanov and L'vov, Khrushchov and Voynitsky; he contrasts and implicitly appraises them; but they do not *change*. To compensate for this deficiency and give the plays shape, Chekhov constructs an almost makeshift and often melodramatic plot of external events. The second and third categories of story, largely developed during the '90s, cried out for transference into drama; for both have the vital element of movement on the inner plane—for Chekhov, the *only* plane of real and significant events.

The Seagull is a play about art and the nature of the artistic personality. Through the medium of the four protagonists—Arkadina, Trigorin, Treplev and Nina—Chekhov re-examines the criteria by which 'artists' are conventionally judged—talent, genius, technique, success—and suggests a better criterion, based on his own concepts of the positive and negative personality.

Arkadina is a successful and, presumably, talented actress, yet is so enveloped in self-interest that she cannot even love her own son. The writer Trigorin also has fame, success and technique (some aspects of which are borrowed, as it were, from Chekhov's own armoury), but is sunk in self-doubt and remains unmoved by his responsibility for the suffering of others. Treplev too has some vestige of originality (his ideas of 'new forms' in the theatre again to some extent coincide with Chekhov's own), but through inner weakness is destined to mediocrity, despair and suicide. Nina alone, though without the benefit of 'talent', is able to survive hardship—particularly the consequences of her affair with Trigorin—to reject finally her self-identification with the tragic symbol of the seagull, and to achieve a perfect awareness of herself and of her own destiny. Arkadina and Trigorin are of the first category, Treplev of the second, and Nina of the third. In the famous 'seagull' speech in Act 4 she describes perfectly the initial downward curve followed by the triumphal ascent:

'I'm so exhausted! If only I could rest . . . yes, rest! I am the seagull . . . No, that's not right. I am an actress. Yes, that's it!

(*Hearing Arkadina and Trigorin laughing, she listens carefully, then runs to the door on the left and looks through the keyhole*) He is here too . . . (*Going back to Treplev*) Yes, that's it . . . Never mind . . . Yes . . . He didn't believe in the theatre, he kept laughing at me for my dreams, and gradually I too stopped believing and lost heart . . . And then there were the cares of loving him, jealousy, the constant fear for my baby . . . I became petty, trivial, my acting became meaningless . . . I didn't know what to do with my hands, or how to stand on the stage. I couldn't control my voice. You can't understand what it feels like to know that you are acting terribly. I am the seagull. No, that's not right . . . Do you remember how you shot the seagull? A man happened by, saw it, and out of sheer boredom destroyed it . . . The plot for a short story. That's not right . . . (*Rubs her forehead*) What was I saying? . . . Oh yes, about the stage. Well, now I'm not like that. Now I am a real actress. I act with pleasure, with delight, I feel wonderful, intoxicated on the stage. And now, while I'm living here, I walk about, all the time I walk about and think, think and feel how with every day that passes I am growing stronger in spirit . . . I know now, Kostya, I understand, that in our business—whether writing or acting—the main thing is not glory, not the glitter of fame, not those things of which I dreamed; it is knowing how to suffer and endure. Know how to bear your cross and have faith. I have faith, things are not painful to me now, and when I think of my vocation, then I have no fear of life.'

The path through personal tragedy and misfortune to the achievement of a new and clearer vision of oneself and of life if mapped again in *Uncle Vanya* and *Three Sisters*. In both the formula is restated: contentment is the perdition of the soul, unhappiness the key to its salvation.

In *Uncle Vanya*, Vanya himself and, even more so, Sonya survive the collapse of their respective hopes of love and the crisis induced by Serebryakov's declared intention to sell the estate. Like Nina, Sonya too perceives the need for endurance, and, more important, glimpses the meaning of immortality in Chekhovian terms: 'Uncle Vanya, we shall live. We shall live through the long, long chain of days, of evenings without end, we shall patiently bear the trials which fate sends us; we shall work for others, now and in old age, knowing no rest . . .'

Astrov too has at one time seen the light: 'When I pass the peasants' forests which I have saved from felling, and when I hear the rustle of young trees planted with my own two hands, I recognize that climate is to some small degree within my control and that if in a thousand years' time man is happy, then I shall bear some slight responsibility for that fact.' But he, alas, now has lapsed from Chekhovian grace. He admits that under the pressure of life's 'boredom, stupidity and dirt' he has become 'a different man'. His increasing intake of vodka is a certain sign of the encroachment of *poshlost'*, but, as is usual in Chekhov, it is his relationships with the opposite sex which provide the acid test. Though irresistably lured by the 'beautiful, fluffy polecat' Elena, he can neither appreciate nor respond to the genuine love of Sonya.

In *Three Sisters* Ol'ga, Masha and Irina, as we meet them in the first act, are all equally obsessed by their own mortality—their age, their lack of achievement, and the implacable march of time. They talk of nothing else. The return to Moscow, of which they dream, is an insubstantial myth: Moscow is childhood, a turning back of the clock, a second chance at life. The arrival of Vershinin, with his memories of them as children and his exclamations echoing their alarm at the swift passage of time, serves first to reinforce the illusion, then to expose it. It is Vershinin who states the truth they cannot yet apprehend: 'You'll be swallowed up by life, but all the same you'll not disappear; you'll have some effect; when you've gone there will appear, perhaps, six people such as you, then twelve, and so on until your kind are in the majority. In two or three hundred years life on earth will be more beautiful and more splendid than we can imagine. Man needs a life like that, and if he doesn't have it now, then he must feel that it is coming, wait for it, dream of it, get ready for it . . .'

The process of awakening is slow: Irina closes the second and third acts with repeated expressions of the illusory dream. Only in Act 4, as a result of tragedy, is the myth rejected, the illusion exposed. Irina and Masha, like Sonya in *Uncle Vanya*, see their hopes of love dashed. All three sisters, symbolically sharing the fate of their doomed class, are squeezed room by room from their house by Natasha, the embodiment of rapacious materialism. Their brother Andrey (a perfect specimen of the second category) is transformed from budding professor to hapless cuckold. Tuzenbakh, for all his dreams of useful work, remains the prisoner of his own pessimism, while Vershinin, though given to bouts of optimistic rhetoric and prognostications of a glorious future, is more defined by his inability to break the bond which ties him to his trivial and hysterical wife: 'Russian man' he admits, 'has an extraordinary capacity for lofty thoughts, but tell me, why is it that in life he never gets off the ground ?'

The three sisters alone triumph, through tragedy: it is upon them that the final curtain closes. Tempered by experience, liberated from illusion, they look now hopefully towards the future and see their own short lives as only part of a greater pattern, which they can accept, if not comprehend. What the sisters' future will be, we do not, and need not, know. The change in the sisters is the dramatic climax: its ultimate impact upon their lives is irrelevant to the play.

The superb balance or inverse relationship achieved in *Three Sisters* between external (apparent) and internal (real) action— between the misfortunes which befall the sisters and the positive shift in consciousness produced thereby—makes it the most excellent of his plays. Contemporary critics and audiences, however, were not equipped to appreciate such theatrical subtleties. Chekhov's despair at the resulting misrepresentations expressed itself first in threats to give up writing for the stage altogether,[1] then in repeated assertions of his intention to write a vaudeville or four-act comedy.[2] Those who took this latter utterance as an ironic jest may have been surprised when *The Cherry Orchard* appeared, duly described beneath the title as *A comedy in four acts*.

In total contrast to *Three Sisters*, Chekhov's last play is packed with the external elements of comedy, vaudeville and farce. The characters of Simeonov-Pishchik, Charlotta Ivanovna, Epikhodov, Yasha, Dunyasha, the passer-by and the post-office clerk hail clearly from the world of farce, while many of the scenes and situations involving these characters and, occasionally, Gaev, Trofimov, Lopakhin and Firs are of like provenance. People swallow bottlefuls of pills, fall downstairs, lose their galoshes etc.

Farce, however, is merely the topmost of three planes on which

---

[1] E.g. in a letter to Ol'ga Knipper (later his wife), 1st March, 1901.
[2] E.g. in letters to Ol'ga Knipper, 7th March, 1901, and M. Lilina-Alekseeva, 15th September, 1903.

Chekhov asks us to react emotionally to his play. Beneath the farce, partly obscured and partly leavened by it, lies the apparent overall tragedy of the external action—the sale and destruction of the orchard. On these two planes alone many scenes invite a complex reaction, consisting sometimes of widely differing emotions. Deeper still lies the third plane, on which we react not to what is actually happening on the stage, but to what this action tells us about the inner worlds of the protagonists and their qualities as people.

Penetration of this third plane leads to an ironic paradox: *Three Sisters* must be seen as Chekhov's most optimistic play, *The Cherry Orchard* as his most pessimistic. If in the former external tragedy cloaks an optimistic inner climax, in the latter the tragi-comic trappings of external action conceal a sombre inner truth. This terrible truth is that no character, in Chekhovian terms, changes for the better; the play is peopled by characters of my first category. M. N. Stroeva[1] has pointed out that in the first three plays the first act presents the hopes and dreams of the protagonists; in the third act these hopes explode in a clash with reality; the fourth act is one of reconciliation and sacrifice. The analysis might seem applicable also to *The Cherry Orchard*; but Stroeva was right to omit it. For Ranevskaya's dream—to rediscover childhood innocence and happiness in the cherry orchard, to shake off the 'heavy stone' of her past,—unlike those of Nina, Vanya, Sonya and the three sisters, is not even an honest dream; it is dishonest self-deception. As the play progresses it becomes clear how essentially uninterested Ranevskaya is in the fate of the orchard. Its final sale and destruction come to her, were she but able to admit it, not as the shattering of hopes, but as a welcome release; now she may do what she really wants—return to Paris and her lover. Her lyrical outbursts of affection for the orchard, her professed distress at its destruction are an emotional indulgence, as idle and imaginary a game as Gaev's billiards. The play *is* a comedy to be sure, but a bitterly ironic one.[2] As the fate of the orchard is settled

---

[1] Stroeva, '" The Three Sisters" in the Production of the Moscow Art Theater', in *Chekhov. A Collection of Critical Essays.*

[2] The first production of the play, by the Moscow Arts Theatre, incurred Chekhov's displeasure. Stanislavsky and Nemirovich-Danchenko advertised the play as a 'drama' and, directing it, insisted that the actors make clear the serious drama underlying the comedy. Chekhov intended precisely the opposite: the play should be acted just as it was written, and the audience left to detect for itself

beneath the hammer, the Ranevskaya household laughs and makes merry. Ranevskaya symbolizes the whole of her disinherited class, dancing with engaging insouciance around its own funeral pyre, into extinction. And in how low a key in this last play ring out the calls to work and to the happy future, voiced as they are by the pathetic and absurd Trofimov!

Some qualities of Lopakhin, perhaps, hold promise for the future. It is typical of Chekhov's refusal to accept the easy stereotypes of socially tendentious literature that his bourgeois entrepreneur is a childishly simple and warm-hearted man. Vaguely aware of the social-economic symbolism of his purchase of the orchard, he is, nevertheless, capable of pity for the decaying class his type has superseded. But ultimately he too is encased in his own acceptance of the unchangeable patterns of life; his intended proposal of marriage to Varya disintegrates with awful inevitability into remarks about the weather.

If a positive or optimistic idea is present in *The Cherry Orchard*, then it enjoys no direct embodiment; it exists only by implication. Meyerhold made the point: 'In *The Cherry Orchard*, as in Maeterlinck's plays, there is a hero who is not seen on stage, but who is sensed every time the curtain goes down . . . For Chekhov, the characters of *The Cherry Orchard* are a means, not the essence in themselves.'[1]

This unseen 'hero' can only be the implied antithesis of the *poshlost'* which in one way or another marks every character in the play.

Much of the technique of Chekhov's drama is based upon that of the later stories. As always, form is a further expression of the artist's view of the true nature of human life, and is thus one with content.

A basic identity between reality and what, at first glance, may appear in his plays to be device, was indicated by Chekhov himself: 'In life, people don't spend all their time shooting each other, hanging themselves or declaring their love for someone. Nor is every

the ironic contrast between the comedy of the action and its melancholy implications. In this way only could the proper impact of the play upon the audience be assured; any reduction or elimination of the play's superficially comic tonality could only mar the effect.

[1] V. Meyerhold, 'Naturalistic Theater and Theater of Mood', in *Chekhov. A Collection of Critical Essays*.

minute spent in saying clever things. Mostly they just eat, drink, flirt and talk nonsense—and this is what should be shown on the stage. A play should be written in which people come, go, eat their dinner, chat about the weather and play cards, not because that is how the author wants it, but because that is how it happens in real life.'[1]

Just as life does not consist of stirring events, so Chekhov insists that meaningful change in life occurs beneath the surface of appearance, within the mind and soul.

'People eat their dinner, just eat their dinner, and at that moment their happiness is being made or their lives are being ruined.'[2]

Thus the meaning of Chekhov's plays, as of his stories, is removed from the surface to what Nemirovich-Danchenko christened the 'sub-text' (*podtekst*); this in turn leads to a withering of external plot and a concentration upon internal development. The Chekhonte anecdote is transformed into the type of story perfectly exemplified by *The Lady with the Little Dog*. This story, far from having any external climax or denouement, ends precisely at that point where events are at their most unfinished and intriguing stage—how will Gurov and Anna resolve the frightful dilemma facing them? But the inner denouement is complete: 'Anna Sergeevna and he loved each other intimately, dearly, like husband and wife, like devoted friends: it seemed to them that fate had meant them for each other, and there was no sense in the fact that each of them was married . . . They had forgiven each other those things in the past of which they were ashamed, they forgave everything in the present and felt that this love of theirs had changed them both.'

So also in the drama, Chekhov gradually and with difficulty rid himself of the encumbering appurtenances of external plot: *Three Sisters* is the first of his long plays to lack a suicide, attempted or accomplished, and only in *The Cherry Orchard* does he dispense with gunshots altogether. The most worn of all dramatic clichés—the love triangle—was an obstruction he also strove to remove. In *The Seagull* the intricate web of mostly unrequited love relationships is used to illuminate the spiritual isolation of the characters, but at the same time inevitably distracts attention from the hub of the play. As Chekhov's dramatic techniques evolve towards final perfection,

[1] *Vospominaniya D. Gorodetskogo*, in *Birzhevye vedomosti* (1904), No. 364.
[2] G. Ars, *Iz vospominaniy ob A. P. Chekhove*, in *Teatr i iskusstvo*, 1904, No. 28.

the quantity and intricacy of love relationships decreases: by *The Cherry Orchard* they are reduced to a few almost self-parodic remnants —the comic flirtations of the servants and the Lopakhin-Varya fiasco.

The traditional highspots of external drama which cannot be altogether excluded, are deliberately toned down to blend with the general temper of the action, or are removed offstage. Thus in *Three Sisters* the shot which kills Tuzenbakh is heard as a muffled sound in the distance, but not even remarked upon at the time; Masha and Vershinin's mutual declaration of love is reduced to the humming of snatches of a tune to each other across the stage and in the presence of others. The impact of the climactic event of *The Cherry Orchard*— Lopakhin's announcement that he has bought the orchard—is dispersed by the slapstick which precedes and follows it, and by Lopakhin's own ironic tone.

Lacking the blatant artifice of event-plot, and reduced largely to the apparently trivial round of everyday life, action in the later plays dissolves into loose, disjointed patterns. Yet, though the picture itself may lack external design, the canvas is given outline and frame: Chekhov marks off the boundaries of his last three plays with the device of arrival and departure. The arrivals no more constitute exposition than do the departures—denouement; both create shape and at the same time give indirect impetus to the inner drama.

Much of the dialogue is of an apparently random nature; conversation is desultory and, because of the total or partial self-encasement of the characters, is often not conversation, but multiple soliloquy. The illuminative and carefully organized dialogue of traditional drama, directed towards the movement and revelation of plot, is barely to be found.

Yet the superior effect of realism created by the apparently inconsequential chatter on Chekhov's stage is, in its way, as deliberate an illusion, as cunning a device—if not indeed more so—as the more obviously purposeful dialogue of conventional drama. It is replete with meaning, communicated to the audience not by direct statement, but by allusion, nuance and the evocation of emotional response: this is its *poetic* quality. Nemirovich-Danchenko's label 'Realism whittled away to symbols' nicely defines the particular process of artistic selection involved. In his dramatic dialogue, as in the prose of his stories, Chekhov is concerned primarily to remove from the broad surface of reality all those parts which are irrelevant to the inner meaning of that reality. What remains is still real, is of reality, but is that part which most perfectly symbolizes the whole, and expresses its essence.

The principle may be applied to any aspect of his writing. Description: one need only quote the famous letter to his brother Aleksandr (10th May, 1886) '. . . nature descriptions must be extemely concise and apropos . . . For instance, you will capture the effect of a moon-lit night if you write that on a mill dam a piece of broken bottle twinkled like a small bright star and the dark shadow of a dog or wolf rolled along like a ball . . .' The emotionally evocative sound effect—the beating of the nightwatchman's iron sheet, the barking dog, the breaking string—is a recurrent feature of both plays and stories. It is mentioned not simply because it happens; it is selected out of the multitude of sounds which the characters hear (as do we all) because it coincides with, or fits—and therefore symbolizes—their mood or thoughts at the time. Characterization: the reader, attuned to Chekhov's manner, and advised that A 'has bought a dacha', B 'likes to argue and talks in a loud voice', or C 'has taken up playing *vint*', knows all that he needs to know about the people concerned.

It is, however, in the application of this technique to dialogue that Chekhov's genius most clearly emerges; hence his excellence as a dramatist. In its most refined form, Chekhovian dialogue represents a series of clues and hints which must be synthesised by the reader or audience into comprehension. There is deliberate artifice here: Magarshack[1] has pointed out that even the intersecting, but entirely independent, conversations of two groups of characters on opposite sides of the stage can be woven by Chekhov into a meaningful whole. But together with artifice, underlying this technique there is a profound knowledge of the true nature of human verbal intercourse. Chekhov knows that much of what we say is merely an indirect, rather than a direct, expression of ourselves and of our thoughts. The multiple soliloquies, though bearing some semblance of conversation, serve only to underline the isolation of the people involved. All men are to some degree in 'cases'; and to that degree they are unwilling or unable to understand their fellows. Total inability or unwillingness to

[1] *Chekhov the Dramatist*, Ch. 15.

communicate is the final hallmark of *poshlost'*, genuine sympathy its antithesis. How eloquently then, as the final curtain falls, does the obvious mutual understanding and sympathy of the three sisters, linked together in mid-stage by Ol'ga's embrace, express their final escape from illusion! And how sterile by contrast seem Ranevskaya's sentimental farewell to the orchard and her profession of concern for the fate of Varya and of Firs when, dashing off in almost indecent haste to the arms of her Parisian gigolo, she leaves Varya to spinsterhood and the dreary post of housekeeper on a nearby estate, and Firs locked, forgotten, in the deserted house!

Chekhov's major achievement in technique is his particular resolution of one of the great problems of the naturalist writer. His literary account of the world, the material of his work, remains to the end strictly limited to the multifarious detail of real life. Yet by developing inside this material a refined system of symbolism and impressionism, he is able to charge his description of the world with a meaning which both unifies and explains it. His greatest contribution to literature as a means by which we may better understand ourselves is his detection and exposure of the many ways in which the external human world—appearance, words, posture—differs from and conceals its inner reality. For Chekhov, appearance does not simply belie reality; more often than not, it is its very opposite. The path to self-destruction lies through happiness, to salvation through sorrow and disquiet. Only the madman is truly sane. In success the spirit dies; through misfortune it is regenerated. Philosophies, policies and theories are means not to explain and change the world, but to escape it.

It is the blend of this ironic scepticism with a dogged idealism which gives Chekhov's work its peculiar flavour. There is precious little in contemporary man of which he can wholly approve or which genuinely augurs the Golden Age to come; but the shift in human consciousness *will* come, and with it, eventually, the Golden Age. Life and the freedom offered by life are good; and man, for all his folly, cannot ignore the fact for ever. Chekhov is intuitively sure, intellectually unsure; he propounds a faith, but no dogma. And that above all is what is captivating about him.

CHEKHOV

SELECT BIBLIOGRAPHY

EDITIONS

Polnoe sobranie sochineniy i pisem A. P. Chekhova, 20 vols., Moscow, 1944–1951.

Works of Chekhov, 15 vols., translated by Constance Garnett, London, 1916–23.

The Oxford Chekhov, 9(?) volumes, ed. and translated by Ronald Hingley, London, 1964–(?). [Six volumes have been published so far.]

Letters on the Short Story, the Drama and other literary topics, ed. L. Friedland, London, 1924.

The Notebooks of Anton Chekhov, translated by S. Koteliansky and L. Woolf, London, 1921.

CRITICAL AND BIOGRAPHICAL WORKS

Balukhaty, S., *Chekhov dramaturg*, Leningrad, 1936.

Berdnikov, G., *A. P. Chekhov*, Moscow–Leningrad, 1961.

Chekhov. A Collection of Critical Essays, ed. R. Jackson, New Jersey, 1967.

Chekhov, M. P., *Anton Chekhov i ego syuzhety*, Moscow, 1923.

    Vokrug Chekhova, Moscow–Leningrad, 1933.

Chekhov v vospominaniyakh sovremennikov, ed. A. Kotova, Moscow, 1954.

Chukovsky, K., *Chekhov the Man*, translated by Pauline Rose, London, 1945.

Corrigan, R., 'The Drama of Anton Chekhov', *Modern Drama: Essays in Criticism*, ed. T. Bogard and W. Oliver, New York, 1965.

Derman, A., *O masterstve Chekhova*, Moscow–Leningrad, 1959.

Elton, O., *Chekhov*, The Taylorian Lecture, Oxford, 1929.

Ermilov, V., *Dramaturgiya Chekhova*, Moscow, 1948.

Fergusson, F., *The Idea of a Theater*, Princeton, 1949.

Gerhardi, W., *Anton Chekhov*, London, 1923.

Hingley, R., *Chekhov. A Biographical and Critical Study*, London, 1950.

Kramer, K. D., *The Chameleon and the Dream*, The Hague, 1970.

Magarshack, D., *Chekhov: a Life*, London, 1952.

    Chekhov the Dramatist, London, 1952.

Mann, T., 'Chekhov', *Russian Literature and Modern English Fiction*, ed. D. Davie, Chicago, 1965.

Mirsky, D., *A History of Russian Literature*, London, 1949.

    'Chekhov and the English', *Russian Literature and Modern English Fiction*, ed. D. Davie, Chicago, 1965.

Nemirovich-Danchenko, V., *Iz proshlogo*, Moscow, 1936. (Translated by John Cournos as *My Life in the Russian Theatre*, London, 1937.)

Paperny, Z., *A. P. Chekhov*, Moscow, 1960.

Peacock, R., *The Poet in the Theatre*, London, 1961.

Shestov, L., *Chekhov and other essays*, translated by S. Koteliansky and J. Middleton Murry, London, 1916.

Sobolev, Yu., *Chekhov*, Moscow, 1934.

Stanislavsky (Alekseev), K., *Moya zhizn' v iskusstve*, Moscow–Leningrad, 1941. (Translated by J. Robbins as *My Life in Art*, London, 1924.)

    A. P. Chekhov v Moskovskom khudozhestvennom teatre, Moscow, 1947.

Valency, M., *The Breaking String. The Plays of Anton Chekhov*, New York, 1966.

Winner, T., *Chekhov and his Prose*, New York, 1966.

Index

347

INDEX

350

351

INDEX

INDEX

INDEX